TROPICAL FISHLOPEDIA

A Complete Guide
To Fish Care

Mary Bailey and
Dr Peter Burgess

Howell Book House

New York

ACKNOWLEDGMENTS

The authors would like to acknowledge the assistance of the following friends and colleagues in the preparation of this book: Bernice Brewster for critically reading some of the chapters on fish health; Gina Sandford for expert advice on catfish; Dr David Ford for information on fish nutrition; Stan McMahon for advice on fish health; and, last but by no means least, the late Dr Keith Banister for invaluable assistance with matters of taxonomy and ichthyology.

In addition MB would like to take this opportunity to acknowledge her incalculable personal debt to Keith for all the advice, information, and encouragement he freely provided over the years of an all too brief but greatly valued friendship, and to dedicate her share in this book to his memory.

While every effort has been made to ensure that the content of this book is accurate and up to date at the time of going to press, it must be accepted that knowledge of fish diseases, the side-effects of treatments (on both fish and humans), and other aspects covered, is an ever-changing science. Moreover, the manner in which the information contained herein is utilised is beyond the control of the authors and publisher, although every effort has been made to warn of the dangers. For these reasons, no responsibility can be accepted by the authors and publisher for any loss, injury, or other problem whatsoever experienced by any person using this book.

Photography (including front cover photo) by Keith Allison unless otherwise credited.

Line drawings by Phil Robinson.

CONTENTS

body structure; Getting around: the locomotory system; A coat of many functions: the skin; Keeping afloat: the swimbladder; Maintaining the salt balance: the osmoregulatory system; Processing the food: the digestive system; Breathing underwater: the respiratory system; Pumping blood: the circulatory system; Fish have brains: the nervous system; In touch with their environment: the sensory system; Combating disease: the immune system; Hormone messengers: the endocrine system; The next generation: reproductive strategies).

6

INTRODUCTION

Fishkeeping is a many-faceted hobby enjoyed by people of all ages and from all walks of life. It offers an opportunity for pet ownership to those who, for reasons of space, exercise, personal health, and so on, cannot keep a dog or cat – almost any home can find space for a small aquarium. At the other end of the scale it can become an absorbing hobby, with a huge display aquarium filled with freshwater tropicals or coral fish in the living room, an array of tanks full of home-bred baby fish in a 'fish-house' (the spare room, garage, shed, or even a purpose-built facility), a huge garden pond, or all three, depending on which way the enthusiast's interests lead him.

This book deals with just one aspect of fishkeeping – the maintenance of freshwater tropical fish. Although some of the information it contains can be applied equally to other branches of fishkeeping (tropical marine, coldwater marine, brackish, cold freshwater aquaria, ponds), the huge number and sheer variety of fish included in the freshwater tropical group warrants this specific coverage. Indeed, many aquarists (fishkeepers) will be quite content to devote themselves to this single branch of the hobby – with a choice of thousands of species to keep, there is little likelihood of boredom.

Fish differ radically from other common domestic pets in that they live in water, and so cannot share our immediate environment. This means we cannot pick them up and stroke them, throw sticks for them to retrieve, or take them for walks or outings in the car. It rapidly becomes apparent, however, that they are aware of human activity in their vicinity and react when their owner approaches – especially at feeding time! At the same time, they are quiet, do not require house-training, do not damage furniture, bite visitors, or steal food from the kitchen. They do, of course, require their owner to provide them with a 'life-support system', their aquarium. This is an additional credit point in their favour, as a well-planned and properly maintained aquarium full of colourful, healthy fish, all going about their daily lives much as in nature, can be the focal point of the living room. Not only is it ornamental, but full of interesting activity, providing an opportunity for underwater gardening (aquatic plants are a fascinating subject in themselves), and an educational tool if there are children in the household.

Establishing this self-contained underwater world can be likened to assembling a jigsaw puzzle. You know what the finished picture should look like, but a number of separate pieces have first to be examined and fitted together to produce the whole. We cannot tell you to start with a particular piece and proceed in a predetermined sequence because there are so many variables. Ideally, you will first decide what fish you would like to keep and then set about accommodating them – but there may be limiting factors, such as insufficient space to house a tank of the requisite size, flooring unable to bear the weight of a large aquarium, or simply the expense.

The fish are the most important piece of the jigsaw, so the first section of this book is devoted to them. It discusses the different types available and how to find out which can be kept together – differences in size, habits, diet (some will eat each other), and environmental requirements mean this topic alone is a separate jigsaw within the overall puzzle. We tell you about fish names, where to obtain fish, how to transport them and introduce them to their new home, what fish eat and how to feed them, showing fish, and how to set about breeding them. We also discuss the motivation behind fish behaviour, and use a special "What if...?" question and answer format to suggest solutions to some common behavioural problems.

Section Two discusses the other pieces of the jigsaw – water, decor, lighting, tank and equipment – and how to assemble them into an aquarium. We also discuss the regular routine maintenance the aquarium will require and provide solutions to some of the problems that may be encountered, again using the "What if...?" format.

The final section deals with fish health. A chapter on anatomy and biology explains the structure of a fish and how its body functions. We explain how to tell if a fish is healthy, so you will quickly realise if it falls sick, and advise on how to prevent this. Because, for a number of reasons, fish illnesses are usually treated by the aquarist rather than the veterinarian, we provide a detailed catalogue of diseases that sometimes affect fish, a list of the medications used to treat them, information on how to treat sick or injured fish, and a further "What if...?" chapter to help link visible symptoms with specific health problems. Information on obtaining professional assistance is provided and safety aspects of fish first-aid are also discussed.

Our intention is that this *Fishlopaedia* should, in the first instance, enable you to make an informed decision regarding the fish and aquarium best suited to your circumstances and to plan and bring into being your own special aquatic microcosm. We trust that thereafter it will serve you as an essential work of reference, helping you to keep things running smoothly and enabling you to deal with any problems that may occur during what we hope will prove to be an enjoyable and rewarding lifetime hobby.

SECTION I
FISH MANAGEMENT

For most people, fish are the main interest in the aquarium, and the choice of fish is commonly the factor that determines the success of the aquarium as a whole.

All too often, however, the beginner decides to set up an aquarium and does so without much thought about what fish he is going to put in it. When the aquarium is ready, he goes to the nearest store and buys a selection of fish that look attractive and are the right sort of size. Miraculously this sometimes works, but more frequently the sequel is disaster. Some of the 'right size' fish were only youngsters, and they rapidly grow and start eating the smaller ones. Some of the fish eat the plants. Some decide half of the aquarium is their private property and attack any other fish that comes near. If the aquarist is sensible, he realises that these are not insurmountable problems, as there are people all over the world with beautiful aquaria full of well-behaved fish; and no-one would keep fish if it were not an enjoyable activity. So, he seeks advice, reads books, and gets back on the right track. Sadly, however, a lot of people become disheartened and give up.

The key to avoiding such problems is to take a totally different approach. The wise aquarist will first decide what fish he would like to keep; next he will find out all he can about them – their eventual size, their habits, and any special requirements they may have. He will probably find that some cannot be kept together because they are incompatible (Chapter 1), and some may be unsuitable for the living quarters he is able to provide (Table 1), but at least he can now look again at his list of 'wants' and decide which species are a viable combination. *Then* he can plan and set up an aquarium suited to their needs.

In this first section of The *Fishlopaedia* we look at various factors that may affect your choice of fish, and at aspects of fish management. We strongly suggest you study not only this section, but also Section 2, Aquarium Management, before making any decisions. Table 1 provides a basic outline of the main points that must be considered.

Remember, careful planning of the entire aquarium project is the key to its success!

Table 1 The Pieces of the Aquarium Jigsaw

- The species of fish you intend to keep (Chapters 1 & 3). You cannot hope to provide for them properly unless you know in advance what they are going to be.
- The available water supply (Chapter 9). Is it suitable for your choice of fish?
- Size of tank (Chapter 12).
- Where the tank is to be sited (Chapters 12, 13).
- Type of base (stand, cabinet, etc, Chapter 12).
- Other equipment (heating, lighting, filtration, Chapter 12).
- Type of decor (substrate, background, plants, rocks, and the like, Chapter 10).
- Type and amount of lighting (Chapter 11).

CHAPTER 1

CHOOSING AND BUYING FISH

1. Suitability and compatibility of species
2. The general community aquarium
3. Sources of fish

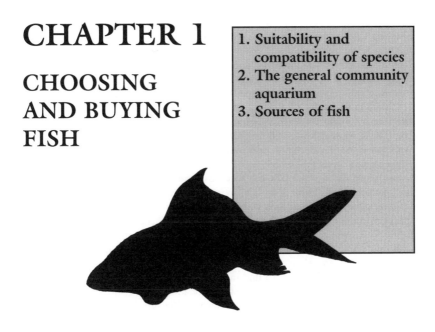

Some scientists believe that the total number of fish species in the world's waters may be as high as 40,000. About 25,000 species have been classified and given a scientific name (Chapter 2), but many more are thought to exist in the oceans and remote freshwaters of our planet. About 8,500 freshwater species have been described, and others are known but as yet unclassified; some of the latter are already being kept by aquarists. It is thought that perhaps 2,000 tropical freshwater species are available to aquarium hobbyists. So there are plenty to choose from!

Your initial choice will probably be based largely on appearance. You will be able to see a number of species by visiting aquarium stores, but in order to get a better idea of what is available it is better to consult illustrated literature. Be warned that not all the species you may find pictured will be readily available locally, or even in your country, and may have to be assigned to a 'future wants' list.

Appearance is not everything, however. An essential lesson to learn, right from the start, is that there are other factors involved in choosing a selection of species for your aquarium, whether you are planning the initial population or considering subsequent additions.

1. SUITABILITY AND COMPATIBILITY OF SPECIES

It is important to bear in mind that fish species are, like mammals and birds, diverse as well as numerous. Few people would consider housing a lion with a gerbil, or an eagle with a budgerigar. Amateurs would not normally consider keeping a lion or an eagle at all! Yet innumerable aquarists make the mistake of trying to keep the finned equivalents in the same aquarium, or of trying to keep fish that really have no place in the domestic aquarium at all. For example, some – such as the piranha (*Serrasalmus* spp.) and electric eel (*Electrophorus* spp.) – are dangerous, while others – such as the red-tailed catfish (*Phractocephalus hemioliopterus*) and pacu (*Piaractus* and *Colossoma* spp.) – are too large.

You might be forgiven for wondering how anyone could be so foolish as to buy a fish that is too big for their aquarium. The problem is that they are sold as small youngsters. Most fish you will find for sale will be about 2.5-10 cm (1-4 in) long, but while some may be almost or completely full-grown, others may be mere babies. A young lion cub is little larger than a good-sized domestic cat!

You might also wonder how fish that are dangerous or too large, or that will not mix, are sold at all. There is, in fact, an increasingly popular view that fish deemed unsuitable for domestic aquaria should be banned, but others say that would be an infringement of personal freedom. Indeed, some experienced aquarists with suitable facilities are quite capable of correctly maintaining these 'problem fish'.

If only those fish that could be housed together were sold, the enjoyment and interest of the aquarium hobby would be dramatically diminished. It is the responsibility of the aquarist to find out all he can about the species he is thinking of buying, so he can make a considered decision as to whether the species is suitable for his aquarium and as a 'tankmate' for other fish he already owns or is thinking of buying. 'Find out *first*' is one of the basic rules of good fishkeeping, and one which will be mentioned repeatedly throughout this book.

AREAS OF INCOMPATIBILITY

Here are some reasons why a species may be unsuitable for a particular aquarium:
• It may be too large for the aquarium (either already, or when full-grown).
• It may be too large (already or when full-grown) to fit in with the rest of the aquarium population. Even if a large fish does not eat smaller ones (see below), the smaller ones are likely to fear for their lives if any significantly larger fish is present.
• It may be too small, even when full-grown, to fit in with the rest of the aquarium population.
• It may be territorial (Chapter 4) and require more private space than the size of the aquarium allows.
• It may be a piscivore (fish-eater) which will eat smaller fish; this is perfectly natural behaviour for fish whose diet consists of other fish in the wild. Many omnivores will also eat fish that are much smaller than themselves. This does not mean piscivores and omnivores cannot be housed with other fish, simply that the other fish should not be 'bite-sized'.
• It may be so small as to be likely to be eaten by other fish already present.
• It may be a fin-nipper – usually not a problem unless species with long, tempting finnage are kept; or it may have long, tempting finnage, irresistible to fin-nippers already present!

- It may be too boisterous to fit in with sedate and/or nervous species, or *vice versa*.
- It may eat plants.
- It may dig – there is nothing inherently harmful in this, but the aquarist may not want the aquarium rearranged.
- It may require different environmental factors – water chemistry, movement, and temperature (Chapter 10); lighting (Chapter 12); cover (i.e. decor, Chapter 11) – to those in the aquarium. These can, of course, be adjusted to suit the fish, but not if this would make the environment unsuitable for tankmates.

It is essential to consider *all* these elements in conjunction. The fact that fish are all the same size does not mean they are compatible – a small but highly territorial fish can wreak havoc. Two species may require the same water chemistry, temperature, and lighting, but be quite incompatible as regards water movement if one comes from a slow-moving stream and the other from a raging torrent. A very common error is to assume that because species are sympatric (found together in nature) they can be kept together in captivity. Most biotopes are populated by both large and small species – predators and prey! Another common mistake is to assume that individuals of the same species will get on together, but in many cases, males, in particular, regard each other as competitors and may fight. The same may apply to related species with a similar appearance (shape and/or colour pattern).

POSITIVE COMPATIBILITY

By contrast, species that naturally live in groups positively need the company of their own kind. Shoaling, in open water species, is a defence against predation, and shoaling fish deprived of this type of security are likely to be nervous and stressed.

Some bottom-dwelling species – e.g. *Corydoras* catfish and some loaches – also live in groups. The reasons for this behaviour are not entirely understood, but such fish appear to do better if provided with the company of their own kind.

HARDY FISH

'Hardy fish' is a term used to describe species which usually manage to survive, whatever the environmental conditions provided. Such fish may be naturally hardy if they have to cope with variable water parameters and/or poor water quality in the wild, or may have been 'acclimatised' to aquarium life – this means only that they survive it, not necessarily that they thrive, and most acclimatised fish do far better (and show better colour) if kept in natural conditions.

Naturally hardy fish include poeciliid livebearers such as the guppy (*Poecilia reticulata*), many (but not all) labyrinth fish, and the Chinese algae eater or sucking loach (*Gyrinocheilus aymonieri*) (Chapter 3).

Acclimatised hardy species include the neon tetra (*Paracheirodon innesi*), and the krib (*Pelvicachromis pulcher*). A number of species collected in the wild (rather than bred commercially) enjoy specialised conditions in nature but survive incorrect ones in captivity, and are also regarded as hardy. These include many catfish as well as the cardinal tetra (*Paracheirodon axelrodi*) and many other tetras. Finally, some species that are commonly regarded as hardy, because they are bred commercially and sold in most pet stores, are in fact not very hardy at all. A classic example is the ram cichlid (*Microgeophagus ramirezi*).

So, it is advisable to look into the background of even supposedly hardy fish, just to be sure. In addition, remember that wild-caught individuals of any species will not have been acclimatised, even if tank-bred strains of the same species have.

A very common error is to assume that hardy species are compatible. Hardy denotes only that they will probably survive whatever environment you provide; it does not mean that they will not grow large, devour each other, eat plants, fight etc!

POPULATION DENSITY

An aquarium can accommodate only a finite number of fish. This is commonly calculated in terms of the total length of all the fish added together relative to the surface area of the aquarium water, though other criteria are used for some species. Details of calculating stocking density are given on P.118. The important point to remember is that stocking density is calculated in terms of the fish length *when fully grown*, and the majority of your fish will not be full-grown when you buy them. Overcrowding can cause stress and is a contributory factor in many health problems.

STRESS

Any incompatibility situation, whether between fish and fish, or fish and their environment, is likely to cause stress, which in turn may lead to serious health problems. Stress is discussed in greater detail in Chapter 21, Section 1.5.2.

Sources of information

Chapter 3 provides an outline guide to the main groups of tropical freshwater fish available to the hobbyist, but it is impossible within the scope of this book to provide the detailed information the aquarist may require on any group, let alone every species he may encounter.

The best source of information is the aquarium literature, which includes a number of encyclopaedic catalogues of species and specialised works on some groups (see Appendix A). When dealing with species new to the hobby, it may be necessary to read up on the natural habitat in order to provide the appropriate environment. Such species are, however, best left to the experienced aquarist familiar with simulating specialised biotopes and will spare tanks in case special accommodation is required.

Other hobbyists may be able to provide useful information. However, it is always worth checking with the literature as well, unless you know the aquarist to be expert and meticulous. Many people may manage to keep a fish alive, but that is not necessarily the same as keeping it properly.

Aquarium stores can be invaluable sources of information, but regrettably some store owners/staff may mislead the unwary aquarist in order to make a sale. Unless you know the dealer is honest, then check in the literature before making any purchase.

---

2. THE GENERAL COMMUNITY AQUARIUM

A community aquarium is any aquarium that, hopefully, contains a compatible group of fish species. Sometimes the community aquarium may be devoted to fish from a particular type of water (a soft water or hard water community), or to a particular group of fish (e.g. a livebearer community or a Malawi cichlid community).

A general community aquarium is one that contains a selection of fish, usually from a wide range of families (Chapter 3), that are compatible in behaviour and size, and tolerant as regards water parameters ('hardy fish' – see above). Fish with very specialised requirements can be kept in a general community if the environment is correct and they are compatible in behaviour and size.

You will often encounter the term 'community fish', and this generally implies a species suitable for the general community aquarium. There are still, however, occasional areas of incompatibility. For example, the tiger barb (*Barbus pentazona*) is notorious for nipping long, flowing finnage, and the sucking loach will attach itself to the sides of flatsided fish such as the angel (*Pterophyllum scalare*). Yet all three species, plus a number with flowing finnage, are regarded as community fish.

An aquarium which is devoted to a single species is termed a 'species aquarium'.

3. SOURCES OF FISH

Aquarists usually obtain fish from aquarium stores, or from each other.

AQUARIUM STORES

Aquarium stores are a source not only of fish, but also of equipment, decor, medications, books and other items. They can be highly variable, both in their stock (some stock chiefly fish, some chiefly equipment, some a balance between the two) and in the quality of their livestock and service.

It may be that you have an excellent aquarium store on your doorstep, glowingly recommended by an aquarist who has introduced you to the hobby. More often, however, you will have to evaluate local suppliers yourself. It is not a good idea to patronise a store simply because it is the nearest, or because it is the only one in your town (although your local store may turn out to be the best for miles around). Visit as many stores as you can. This will not only give you an opportunity to compare and contrast, but to see a far wider selection of fish than you are likely to find in a single store. If the shop with the best fish stocks only a small selection of equipment, you may end up shopping at several stores.

It is worth doing some research before visiting a single store, so you will be in a better position to make the necessary judgements. Points to consider are:
• Cleanliness and tidiness of the shop.
• Cleanliness of the tanks. There should be no large accumulations of detritus ('mulm'), no dead or dying fish, no algae coating the front glass so you cannot see the fish (algae on other glasses is quite acceptable).
• Health of the fish (Chapter 18). If a tank is infected with an obvious disease, it should be clearly marked 'Not For Sale'.
• Decor (Chapter 10) used in the tanks. Some shops leave all their tanks bare to make it easier to catch fish, but totally bare tanks are stressful, particularly if the light from the tank below is shining through the bottom glass so the fish are subjected to glare from below as well as above. There is no excuse for tanks having no background. But because shop tanks are subject to constant disruption and fish do need to be caught, it is unreasonable to expect each tank to be fully decorated. Full marks should be given to the store that has provided essential cover for the fish each tank contains, in the form of caves or (plastic) plants, for example.
• Labelling of the tanks. Each tank should be clearly labelled with what the tank

contains and the price. Common names are acceptable if truly in general use (Chapter 2), but otherwise the scientific name should be given and spelt correctly. Scientific names may be difficult to spell, but they can be copied from books! Unlabelled tanks and tanks with labelling half worn away (and probably referring to what the tank contained months ago), are minus points. The same applies to tanks with signs for 'mixed tetras' or 'mixed Malawi cichlids'. Some stores, however, not only provide the name and price of their fish, but also brief details of its eventual size, requirements, and suitability for the general community or for beginners. Top marks to these!

• Staff attitude and efficiency. Are the staff willing to offer advice and information? Is the advice and information correct? It is worth going armed with a few test questions based on your background reading (see also below). Watch the staff at work with other customers. Are they catching the fish quickly and efficiently, or chasing them round? Are they packing the fish properly? (Chapter 6).

• Some tanks may be marked 'Q' or 'Quarantine', and 'Not for Sale'. This shows that the shop quarantines (Chapter 20) fish (in case they are infected with a disease) that have recently arrived from the wholesaler. Some shops have a special quarantine facility away from the customer area, so if no tanks are marked 'Q' etc, then enquire what the store does about quarantine. If they do not quarantine fish, or if you see them unpacking newly-arrived fish and immediately offering them for sale, this denotes an irresponsible attitude towards customers. So does using the same net in every tank, unless it is dipped in disinfectant (and rinsed in fresh water) between tanks. Top marks for a separate net for each tank, hanging by or kept in the tank in question.

• Reference material. The very best shops will have a selection of reference books, so they can find out about the fish they are selling (no-one can be expected to know everything about all the species that might pass through the shop) and answer obscure questions from customers. If the shop sells books, that too is a plus point.

A few questions to ask (you will have researched the correct answers beforehand):
• Ask the eventual size of a fish you know grows far too large for a general community: e.g. the Oscar (*Astronotus ocellatus*, about 30 cm/12 in), the common plec (*Hypostomus plecostomus*, 30-40 cm/12-16 in), or the tinfoil barb (*Barbus schwanenfeldi*, about 40 cm/16 in).
• Ask if a fish is suitable for a community (knowing that it is not). The Oscar will again do nicely – it is aggressive, destructive, and eats smaller fish!
• Ask how long you must wait, you buy a tank and equipment then and there, between setting up your aquarium and putting fish in it (at least three to four weeks).

If you get the right answers, that is a good indication that the store is interested in helping you keep fish properly, and not just in making a quick sale. If you can find a good and honest retail outlet that can supply most of your needs, then it is a wise policy to shop there. A good dealer can become a good friend, who will obtain unusual fish to special order, buy young fish from you, sell you equipment out of hours in an emergency, and provide other assistance beyond the call of duty.

OBTAINING FISH FROM OTHER AQUARISTS

Obtaining fish from other aquarists can be tempting as they are often free, or at least cheaper than those from the store. But it is unwise to buy from anyone unless you know them to be a good fishkeeper and have inspected their tanks. Bear in mind that any young fish they supply are likely to be brothers and sisters, which is undesirable if you are planning to use them as broodstock (Chapter 8).

SELECTING STOCK

There must be a delay of at least several weeks between deciding what species to keep and actually buying them – you have to acquire all the equipment, set up the aquarium, and mature it properly (Chapter 14) before introducing a single fish. Nevertheless, it is important to consider stock selection at this early stage.

Assuming you follow our advice and visit several aquarium stores, perhaps repeatedly, then you will have an opportunity to learn to spot poor-quality or sickly fish and differentiate them from good-quality, healthy ones. This may help you in your eventual choice of supplier, as you should buy from the shop which sells what you have learned to recognise as the best fish.

It is important to buy only healthy stock if you are to get off to a good start. Almost inevitably, every aquarist will experience a disease outbreak sooner or later, but the risk can be minimised by careful stock selection. Chapter 18 provides information on how to determine whether or not a fish is healthy, and some typical signs of ill health are dealt with in Chapter 20. The information on selecting breeding stock in Chapter 8 is also worth consulting. Only the very best stock should be used for broodstock, but there is no reason why you should not select top-quality stock even if you have no intention of breeding your fish.

Do not make the common mistake of buying a fish because you feel sorry for it – because it is thin, smaller or a different colour to the others, injured, harassed, or in any way substandard. Equally, the largest fish in a batch may be a bully that has been chasing the others away from the food. Individuals of average size are less likely to prove troublesome, but note that males and females are different sizes in some species.

You are entitled to expect the assistant to catch the individual fish you select; however, it is not reasonable to expect him to catch a particular small fish out of a shoal of 50 or 100. In such situations it is more usual either to accept or reject individuals caught at random. The assistant will normally trap fish between the net and the front glass so you can inspect them (if he does not, ask him to). Never be afraid or embarrassed to reject a fish. You may find the assistant himself rejects some fish because he regards them as inferior quality, and it is sensible to accept his judgement in such instances. Once the fish is in the plastic bag, inspect it again – you will have seen only one side when it was trapped in the net.

Never be afraid to change your mind about buying, for example if the assistant stresses the fish by chasing them endlessly (competent staff will catch fish quickly and efficiently), or if you are dissatisfied with the standard of packing. Once the fish are paid for they become your responsibility and it is up to you to transport them home safely and introduce them to their new home. These topics are all covered in Chapter 6.

CHAPTER 2

THE CLASSIFICATION AND NAMES OF FISH

1. Taxonomy and scientific nomenclature
2. Scientific and common names

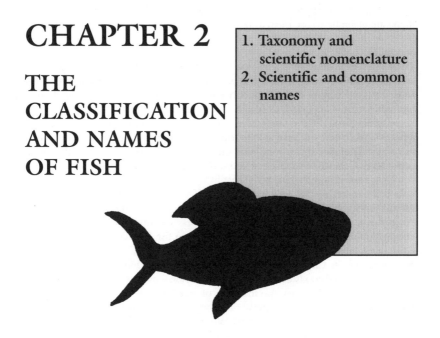

Our planet is inhabited by a very large number of fish species classified under various groupings, and, even though a comparatively small portion of these are likely to be encountered by the aquarist, the sheer variety is likely to prove confusing, at least initially. So too will be the different names used to identify the groups and species. Accordingly, in this chapter we provide a basic introduction to the taxonomy (classification) and nomenclature (naming) of fish.

Many aquarists fight shy of taxonomy and nomenclature, regarding them as complicated, difficult, and irrelevant. Getting to grips with scientific nomenclature may not be easy, but it is useful to have a basic knowledge of where a particular fish fits into the scheme of things (for example, aquarium 'sharks' are not close relatives of 'Jaws'!). Except where a few commonly kept species are concerned, it is essential to know the correct scientific name – at least if there is to be any reasonable hope of finding out about its habits and requirements.

1. TAXONOMY AND SCIENTIFIC NOMENCLATURE

Taxonomy (or systematics) is the science of the classification of living things (including extinct species), while scientific nomenclature is the system employed by taxonomists to give unique names to those same living things.

SYSTEMATICS

The classification of the animal kingdom consists of a progressive system of subdivisions based on known or presumed relationships between organisms or groups of organisms. It can be thought of as resembling a family tree, but without any suggestion of time or descent. At the top of this 'taxonomic tree' we have the entire animal kingdom (Animales), and at the bottom each individual species (Table 2). Whenever a new group (termed a taxon; plural taxa) is discovered and catalogued, a scientific description of it is published, providing details of its characteristics (so other people will be able to recognise it) and assigning it a unique scientific name which applies to that taxon and no other. Thus, using the example in Table 2, there is only one phylum called Chordata, one class called Actinopterygii, and so on down to the one and only species called *Poecilia reticulata* (the guppy).

As far as the aquarist is concerned, for identification purposes it is generally sufficient to know to what genus and species a fish belongs. To evaluate form, habits, and general requirements, however, he will often find it helpful to know the family and/or order as well. For example, the order Siluriformes (generally known as catfish) consists of largely bottom-oriented, scaleless fish with highly sensitive barbels. This major group is subdivided into a number of families, each with its own special features, but all with the characteristics of the order, i.e. all clearly catfish.

Another example is the family Cichlidae (cichlids) (order Perciformes). Cichlids have achieved a huge degree of popularity – or notoriety – on account of their universal habit of caring for their young, unfortunately to the detriment of any other fish foolish enough to get in the way. Thus, the aquarist who is aware that a potential purchase is a cichlid, will be forewarned that it is likely to be interesting but possibly problematical in its behaviour.

The final stage in the family tree, the subspecies, may be encountered occasionally. A subspecies is a distinct form of a species, often geographically isolated, which is not yet deemed to have become a species in its own right, though it may eventually do so. Only a relatively small number of fish species have subspecies.

Table 2 The Taxonomic Family Tree

The chief subdivisions of the Animal Kingdom, using *Poecilia reticulata* (the guppy) as an example.

Subdivision	Example
Kingdom:	Animales
Phylum:	Chordata
Subphylum:	Vertebrata
Superclass:	Gnathostomata
Class:	Actinopterygii
Subclass:	Neopterygii
Division:	Teleostei
Superorder:	Acanthopterygii
Order:	Cyprinodontiformes
Family:	Poeciliidae
Subfamily:	Poeciliinae
Genus:	*Poecilia*
Species:	*reticulata*
Subspecies:	none

(Note: Different authorities may cite slightly different subdivisions, not all of them recognised by all authorities. The following schematic follows Nelson, 1994.)

2. SCIENTIFIC AND COMMON NAMES

The system used for the scientific naming of fish and other animal species is called the trinomial system, trinomial meaning 'having three names'. The three elements – the names of the genus (the generic name), of the species (the specific name), and of the subspecies (the subspecific name) – represent the final three stages in the 'taxonomic tree' in Table 2, and together make up the unique scientific name of the species or subspecies concerned. The subspecific name is, however, normally used only when appropriate, i.e. when subspecies actually exist. In such cases, the first described subspecies is called the nominate subspecies, and its subspecific name is always the same as the specific; subsequently classified subspecies have subspecific names which differ from the specific name and, of course, from each other.

The scientific name of a species is conventionally printed in a different typescript (usually italics) to that of the text containing it, or underlined when handwritten. In scientific literature, the name of the author of the paper describing the species, and the date of the latter, are appended in normal script. If the author and date are placed in brackets this indicates that the species was originally assigned to a different genus to the one it is now. Thus the full name of the guppy is *Poecilia reticulata* Peters 1859; but in the case of *Pelvicachromis pulcher* (Boulenger, 1911) the author's name is shown in brackets because Boulenger originally described this fish as *Pelmatochromis pulcher*.

The essence of a scientific name is that it is unique, belonging to one plant or animal alone, and that it is universal to all countries in the world, whatever their language. Many fish have common names as well, for example guppy, angelfish, tiger barb. But those particular names are current only in some English-speaking countries. A German aquarist will have no idea what an angelfish is, as he calls it a Segelflosser ('sail fin') and yet this is one of the most common aquarium fish worldwide. Use the scientific name, *Pterophyllum scalare*, and anyone, in any country, will know – or can easily find out – exactly which fish is meant.

Sometimes a common name may be used in different languages – but applied to different fish! One example is the name zebra cichlid, which to English-speakers denotes *Metriaclima zebra*, a Lake Malawi species, but in Germany refers to a Central American species, *Archocentrus nigrofasciatus*, known in England and the USA as the convict cichlid. The increasingly common publication of fishkeeping books in multiple languages, with translations often using the wrong common name, reinforces the need to know the scientific name.

Even within a country, common names can cause confusion. Some fish have more than one. Some common names – e.g. butterfly cichlid, flag fish – are used for more than one species. Worst of all, some are made up by wholesalers, retailers, and publishers to cater for public dislike of scientific names. Thus the aquarist may be unable to find information on the fish he has purchased because no book uses the made-up name; or unable to find the fish he has read about, because the aquarium trade calls it something quite different. Later on, he may be unable to sell any fry his fish produce, because the name he uses is meaningless to his potential customers.

Unfortunately, scientific names can also sometimes be confusing, because occasionally some of them require amendment, as scientists learn more about the organisms they are classifying. Thus it may be discovered that two names have been applied to one taxon, in which case the first one remains valid and the later one becomes a synonym. Sometimes it is realised that a species has been assigned to the wrong genus, or that a genus needs to be divided into two. But the latest, up-to-date name of each taxon remains unique, and if advice is sought from an expert, then he or she should be able to indicate what fish is meant and what other names it can be found under in reference books. But you are unlikely to get very far seeking information, even from an expert, on names such as 'spotted catfish' and 'striped cichlid', which could apply to any of a large number of species.

So, as a general rule, it is unwise to buy a fish unless it is properly identified with its scientific name, or you are able confidently to identify the species from previous experience. If the name is unfamiliar, it should be written down for future reference. Do not be put off if you cannot pronounce it – that is not essential. Even experts have difficulty pronouncing some scientific names, such as *Tahuantinsuyoa macantzatza*!

CHAPTER 3

THE MAIN FAMILIES OF TROPICAL FRESHWATER AQUARIUM FISH

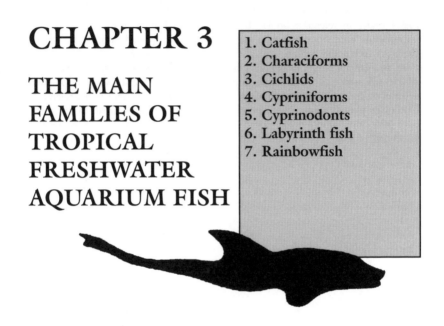

1. Catfish
2. Characiforms
3. Cichlids
4. Cypriniforms
5. Cyprinodonts
6. Labyrinth fish
7. Rainbowfish

The aim of this chapter is to introduce the aquarist to some of the groups of fish he may encounter. Because of considerations of space, the detail provided can only be very limited, but it is hoped it will provide the aquarist with general guidelines as to what to expect in each case, enabling him to decide which group interests him, or includes members possibly suited to his aquarium. Table 3 (P.33) shows many of the fish families whose members – or some of them – are sometimes kept in tropical freshwater aquaria, while the text of the chapter provides a brief introduction to the most popular groups. As regards the latter, unless otherwise specified, a temperature in the range of 23-26.5 °C (74-80 °F) is appropriate. Breeding details are normally given only where captive breeding is likely (for fish-breeding terminology and captive breeding techniques see Chapter 8).

Some of the groups covered below are the subject of a number of specialist publications, and encyclopaedic catalogues of aquarium fish species are also available. A list of additional reading matter will be found in Appendix A.

We cannot stress too highly, or too often, the need to research each species before deciding whether to keep it. Even closely-related fish may differ considerably in size, requirements and behaviour, and many an aquarist has learned this the hard way.

You may not understand some of the terms used in this chapter, but you will when you have read and absorbed Sections 1 and 2 – only then will you be ready to make an informed choice as to the fish suited to the conditions you are able to provide. For an explanation of anatomical terms see Chapter 17 and Appendix B.

1. CATFISH (Order Siluriformes)

Catfish are an extremely diverse group of fish, found all over the world in all temperature zones and in salt as well as freshwater. Unlike most other fish they do not have scales; some types are 'naked', while others are 'armoured' with scutes, bony plates, often equipped with formidable spines, running along the flanks. Other defences include very strong sharp spines in some of the fins. Another feature in common is the possession of sensory barbels around the mouth, used to 'taste' the environment and to seek out food.

Catfish are highly variable and generally bizarre in form, bearing little or no resemblance to the usual concept of what a fish should look like. This is, however, a major part of their charm. Their habits are almost as diverse as their appearance, making them interesting as well as attractive. As a group, freshwater tropical 'cats' are extremely popular with aquarists, from beginners looking for a scavenger to clean up leftover scraps of food in the community aquarium, to the specialist *aficionado* – with all possible stages of enthusiasm in between.

With more than 2,000 species known to science, most of them living in tropical freshwaters, we cannot hope to provide more than a brief summary here. Background research is important before purchasing any catfish, as these creatures, perhaps more than any other group of fish, are the victims of a number of misapprehensions by aquarists. Despite their immense variation in appearance, many fishkeepers assume they are all the same as regards behaviour and requirements.

Common mistakes include:

• Not realising that some catfish grow *big*. These fish range in size from a few centimetres (1-2 in) to two metres (seven feet) or more in length, and the large ones can live for very many years. This type of size range can be seen within some of the individual families, so the fact that one species is known to be small is not an invariable guarantee regarding its close relatives. Zoos and public aquaria are bursting with cast-off giant aquarium fish that have outgrown the largest accommodation their former owner could provide. In particular, aquarists should beware of the red-tailed catfish (*Phractocephalus hemioliopterus*), often available as very attractive youngsters of 8-10 cm (3-4 in), but which quickly grows to a monster well over a metre (39 in) long, and ultimately much larger.

• Forgetting that many catfish are nocturnal and require feeding after 'lights out'.

• Assuming that all species will scavenge all types of food, and thrive on scraps. Many are specialised feeders, and the larger species are often formidable predators.

• Assuming that all suckermouth species feed on algae. Not all are vegetarian, and the average aquarium does not provide enough algae for even a single individual.

• Using coarse gravel with bottom-dwelling species such that their delicate sensory barbels and unprotected undersides become abraded and open to infection.

• Not knowing that some species are gregarious and need to be kept in groups.

• Assuming all are armour-plated and invulnerable to attack by other fish.

• Not knowing that some freshwater species are very intolerant of salt.

• Not realising that the spines on the scutes and in the fins can puncture not only natural enemies but also polythene bags and aquarists' hands! Sometimes the spines are coated with poison, and this makes any wound extremely painful (it should be soaked in the hottest water bearable, and medical attention sought). The spines can easily become entangled in nets, and the barbels damaged by clumsy handling. Catfish must be handled with care!

However, although the last of the above points may sound daunting, if properly researched, suitably maintained, and handled with care and respect, catfish are some of the most interesting and rewarding of all aquarium fish.

The following are a few of the most popular tropical freshwater catfish families, but there are about 30 others, any of which may occasionally be encountered.

MOCHOKIDAE (upside-down catfish, synos)
Genera include: *Synodontis*, *Chiloglanis*, and *Mochokiella*.
A popular family of small to moderately large (7.5 cm/3 in to 38 cm/15 in), naked, African catfish, some with very attractive markings. Most are members of the genus *Synodontis*. Although one species, *S. nigriventris*, spends much of its time upside-down near the surface, many of the others tend to be bottom-dwellers and more conventional in their orientation, though they may sometimes swim on their sides or upside-down. Water chemistry requirements vary. Unfortunately, aquarists familiar with either the fluviatile acid-water species, or the alkaline-water East African lacustrine types, commonly assume that all 'synos' will be equally at home in the same tank, which is not the case. The smaller species are gregarious, the larger ones can be very territorial towards conspecifics. Little is known of their breeding habits, except that one species, the cuckoo catfish, *S. multipunctatus*, from Lake Tanganyika, substitutes its eggs for those of mouthbrooding cichlids at spawning time. There is no evidence that other synos are cuckoos – in fact most have no mouthbrooding cichlids available.

DORADIDAE (doradids, talking catfish)
Genera include: *Megalodoras*, *Amblydoras*, *Platydoras*, *Pseudodoras*, *Opsodoras*, *Oxydoras*, *Agamyxis*.
The name 'talking catfish' derives from the ability of doradids to produce sounds using their pectoral fins or swimbladders. All doradids come from South America, are armoured, and can lock their fins in the erected position if they feel threatened. This makes them difficult to net and handle. They range in size from about 7 cm (3 in) to more than 75 cm (30 in), and only the small types are suitable for the general community. They are rather peaceful carnivores, which may eat tankmates small enough to fit into their mouths. They require somewhat acid to neutral or slightly alkaline water.

CALLICHTHYIDAE (mailed catfish)
A South American family of armoured catfish, some extremely popular community fish. Genera include: *Corydoras*, *Brochis*, *Callichthys*, *Aspidoras*, *Hoplosternum*, and *Dianema*, of which the first is by far the best known and most popular. Size range is 2.5 cm/1 in to 20 cm/8 in, with the 'corys' among the smaller species (to 7.5 cm/3 in).

Many of these cats are shoaling fish, and the concept of keeping a single *Corydoras* as a scavenger is actually rather unkind. They are far happier in a small group, ideally of the same species, but a mixed group is better than just one individual. Because they are so often kept in community aquaria with dubious hygiene, inappropriate substrate material, and poor water quality, they have a reputation for suffering damage and infections to their barbels and undersides. This reflects poor fishkeeping rather than an inherent weakness in the fish. They have the ability to breathe atmospheric oxygen and can commonly be seen visiting the water's surface to do so, even in well-oxygenated aquaria – this does not necessarily mean there is anything amiss. Another common error is to assume that their armour makes them invulnerable – constant harassment can cause physical damage and very serious stress.

Breeding *Corydoras* is fairly easy – a group may well do so in the community aquarium. Spawning sites include the aquarium glass and plants. Some mailed catfish practise parental care. Breeding method 3 (Chapter 8), removing the adults if they show no interest in guarding the spawn.

LORICARIIDAE (loricariids, suckermouth catfish)
Another family of South American armoured catfish, again extremely popular. Genera include: *Ancistrus*, *Hypancistrus*, *Farlowella* (twig catfish), *Otocinclus*, *Peckoltia*, and *Rineloricaria*, whose members are fairly small (10-20 cm/4-8 in) and suited to the community aquarium. There are also larger types belonging to the genera *Hypostomus*, *Leporacanthicus*, *Sturisoma*, *Panaque*, and *Pterygoplichthys*. These include the 'plec', *Hypostomus plecostomus* (30 cm/12 in), small specimens of which are often purchased as algae-eaters for the community, which they eventually outgrow.

All these catfish have a suckermouth on the underside of their heads, used in nature to attach themselves to rocks in fast-flowing, well-oxygenated rivers. Rarely do they enjoy natural conditions in captivity! Although they are often regarded as herbivores by hobbyists, some are meat-eaters and will not do well on a diet of algae supplemented by lettuce leaves. Some are difficult to handle because of their spines.

Many loricariids have not been spawned in captivity, but *Ancistrus* are quite easy to breed. They practise parental care, laying their eggs in a hollow in bogwood (or other 'cave'). The male guards the spawn. As they are not easy to handle, they are best bred in their normal quarters; otherwise breeding method 3 (Chapter 8).

2. **CHARACIFORMS** (Order Characiformes)

Also popularly known as characins, although strictly speaking this name applies only to the family Characidae. A very large group of fish, found mainly in tropical freshwaters in the Americas and Africa. Some of the small characiforms are among the most popular fish for the community aquarium, while others, (e.g. piranhas), are best left to the expert. Most, including many large types, are shoaling fish. Small species tend to feed on aquatic invertebrates or insects that have fallen on to the water's surface, while larger types are more likely to be predatory or herbivorous. Water chemistry and other water conditions (Chapter 10) are variable with geography, but commonly are soft, acid, and slow-moving/still. Tank-bred stocks of some of the most popular softwater types have been acclimated to harder, more alkaline waters, in which they are, however, generally unlikely to breed. Many characiforms offered for sale (including popular species) are wild-caught and will benefit considerably from correct water conditions for general maintenance.

The following families of characiforms are particularly popular with aquarists, and most species are suitable for community aquaria provided water conditions are appropriate:

CHARACIDAE (true characins, tetras)
Generally small (up to 10 cm/5 in total length, usually smaller), often colourful, shoaling fish. They are suitable, in terms of temperament, for the general community, with plants for shelter and open midwater spaces in which the shoal may swim. Their natural diet is largely small invertebrates, but they will readily take flake, small pellets, and frozen foods. They are egg-scatterers which do not practise parental care; some are quite easily bred (breeding method 1a, Chapter 8, using a small shoal). Most species are neotropical, but there are also a fair number of African species, some available in the hobby. Most prefer, and will show far better coloration in, soft acid water, and under moderate rather than bright lighting (Chapter 12).

GASTEROPELECIDAE (hatchetfish)
Named in reference to their shape, these small (up to 6 cm/2.5 in) shoaling fish swim just below the surface, and can 'fly' out of the water to elude pursuit. They are exclusively South American in origin, and benefit from soft acid water (some species unconditionally require it). They are noted for being particularly sensitive to nitrogenous wastes (Chapter 10) and are sometimes used as 'pollution indicators' in tanks containing rarer and/or more expensive fish.
They are surface-feeders which may take flake, but sometimes require live invertebrate prey. The aquarium should be tightly covered, in case they take flight! A layer of small floating plants such as *Riccia*, duckweed (*Lemna*), and *Salvinia* reduces this danger. They attach their eggs to the roots of floating plants, or scatter them, but do not practise parental care (breeding method 1a, b, or c (Chapter 8), using a small group and additional floating plants).

LEBIASINIDAE (pencilfish and splash tetras)
A strictly South American family.
Among the pencilfish (genera *Nannostomus, Nannobrycon*), 6 cm/2.5 in is large! Although just as suitable for community life as small tetras, pencilfish have failed to achieve the same popularity, which is a pity. They should be kept in a shoal, and require water that is low in nitrogenous wastes and, ideally, soft and slightly acid. Bright light should be avoided, or areas of shade provided, and a dark-coloured substrate is preferable. Depending on species, pencilfish may swim at any level in the aquarium, but not normally right at the surface. They sometimes swim at strange angles (in a shoal), and change colour at night; neither behaviour is cause for concern. They have very small mouths. Flake and frozen foods may be accepted, but wild-caught individuals may require small live foods such as *Cyclops* (Chapter 7). They are egg-scatterers that will avidly cannibalise their spawn (breeding method 1a or 1b, Chapter 8, small group, with a dark bottom to the breeding tank – substrate, or, ideally, dark paper/cloth or similar beneath the tank).
Splash tetras (genera *Copeina, Copella, Pyrrhulina*) are sometimes larger (up to 15

cm/6 in) and are surface-dwellers, likely to jump at any provocation, so a tight-fitting hood is essential. *Copella arnoldi* actually leaps out of the water to spawn on the underside of a leaf just above the surface. The male then hovers below the eggs, splashing them sporadically with his tail to keep them moist. The other members of this group also practise parental care, but spawn more conventionally, on large aquatic plant leaves, the male once again guarding the spawn (breeding method 3a, Chapter 8, in pairs).

3. CICHLIDS (Order Perciformes, Family Cichlidae)

An extremely diverse family found mainly in Africa and the tropical Americas, with a small number of representatives in Asia, occurring in all types of water conditions including brackish. Aquarists recognise a number of major groups – 'Rift Valley Cichlids' (East Africa), 'Central Americans', 'West Africans', 'South American dwarfs' – as well as a number of smaller ones. Size range 2 cm/0.75 in to 90 cm/36 in.

It has been said that if an ecological niche or a food resource exists, somewhere a cichlid will have evolved to exploit it. Indeed, the diversity of their habits, together with their often bright coloration, are two of the reasons for their popularity with aquarists. Above all, they are noted for their interesting breeding behaviour: all cichlids practise parental care. Two main strategies are involved:
• Substrate-brooding, where the eggs are laid on a rock, root, plant, or other surface and guarded by both parents (community tank or breeding method 3, Chapter 8).
• Mouthbrooding, where eggs and fry are brooded in the mouth of one or both parents (usually the female). These cichlids are normally bred in their usual quarters rather than a special tank, but the brooding female is often removed to a special small tank.

Unfortunately, while aquarists are attracted by this parental behaviour, many fail to realise that the downside of a fish that defends its eggs and fry is that this involves attacking any potential enemies that come close. In captivity, 'enemies' mean tankmates, and 'close' may mean the other end of the aquarium. The area defended is termed the 'breeding territory' and may be guarded even when the fish are not breeding. Thus many cichlids require their own quarters, with no other fish. However, a number of smaller species ('dwarf cichlids') can be kept in a general community provided the aquarium is large enough (90 cm/36 in minimum length) and the water parameters appropriate. One cichlid, the angelfish (*Pterophyllum scalare*), is an extremely popular and usually trouble-free community fish; another, the discus (*Symphysodon* spp.), is virtually a cult fish, with two species. Both angels and discus are available in a number of colour types, mostly produced by selective breeding.

Successful cichlid-keeping depends largely on circumventing territoriality, and aquarists have devised various methods of so doing to suit different breeding behaviour patterns. Because of this, as well as their diversity of behaviour, diet, and water requirements, it is essential to research any cichlid before purchase.

4. CYPRINIFORMS (Order Cypriniformes)

Also popularly known as cyprinids, although strictly speaking this name applies only to the family Cyprinidae. This large group, found in Africa, Asia, Europe, and southern North America, is not restricted to tropical waters, and includes such familiar coldwater species as the goldfish (*Carassius auratus*) and Koi (*Cyprinus carpio*). It contains a number of families, some of whose members are long-time aquarium favourites, noted for their hardiness and ease of maintenance, and in some cases, breeding. Many cypriniforms are shoaling or sociable fish. The following families contain many popular species, often suited to the community aquarium:

CYPRINIDAE (cyprinids – including barbs, danios, rasboras, 'sharks')
Barbs range in size from about 2.5 cm/1 in to 30 cm/12 in. They are shoaling fish found in all types of fresh water in Africa and Asia and are generally unfussy about water chemistry in captivity. They are omnivorous and will readily accept prepared foods.

Danios (size range 5-10 cm/2-4 in) come from Asia. Their requirements are similar and they too are excellent beginners' fish.

The White Cloud Mountain minnow (*Tanichthys albonubes*) is another very popular hardy cyprinid, which requires cooler than normal temperatures and well-oxygenated water, as it comes from a higher altitude than many tropicals. Temperature range 16-23 °C (60-74 °F).

Barbs, danios and White Clouds are egg-scatterers that do not practise parental care, and barbs and danios may eat their eggs in the confines of the aquarium (breeding methods 1a, b, c, Chapter 8, using a pair or small group).

Rasboras are found in south-east Asia and Indonesia. They are excellent community fish, being small and peaceful, but some require more attention to water chemistry than other cyprinids and prefer live foods. Soft acid water is required for breeding some otherwise hardy species. They are plant-spawners with adhesive eggs; some scatter their eggs among fine-leaved vegetation, but others, including the popular harlequin rasbora (*Rasbora heteromorpha*), stick their eggs to the underside of broader leaves (breeding methods 1a, 1d, Chapter 8).

'Sharks' are not true sharks, but look like miniatures of their very distant marine cousins (the similarity relates mostly to the pointed dorsal fin). They range in size from about 10 cm/4 in to 60 cm/24 in. The smaller ones are popular community fish, but most – the exception is the flying fox (*Epalzeorhynchus kallopterus*) – can be troublesome, acting territorially and bullying tankmates (and each other if kept in groups). Hence they should be kept only with fish of similar or somewhat larger size and robust temperament. They are hardy as regards water chemistry, and omnivorous. The larger species are more peaceful but their size precludes their inclusion in the general community. They are not normally bred in domestic aquaria.

COBITIDAE (loaches)
Loaches are bottom-dwelling cypriniforms. They require a fine, soft substrate (e.g. sand) to avoid damage to their often scaleless undersides and sensory barbels; some, notably khuhli loaches (*Acanthophthalmus* spp.) and the horse-faced loach (*Acanthopsis choiorhynchus*) like to burrow in the substrate. Most species appreciate hiding places among plants, or in 'caves' (Chapter 11). They come from a variety of water conditions in nature, but most species are hardy as regards water chemistry.

Their natural diet is aquatic invertebrates, but most will accept manufactured or frozen foods (Chapter 7). Some, including the most popular species, the clown loach (*Botia macracanthus*) are gregarious and benefit from being kept in a small group, but a number are quarrelsome among themselves or may harass other fish species.

Probably the most popular genus of loaches is *Botia*, which contains a number of attractively patterned, sometimes colourful, smallish species. Loaches are rarely bred in captivity. Some species are noted for sensitivity to some disease remedies.

5. CYPRINODONTS (Order Cyprinodontiformes)

Also commonly known as toothcarps, this order of generally small, usually surface-dwelling and feeding, fish comprises two major groups: those which reproduce by laying eggs (egg-laying toothcarps), and those which produce live young (live-bearing or viviparous toothcarps). The latter group, the livebearers, includes some of the most popular and easy-to-keep freshwater tropicals, while some of the egg-layers are rarely seen and regarded as very difficult fish, reserved for the specialist. Two families are particularly popular:

FAMILY CYPRINODONTIDAE (egg-laying toothcarps, killifish)
Killifish are found throughout tropical zones and are small, often very colourful, fish, ranging from 2.5-10 cm/1-4 in. They fall roughly into two groups: those from pools that dry up each year ('annual killies') and those from more permanent waters. The former are short-lived and normally maintained only by specialists; it is rare to see them offered for sale and stocks normally have to be obtained from other hobbyists. The same is often true of the second group, although a few of the 'easier' species (*Pachypanchax* spp., *Aplocheilus* spp., *Jordanella floridae*) are sometimes found in retail outlets as they make good community fish. So, too, do many of the others as long as water conditions and diet are appropriate. They are not aggressive fish.

Many – but not all – killies originate from soft acid water, which is required for successful spawning. However, most will thrive in neutral conditions. Another requirement is abundant live food (especially if they are to be bred), though many will accept flake. Many tolerate slightly cooler temperatures than most tropicals.

Breeding killifish is a complex hobby in itself, requiring a collection of small aquaria for conditioning, spawning, and resting adults, and rearing fry. Most killies are easy to sex – males are generally more colourful than females. In fact, the females of the species within a genus are commonly very similar in appearance, so it is unwise to mix such species: you may not be able to tell them apart when you want to separate them, and hybrids may occur. Male killies are noted for 'driving' females hard in their eagerness to keep spawning. This can fatally stress or exhaust the female, so it is usual to have two females to a male; and, unless they are kept, when not breeding, in a large aquarium where the females can evade the male, it is usual to keep him separate until the time comes to breed them, and again afterwards. The fish need to be extremely well fed on live foods before and during spawning, in order to maintain their strength and female egg production.

The annual species (e.g. *Nothobranchius* spp., *Cynolebias* spp., *Pterolebias* spp., and some *Aphyosemion* spp.) spawn, in nature, in the mud at the bottom of their pools. The eggs survive the drying-up of the water, and most hatch when the rains come. But in case the rain is just a short shower, to be followed by further drought, a few eggs will not hatch until they have been wetted twice – or maybe three or four times.

Thus the future of the species is assured. In the aquarium, peat is used as a mud-substitute, with the aquarist subsequently simulating the dry and rainy seasons to induce the eggs to hatch (breeding method 2a, Chapter 8).

The 'perennial' killies often spawn almost daily for a period of weeks, usually either attaching their eggs to plants or scattering them on the bottom. They can be bred in the community tank, but the fry are usually eaten, so any serious breeding attempt should take place in a special tank. Because the eggs are laid over a period of time, the fry hatch in sequence. Without the aquarist's intervention the larger ones may cannibalise their tinier siblings, so the eggs are generally removed at regular intervals and hatched in separate batches (breeding method 2b, Chapter 8).

POECILIIDAE (live-bearing toothcarps)
These fish originate from the Americas and some of the Caribbean islands. They include some of the most popular hardy species – guppy, molly (both *Poecilia* species), swordtail, and platy (both *Xiphophorus* species), available in many fancy colour varieties. The family also includes the limias (*Poecilia* spp.) and mosquito fish (*Gambusia* spp.). Poeciliids range in size from just 2 cm/0.75 in (e.g. the male *Heterandria formosa*, also known as a mosquito fish), up to 20 cm/8 in (e.g. female *Belonesox*, a voracious piscivore). Females are larger than males on an age-for-age basis.

Most poeciliids prefer neutral to slightly alkaline water. Several species, such as some mollies and some gambusias, come from brackish water, while others have both freshwater and brackish populations in the wild. Contrary to popular belief, the original guppies from which cultivated stocks are descended are freshwater fish (from the rivers of Trinidad), although brackish guppy populations do also exist.

Poeciliids will accept and thrive on manufactured foods but many require vegetable matter in their diet, which can be furnished by vegetarian flake or granules. The fact they can survive on manufactured foods does not mean that they will not enjoy and benefit from other types of food.

These fish give birth to live young which are immediately able to swim, feed, and fend for themselves. There is no parental care. Fertilisation is internal – males possess a modified anal fin, the gonopodium, which is used to inseminate the female. The presence of the tube-shaped gonopodium in mature males makes sexing these fish very easy. The female can store sperm in her body, so a single mating can give rise to several broods of young. Average brood size varies between species, and according to the age and size of the female, ranging from two or three babies to 200 or more. Species such as the guppy can give birth every three to four weeks. Most species will readily breed in captivity (breeding method 4, Chapter 8)

6. LABYRINTH FISH (Order Perciformes, Suborder Anabantoidei)

The families Anabantidae, Belontidae, Helostomidae, and Osphromenidae are commonly referred to as anabantids by aquarists, although strictly, that name should be reserved for the members of the family Anabantidae. The alternative name 'labyrinth fish' refers to their shared character of possessing an accessory respiratory organ, the labyrinth (so called because of its structure), which enables them to survive in waters with a minimal oxygen content by breathing atmospheric air. They are African and Asian fish – there are no anabantoids in the Americas. Most of the popular species, and those suited to the general community, are members of the family Belontidae. Most labyrinth fish practise parental care, usually by the male. A few brood the eggs in their mouths, but the brood-guarding method commonly associated with the group is bubblenest-building. By passing atmospheric air through his gills, the male creates a mass of mucus-coated bubbles at the water's surface, commonly among surface vegetation. The pair spawn beneath the nest, and the eggs, which are lighter than water, float up to the surface. After spawning, the male guards the nest (including against the female, who must be removed if the tank size is such that she cannot keep well away), and tends the eggs. When they hatch, he continues to tend the larvae, retrieving any that fall out of the nest. Once they are free-swimming, however, he is likely to eat them. This fascinating behaviour can be observed in their normal aquarium or a special breeding tank (breeding method 3a, Chapter 8).

Labyrinth fish are extremely popular with aquarists. Many are small, colourful, peaceful, hardy fish suited to the community aquarium. If problems do occur, this is commonly because their sometimes long, flowing finnage proves irresistible to fin-nipping tankmates, so it is especially important to consider the possible effect of tankmates on the labyrinths and *vice versa*. Some anabantoids are large, and some are aggressive among themselves and/or towards other fish, so do not assume that any member of the group is a community fish.

Water chemistry requirements vary from species to species within each family; many species are hardy in this respect, but a few have very stringent requirements. A general requirement is for a warm and humid air space above the water's surface, especially in breeding tanks – breathing cold air may kill the fry.

FAMILY BELONTIDAE (gouramis, fighting fish, combtails, paradise fish)
The gouramis in this family (genera *Trichogaster*, *Trichopsis*, *Sphaerichthys*, *Colisa*) include some of the most popular anabantoids, all suited to community life, provided, in some cases, that the water chemistry is suited to their special needs. They are omnivorous and will take manufactured foods, but should also be offered small live foods. *Sphaerichthys* are mouthbrooders, while the others are bubblenest-builders. All originate in Asia.

The fighting fish, genus *Betta*, are represented in the aquarium chiefly by *B. splendens*, the Siamese fighter, although a number of others are occasionally available. You will never see two male fighters in the same tank in an aquarium shop, and they may be housed in jars on a shelf (a widespread practice which must be regarded as unkind). If kept together, they will fight to the death, so only one male can be kept in the home aquarium. Females are not belligerent and lack the splendid flowing finnage of the males. Siamese fighters have been selectively bred to improve their finnage and to produce a number of colour varieties. They are bubblenest-builders, but some other *Betta* species are mouthbrooders.

Combtails (genus *Belontia*) are not good community fish, as they tend to be aggressive when adult. They are bubblenest-builders.

Paradise fish (*Macropodus*, *Parosphronemus*, *Pseudosphronemus*) are also bubblenesters and tend to aggression – males may fight almost as single-mindedly as those of *Betta splendens*. The species usually seen, *Macropodus opercularis*, is tolerant of quite low temperatures, and hence was the first tropical ornamental fish to reach Europe alive back in the 19th century. Its general tolerance of low temperature and poor water quality enabled it to survive the long voyage from Asia.

7. RAINBOWFISH (Order Atheriniformes)

Members of the Melanotaeniidae, Atherinidae, and Pseudomugilidae families are all commonly referred to as rainbowfish, because their iridescent sheen makes them appear to change colour as they catch the light from different angles as they swim around the aquarium. All are relatively small (5-15 cm/2-6 in), peaceful, colourful fish. *Pseudomugil* species (blue-eyes) are difficult and best kept by the specialist, but the others are suitable for a community aquarium. Different species may come from quite different habitats, and must be individually researched as regards water and habitat requirements, which are important to their wellbeing. Most are omnivorous, but benefit from plenty of live foods. They are quite easy to spawn, and scatter their eggs among fine-leaved plant foliage (see breeding method 1a, Chapter 8). They do not practise any parental care.

FAMILY MELANOTAENIIDAE (rainbowfish)
A family of rainbowfish found in Australia and the island of New Guinea. The family includes the genera *Melanotaenia*, *Chilatherina*, and *Glossolepis*, and these are generally regarded as the easiest 'rainbows' to maintain.

FAMILY ATHERINIDAE (Silversides)
Atherinids are found in Madagascar and parts of Indonesia. Two species are relatively popular: the Madagascar rainbow (*Bedotia geayi*) and the Celebes rainbow (*Telmatherina ladigesi*). Their flowing finnage makes them vulnerable to fin-nipping.

Table 3 The Main Groups of Tropical Freshwater Aquarium Fish

Groups are arranged in the order normally used by systematicists (See Chapter 2), rather than alphabetically, as this best illustrates the relationships between them. Common names have been given where available.

Abbreviations: pg = panglobal (except polar regions); pt = pantropical; nt = neotropical; Af = Africa; As = Asia; Au = Australia; SA = South America; CA = Central America (and extreme southern USA). * denotes further details in the text of Chapter 3.

Order/Family	Common Name	Range	Size	Water	Notes
Osteoglossiformes					
Osteoglossidae	Arawanas	Af,SA,As,Au	to 120cm/48"	varies	Too large for domestic aquaria
Pantodontidae	Butterflyfish	Af	10cm/4"	soft/acid/calm	Peaceful, delicate, surface dweller, live food; jump
Notopteridae	Knifefishes	Af,As	20-60cm/8-24"	soft/acid	Nocturnal, not for general community
Mormyridae	Elephantnoses	Af	23 cm/9"	varies	Crepuscular, need sand substrate
Characiformes*					
Characidae*	Tetras	Nt,Af	2-10cm/1-4"	varies	Most shoal; most are excellent community fish; planted aquarium
Serrasalmidae	Piranhas,pacu, & merynns	SA	10-100cm/4-39"	soft/acid	Many unsuitable for domestic aquaria; many shoal; piranhas dangerous
Gasteropelecidae*	Hatchetfish	SA	2-6cm/1-2.5"	soft/acid/calm	Shoaling surface-dwellers; jump; may need live food; floating plants
Lebiasinidae*	Pencilfish	SA	to 6 cm/2.5"	soft/acid/calm	Shoaling; ideal for general community; planted aquarium
Anostomidae	Splash Tetras	SA	to 15cm/6"	soft/acid/calm	Planted aquarium
	Headstanders	SA	10-30cm/4-12"	soft/acid/current	Rocks with vertical crevices; groups of 6+
Gymnotiformes					
Electrophoridae	Electric eels	SA	Large	not critical	Can deliver lethal electric shock, unsuitable for home aquaria
Apteronotidae Rhamphichthyidae Gymnotidae	American knifefish	SA	30-60cm/12-24"	soft/acid/calm	Difficult fish, for the specialist experienced aquarist only

	Common name	Distribution	Size	Water	Notes
Cyprinodontiformes*					
Cyprinodontidae*	Toothcarps / Killifish	pt	up to 10cm/4"	variable	Very diverse group; some specialist fish with stringent requirements; some suitable for community
Goodeidae	Goodeids	CA	5-20cm/2-8"	hard/alkaline	Some suitable for community, some specialist fish; some livebearers, some egg-layers
Poeciliidae*	Livebearers	SA,CA	5-10cm/2-4"	hard/alkaline	Includes some of the most popular, hardy, community fish and cichlid foods - guppies, platies, mollies, swordtails
Atheriniformes*					
Melanotaeniidae	Rainbowfish	Au,As	to 10cm/4"	variable	Excellent community fish; shoaling; planted tank
Atherinidae	Silversides	Af,As	to 10cm/4"	variable	Good community fish; shoaling; planted tank; avoid mixing with fin-nipping species
Pseudomugilidae	Blue-eyes	Au,As	to 7.5cm/3"	variable	Difficult; shoaling; planted tank; best kept by experienced aquarist in single species tank
Perciformes					
Channidae	Snakeheads	Af,As	20-100cm/8-40"	neutral/calm	Predators; unsuitable for community; may bite fingers; can breathe atmospheric air and may climb out of tank; good pets if kept alone
Monodactylidae	Monos	As	to 25cm/10"	brackish	Biotope aquarium necessary; mix well with scats (below)
Toxotidae	Archerfish	As	to 10cm/4"	brackish	Require highly-specialised accommodation (paludarium)
Scatophagidae	Scats	As	to 30cm/12"	brackish/salt	Biotope aquarium essential; mix well with monos (above); adult scats are marine fish in nature!
Nandidae	Nandids, leaffish	pt nt,Af,As	8-10cm/3-4"	varies	Highly predatory; unsuitable for community
Cichlidae*	Cichlids	nt,Af,As	2-90cm/1-36"	varies	Extremely diverse group; popular with aquarists on account of advanced parental care; most territorial; many require specialised maintenance; only a few suited to general community - ALWAYS check, small size not reliable indicator!
Eleotridae	Sleeper gobies	Pg	7.5-51cm/3-20"	varies	Very few suited to general community; some require brackish water
Gobiidae	Gobies	Pg	to 15cm/6"	varies	Very few suited to general community; many are brackish-water fish, and some marine.
Periophthalmidae	Mudskippers	As	8-20cm/3-8"	brackish	Highly specialised paludarium essential; difficult
Anabantidae	Climbing perch and bush fish	As,Af	5-12cm/2-5"	variable	Peaceful but predatory - will eat smaller tankmates; can breath atmospheric air; climbing perch may climb out of tank

Cypriniformes*					
Cyprinidae*	Barbs,danios,rasboras	Af,As	2-60cm/1-24"	variable	Many are popular community fish
Gyrinochelidae	Sucking loach	As	12cm/5"	not critical	Common community fish; may attach to flat-sided fish using suckermouth, causing damage/stress
Cobitidae*	Loaches	As	8-12cm/3-12"	variable	Bottom-dwellers requiring fine substrate; many good community fish; some need to be kept in groups
Balitoridae	Hillstream "loaches"	As	5-10cm/2-4"	acid-neutral/current	Also known as Hong-kong "loaches"; require special biotope aquarium
Siluriformes*					
Bagridae	Bagrids, naked catfish	Af,As	5-60cm/2-24"	variable	Predators; small species suitable for community if tankmates too large to eat
Siluridae	–	Af,As	8cm-2m/3"-6" or more	variable	Most unsuitable for community aquaria; not all tropical
Claridae	Walking catfish	Af,As	30cm/12" or more	not critical	Predatory; unsuitable for community; can breathe atmospheric air and may climb out of aquarium!
Malapteruridae	Electric catfish	Af	large	not critical	Can deliver a lethal electric shock, hence unsuitable for domestic aquaria
Mochokidae*	Upside-down catfish	Af	7-38cm/3-15"	variable	Small species suitable for community aquaria; popular group; not all swim upside-down
Doradidae*	Talking catfish	SA	7-75cm/3-30"	variable	Carnivores; many are strictly specialist fish; difficult to handle because of erectile spines
Aspredinidae	Banjo catfish	SA	up to 15cm/6"	variable	Crepuscular; require dimly lit aquarium or will hide; otherwise suitable for community
Auchenipteridae	Driftwood catfish	SA	up to 20cm/8"	variable	Peaceful; require hidingplaces and peaceful tankmates
Pangasiidae	–	As	large	variable	Specialist fish; too large for community aquaria
Pimelodidae	"Pims"	SA	mostly very large	variable	Carnivores; red-tailed catfish (*Phractocephalus haemaliopterus*), often sold as attractive juveniles, attains 100cm or more!
Callichthyidae*	Mailed catfish	SA	2-20cm/1-8"	variable	small types (eg *Corydoras*) ideal community fish; many need to be kept in shoals
Loricariidae*	Suckermouth catfish	SA	10-30cm/4-12"	variable	Popular group, not all suited to community or for beginner; not all herbivores as sometimes thought

Belontidae*	Gouramis, fighting fish, combtails, paradise fish	As	to 15cm/6"	variable	Very popular group; some, but not all, are good community fish; some can be aggressive; some are delicate
Helostomatidae	Kissing gouramis	As	to 45cm/18"	not critical	Often kept in community aquaria but not ideal occupants; "kissing" behaviour is actually a trial of strength!
Osphronemidae	Giant gourami	As	to 45cm/18"	not critical	Ultimately very large, ugly fish, with little to recommend it; public aquaria are full of specimens that have outgrown domestic aquaria
Synbranchiformes					
Mastacembelidae	Spiny eels	As,Af	30-100cm/12-40"	variable	None suited to general community; large specimens aggressive, may bite owner
Tetraodontiformes					
Tetraodontidae	Puffers	pt	5-100 cm/2-40"	variable	Most are marine or brackish, only a few freshwater; may need veterinary attention to teeth unless fed natural diet of snails

CHAPTER 4

MOTIVATION AND INTELLIGENCE

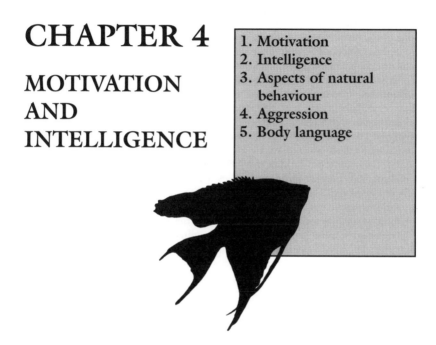

Because the aquarium is a self-contained unit, the behaviour of its occupants does not directly affect the household, unlike that of pets such as cats and dogs, which roam freely around the house. Nevertheless, the keen and observant aquarist cannot help but take an interest in the activities of his fish and in the motivation behind them. Sometimes, if the behaviour is destructive or otherwise 'antisocial', an understanding of what lies at its root may render it at least tolerable, and even suggest methods of accommodating or countering it. In fact, a number of aquarium techniques, especially as regards breeding (Chapter 8), have been evolved by aquarists simply to deal with some of the problems associated with trying to simulate nature in a small glass box.

1. MOTIVATION

The motivation of all creatures centres on a powerful instinct for individual, genetic, and species survival. The objective of individual survival is to live long enough to pass on genetic material to a new generation and to perpetuate the species. This applies equally to fish, so we may expect to find these various types of survival at the root of their behaviour.

Individual survival depends largely on finding sufficient food for energy and growth, and on avoiding being eaten or killed in any other manner. Moreover, scientific evidence suggests that fish suffer both stress and pain, confirming what has been suspected by observant aquarists for decades. Thus it is now known that avoidance of pain is a stronger stimulus than hunger. Feeding and escape/evasion behaviour are thus everyday aspects of life, in fish as in other animals.

Genetic survival depends on reproductive success and the survival of at least one of the offspring to adulthood, to breed in its turn.

Species survival requires breeding success by a number of pairs in order to ensure a viable breeding population with sufficient genetic diversity.

It is assumed that a fish's motivation to feed, survive and breed is purely instinctive, although some species are capable of learning to exploit new food sources or habitats (in both the aquarium and the wild), and of recognising and evaluating new potential dangers (e.g. vacuum cleaners, cats!) and using unnatural types of cover (e.g. flowerpots, pieces of pipe, coconut shells). Fundamental reproductive techniques (Chapter 8) and courtship behaviour change only very slowly (over centuries or millennia), but the finer details, such as where the eggs are laid, may depend on circumstances and include an opportunistic element. There is a recorded case of eggs being attached, in the wild, to a floating biscuit (cookie) wrapper instead of the more normal floating vegetation, and the use of artificial 'spawning media' is commonplace in the aquarium.

The aquarist must learn to accept the immutability of his fishes' basic survival instincts. He will not change them, though he may find ways of circumventing their undesirable aspects.

2. INTELLIGENCE

Newcomers to the aquarium hobby often assume that fish are unintelligent and unresponsive pets. Indeed many aquaria are initially intended as purely decorative objects, with little or no regard for the welfare of the occupants as living creatures. Fortunately, the majority of aquarists come to appreciate that fish are not only attractive to look at, but interesting as regards their behaviour. They realise that their fish are aware of the world outside their aquarium, capable of learning, and able to adapt their behaviour in response to quite unnatural stimuli they encounter in captivity.

The degree of responsiveness and learning ability displayed varies considerably between families, and even species, but in some cases is clearly greater than that of mammals of equivalent size. Indeed, in some cases, behavioural adaptability has proved so great as to cast doubt on the validity of aquarium observations in the study of behaviour, because it is difficult to evaluate the extent to which the behaviour exhibited reflects adaptation to the artificial environment.

3. ASPECTS OF NATURAL BEHAVIOUR

Not all fish species behave in the same way in response to their survival instincts. However, depending on the species, the following are all elements of natural behaviour. Those which the aquarist may find antisocial or destructive are not motivated by any intention to annoy, but are simply part of the normal instinctive repertoire of the 'guilty' fish. A number of problems arising from these basic behavioural elements are discussed in Chapter 5.

Note that some behavioural elements may have more than one function. For example, a predator that uses camouflage to entrap its prey (feeding behaviour) is also protected from predation by that same camouflage (escape/evasion behaviour).

FEEDING BEHAVIOUR

• Eating other fish or plants. Even non-piscivorous species will commonly eat small fish that fall into their preferred size range for food items, and most adult fish will eat eggs and fry if the opportunity arises.

• Digging in the substrate. Some fish simply forage in the uppermost layer of the substrate, but some may sift it through their gills, sometimes taking in large mouthfuls in the process.

• Defending a feeding territory. In the aquarium it is quite common for a fish to lay claim to the area of the tank where feeding takes place, or to defend a worm-feeder against tankmates.

• Lurking. Hiding among cover, lying in wait for prey – even if the prey is inanimate aquarium food!

• Camouflage. Some fish, for example some nandids, are cryptic in coloration or shape to enable them to remain unnoticed by potential prey, and actively position themselves to take advantage of their camouflage when hunting. The pike characin (*Acestrorhynchus microlepis*) and pike livebearer (*Belonesox belizanus*) are slender so as to present a minimal frontal profile when facing their prey.

ESCAPE/EVASION BEHAVIOUR

• Hiding among plants, rocks, and other decor items.

• Digging to enlarge a cave or partially block the entrance.

• Burrowing in the substrate to hide from possible danger or to elude an actual threat (including a net-wielding aquarist!).

• Camouflage. Cryptic shape or coloration enables the fish to merge into its surroundings and be less visible to predators.

• Shoaling. The swimming pattern of the shoal may be visually confusing to predators, and by swimming in a group each fish reduces the statistical likelihood of being singled out as prey.

• Jumping and skimming along the surface to evade actual or expected attack/pursuit. Again, fish may behave in this way when threatened by the net.

• Erecting their fin spines makes fish difficult and painful to swallow.

BREEDING BEHAVIOUR

• Fighting: for a mate, or breeding territory, or both.

• Chasing:

– the opposite sex prior to and during spawning (usually male chasing female). The chasing is often interspersed with episodes of courtship display, e.g. fin spreading, quivering.

– other fish. This may involve chasing away competitors for a mate or spawning territory, or (in species that practise parental care) chasing away potential egg/fry predators.

– the partner away after spawning (in parental species where only one partner

guards the spawn, for example, gouramis).
- Hiding, in species which guard their eggs/fry in a sheltered or secluded spot.
- Digging, to enlarge a spawning 'cave', or to prepare a spawning 'nest' or pits in which to guard larvae/fry. Plants, and sometimes equipment, such as heaters, may be cleared away from the 'site'.

4. AGGRESSION

Aggression can be a serious problem in the aquarium. It is the commonest cause of injuries (Chapter 21, section 1.6.1) – either damage caused directly by an attack, or through collisions with decor/equipment during flight. Both injuries and stress (*ibid*, 1.5.2) can lead to fish deaths. Sometimes a particular fish may be seen to be acting aggressively, but sometimes only the results of aggression (injuries) are apparent, in which case the aquarium needs to be closely monitored to establish which fish is/are responsible.

It is rare for a fish to attack another without some sort of provocation. An attack may appear to be unprovoked from the aquarist's viewpoint, but this is simply because he fails to appreciate the underlying motivation.

TERRITORIALITY AND GUARDING
Some fish establish feeding and/or breeding territories. The latter may be simply for spawning, or, in species that practise parental care, a sometimes substantial area, which acts as a nursery for the fry, and from which all other fish are violently excluded. Some of the chasing behaviours listed earlier are territorial, and commonly regarded as aggressive by aquarists, even though they are in fact defensive.

A defensive attack is usually preceded by threatening behaviour, which in nature would normally be sufficient to warn off the intruder, whose natural reaction is flight. The defending fish is unlikely to pursue beyond the boundary of the territory, as this would leave the mate/territory/eggs/fry unguarded. Problems stemming from guarding behaviour occur in the aquarium only because there is insufficient space for the intruder to distance itself from the attacker, who thus continues attacking relentlessly. Parentally-motivated individuals will often launch near-suicidal attacks on larger enemies, including nets, siphon tubes, and the aquarist's hands.

Actual fights do sometimes occur, where fish are competing for a mate or territory. Such fights can be serious. Again, the usual reaction of a loser is to flee; and, again, this may lead to problems in the aquarium because there is insufficient space to escape the victor, to whom the continued presence of the loser suggests that it is still trying to compete. Another situation where fights may occur is at shared territorial boundaries; however, these are usually largely ritualised battles between well-matched and equally motivated individuals. The serious fighting will have occurred when the territories were first established.

When new fish are introduced into a new aquarium containing territorial species, they are commonly attacked. The aquarist finds this particularly puzzling when the new fish is intended as a mate for a resident of the same species, and hence (in the aquarist's view) a desirable tankmate. However, the territorial fish sees only an intruder, unless the new fish is ready to spawn immediately.

Territoriality and pair-bonding commonly go hand-in-hand in some groups where the bonding often precedes the carving out of territory, or requires the non-territorial partner to approach the territorial one while giving the correct courtship signals. This does not happen when a confused (by new surroundings) and stressed (by transportation) fish is unceremoniously tipped into the existing territory of another.

Another apparently inexplicable form of aggression is where, after spawning, one partner attacks the other. This may be because, in nature, the partner would not remain in the territory (as in the case of gouramis and fighting fish, and mouthbrooding cichlids). This problem sometimes also occurs where normally both parents would remain together to guard the brood, and usually if no other fish are present. It is thought that this occurs because the aggressive partner has a very strong instinct to defend the territory, and, lacking any real enemies, it attacks the partner instead.

PREDATION

Aquarists also commonly mistake predation for aggression. However, it is no more aggressive for a piscivore to eat another fish than it is for a herbivore to eat a plant. The fault lies with the aquarist for mixing incompatible fish.

A few fish eat parts of other fish rather than the whole individual; scales and fins are the parts most commonly consumed. In nature, the predator will move from victim to victim across a sizeable area containing a multitude of fish, such that no individual is likely to be seriously damaged. In the aquarium, however, immense damage can be done in a short space of time. Obviously there is no place for these specialised feeders in an aquarium containing other fish. This type of behaviour should not, however, be confused with fin-nipping, which usually affects species with long, flowing finnage, whose extremities are nipped off. It is thought that the attacker sees the fin tip moving and mistakes it for a food item. Fast reactions are necessary to capture some small prey items, and the fish does not have time to stop and see exactly what it is grabbing.

5. BODY LANGUAGE

Fish are known to communicate in a number of ways. Some, such as knifefish, produce electrical impulses which it is thought are used for communication, *inter alia*. Some emit audible sounds, while scientific studies have shown that others produce sound-waves inaudible to humans. But fish also have a varied repertoire of visible signals, involving both movement and colour patterns.

Some of these signals seem to be fairly universally understood, whatever the species. For example, a fish which faces another, flares its gills, and opens its mouth wide, is making what is called a 'frontal threat' display. This may be an aggressive move, to defend territory, or a defensive one, to make the displaying fish look large and nasty, hence too big to eat or attack. In some species males may use this display to impress females.

Lateral display of the body, sometimes with simultaneous quivering and/or body/tail slapping, is another common gesture of a courtship display, although in some fish it is also an aggressive/defensive signal ('lateral threat'). Spreading (sometimes with quivering) of the fins often accompanies lateral display, and is another expression of courtship or threat. In some territorial fish, lateral display, with quivering and fin-spreading, seems to fill a dual and simultaneous role when dealing with individuals of the same species, perhaps translating as: "See how big and colourful I am. Come and spawn with me or else get out of here." In species that spread their fins in threat, folding of the fins by the opponent appears to indicate submission/deference, while erecting the fins and quivering back is to accept the challenge.

Coloration, including the colour pattern, is also an extremely important signal. At its most basic level it helps members of the same species locate or identify each other as potential mates, competitors, and/or members of the shoal. It may go no further than that; however, many species exhibit different coloration to signal that they are in breeding condition and impress potential mates with their fine colours. Sometimes a ripe female develops a brightly-coloured area on the abdomen, accentuating its round, egg-filled, shape. Fish with special breeding colours are sometimes quite drab and inconspicuous when not breeding, as visibility can be a disadvantage, rendering the fish more prone to predation; or, if it is a predator, more obvious to potential prey. Breeding coloration may also serve as a stimulus to competition, such as fighting for mates or breeding territory, which would be pointless, and probably disadvantageous, outside the breeding season (e.g. in shoaling fish).

Some types of fish have an even more highly-developed colour 'language', which they may use, for example, to indicate their status within the species group – the brighter/bolder the colour and pattern, the higher the status. They may also use colour to threaten (bright colour) or indicate submission (drab or reduced colour), often with gestures of the type described above. Some parental fish have special coloration while guarding young; this may be used to warn off intruders, or to draw attention to the adult and hence away from the fry. Some brood-care patterns have been shown, by scientific experiment, to act as attractants for the brood (easy location of parent). Even more remarkable, in some fish, fin/body movements and coloration are used to communicate different instructions to the fry, for example "Come here", "Follow me", "Hide on the bottom".

We must assume that each species has its own 'language' pertaining to its own particular life patterns. There are, however, strong indications that closely-related species clearly understand each others's basic signals, though they may not have the faintest idea what members of a quite different fish family are 'talking about'.

Although the aquarist cannot communicate back, he can learn to recognise some of the signals his fish are making. This may enable him to predict their actions, for example to spot imminent breeding or trouble brewing. It can also add an extra dimension to his enjoyment of his aquarium.

CHAPTER 5

BEHAVIOURAL PROBLEMS
(What if my fish...?)

1. Feeding behaviour
2. Escape/evasion behaviour
3. Breeding behaviour
4. Behaviour with multiple causes

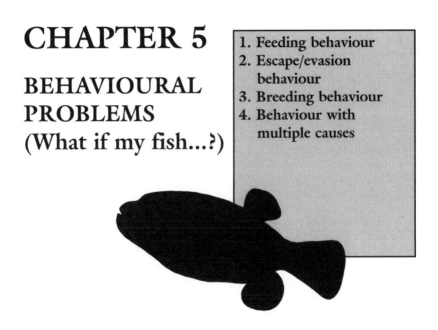

This chapter examines some of the fish behavioural problems that aquarists commonly encounter, using a question and answer format: "What if my fish...?" It is not intended to be a definitive catalogue, as that would require a book in itself.

The secret of dealing with this type of problem is to try to establish the underlying motivation. Understanding why a fish behaves in a particular fashion will often suggest a method of accommodating or countering its behaviour. Of course, many problems can be avoided by the simple expedient of finding out about the likely behaviour of each fish species *before* purchasing it, and not buying it at all if its habits are likely to prove disruptive or inconvenient.

One thing is certain – the fish is not to blame for behaving according to the instincts instilled in it by thousands or millions of years of evolution, nor does it have any intention of annoying its owner. The guilty party is invariably the aquarist who failed to do his homework. For this reason, if behavioural problems do occur, the aquarist has a moral responsibility to solve the problem in a manner that ensures the wellbeing of all his fish, including the 'difficult' individuals. Sometimes the only solution may be to rehome the offending fish (with another aquarist, or ask the dealer to take it back) or else to provide it with its own private quarters. If the latter alternative is the only option, then the aquarist must accept the possible inconvenience and undoubted expense. Destroying an innocent creature is not an acceptable way out.

Not all the behaviours listed below are likely to cause difficulties; some are included because the aquarist may be concerned at a departure from normal behaviour, or simply wish to understand why his fish are doing the things they do.

Note: the groupings used in Table 4 and in the text correspond to the motivational groupings used in Chapter 4.

Table 4 Behavioural Problems Discussed in Chapter 5

FEEDING BEHAVIOUR
What if my fish...?
1... eats tankmates?
2... nips the fins of other fish?
3... attaches itself to other fish?
4... eats plants?
5... eats faeces and corpses?
6... eats equipment and decor?
7... won't let other fish near the food?

ESCAPE/EVASION BEHAVIOUR
What if my fish...?
8...... hides?
9...... jumps out of the water?
10... climbs out of the tank?
11... buries itself in the substrate?
12... swim in a group?

BREEDING BEHAVIOUR
13... locks mouths with other fish?
14... won't let other fish go near part of the tank?
15... attacks the opposite sex?
16... won't breed?
17... breeds with a member of another species?
18... eats its eggs or fry?

BEHAVIOUR WITH MULTIPLE CAUSE
What if my fish...?
19... chases other fish?
20... digs?
21... uproots plants?
22... interferes with equipment?
23... attacks or kills other fish?
24... dashes about, upsetting other fish?
25... blows bubbles?
26... bites me?!

---

1. FEEDING BEHAVIOUR
What if my fish...?

1. What if my fish eats tankmates?
This is a common problem where piscivorous (fish-eating) species have been housed with fish small enough to be eaten, and is to be expected. Omnivorous fish will also sometimes eat smaller tankmates, and, again, this is quite natural. Most fish will eat fry, including their own. Humans tend to regard this as cannibalism, but the fish is simply exploiting an available food source in the interests of its own survival.

Sometimes the problem does not manifest itself initially, for example where a juvenile piscivore is housed with adults of a smaller species. The predator grows and ultimately becomes large enough to feed on its tankmates. Rather more unexpected are cases where the large fish, usually an omnivore rather than an out-and-out piscivore, does not eat its now smaller companions. It is thought that this is because it recognises them, and does not equate them with food, which it knows arrives from above when the aquarist approaches. The smaller fish are usually shorter-lived than the large one, and when they die are replaced with others of the same species – which are promptly eaten! They are unfamiliar, and they arrive via the normal food route. This scenario, which commonly involves the angelfish (*Pterophyllum scalare*), preying on species such as the neon tetra (*Paracheirodon innesi*) and a number of other small characins/cyprinids, is a source of confusion for many hobbyists.

Avoid problems of this kind by avoiding the circumstances that lead to them.

2. What if my fish nips the fins of other fish?

A common problem, especially where fish are kept that have long or flowing finnage. Favourite targets are the long fins of the Siamese fighting fish (*Betta splendens*) and the angelfish, the tails of some guppy (*Poecilia reticulata*) varieties, and the long, feeler-like pelvic fins of gouramis and some other anabantoids. Fin rot (Chapter 21, section 3.2.2) may develop on the damaged fins but is generally not a problem if the fish are in good health and water quality is excellent.

• The offending fish may instinctively snap at some moving objects, perceiving them to be potential food items. There is no real answer to this problem except to keep long-finned fish by themselves, as the nipping is a reflex action. Unless the damage is serious, or the victims appear stressed through constant attacks, it is probably best simply to regard it as a fact of life.

• Some small barbs, notoriously the tiger barb (*Barbus tetrazona*), are often persistent fin-nippers if kept in ones or twos. If kept in a shoal, as nature intended, they generally do not harass tankmates in this way. The reasons for the behaviour and the cure are unknown.

• A few species, e.g. *Genyochromis mento*, a Lake Malawi cichlid, are specialised feeders whose natural diet is pieces of fin. Such fish should not be kept with others.

• Fins may be bitten during a territorial attack by one fish on another. See What if? nos. 19, 14, and 15.

3. What if my fish attaches itself to other fish?

The Chinese algae eater, or sucking loach (*Gyrinocheilus aymonieri*), and, less frequently, some suckermouth catfish, may sometimes attach themselves to the sides of large flatsided tankmates. This may be purely accidental initially (sucking loaches will attach to other flat surfaces), but sometimes the loach or catfish develops a taste for the body mucus of its victim and attaches itself repeatedly. This can be extremely stressful for the victim and can cause damage to the underlying skin, as well as breaching the protective mucus coating that protects the fish against infection by pathogens and parasites (Chapter 21, sections 3, 4, 5).

The offending fish and its victim(s) must be separated.

4. What if my fish eats plants?

This is normal behaviour if the fish is a herbivore. Notorious plant-eaters are generally well documented in the aquarium literature, so a little preliminary research will warn of the problem. Feeding alternative green foods such as lettuce and spinach (Chapter 7) may distract the fish from living vegetation. Some plants, notably Java fern (*Microsorium pteropus*), have tough and bitter-tasting foliage which is more herbivore-resistant than softer growths. Plastic plants are another option.

Some fish will forage on algae attached to plant leaves, and this should not be confused with eating the leaves themselves.

5. What if my fish eats faeces and corpses?

Most fish will forage on corpses, which they see only as a piece of food, not as a dead friend! They will also commonly nibble at dying tankmates. The moribund fish should be removed to a private tank where it can die in peace, or be humanely despatched (Chapter 25). Feeding on faeces (coprophagy) is another habit which the aquarist may find distasteful, but which is perfectly normal in some species. It is important to remember that in nature it may be necessary to exploit such resources in order to get enough to eat and survive. The behaviour does not mean that the fish is underfed, simply that it is following its survival instincts.

However, feeding on corpses and faeces may transmit diseases and parasites; decaying corpses may also cause organic pollution of the aquarium. Corpses should always be removed as soon as they are seen, and any accumulations of faeces siphoned off regularly. In any case, this is simply part of good aquarium husbandry.

6. What if my fish eats equipment and decor?

It is not unknown for some large fish to swallow small pieces of equipment (airstones, air valves, plastic suckers, etc). We can only assume the fish thinks they are food. Such objects should not, of course, be loose in the aquarium.

A number of fish, notably some loricariid catfish and *Uaru* cichlids, will gnaw at bogwood. It is believed that dead wood forms part of their natural diet. Avoid using varnished bogwood if such fish are kept, as the varnish may poison them.

7. What if my fish won't let other fish near the food?

The offender is usually a member of a species that defends a feeding or breeding territory in nature. The problem can generally be solved by varying the feeding place, scattering the food around the aquarium, or using foods that disperse naturally, e.g. flake, *Daphnia*.

2. ESCAPE/EVASION BEHAVIOUR

8. What if my fish hides?

Hiding is the normal method of self-preservation for many fish, and some hide in order to lie in wait for prey. Such fish can thus be expected to spend at least part of their time in caves, among plants, or in other favourite places of concealment. Some fish, especially species that practise parental care, may become secretive when breeding. Some fish hide at night, while nocturnal species commonly go to ground during the day. Newly-introduced fish often hide until they have evaluated their surroundings and feel confident enough to come out into the open.

If fish that do not normally hide start to do so, and this cannot be attributed to breeding behaviour, then the fish may be unwell (see Chapter 20, What if my fish hides?).

9. What if my fish jumps out of the water?

This is a common escape behaviour for some fish species, especially those that usually live near the surface. In nature, the object is normally to escape predation, but, in the aquarium, this behaviour is sometimes a response to aggression by tankmates. Some fish also jump for food, and the splash tetra (*Copeina arnoldi*) jumps to spawn out of water.

Small, surface-dwelling fish such as hatchetfish and killifish have an uncanny knack of finding even the smallest aperture in the tank cover and ending their days as matted, dehydrated corpses on the carpet. Where such fish, and others, are known to jump (usually stated in the aquarium literature), then all likely escape routes must be carefully blocked. Floating plants can also be used to discourage jumping. The aquarist should also aim to provide an environment where fish do not need to jump in order to evade real or imagined danger.

Jumping may also be a reaction to poisoning or some diseases. Hence regular jumping, or jumping by fish that do not normally do so, is a cause for concern (see Chapter 20, What if my fish jumps?).

Fish may jump when threatened by the net. As netting commonly involves removing the hood, there is a danger they could jump out of the tank. Although sick fish are rarely that athletic, it may be a sensible precaution to lower the water level before netting healthy fish. An additional partial water change will do no harm!

10. What if my fish climbs out of the tank?
Some fish, notably *Clarias* catfish, climbing perch, and snakeheads, are able to breathe atmospheric air and to cross dry land to find water if their native pool dries up. Although there is little likelihood of the aquarium drying up, its size and volume is probably rather less than the (diminishing) pool size required to trigger this type of migration in the wild. Whatever the reason, these fish are quite likely to set off around the house unless preventive measures are taken. Large specimens may even be able to dislodge lightweight metal or plastic hoods. Hence the hood should not only offer no gaps through which the fish may escape, but it (and the access flap) should be heavy and/or fixed in place. Fishkeeping often requires the aquarist to improvise, and this is one such situation!

11. What if my fish buries itself in the substrate?
This is simply a form of hiding. Some loaches regularly practise this form of concealment. Keeping them in an aquarium with no substrate is not an option, as to deprive them of their natural cover is unkind and likely to cause nervousness and considerable stress. Instead they should be provided with a fine substrate with no sharp edges so they can behave naturally.

12. What if my fish swim in a group?
Some fish swim in a shoal for protection. The movement of the shoal is thought to confuse predators, and statistically each fish is less likely to be the victim of predation than if it swam around by itself. Shoaling is also thought to be an important part of feeding behaviour in such species. Species that normally live in shoals in nature should always be kept in groups, to avoid nervousness and stress.

Fish that do not shoal for protection may also form a feeding shoal (sometimes containing more than one species), for example, to exploit an unusually rich food source. Some fish breed in groups, even if they are normally solitary.

3. BREEDING BEHAVIOUR

13. What if my fish locks mouths with other fish?

This behaviour is commonly seen in cichlids, as well as in kissing gouramis (*Helostoma temminckii*) and some gobies. It is not a gesture of affection, but a trial of strength. Male fish (and occasionally female cichlids) wrestle in this way during disputes over territory and potential breeding partners. Courting pairs of cichlids also sometimes mouth-fight, and it is thought they are testing each other's strength and resolve, to establish suitability as a partner – capable of defending the brood and not likely to flee when danger threatens.

14. What if my fish won't let other fish go near part of the tank?

This generally means the fish is/are defending a breeding territory or eggs/fry. This can cause immense problems if the tank is not large enough to provide the space the breeding fish (usually cichlids) require and still leave room for the rest of the tank population. It is not uncommon for the other fish to be badly harassed, injured, or even killed in such circumstances. A temporary solution is to partition the tank into two parts using a divider. In the long term, a better remedy is to use a larger tank or to provide the breeding fish with their own private tank (Chapter 8).

15. What if my fish attacks the opposite sex?

Such attacks can have serious consequences, with the victim being badly stressed, physically injured, or even killed. The root of the problem is the confined space offered by even a large aquarium; in nature the harassed fish would simply swim away, but may not be able to get out of sight/range in the aquarium.

The solution will depend on the type of fish, its breeding behaviour, and the size of the aquarium. The aquarium literature on various species and/or families contains specific advice. As a short-term solution, the fish can be separated using a divider or by moving one of them to another tank.

The following are some of the scenarios in which such attacks occur:

• Firstly, establish whether one fish is actually attacking the other, or simply courting it. Courtship can look – and be – rather a rough affair in some types of fish. A good guide is whether the fish being 'attacked' is standing its ground (i.e. is interested in being courted) or trying to get away. However, chasing is itself commonly a part of courtship in some types of fish (usually non-territorial species).

• If a fish that is being courted is not ready to spawn, it may flee, or else show initial interest but then flee. If there is insufficient space for it to make good its escape, then courtship may well degenerate into harassment. Particularly serious problems can occur in fish that breed all year round rather than seasonally, as the male (usually the aggressor) will always be ready to spawn, but the female only when she is ripe (full of mature eggs). In nature, she would not go near the male until ready to spawn, but in the confines of the aquarium she may have no choice. Her presence will, however, signal to the male that she is ready to spawn.

• Sometimes the male may wish to continue spawning after the female has laid all her eggs.

• In some fish that practise parental care but only one parent guards the spawn (e.g. gouramis, the guarding adult will usually chase away the non-guarding parent soon after spawning.

• Male cichlids sometimes attack the female during brood care in situations where the pair are housed in a tank of their own. It is thought this is because the male has a very strong instinctive need to defend the breeding territory, and the female is the only fish available to attack. This can be solved, if the tank is large enough, by partitioning off one end of the tank with a clear divider, and putting a 'target fish' in the compartment created, to divert the male. Target fish must always be provided with enough space and suitable decor (e.g. a hiding place), and *never* exposed to actual contact from the breeding pair.

• Male poeciliid livebearers often harass females that have recently given birth, which can exhaust the already weakened female and even lead to her death. It is thus a wise precaution to isolate the female for rest after parturition.

16. What if my fish won't breed?

This can be a source of considerable frustration to would-be fish breeders, and has many causes. The following are a selection of those commonly encountered:

• They may all be the same sex.
• They may not be sexually mature.
• They may be too old.
• They may be sterile.
• They may be seasonal breeders.
• The oocytes (egg cells) may not be developing in the ovaries due to incorrect diet (Chapter 7) or water conditions (chemistry and/or quality, Chapter 10).
• The oocytes may be developing normally, but are not yet ready to be laid.
• They may require one or more special triggers to stimulate spawning by stimulating the natural conditions at the beginning of the spawning season.
• They may lack a suitable spawning substrate (surface on which to spawn). Plant-spawners will not normally spawn on rocks, or rock-spawners on plant leaves.
• In territorial species, they may not be able to secure a suitable breeding territory (too many other fish present, other fish dominant).
• The water chemistry (Chapter 10) may be incorrect.
• The lighting (Chapter 12) may be unsuitable. Insufficient light usually leads to underdevelopment of the gonads due to lack of stimulation of the pituitary gland.
• They may be stressed by a multitude of causes: poor water quality, aggression from tankmates, unsuitable surroundings, or even the aquarist constantly fiddling with the tank to try to get them to spawn!

17. What if my fish breeds with a member of another species?

This is called hybridisation and may occur if closely-related species are kept together.

• If only one individual of a species is present, it may mate with a related species.
• Even if both sexes of closely-related species are present, they may still interbreed in the absence of factors – commonly geographical separation – that would keep them from so doing in nature.
• If the male of the correct species is unable to repel one or more competing males of other species, the other male(s) may fertilise the eggs.

In all instances, prevention is the only sensible course. If hybrid matings do occur, the eggs/fry should be destroyed, and steps taken to avoid further mis-matings (i.e. the fish in question should be separated).

18. What if my fish eats its eggs or fry?

A common problem, possibly even more frustrating to the aquarist than failure of his fish to spawn in the first place. There are a number of possible causes:

• Many fish do not practise parental care, and although they have a strong reproductive urge, do not recognise their own eggs and fry as anything other than food. It is normally necessary to rescue the eggs/fry in order to rear the brood (Chapter 8), although a few may survive the attentions of their parents and tankmates in an aquarium with plenty of plant cover or rocky nooks and crannies.

• Fish that do practise parental care may eat their eggs if the latter are infertile. This may occur if the male is too young/old to produce milt, or otherwise sterile; if no male is present; and if water chemistry and quality are incorrect.

• Young pairs of parental species may need trial attempts before they get it right.

• Parental species may eat their eggs or fry if stressed or disturbed. Hatching and rearing a brood involves a considerable investment of time and energy, and, if success seems unlikely, the sensible course is to recycle the protein (rather than letting it go to waste or be eaten by other fish) and try again when circumstances may be more favourable. Aquarists who shine torches into breeding caves, or move decor to have a look, have only themselves to blame if eggs are eaten.

• There is increasing evidence that parental care is learned, rather than inherited, in some species, such that, if the eggs are hatched and the fry reared away from the parents, the offspring will not look after their own eggs/fry but eat them. The best-known example is the angelfish (*Pterophyllum scalare*), which has been artificially hatched and reared almost since it was first imported.

• Sometimes the parent fish are blamed for the activities of tankmates! Nocturnal catfish are commonly the villains of the piece, enjoying a midnight feast at the expense of diurnally-active parental species.

4. BEHAVIOUR WITH MULTIPLE CAUSES

19. What if my fish chases other fish?

Assuming the pursuer is not trying to catch and eat potential prey, chasing may be part of either courtship behaviour or territorial behaviour.

• Some fish chase each other as part of their normal courtship ritual.

• Some fish will chase a potential mate who does not respond to their courtship.

• Some fish will chase their breeding partner away after spawning.

• Territorial fish will chase other fish away from a feeding or breeding territory.

• If two fish fight then the winner will commonly chase the loser.

In all instances, if the chasing is persistent and causes undue stress or physical damage, it may be necessary to separate the individuals concerned.

See also What if nos. 7, 14, and 15.

20. What if my fish digs?

This is perfectly natural for some species, but causes immense distress to aquarists whose vision of an idyllic underwater garden is converted into a miniature quarry!

Fish may dig for a number of reasons:

• As part of their feeding behaviour. Some forage in the surface layer of the substrate, while some (sifters) pick up mouthfuls of substrate and either spit them out again, or eject non-edible material via the gills.

• As part of their escape/evasion behaviour. Some fish (e.g. some loaches, and spiny eels) bury themselves in the substrate; others will excavate hiding-places under decor or enlarge existing aquarist-constructed caves to suit their personal preferences.

• As part of their breeding behaviour. Some killifish spawn in the substrate. Many cichlids dig nursery pits in which to guard their larvae/fry.

• Boredom may play a part where fish with a natural tendency to dig are kept alone.

In all cases, the best solution is either to avoid fish that dig, or accept the inevitable. It is unkind and stressful to keep fish without substrate to prevent digging. Fish with a strong instinctive need to dig when breeding may not breed at all if thwarted in this respect. Enlargement of (non-breeding) caves can, however, be avoided by creating caves with solid (e.g. rock) floors.

21. What if my fish uproots plants?
This is commonly a concomitant of digging (See What if no. 20). Plants are sometimes also seized in the mouth and pulled up, sometimes to clear the way for digging. Plants added to the aquarium and sited in a fish's territory may sometimes be pulled or dug up, presumably because they are regarded as intruders (the same fish will usually ignore plants that were there first!). Plants may be uprooted as fish swim through them, usually if the plant is not properly rooted, or if the fish is large. Plants may also be uprooted by herbivores feeding on them. (See What if no. 4).

22. What if my fish interferes with equipment?
Some large fish, may move equipment such as heaters and filter pipes, sometimes pulling them free of holders. This may be part of 'site clearance' prior to breeding (See What if nos. 20, 21), but may also be due to boredom. Providing 'toys' (plastic plants, ping-pong balls) has proved effective where boredom is suspected. Otherwise it may be necessary to fix equipment semi-permanently in place with silicon sealant or to house it in a special compartment partitioned off with a sheet of perforated (to permit water circulation) rigid non-toxic plastic, again fixed in place with silicon sealant.

23. What if my fish attacks or kills other fish?
The reasons for this are generally as for What if no 19.

If the victims have just been introduced to an aquarium containing territorial fish, the assault may be because the new fish are seen as intruders. Introducing a number of fish simultaneously will usually minimise the likelihood of serious harm. Turning the aquarium light off and excluding room light is also helpful. Other options involve rearranging the decor to disrupt existing territories, partitioning the tank, or removing the aggressor to another tank while the new fish settle in.

24. What if my fish dashes about, upsetting other fish?
Some fish move around the aquarium in rapid dashes, and some other fish, usually slow-moving species, often find this disturbing. The solution is to avoid mixing the species concerned. Books which catalogue aquarium fish will normally indicate which species may cause this type of upset, and those particularly susceptible to it.

25. What if my fish blows bubbles?
• Many labyrinth fish build a nest of bubbles in which they protect their eggs.

• Some fish with the ability to take in atmospheric air may emit bubbles from their gills after so doing. This is often seen in *Corydoras* catfish.

• Some large-mouthed fish which do not normally feed from the surface may take a gulp of air along with floating food, and proceed to 'blow' bubbles from mouth and gills. This is not known to cause any physical harm, but it is probably better to avoid feeding floating foods to fish with this tendency.

26. What if my fish bites me?!

Many fish will nip or suck at their owner's fingers if these are placed in the water at feeding time, or even during tank maintenance when the hand first enters the tank, because they have learned to associate the appearance of fingers with the arrival of food. Such nipping may tickle a bit, but is harmless, and most aquarists enjoy it! Many even train their fish, especially larger ones, to take pieces of food from the hand, finding this makes the fish seem more like a pet.

Some large predators, however, notably piranhas, are quite likely to mistake fingers for food and can inflict serious injuries. If such fish are kept, then the aquarist should keep his hands out of the aquarium, visitors should be issued with dire warnings, and, if there are children in the household, the hood must be fitted with a lock. Indeed, it is strongly recommended that piranhas and other dangerous fish not be kept in households with children, if at all.

Territorial fish may also attack hands, and, if they are protecting fry, may do so with considerable violence and almost suicidal vehemence. Although the effect is normally more of a surprise than anything else, some fish, even small ones, have sharp teeth and will use them, regardless of the size of the threat to their offspring. Obviously, the fish are not to blame for following their most basic parental instincts, and most aquarists regard a nipped finger, even if blood is drawn, as a mere trifle compared to the pleasure of finding they have a new family!

CHAPTER 6

TRANSPORTING FISH

Every aquarist should be familiar with the correct procedures for moving a fish from one tank to another, whether it be the short distance from the quarantine tank to the main aquarium, the trip home from the aquarium store, or a long trip of several hundred miles. Any handling of this kind is inevitably stressful, and may result in physical injury and even death if conducted without due attention to detail.

1. MATCHING WATER PARAMETERS

Whenever fish are introduced to a different aquarium it is essential that the water in their new home should match that which they are used to as closely as possible, otherwise they may experience severe shock (Chapter 21, section 1.5.1) and die. The parameters involved are water chemistry, water quality, and temperature (Chapter 10). Particularly dangerous are a sudden change in pH (pH shock), an increase in nitrate level (nitrate shock), or a change in temperature (temperature shock). Very many fish die because careless or ignorant aquarists have failed to realise the danger, and usually the innocent aquarium dealer is accused of selling poor-quality fish. Careful water matching is necessary not only with newly-purchased fish, but also if fish are moved from tank to tank in the home.

Newly-purchased fish should always be quarantined to minimise the risk of introducing disease into the main aquarium. The quarantine aquarium should be set up with water that matches that in which the fish have been kept, and any necessary adjustments made during the quarantine period.

TEMPERATURE EQUALISATION

To avoid temperature shock, a fish is normally floated, in a container of its previous water, in the new aquarium for a short period, so that the temperatures may equalise. The container may be that in which the fish was transported home, or a plastic bowl or box if it is being moved from tank to tank at home. The tank light should be switched off before equalisation to avoid stressing the fish.

Use a thermometer to check temperatures at the start of equalisation – it may not be necessary at all! With a little experience you will soon be able to gauge how long is required for equalisation, but always check the temperatures again before releasing the fish. It is sometimes suggested that equalisation should take about half an hour, but, in practice, five minutes is normally the maximum required, and it can be extremely stressful for a fish to be left floating for a long time.

CHEMICAL EQUALISATION

If you are buying fish locally, then they will normally have been kept in local tap water, whose parameters should already be known. If buying further afield, then ask the store about hardness and pH, or test a sample of the water in which the fish is packed. During the quarantine period the chemistry of the water in the isolation tank can gradually be adjusted to that of the main aquarium. Details of preparing, adjusting, and testing water will be found in Chapter 10.

There is a myth that chemical shock can be avoided by repeatedly mixing small amounts of water from the new aquarium into the container used for temperature equalisation. Theorefically this is true, but only if the process is continued using very small amounts at a time, for 48-72 hours, which would be totally impracticable and highly stressful for the confined fish. Doing it for the 30-60 minutes normally suggested is also stressful, and pointless.

NITRATE LEVELS

The water in aquarium shop tanks is usually of very good quality (Chapter 10) as it is subject to constant small changes (because water is taken out to pack fish) and routine larger ones. Regrettably, the water in domestic aquaria is not always as healthy. The nitrate level of the main aquarium should be tested before new fish are exposed to it. Although some books advocate filling the quarantine tank with water from the main tank, this is inadvisable if its nitrate level is high – use suitably prepared tap water instead. In such cases, it is normal to adjust the main aquarium to the new fish rather than vice versa, using partial water changes to reduce the nitrate level before the new fish are introduced. Of course, if the main aquarium is properly maintained, it will not have a high nitrate level anyway!

2. CATCHING FISH

Nets can be purchased from the aquarium store for this purpose. Two nets are required so the fish can be caught using a 'pincer movement' to bring it to the front of the tank and trap it against the front glass. Alternatively, the fish can be guided into a single net using the free hand. Chasing with a single net is stressful for the fish. Panic can lead to fish colliding with rocks or getting stuck in small gaps in the tank furnishings, and may result in injury. Likewise be careful to trap the fish only in the material of the net, never with the hard frame.

Some fish, particularly surface-dwellers, may jump when frightened by the net. If the aquarium contains such fish, it is wise to siphon off some water to lower the level in the tank, making it less likely that they will jump out of the aquarium.

Tip: learn how to catch fish by watching an experienced aquarist or store assistant.

3. MOVING FISH FROM TANK TO TANK

As when introducing new fish, the water of the two tanks should be a good match in order to avoid shock. If not, the quarantine tank should be set up with water from the fish's old home and gradually adjusted to match that of the new.

Some aquarists simply catch a fish and carry it in the net, popping it unceremoniously into the new aquarium. It is far better to put the fish in a plastic bowl or box, filled with water from its original tank, and float this in the new aquarium so that the inevitable small difference in water temperatures can equalise. The container can then be gently tilted, allowing the fish to see where it is going and swim out when it is ready. It is best to use an opaque container rather than a clear one, otherwise the fish will try to get out through the plastic to the more amenable environment it can see below, while any resident fish are likely to crowd around inquisitively. All very stressful for the new fish.

4. PACKING FISH

You may need to do this if you give or sell fish to someone else, if you take fish to a show, or if you move house. Even if you never do any of these, it is still advisable to learn the correct method, so that you can ensure those you buy are properly packed. You should not be afraid to insist on correct packaging.

SUITABLE CONTAINERS
Fish are normally packed in plastic (polythene) bags. Note the following:
• Double bags (one inside another) should be used, in case one leaks or is punctured by fish spines.
• The pointed corners of the bags should be tied off (with rubber bands) or taped back upon themselves to create round corners which will not trap fish. Otherwise it is all too common for fish, especially small ones, to get trapped in corners and be crushed or suffocated. Some shops use bags manufactured with rounded corners specially for fish use.
• The bag should be large enough; bag width should be at least twice fish length.
• Bags should be at least three times as deep as wide, to allow adequate air space.
• Small adult fish of non-territorial or non-aggressive species, and juveniles of most species, can be packed several to a bag (as long as the bag is large enough). Adults and sub-adults of territorial/aggressive species, and fish longer than about 6 cm/2.5 in, should be packed separately.

It is also possible to pack fish in lidded plastic buckets (if designed for food use) or plastic jars (e.g. large sweet jars – usually free from sweet shops. Aquarium stores usually pack fish in bags, but there is no reason why you should not take your own containers when buying fish.

Rigid containers have a number of advantages:

- They are unlikely to be punctured by fish spines or knocks.
- There are no tight corners in which fish may become trapped.
- The lid can be removed during the journey to admit fresh air (see below).
- They are much easier to open to release the fish into their new home.

The only disadvantage is that they can be difficult to fit into a fish box (see below).

THE PACKING WATER

The water needed to pack all the fish from a particular tank should be put in the requisite containers before netting begins and any debris is stirred up. Suspended detritus in the containers may cause gill irritation.

If you are packing fish yourself, always check that the ammonia and nitrite content of the water is zero, and its nitrate content as low as possible. It is no bad thing to perform a partial water change (Chapter 15) the day before packing fish, or to use two-thirds tank water, one-third new in the containers. Except for short journeys, a good idea is to place a little zeolite in each container to remove the ammonia excreted by the fish in transit.

Enough water should be used comfortably to cover the fish (three times fish body depth suffices for most species).

OXYGEN

Many aquarists think only of maintaining the right temperature when transporting fish, but more die in transit through pollution, or lack of oxygen, than from chilling or overheating. The dissolved oxygen that fish breathe is absorbed into the water from the atmosphere; the amount of air in a sealed container is finite, and all the oxygen may be used up before the fish reaches its destination.

The air space in a fish bag should be at least twice the volume of the water. If you are purchasing fish and have a long journey ahead, ask to have the bags filled with oxygen. In fact, some shops will ask you how far you have to go, and use oxygen automatically if they think this necessary. Remember that it is time, not distance, that is important – a comparatively short journey can take a long time if traffic conditions are bad, or if you have to wait two hours for your train.

Aquarists do not normally have access to oxygen, but can still minimise the risk of oxygen starvation. Use as deep a bag as possible, or a lidded container so the air supply can be renewed at intervals (it is possible, but difficult, to undo bags if necessary). Aerate the water in the containers vigorously for several minutes – *before* putting fish in them. Violent aeration in a small space is highly stressful.

SEALING THE BAGS

This involves trapping as much air as possible in the bag while twisting its neck, then either knotting the neck or doubling it over and securing with two stout rubber bands (two, in case one breaks). It is quite impossible to describe the technique required to trap air in a plastic bag, but if you have a helpful dealer, he may be prepared to teach you. Oxygen is put into bags by inserting a tube through the partially-twisted neck, and if you cannot master the knack of trapping air, there is no reason why you should not use your airpump (Chapter 13) and airline to inflate bags, provided you keep the airline out of the water.

Never inflate bags by blowing into them, as you will be filling the vital air space with used air, from which your lungs have already extracted the oxygen!

Shops will commonly pack sealed plastic bags in brown paper bags, an opaque carrier bag, or even newspaper, so the fish are not exposed to light and other stressful external stimuli while in transit. This is not, however, necessary if they are to be transported in an insulated, often opaque, container, which is the ideal situation.

Tip: if travelling some distance, ask for some spare bags for emergencies.

INSULATION

Fish are usually transported in insulated boxes to ensure they do not become chilled (or overheated, in hot weather/climates). The container most often used is a 'fish box' made of expanded polystyrene ('styrofoam'), but any insulated container (e.g. insulated picnic boxes or bags) can be used. Most aquarium stores will give you a fish box if you ask, but do not expect to be given another each time you shop; keep the one you are given and take it with you next time.

If the containers of fish do not fit the box snugly, pack the empty spaces to stop them rolling or sliding around. Crumpled newspaper is ideal. Take newspapers with you, as not all shops will have any. Alternatively, plastic bags, filled with air and sealed, will do the trick. If all else fails, any soft padding (such as clothing) will do.

Tip: a fish box can have other invaluable uses. Provided it is clean and does not leak, it can be used by itself to transport a large fish or as an improvised temporary aquarium if the main aquarium leaks or breaks.

5. TRANSPORTING FISH

The fish, once bagged, should ideally be transported to their destination immediately and unpacked as soon as possible. Other business should be conducted before the fish are purchased. If you see fish you want early in the day, and are worried that they may be sold to someone else if you do not buy them at once, it is generally possible to reserve a number, or even specific individuals. Expect to pay a deposit, or the full price, when reserving fish. Some stores will have your fish packed and waiting for you at a specific time, but unless you trust the store and its staff completely (from long experience), it is wiser to supervise the catching and packing.

Even if the fish are in an insulated container, avoid exposing them to undue heat (e.g. noonday or tropical sun) or cold. Do not keep checking the fish during the journey. Every time you let light into the box you will terrify the fish. Open the box only on long journeys if you think fresh air may be required in the bags/buckets.

6. UNPACKING

It is unwise to buy fish on impulse (even if you know they are suitable) with no quarters ready for them; but it happens. If the quarantine tank is not set up and waiting, then leave the fish undisturbed in their box until you are ready for them. Do not get them out to show the family – they can see them later.

If possible, undo the bags before removing them from the box and then transfer them quickly to the quarantine tank for temperature equalisation. This is far less stressful than holding the bags in mid-air while you struggle to undo them, exposing the occupants to strange visual stimuli. It is even more stressful if the bags are floated, still sealed, and then taken out of the tank again for opening. The shorter the period of time between being removed from the box and released into the tank, the better.

Once the temperatures have equalised, gently submerge the necks of the bags and allow the fish to swim out, gradually lifting the bottoms of the bags to encourage them to do so. Always check that none are left behind in the bags.

Newly-introduced fish may hide or rest on the bottom, because they have been stressed by their recent experiences. This is inevitable – you can only minimise the stress, not avoid it completely. The fish will be disorientated, so leave them alone and never try to coax them out of hiding, as this will only cause more stress. Leave the light off (and keep activity near the aquarium to a minimum) until the next day, when, if you have managed the transportation and introduction process correctly, the new arrivals will be acting as if they had been in their new home for years.

CHAPTER 7

NUTRITION

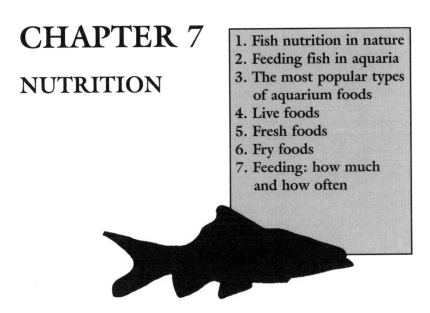

Fish, like all other animals, must obtain food in order to live, grow and reproduce. Food serves two major purposes: it provides energy to drive the fish's metabolic processes and it contains essential building blocks for tissue growth and development.

The major categories of nutrients required by fish are proteins, lipids (fats), and carbohydrates, plus small quantities of certain minerals and phytochemicals such as vitamins. Fish differ from other vertebrates in the relative amounts of these nutrients they require. In particular, many groups of fish (notably the carnivores) are able to utilise a high percentage of dietary protein (between 35-55%), compared with a maximum of just 25% protein in the case of birds and mammals.

There are also subtle qualitative differences between the dietary requirements of fish and those of other animals, and dietary differences also exist between fish species, as discussed below.

1. FISH NUTRITION IN NATURE

To feed fish properly in captivity it is important to be aware of the natural diet and feeding habits of the species concerned.

NATURAL FOODS

In the wild, a wide variety of food materials are exploited by fish. Potential food items include: decomposing organic matter; bacteria, protozoa and other micro-organisms; aquatic plants and algae; fruits and seeds; invertebrates (e.g. insects, worms, snails, crustaceans); other fish; amphibians; sometimes even birds, reptiles and mammals. Not all species consume all types of foods – most specialise to varying degrees. For example, some fish consume mostly vegetable matter and are termed herbivores (plant-eaters). Others, including many large catfish and some characins, have a preference for animal matter (live or dead), and these are termed carnivores (meat-eaters). Probably the most famous (or infamous!) freshwater carnivore is the red-bellied piranha (*Serrasalmus nattereri*), a large relative of the tetras.

In fact, most fish have a fairly wide-ranging diet which includes both vegetable and animal foods, and these are known as omnivores (*omni* meaning 'all'). The barbs (family Cyprinidae) are often regarded as herbivores by aquarists, yet anyone who has observed small barbs in the aquarium will know that they readily take *Daphnia, Tubifex*, and other live prey (see below). There are also some fish species which exhibit very specialised feeding behaviour, and, in a few cases, the actual types of food eaten are bizarre, as in the case of *Genyochromis mento* and a few other cichlid species which feed, apparently exclusively, on the scales and fins of live fish and are termed lepidophages (scale-eaters). Much of our knowledge of the natural foods of fish is gained through careful analysis of the gut contents of wild-caught specimens.

Although most fish will accept 'unnatural' food items under aquarium conditions, it is important to offer foods which are suitable for the fish's digestive system. For instance, herbivorous and omnivorous species typically possess very elongated guts and no true stomach, so their digestive systems are equipped to deal with a steady throughput of small portions of food. Carnivores, on the other hand, commonly possess a stomach which can accommodate and partly digest bulky foods before they are further processed along the relatively short intestine. Clearly, feeding large items of food (such as whole dead fish) to a herbivore would be as inappropriate as offering lettuce to a carnivore. (See also Chapter 7).

The food preferences of a fish may also change during its lifetime. The size and types of food eaten will depend on the fish's size (i.e. mouth size) and stage of development. The fry of piscivores, for example, are unlikely to be able to find other fish small enough to eat. Similarly, juvenile molluscivores are generally unable to crush snails until adult. Moreover, in the wild, environmental factors such as water temperature and season will affect the types and abundance of foods which are available to fish, and hence influence their diet.

FEEDING STRATEGIES

Fish differ not only in their dietary preferences (i.e. the types of foods eaten) but also in their feeding behaviour. Ambush piscivores stalk their prey or lie in wait until suitable prey passes by. Pursuit predators, by contrast, rely on speed to hunt down and capture their quarry. Other types of fish, for example the molly (*Poecilia sphenops*), may spend many hours each day foraging on algae and other vegetable matter.

The physical means by which food is secured vary considerably. For example, some fish use suction to snap up small food items which are generally swallowed whole. Many aquarium species exhibit this snapping behaviour when free-swimming live foods such as *Daphnia* and *Artemia* (see below) are fed. The food of herbivores includes live or decaying plant material (sometimes including leaves which have fallen into the water), such foods being secured by biting off pieces or picking up the whole item. Some herbivores are primarily algae-eaters, an example being the plecostomus catfish, which has a modified suckermouth for attaching to rocks over which it grazes on algae. Large predatory carnivores may need to grasp their struggling prey until it can be swallowed whole or is broken into bite-sized chunks, and this is typically achieved with the aid of one or more rows of sharp teeth which impale the victim's flesh to prevent it from escaping.

OTHER ASPECTS OF FEEDING BEHAVIOUR

The size and frequency of meals varies between species and is commonly a function of prey size. For example, large predatory species such as the red-tailed catfish (*Phractocephalus hemioliopterus*) are accustomed to taking a single large meal, such as another fish, which can last them several days. At the other extreme, some of the grazing species, such as the mollies (*Poecilia sphenops, inter alia*), spend a lot of time nibbling on algae or snatching small food items from the water. The amount of food required, and the frequency of feeding, may also depend on the stage of development or reproductive status of the individual, as well as environmental factors such as the seasonal availability of some foods, and water temperature.

Another important aspect of feeding behaviour which must be taken into account by the aquarist is the fish's feeding position in the water column. For example, most loaches and catfish feed mainly on the substrate, whereas some of the livebearers and killifish are surface-feeders. Between these extremes are the mid-water feeders which comprise the majority of popular aquarium species, and include most of the barbs, rasboras, and tetras. The position of the fish's mouth is a useful (but not infallible) clue to its feeding level: species with downward-pointing or underslung mouths are generally bottom-feeders; those with forward-pointing mouths are mid-water feeders; and those with upturned mouths are surface-feeders.

Many fish are able to feed at all levels, but some, especially those with underslung mouths, may find it difficult to take food from other levels, particularly if obliged to feed at the surface, as this may require a totally unnatural swimming position. Furthermore, some species may be reluctant to leave their preferred level (perhaps due to innate predator-avoidance behaviour) such that certain bottom-dwellers may be inhibited from rising to the surface to take floating foods, while some surface-dwellers may be reluctant to follow sinking foods down through the water.

2. FEEDING FISH IN AQUARIA

Natural feeding habits should be taken into account when considering compatible species for the community aquarium. Fish which require special diets or which exhibit unusual feeding behaviour are sometimes best kept in single-species aquaria where their needs can be specially accommodated. It is unwise to ignore such special needs or to expect a species to adjust to what is on offer – this is likely to lead to ill health and perhaps death for the fish concerned.

It is vital to ensure that all aquarium inhabitants are receiving adequate quantities of food and that the type of food offered is suitable for the species in question. There is no point offering lettuce to an obligate piscivore, or feeding large pieces of fish to a strict herbivore. This 'food incompatibility' may relate to feeding behaviour (e.g. piscivores may not recognise non-moving foods as edible) and/or digestive differences (e.g. a herbivore's gut is not equipped to handle large pieces of food or a carnivore's to break down plant material).

These considerations are especially important in community aquaria housing species with different dietary requirements and feeding behaviours. For example, bottom-dwelling catfish and loaches can easily lose out at feeding time since the mid-water and surface-feeding fish are usually first to encounter the food. Fast-sinking foods (pellets, tablets and wafers) are commercially available for the benefit of bottom-dwelling species, but such foods should not be used exclusively if obligatory surface-feeders are also housed in the aquarium.

The nutritional quality of the diet is crucially important to the general wellbeing of the fish. Fish which have been routinely fed on a poor diet may exhibit retarded growth, and in severe cases can develop nutritional deficiency symptoms such as skin or eye disorders. A healthy diet is also important for maintaining the fish's natural immunity to infections. (See also Chapter 21, section 2.0.)

3. THE MOST POPULAR TYPES OF AQUARIUM FOODS

It is virtually impossible to provide fish with their complete range of natural foods under aquarium conditions. To do so would require a ready supply of tropical aquatic invertebrates, plants and algae, etc, and these would have to be collected from the fish's natural environment in order to ensure that the correct food species were supplied. More easily available sources of food must be sought instead.

Fortunately, most fish species purchased through the aquarium hobby, especially those which have been raised on fish farms, will readily accept dry and non-living foods. A small proportion of wild-caught fish may require a period of weaning from natural foods to artificial diets. In a few cases, the fish may refuse all but live foods (see below). Predominantly piscivorous species, such as the pike livebearer (*Belonesox belizanus*), are notoriously difficult to wean on to non-living foods, and the aquarist must be sure of a year-round supply of suitable live prey before considering such species for aquaria.

COMMERCIAL AQUARIUM FISH FOODS

During the early days of the aquarium hobby, fish foods were usually collected or prepared by the aquarist. Popular food items included kitchen scraps such as beef heart, hard-boiled egg yolk, and vegetables, as well as live foods such as earthworms and *Tubifex*. Many of these foods are still as popular today. One well-known fish food was ants' 'eggs', which were commercially available in dry pack form. These 'eggs' were in fact the dried pupal cases and of virtually no nutritional value!

Nowadays, a large array of good-quality dry, frozen, and live foods for tropical aquarium fish are commercially available, examples of which are given below.

Dry Foods – Flake, Granules, and Pellets

The most popular foods for tropical fish are the so-called dry foods, notably flake (ideal for many small and medium-sized fish), as well as granules and pellets, both of which are available in various grades to suit different sizes of fish. These have a low moisture content (below 4%) which prevents spoilage by micro-organisms such as moulds or bacteria. Their dry state also ensures a long shelf-life and they are less messy to feed than moist diets such as paste foods.

Fortunately, most fish species sold for aquaria will, when kept in captivity, readily adapt to 'unnatural' dry foods. Many popular aquarium species such as the guppy (*Poecilia reticulata*) and angelfish (*Pterophyllum scalare*) have been farm-raised and bred for many generations on a mix of artificial dry and live diets.

When selecting a dry food it is important to choose a quality brand rather than a cheap product which could be nutritionally inadequate. Good-quality dry formulations meet the nutritional requirements of a wide range of fish, and are suitable for feeding to most tropical community fish. In addition, there are specialised products on the market which have been formulated for a particular species or fish group, examples being cichlid foods, catfish foods, discus foods, herbivore and carnivore foods, and the sinking pellet or wafer foods sold for bottom-feeders. However, while some of these foods are intended for a dietary type or a particular species, it should be borne in mind that the order Siluriformes (catfish) and the family Cichlidae encompass a vast number of different dietary types, such that no one food can possibly be suitable for them all (and some types of cichlids are prone to digestive disorders, e.g. Malawi Bloat (Chapter 21, 6.4), if fed unsuitable foods). Likewise, sinking foods may not suit the varied nutritional requirements of bottom-dwelling catfish and loaches, some species within these groups being primarily carnivorous and others primarily herbivorous.

Other specialist dry foods include those which enhance fish coloration, and high-protein formulations which are used for growing on young fish.

Freeze-dried foods

In addition to flake and pellet dried foods, some of the popular live-food organisms (discussed below) are also available in freeze-dried form, examples being freeze-dried bloodworms and *Tubifex* worms. Freeze-drying involves the removal of the moisture content of the food without significantly affecting the nutritional content.

Storage of dry foods

Quality brands of dry fish foods are packed in a low-oxygen atmosphere to prevent deterioration during sealed storage. Sealed pots of food should be stored under cool, dry conditions in order to avoid spoilage and also to prevent vitamin degradation (certain vitamins, such as vitamin C, can be destroyed by exposure to heat, high humidity, and even intense light). The pot of fish food should therefore be light-proof, and the lid replaced immediately after use to minimise atmospheric exposure. Dry-food containers should never be kept on the aquarium hood as it gets too hot because of the light inside, nor should they be kept in a tropical fish-house, which is typically warm and very humid.

It is sensible to purchase only sufficient quantities of dry food to last no more than three months, because vitamin degradation may occur with time. For similar reasons, do not use foods which have significantly passed their sell-by date.

Frozen foods

Although many fish species are fed dry foods exclusively, they will benefit from a varied diet including occasional supplements of fresh or frozen foods, the latter being particularly popular with many aquarists.

Many of the popular live foods (see below) are also available in fresh-frozen form, specially prepared for the aquarium hobby. These must be stored in a freezer, or the freezer compartment of a refrigerator, so they remain frozen. The commercial freezing process, which sometimes includes gamma-irradiation, kills most fish pathogens, so the gamma-irradiated 'live' foods are much safer to feed than when given alive.

Some of the foods mentioned under 'fresh foods' below are also available frozen for aquarium fish. As with fresh foods, not all are actually suitable for fish, and the warnings given below should be heeded equally as regards the frozen product.

It is recommended that frozen foods be allowed to defrost, or be quick-thawed in a fine net under the cold tap, before feeding to the fish. Failure to do so could theoretically result in the fish's stomach being excessively chilled and there is a possibility that ice crystals in the frozen food could puncture the gut wall of small fish. The liquid content should be strained off – it cannot be consumed by the fish, so its nutrients will simply pollute the aquarium.

4. LIVE FOODS

Live foods, particularly aquatic invertebrates, form an important part of the diet of many wild fish. Surface-feeding species, for example, may consume large quantities of aquatic and terrestrial insects, the latter having fallen on to the water's surface and become trapped by surface tension. Conversely, many bottom-dwellers forage over the substrate for aquatic insect larvae, crustaceans, and sediment-dwelling worms. As stated earlier, it is not feasible to supply aquarium fish with the actual species of organisms which they encounter in the wild, but in many cases we can provide the same types of prey, such as mosquito larvae and small crustaceans.

Live foods have many benefits. Most are of high nutritional quality, and the essential vitamins and other nutrients which they contain will be intact and not destroyed by food processing or leaching into the water as occurs in some dry-food formulations. The natural feeding instincts of fish (even those bred on fish farms) mean they usually respond more eagerly to living, moving prey than to inanimate foods. In fact, the fry of many species, and even some species when adult, will recognise only moving foods as being edible, such that they may starve to death if given only dry or dead foods. Some novel attempts by the foodfish industry have been made to animate dry foods by incorporating effervescent chemicals so as to propel the foods in the water, but these have not proved successful!

The major negative aspect of feeding live foods is the risk of introducing diseases (Chapter 21) and pests (Chapter 22). Microbial pathogens (e.g. bacteria, viruses) and parasites may be present in the gut or body tissues of the live food organisms, and the water in which these foods are collected may itself be a source of disease or pests. Freshwater crustaceans such as *Cyclops* may harbour larval stages of parasitic helminths ('worms'), and *Tubifex* worms are renowned for carrying viral and bacterial pathogens, and even certain protozoan parasites. Live foods which are cultured under intensive conditions, in open systems where fish are not present, are far less likely to carry such diseases; however, the aquarist has no reliable means of distinguishing cultured live foods from those taken from the local pond or river. Treating the water or purging live foods may rid them of some parasites and

BREEDING

Mouthbrooder *Orthochromis machadoi*, found in West African rivers.

Steatocranus irvinei (River Volta, West Africa), female with fry.

Mary Bailey.

Uaru amphiacanthoides fanning its eggs.

Mary Bailey.

Teleogramma brichardi female guarding eggs on the ceiling of a cave.

Cockatoo dwarf cichlid, *Apistogramma cacatuoides*, female with fry.
Note the white plastic divider to protect the other (much larger) fish from her
protective instincts!

Blue-eyed or jade-eyed cichlid, *Archocentrus spilurus*, pair with fry.

NETS

Choosing the right net makes it considerably easier to catch your fish.

Step 1.
The best way to net a fish is to trap it between the net and the glass so that you do not end up playing a very stressful game of chase around the aquarium.

Step 2.
Angle the net and move it under the fish.

Steps 3-6:
Bring the net
up and under
the fish, and
bring it to the
surface.

Step 3.

Step 4.

Step 5.

Step 6.

FEEDING

Most fish look forward to the approach of the aquarist's hand at feeding time; some, such as these cichlids, can learn to be hand-fed.

Staple diet flake food.

Floating food sticks for large fish.

Algae wafers which sink for bottom-feeders.

Sinking granules.

Cichlid with an earthworm in its mouth, and another cichlid thinking about pinching it. Tugs-of-war do occur!

Frozen food: bloodworms, glassworms, brine shrimps, and *Daphnia*.

Freeze-dried *Tubifex*.

Live brine shrimps.

Live bloodworm.

INTRODUCING NEW FISH

Mary Bailey.

To avoid temperature shock when introducing new fish to the tank, they are floated, in a container of their previous water, in the new aquarium, so that the temperature may equalise.

SHOWING FISH

Peter Burgess.

Some consider the conditions in which fish are shown to be cruel and stressful. (See Chapter 9)

pathogens, but these procedures cannot be relied upon completely to eliminate any diseases which may be present. The potential of introducing diseases along with live foods is thus a significant risk, of which the aquarist should be aware.

> **Note:** for conservation reasons some creatures formerly used as live foods, and mentioned as such in older aquarium literature, should not be collected; notably the spawn and tadpoles of frogs, toads, and newts, all of which are currently threatened by various factors in the wild. It is also important to respect property-owners' rights when collecting foods from the wild – always ask permission first.

SOME TYPES OF LIVE FOODS

Freshwater crustaceans:

Daphnia (water fleas), *Bosmina, Cyclops,* and other free-swimming freshwater copepods can sometimes be found occurring naturally in ponds, and *Daphnia/Cyclops* can sometimes be purchased from aquatic retailers.

Domestic ponds, water butts, and other large containers can be 'seeded' with purchased or wild-caught *Daphnia* to provide a convenient supply. Their natural diet is micro-organisms, including free-floating unicellular algae ('green water'). Duck/goose ponds are ideal sources because constant fertilisation by the birds ensures a steady supply of food for the crustaceans. The aquarist must use his imagination regarding the fertilisation of other containers, but water in which horse manure has been steeped (the water should be strained before use!), and hay infusions, have been used with success. Provided the pond/container is sunlit for part of the day, algae and crustaceans should prosper, but overheating must be avoided.

A net of suitable mesh size is used to capture the food. When dealing with ponds a long handle is useful, though not always essential as crustaceans often gather in the sunny shallows near the edge. An aquarium net securely lashed to a long bamboo cane will suffice for the average aquarist's needs. These creatures will not survive long in small containers of water, and for only a day or two once deprived of their food supply, so it is best to catch only what is needed for immediate use. The food should be transported in a bucket of clean water – not pond water.

It is important, especially when feeding small fish, to check the 'harvest' for the presence of predatory 'nasties' such as dragonfly larvae and glassworms (see below).

'Pond foods' can be graded to provide several sizes of foods for various sizes of fish, using strainers of different mesh size, which can be home-made (nylon net curtain, or a variety of aquarium nets) or purchased (live-food sieves).

If the crustaceans have been kept in a bucket for a day or more, the residual water will usually be rich in very small individuals, which can be strained out using a very fine sieve or piece of cloth, and used as foods for fry. Alternatively, the food-bearing water can be fed direct to the fry, but only in small amounts to avoid chilling.

Larger crustaceans, notably *Gammarus* (freshwater shrimps) and *Asellus* (water hog-lice or water lice) can be collected from heavily vegetated waters, and under stones. Pond filters are also favourite hiding-places for these critters, and can be 'seeded' to produce a convenient supply.

Salt-water crustaceans:

Newly-hatched *Artemia* (brine shrimp) nauplii are commonly used as a fry food (see below). In recent years some retail outlets have stocked live adult *Artemia* for feeding to larger fish, and, although quite expensive, they are an excellent food (be sure to rinse *Artemia* under the tap before feeding, to avoid salt accumulation in the aquarium). It is possible to grow *Artemia* nauplii to maturity using a small aquarium filled with salt water, the salinity matching that used for hatching (see below); they can be fed on infusorians and/or liquid fry food, and will also feed on naturally-occurring micro-organisms. However, the process is rather time-consuming, and not really practicable as a viable source of live food.

Aquatic insect larvae

Blood worms (red mosquito larvae) are the larvae of chironomid midges and are generally found in the detritus at the bottom of ponds or other bodies of slow-moving or static water with silt/organic material on the bottom, or in thick growths of algae ('blanket weed'). They are about 1-2 cm (0.5-0.75 in) in length, and, as the name suggests, blood-red in colour. They can sometimes be purchased from aquatic retailers, but this is inadvisable as some commercial sources are polluted and contaminated bloodworm can introduce pathogens. The dedicated aquarist can collect his own from safe sources, but as this commonly requires picking individual larvae from the detritus with forceps, it is easier to buy the frozen (gamma-irradiated) product, which is safer.

   Glassworms (white mosquito larvae) are the transparent larvae of the phantom midge (*Chaoborus* sp.) and are about the same size as bloodworms. They are occasionally found among pond-living crustaceans (*Daphnia,* etc, see above), but rarely in sufficient quantity to constitute a separate food type. Fish enjoy them, but they are predatory and should not be fed to tanks containing small fry.

   Mosquito larvae (black mosquito larvae) can measure up to about 1 cm (0.5 in) and are commonly found hanging just below the surface of stagnant water. They are air-breathers, using a small tube to take atmospheric air from just above the surface. At any hint of danger – including a shadow falling on the water – they dive to safety, so the net must be wielded stealthily. Horse and cattle troughs, ponds, and even buckets of rainwater can be rich sources of these larvae, which can be caught and transported as for *Daphnia,* etc. Fish greatly enjoy this food, which is not known to have any attendant dangers. But, do ensure all the larvae are eaten – in the tropical conditions of the aquarium they quickly metamorphose into mosquitoes!

   Whiptail larvae (drone-fly larvae, also known as rat-tailed maggots) are greyish with a body about 1 cm (0.5 in) long and 3 mm (0.125 in) in diameter, with a long air tube (the 'tail'). They are occasionally found in ponds and other stagnant waters and are much enjoyed by any fish whose mouths are large enough to cope.

Worms

A number of different worms are used as foods for aquarium fish, and include cultured, collected, and purchased types:

   Earthworms are an excellent food for fish and much enjoyed by the recipients. They should be rinsed free of soil before use, then fed whole or chopped, depending on the relative sizes of worms and fish. They can also be minced in a kitchen blender (ideally one reserved for the purpose!) to produce an excellent fry food. Although it is sometimes possible to buy worms (mail order), most aquarists regard this food as a free side-benefit of gardening activities. Note that worms should not be harvested from ground recently treated with pesticides or other chemicals.

Worms can also be cultured in large boxes, usually of wood, filled with compost rich in organic matter. The culture is fed on vegetable wastes from the kitchen, spread on the surface of the compost. If the box is bottomless and sited on soil, it will be colonised readily and recolonised as harvested, provided the food supply is maintained; if there is no food, of course, resident worms are equally free to leave. Alternatively, fully-enclosed boxes can be used, but will provide a smaller crop due to the need to let the worms breed to replenish the population. The advantage of cultures is that it is possible to keep up a supply of worms even when the garden is frozen (by insulating) or rock-hard with drought (by watering). Cultures should be shaded to avoid overheating in hot sunny weather.

Tubifex are small (about 2-2.5 cm/1 in long) red worms which are harvested from the wild, where they are typically found in foul mud – around sewage outfalls, for example. Harvesting them is not normally regarded as a suitable pastime for the aquarist, who instead can buy these worms from some aquatic retailers. Despite claims for various disinfectants and mechanical methods of cleansing *Tubifex*, it must be stressed that, whatever the sanitising method used, feeding live *Tubifex* is one of the best ways of introducing disease into the aquarium. So, although there is no denying that fish enjoy this food, it is simply not worth the risk. Freeze-dried, bottled, and frozen (gamma-irradiated) *Tubifex* is safer.

Whiteworms (*Enchytraeus* spp.) are about 1-3 cm (0.5-1.25 in) long and, as their name implies, white in colour. They are sometimes found in soil rich in organic matter but for aquarium use they are normally cultured using a culture purchased from a retail outlet or mail order supplier. They are cultured in a shallow (4-5 cm/1.5-2 in deep) plastic or wooden box of reasonable size (e.g. 20 x 30 cm/ 8 x 12 in) containing loamy soil (the 'compost') often mixed with peat. The soil must be kept moist but never wet, to which end the culture is usually covered with a sheet of glass topped with thin plywood, cardboard, or similar, as darkness is also required. The culture should not be airtight, or the worms will suffocate.

Whiteworm cultures can be fed using one or more pieces of bread pre-moistened with water or low-fat milk. Other culture foods include cereals such as porridge oats, and some aquarists feed their whiteworms with best-quality aquarium flake foods, on the basis that what goes into the worms will subsequently go into the fish. Whatever the food, it must be moist. How much and how often to feed must be established by experiment, and the food replaced if it starts to go mouldy.

It is important not to harvest worms until the culture is thriving, which will be evident from the numbers of worms around the food when the lid is lifted. Equally do not over-harvest. The worms can be removed with forceps. If the compost is the right consistency and has just the right moisture content, the worms will generally come out clean and can be fed straight to the fish, otherwise they should be rinsed. They can be fed using a worm feeder (available from aquatic stores) for surface- and mid-water feeders, or simply dropped into the aquarium for bottom-feeders.

Old cultures tend to become 'caked' and less prolific, and should either be stirred up thoroughly (it will take a week or so for yields to improve again), or a new culture started using some of the old one to seed it.

Grindal worms are a smaller (0.5cm/0.25 in) *Enchytraeus* species sometimes used for older fry or small fish species such as dwarf cichlids, small tetras, etc. They are home-cultured, and starters are generally available only by mail order from specialist suppliers. The compost should be as for whiteworm, but usually in a smaller container, such as a plastic sandwich box. The culture should again be covered and kept dark. A very small amount of cereal (e.g. porridge oats) should be sprinkled on a small area (diameter circa 3-4 cm/1.25-1.5 in) of the compost surface, slightly moistened, and covered with a small piece of glass. When the worms have eaten the food, many will remain congregated on the underside of the glass and can be rinsed off into the tank (the worms are too small to be rinsed of soil). Experience is required to achieve the right consistency and moisture content of the compost, so that it does not stick to the glass. Grindal worms are not very prolific, so care is required not to harvest too many at once, for fear of over-depleting the culture.

Microworms are generally used as a fry food but can also be fed to very small adult fish (see section on fry foods, below, for culture instructions).

Other possible live foods
Woodlice are enjoyed by medium to large fish, although they may take a while to learn how to tackle them. Larger fish may enjoy **crickets**, which can be purchased from pet shops specialising in herptiles (lizards, etc).

Flies and other insects, both terrestrial and aquatic types, are sometimes enjoyed but must be insecticide-free, i.e. swatted, not sprayed! Suitable flies include the housefly, whitefly, greenfly, and blackfly. Stinging insects are best avoided. **Maggots**, as sold for angling bait, are sometimes used as live food for aquarium fish, but avoid dyed ones due to possible toxicity of the dye. Maggots are best kept in a bait box or other plastic container with a tight-fitting lid, which must, however, be perforated to admit air. Like mosquito larvae they may metamorphose, especially in warm conditions, filling the house with flies when the container is opened. For this reason, anglers sometimes slow their development by keeping them in the fridge! **Fruitflies** (*Drosophila*) – preferably the wingless type – can be cultured for obligatory surface-feeders. Starter cultures with instructions are available from a few pet suppliers (e.g. herptile specialists). Fruitflies are usually cultured in sponge-plugged glass bottles filled with a porridge/sugar/yeast mix. Among the aquatic insects, the **water boatmen** (*Notonecta* spp.) and **pondskaters** (*Gerris* spp.) are acceptable fish foods.

Crushed **aquatic snails** are enjoyed by some fish, but only aquarium snails should be used; wild ones may be host to parasites.

Live fish
Live fish may be required as food by piscivorous species, although most can be 'weaned' on to dead fish (see fresh foods, below) and other carnivore foods once they have learned to associate what their owner puts into the tank with food. Some aquarists, however, appear to enjoy the spectacle of feeding live fish (e.g. goldfish) or even live animals (e.g. mice) to predatory species, particularly piscivorous piranhas. Fortunately, the use of 'feeder fish' – healthy fish purchased purely as food for predators – has not gained wide acceptance in some countries (for example, the UK) and many feel that the practice should be universally condemned.

Breeder hobbyists sometimes use genetically deformed and/or stunted, and otherwise surplus, fry as food for other fish – which is, after all, the fate of most fry in the wild. The culling of fry may be necessary when breeding species which produce large broods, particularly where demand for young stock is low – as with many Central American cichlids. Using culled fry as food is generally regarded as acceptable, given that they have to be disposed of in some fashion.

It is important never to dispose of diseased fish by feeding them to others, as this can result in the disease being transmitted. For the same reason, do not allow fish to forage on the bodies of dead or dying tankmates.

5. FRESH FOODS

Many human foods are equally suitable for fish. Fresh or frozen green vegetables, such as cucumber, peas, spinach, and lettuce, are ideal supplementary foods for omnivore and herbivore species. Some fresh or frozen vegetables are not easily digested by fish and must be pre-treated before being used. Peas should be cooked to soften or remove their skins, and lettuce and spinach should be blanched to break down the indigestible cellulose.

It is best to avoid feeding mammal/bird meats to fish as this can lead to the accumulation of harmful fatty deposits in the liver and other tissues. Despite such risks, the feeding of beef heart or liver is still advocated by many aquarists, but, if used at all, the golden rule is to feed such meats very sparingly. On the other hand, fresh or frozen fish, shellfish (e.g. mussels), and shrimps/prawns are excellent foods for fish.

Warning: never feed bread, biscuits, cheese or cheese products, as they all contain saturated fats that will harm fish.

6. FRY FOODS

The fry of many fish species will accept only live prey, largely because they may not perceive non-moving foods as being edible, at least initially. In some cases, however, the fry will learn to associate the approach of the aquarist with food, and will then try whatever is offered. Suitable small live foods for raising fry include infusorians, *Artemia* nauplii and microworms:

Infusorians (micro-organisms) are required as a first food by very tiny fry. Mature aquaria, especially if containing plenty of algae, may contain sufficient naturally-occurring organisms, but in special breeding aquaria, where conditions are generally more sterile, cultured infusorians will be necessary. These can be cultured by placing vegetable matter (commonly a crushed lettuce leaf) in a jar of water in a warm sunny place, such as a window ledge. The culture water must be de-chlorinated (e.g. aquarium water), otherwise it may kill the infusorians. When the water becomes cloudy, small quantities (to avoid chilling the fry) can be added to the fry tank using a pipette. Commercial infusorian substitutes are available from aquatic retailers.

Newly-hatched *Artemia* (brine shrimp) nauplii are a suitable first food for many fry, or second food for those initially requiring micro-organisms. They have the twin advantages of being mobile in the open water (attractive and visible), and of their orange colour being apparent in the normally transparent bellies of the fry that have eaten them, indicating that the fry are feeding and receiving adequate food.

They are hatched by the aquarist from 'eggs' (actually cysts) purchased from aquatic retailers or by mail order. Hatching is achieved in a container (a large sweet jar, two-litre plastic lemonade bottle, or purchased hatcher) of salt water. The salinity required will vary depending on the source of the cysts (see the instructions on the packet). The culture must be vigorously aerated to keep the cysts circulating, and the container should be kept in a warm place, 18.5-26 °C (65-80 °F). Hatch time will depend on temperature, but is usually 36-72 hours.

To harvest the nauplii the aeration is turned off and a light source positioned close to the container at about half-way up its height. The shrimps will congregate near the light, while unhatched cysts and discarded shells normally float on the surface or sink to the bottom. The shrimps can thus be siphoned off or removed with a pipette, without unwanted debris; some fry will die if they ingest shells or cysts. The nauplii must be strained (using a live-food sieve or a small fine-meshed net), and rinsed in fresh water. *Never* add shrimps in culture water as the salinity may kill the fry. The aeration must be turned on again after harvesting. A culture will supply food for two to five days depending on how much is required, and a succession of cultures may be required to ensure sufficient food.

Microworms are suitable for feeding in parallel with, or instead of, *Artemia* nauplii. They are much more economical to feed than *Artemia* since a microworm culture is cheap and easy to propagate, offering a permanently available supply. Starter cultures can be obtained by mail order (look for ads in aquarium magazines) or from another hobbyist. One disadvantage is that the worms sink – albeit slowly – instead of swimming, but most fry catch on quickly and chase the food down to the bottom. Microworms are more suitable than *Artemia* for bottom-oriented fry.

Microworms are usually cultured in a plastic container (margarine tub, sandwich box). A 1 cm (0.5 in) layer of porridge oats is placed in the container then moistened with boiling water to form a stiff paste. Do not stir as this is likely to spread the paste up the sides of the container, which must be kept clean. When the porridge is cool, add the starter. Rest the lid on the container so the culture does not dry out, but air can get in, and stand in a warm place (e.g. on top of a tank). After a few days the worms will have proliferated to the extent that they start to crawl up the sides of the container, and can be harvested from the porridge-free plastic using a finger, cotton bud, or artist's brush, which is then rinsed in the aquarium.

A culture may remain active for three to six weeks, but will often smell unpleasant after about ten to twenty days. It is politic to start a new culture (porridge oats are cheap, divorce expensive!) before the old one reaches the foul-smelling stage, this time simply using a spoonful of old culture as starter. If many fry are hatched, then two or more cultures can be run simultaneously.

Tiny *Daphnia*, *Cyclops*, and *Bosmina* can also be used as fry foods. See Live Foods (freshwater crustaceans) above.

7. FEEDING: HOW MUCH AND HOW OFTEN

The inexperienced fishkeeper often makes the mistake of overfeeding his fish, usually with dire consequences. Excessive feeding may not necessarily cause any direct harm to the fish, but it can lead to serious water quality (Chapter 10) problems which may stress or kill the aquarium inhabitants.

The deleterious effects of overfeeding are basically two-fold:
• Uneaten food will quickly decompose leading to ammonia production.
• Excess quantities of food consumed by the fish, in particular an excess of protein, will result in increased ammonia excretion.

The resulting surge in ammonia from these processes may overwhelm the biological filter (Chapter 10), leading to a build-up, in the aquarium water, of ammonia, which is toxic to fish. In the case of regular overfeeding, the biological filter may adapt and cope with the raised ammonia level. However, the net effect will be increased organic pollution (which can cause epidemics of pests such as planarians and snails, Chapter 22), including increased nitrate production. The latter will necessitate more frequent water changes (Chapter 15) to prevent toxic effects on the fish and nitrate-related environmental problems such as algal and bacterial blooms.

It should be borne in mind that fish require much less food than other animals of similar size. This is partly because fish are cold-blooded (poikilothermic) and do not, therefore, need to convert food into heat. Many fish are capable of neutral buoyancy and therefore do not require energy to counteract the force of gravity. Weight for weight, fish require less energy than other animals.

With experience, the aquarist will learn to gauge the correct amount of food. However, for newcomers to the hobby, one useful rule is to feed only as much per meal as the fish will consume in about five minutes. If the fish are inadvertently overfed, or an accident occurs (for example the tub of food is knocked into the water), then it is imperative to siphon out as much as possible of the excess before it decomposes.

As mentioned earlier, the range of food items consumed by fish, and the frequency of their feeding, will vary from species to species and may be influenced by environmental factors. Most fish species, and the fry of virtually all types, are continuous feeders in nature, and it is better to feed them a small amount several times per day rather than one big feed. In the case of community aquaria housing many different types of fish, two or three small feeds per day are generally recommended. Exceptions are fish which take large prey items. For example, some piscivores which may eat whole fish half their own size. Such fish require feeding only two or three times per week and may even refuse any additional food offered.

Careful observation is necessary to ensure that all the fish in the aquarium get a fair share of the food: slow-moving, shy, or nocturnal species can easily lose out at mealtimes, as can individual fish at the bottom of a 'pecking order'.

Finally, feeding time is an excellent opportunity to check that all the aquarium occupants are present and in good health; loss of appetite should always be regarded as a warning sign that something may be amiss.

CHAPTER 8

BREEDING

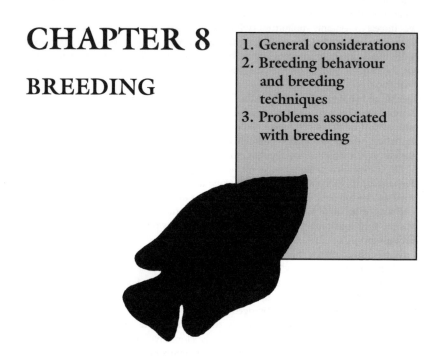

1. General considerations
2. Breeding behaviour and breeding techniques
3. Problems associated with breeding

As we have seen in Chapter 4, reproduction is one of the main motivational forces in fish, as in other creatures. The aquarist may initially have no interest in breeding his fish, but if individuals of both sexes are present and environmental conditions are appropriate, then many freshwater tropical fish will endeavour to breed in captivity without any intervention from their owner. We say 'endeavour' because in the community tank it is probable that most, if not all, of the eggs or fry will be eaten by other fish, and unless the parents belong to a species that practises parental care (see below), they will commonly cannibalise their own offspring. However, the fact that they are trying to breed is often enough to encourage the aquarist to turn his hand to breeding.

In this chapter we look first at some general aspects of breeding aquarium fish; then at some of the various techniques used depending on natural breeding behaviour (which is highly variable); and finally at some of the problems that may occur. This can, however, be at best a mere introduction to a highly complex subject – one which no book, let alone a single chapter, can hope to cover fully, given the vast number of different fish species, with different breeding habits, that exist.

1. GENERAL CONSIDERATIONS

WHY BREED FISH?

Aquarists usually breed their fish because it adds a new dimension to their hobby. Once the aquarium has been set up, then, providing the job was done properly, it requires only a few minutes' attention most days, with a weekly maintenance session (Chapter 15). It is interesting to look at, but there is not much to *do*. Breeding offers the opportunity for increased aquarist participation, and for observing a whole new aspect of fish behaviour.

It is unwise to regard breeding as a potential source of income. Many popular species are commercially bred or collected in vast numbers, while demand for more unusual types may be limited, at least locally. The aquarist may find he is offered little or nothing for commonplace species, or that he can sell only small numbers of the more exotic ones. However, mass-produced stock is sometimes of inferior quality, so the amateur producing good-quality stock may be able to carve out a niche market, and perhaps cover the costs he has incurred in producing his youngstock. If he breeds species not yet produced commercially, then he will be doing his bit for conservation by reducing pressure on wild populations.

PLANNING AHEAD

As we have already seen, fry produced in the community aquarium are unlikely to survive because of predation, so if a serious breeding attempt is to be made, at least one extra tank will be required. Commonly, small species can be spawned by placing a pair or small group in a small aquarium, say 30 x 20 x 20 cm (12 x 8 x 8 in) (some small species, and, of course, larger ones will require larger breeding tanks) but not many fry can be reared to saleable size (usually at least 2.5 cm/1 in) in such a small container. So, already we are looking at two extra tanks instead of one. Breeding several species may require yet more tanks, or a long wait before the next breeding attempt, while the first batch of fry are grown on and sold. Unless the aquarist is a master of self-restraint, the house may very soon be filled with tanks in every available corner. Make sure you think ahead. You do not want to breed fish then have to destroy the fry because accommodating their needs is going to lead to divorce!

For the same reason, it is wise to canvass potential markets, usually other aquarists and local dealers, before breeding any species, as there are few things more disheartening than having to destroy healthy young fish because no-one wants them. The species you are considering breeding may be one for which there is no market; or you may need to cull the brood to saleable numbers, or to the number for which you have growing-on accommodation.

SELECTION OF BREEDING STOCK

If you are to establish yourself as an amateur breeder from whom dealers and other aquarists are happy to buy youngstock, then you must produce healthy young fish which are typical of their species or variety. Nobody will want fish that are deformed, too small, poorly-coloured, or in any way unhealthy.

In order to produce offspring that are true to type, whether for the naturally-occurring form of a species or for a 'fancy' variety, it is important to select only healthy individuals, typical of the relevant species or variety, as breeding stock. Do not use individuals which are atypically small or large, deformed, or which exhibit aberrant coloration, in case their abnormality is heritable. Breeding stock that repeatedly produces aberrant offspring should not be used again. For normal purposes, it is best to mate unrelated fish in order to avoid inbreeding, which, over a number of generations, can lead to general deterioration from type, ill health (through loss of vigour), and an increase in the likelihood of uncovering harmful genes. Careful stock selection will not guarantee the absence of deformities and other aberrations in the offspring, but will reduce the probability of these occurring.

When purchasing broodstock, remember that there is a possibility that any batch of captive-bred stock may be closely related, hence it is preferable to obtain breeding stock from two or more different sources. Avoid buying even normal individuals from batches containing deformed or otherwise aberrant specimens, as the presence of abnormal siblings may be an indication of inbred stock.

It is also important to make sure you know the identity of the species you plan to breed. This should be its scientific name (Chapter 2), or, if it does not yet have a scientific name, the accepted temporary name it has been given in the hobby. Buy your broodstock from dealers or breeders who label their stock correctly, not from tanks marked, for example, 'mixed tetras' or 'mixed Malawi cichlids'.

If you are breeding a species which has numerous 'fancy' varieties – notable examples being the guppy (*Poecilia reticulata*) and the angelfish (*Pterophyllum scalare*) – then buy a specific variety; if you buy individuals of several varieties they will probably interbreed (because they are still the same species) and produce a batch of youngsters which are neither one parent type nor the other. Generations of careful selective breeding have gone into producing fancy varieties, but all that work can be undone by a single ill-considered cross-mating. Many aquarists make this mistake, and find themselves stuck with a brood of unsaleable crossbreeds.

The same applies to species which have natural varieties (e.g. differing colour patterns based on different geographical ranges). Likewise, always make sure that you are mating male and female of the same species. Some species, particularly the females of some species, are very similar; if you mix them, hybrid crosses may occur. These too are undesirable and unsaleable.

CONDITIONING FOR BREEDING AND TRIGGERING SPAWNING

Before fish will breed, they must be in breeding or spawning condition – females must contain ripe eggs and males milt. Whether a fish is in breeding condition may depend on its age (it may not be old enough, or too old), its diet (eggs will not normally ripen in a poorly-nourished fish), and/or seasonal factors (which may affect hormones and food supply).

Species which breed all year round and those that produce live young do not normally require any special treatment to bring them into condition. If they do, this is usually a sign that normal maintenance is incorrect.

In nature, seasonal spawners typically experience a series of events which combine to produce physical and psychological readiness to breed. These may include changes in temperature, water chemistry, and diet/food supply, and sometimes photoperiod and light intensity, although in the tropics, where day and night are of similar length all year round, photoperiod is probably of lesser importance.

Seasonal spawners may require a special diet – more food than normal, and/or different foods, particularly live foods. A slight rise in temperature is used to trigger spawning in some species; while in other cases it may be necessary first to lower the temperature and increase oxygen content (to simulate the rainy season or an influx of melt-water from the mountains), then to feed live food while gradually raising the temperature over a period of weeks, again to simulate seasonal events. But this is commonly quite unnecessary, and such triggers should be tried only if spawning fails to occur in fish which are properly fed and maintained. Some species may even be deterred from spawning by gratuitous alterations to their environment.

2. BREEDING BEHAVIOUR AND BREEDING TECHNIQUES

One of the things that makes breeding fish so rewarding is the variety of different strategies they use, and the different behaviours involved. While the breeding habits of many are already known, others remain a mystery because they have not been studied in the natural habitat and no-one has yet spawned them in captivity. Indeed, herein lies one of the great challenges of fishkeeping – to be the first to breed a species and record the details for the benefit of other aquarists and the fund of scientific knowledge. It is a good idea always to keep notes; even if you are breeding a species that has been spawned several times before, you may observe some facet of behaviour that has yet to be recorded. If you are lucky enough to achieve a 'first', your observations will be invaluable.

Where your chosen species has been bred before, find out all you can about its breeding habits, and techniques that have been used successfully, before making your own breeding attempt. If the species has not been bred previously and no information is available, then data regarding a close relative may prove helpful.

BREEDING STRATEGIES IN FISH
Fish have a huge variety of breeding strategies, but, from the aquarist's point of view, it is normally adequate to consider just the major distinctions:
• Fish may lay eggs which are fertilised after spawning and subsequently hatch into fry (egg-layers) or they may be fertilised internally and give birth to fry (livebearers or viviparous fish).
• Fish may either protect their eggs and young (species that practise parental care, 'parental species' for short) or abandon them to their fate ('non-parental species'). Non-parental fish may even eat their own eggs/fry soon after spawning or giving birth. Parental species generally have only a limited period during which they guard their offspring, after which they too may indulge in cannibalism. Parental species may also eat their eggs/fry during the guarding period for a number of reasons – typically because they have been disturbed or because their natural behaviour has been modified by unnatural factors in captivity. Parental fish are often territorial and aggressive when defending their brood (Chapters 4, 5).

No livebearers are known to practise post-parturition parental care, hence we are left with three main groups: livebearers, non-parental egg-layers and parental egg-layers. The last group can be further subdivided into species that lay their eggs and stand guard over them, those that carry eggs and fry around (commonly in their mouths), and those that practise a combination of the two techniques. Non-parental egg-layers commonly scatter their eggs among plants or on the bottom (egg-scatterers), or attach them to plants or other surfaces (egg-hangers or substrate-spawners); others, for example some killifish, bury them in the bottom substrate (in nature, usually mud), or hide them in crevices or other safe places.

Producing live young, or guarding fry hatched from eggs, means that the fry are larger when they embark on life alone (without parental protection, inside or outside the body), and so stand a better chance of survival. Guarded fry will also have learned their way around their environment, under parental supervision, before becoming independent.

BREEDING TANKS AND METHODS

These will vary according to the species concerned. Livebearers will mate and produce young with little regard for surroundings. Non-parental egg-layers are often spawned in temporary quarters with minimal decor, to which a pair or small shoal is introduced when thought to be ripe; while parental species may require a reasonable simulation of their natural habitat, and sometimes a private tank, long-term, for the breeding pair. Parental species may also attempt to rear their brood in the community aquarium, but their defence of their family may cause immense disruption and possibly injury to other fish.

It must be noted that many so-called hardy species, which can be maintained in water with a chemistry different to that encountered in their natural habitat, may require the correct (natural) water chemistry to induce them to spawn or to ensure viable eggs and milt, not only at spawning time but for some time previously.

The following are some breeding methods and set-ups often used (they are numbered to permit reference from Chapter 3). The list is not exhaustive; there are many other variations.

Method 1: Temporary quarters with minimal furnishings, commonly just a spawning medium; this may offer natural cover in/on which the fish may lay their eggs, prevent them from immediately eating their eggs, or both. The fish are placed in the breeding tank for a short period only – a few hours to a few days. In the latter instance, a small air-driven filter should be included. If they do not spawn, they are usually returned to their normal accommodation and another attempt made later; if they do spawn, they may require a post-spawning rest (see below) in another special tank before return to their normal quarters. The eggs are hatched artificially (see below), in the breeding tank or in another, usually smaller, container.

There are a number of variations on this basic method:

• 1a, Java moss or fine-leaved plants are used as the spawning medium. Used for egg-scatterers or egg-hangers that spawn amongst vegetation.

• 1b, Plastic mesh (e.g. greenhouse shading mesh) is suspended from the rim of the tank. The fish spawn above the mesh and the eggs fall through to safety. Used for cannibalistic egg-scatterers that do not require a particular spawning medium.

• 1c, The tank bottom is covered with glass marbles (glass balls). Used as for 1b.

• 1d, Broad-leaved plants are used as the spawning medium, for egg-hangers that prefer this type of vegetation.

Method 2: Slightly longer-term accommodation with minimal furnishings, usually for killifish, which commonly lay a few eggs per day over a period of weeks. The tank is equipped with a small, low-turnover, air-driven filter and a suitable spawning medium. The fish remain in the tank until the female has stopped spawning, when another ripe female may be substituted. Two main variations:

• 2a, Peat spawning medium, for annual species that lay their eggs in the mud on the bottom of their pool, in nature. The fish are removed after spawning, the water is drained off, and the peat is removed and stored in a plastic container in a warm place. The container is labelled with the species name and date of storage. When the period of time appropriate to the species has elapsed, the eggs are wetted and hatched.

• 2b, The spawning medium is a 'mop' made from strands of nylon wool attached to a cork or stone, depending on whether the species spawns on surface or bottom vegetation in nature. The eggs are pulled off gently each day and kept in water until they hatch. (In nature, of course, the fish spawn on plants, but these do not take well to daily handling for egg-collecting!).

Method 3: Medium to long-term accommodation for parental fish; with suitable decor and filtration. Three variations:

• 3a, Egg/fry guarders where only one parent practises brood care. The pair are placed in the tank and left to spawn when ready. The non-guarding parent is removed afterwards. The guarding parent is removed when it ceases guarding.

• 3b, Egg/fry guarders where both parents practise brood care. The pair are placed in the tank as for 3a, but both are left to guard the brood. Both are removed when brood care is over, or the pair may be left to breed again and the fry removed.

• 3c, Egg/fry brooders (e.g. mouthbrooders) are often bred in their normal quarters, but the brooding fish is removed to a 'brooding tank' where it will not be disturbed or harassed. It is removed once brooding, and any subsequent guarding, is over.

Method 4: Breeding traps, for livebearers. Livebearer fry are likely to be eaten by tankmates (including their mother) immediately after birth. The usual method of preventing this is to use a 'breeding trap', a special container (from the aquatic store) in which the pregnant female is placed when she appears about to give birth. The fry can elude their mother by swimming through small apertures in the container. Two types of breeding trap are available: one type is designed for use in the community tank, and has a special chamber into which the fry pass from the 'maternity ward'; the other allows them to escape into the tank, and is intended for use in separate breeding tanks with no other fish present. Females and fry should not be kept in traps for any longer than necessary; traps are not intended for rearing fry, simply for very temporary protection.

POST-SPAWNING/PARTURITION REST
Spawning and parturition can be exhausting and stressful. Females in particular may need to recuperate afterwards, in isolation, before being returned to their normal quarters. Note that not all species require this rest period, and that parental species should be allowed to remain with their offspring.

HATCHING
In the case of tropical freshwater fish, the eggs normally hatch into larvae between one and five days after spawning (depending on the species and the water temperature). The larvae are unable to swim for a few days more, during which they are nourished by, and absorb, their yolk sacs. At the end of this period they become free-swimming and start to search for food.

Parental species should be allowed to guard their eggs themselves; removing the eggs is likely to stress to the adults, and there is some evidence that parenting is learned rather than inherited – individuals that have been hatched and reared away from their parents sometimes lack parental instincts and cannibalise their own spawn.

The eggs of non-parental species must be hatched by the aquarist. The hatching container (the breeding tank or any suitably-sized non-toxic container such as a plastic sandwich box or glass jar, floated in an aquarium to keep it warm) must be filled with water taken from the breeding aquarium, to ensure water chemistry is an exact match. The eggs must not be exposed to air during any transfer, and if they are attached to a spawning medium, that will generally be transferred too. The water in the hatching container should be oxygenated and circulated using a diffuser, but the current should be gentle and the bubbles of air must not come into contact with the eggs (this can damage them). It is usual to add methylene blue to guard against egg fungus (Chapter 21, section 3.3.4).

CARE OF NEWLY-HATCHED FRY
No food should be offered until the fry are free-swimming – as larvae they will live on their yolk sacs, and adding food at this stage will contaminate the hatching container, with possible loss of the brood. If the eggs were attached to a spawning medium, this should be removed when the larvae or fry become detached.

Fry hatched in a mature aquarium, e.g. with their parents, will often find sufficient naturally-occurring micro-organisms to serve as their first food, and will be seen foraging for this type of food when nothing else is available. Fry hatched artificially in a relatively sterile hatchery must be fed as soon as they become free-swimming. Suitable foods are described in Chapter 7. Water quality should be monitored at least daily, and small partial water changes made on a daily or twice-daily basis, always using water of matched chemistry and temperature. Siphon new water into the container through airline tubing, to avoid battering the delicate fry.

The fry of some species need to fill their swimbladder (Chapter 17) with atmospheric air; others, for example, those of labyrinth fish need to breathe it. Their quarters must have a tight-fitting cover so that the air above the water is warm – cold air may cause permanent, or fatal, damage to delicate organs.

REARING
Attention must be paid to a number of essential points when rearing fry:
• First-rate hygiene. Water quality should be excellent, with minimal nitrate.
• Good-quality, balanced nutrition (Chapter 7). Heavy feeding with growth (protein-rich) foods will promote rapid growth, but may cause water quality problems, which may limit growth and cause ill health. Rapid growth is not of paramount importance, good water quality is! A balance should be achieved – sensible feeding, no water problems, and healthy fry.
• Growing space. The more space the better. Overcrowding may lead to poor hygiene and water quality, and stress.
• Culling. Any fry that are stunted, or abnormal in form, colour or behaviour, should be euthanased (Chapter 25), but note that sexual dimorphism as regards size may manifest at an early stage, and if half the brood appear to be runts, they may in fact be the smaller sex! If numbers exceed the market demand, or rearing space is limited, then excess numbers of fry should also be culled. Culling should take place at the earliest stage possible.

3. PROBLEMS ASSOCIATED WITH BREEDING

These are legion. The following are a few of the most common:
• Failure to spawn or eggs fail to hatch (See Chapter 21, section 6.6).
• Egg/fry cannibalism.
• Aggression between breeding partners and towards other fish. This problem is covered in Chapters 4 and 5.
• Hybridisation.
• Spawn binding. This usually occurs where a female fish lacks a mate or fails to spawn for some other reason (e.g. incorrect environment) although she is ripe. Unless she can reabsorb or shed the eggs, they will decay inside her, causing bacterial infection of the reproductive tract, usually resulting in death. Prevention is the optimal solution, by providing a partner and suitable environmental conditions. If spawn binding does occur, the vet may be able to 'strip' the female of her eggs, although this is impracticable for small fish (say, less than 5 cm/2 in).
• Paternity in livebearers. Female livebearers are able to store sperm for some time, using it to fertilise eggs over a period of months. Thus, unless a female is known to be virgin, or has been isolated until she ceases producing fry (sperm used up), there is no guarantee that the partner chosen by the aquarist will be the father of any fry produced. Young males commonly inseminate their sisters at an early age, so it is wise to separate the sexes as soon as possible to avoid undesirable matings.
• Precocious breeding. If female fish breed at too young an age, this can have a deleterious effect on their growth, by diverting energy to egg/fry production. If combined with overbreeding (below), the retardation can be serious and the female's health may be affected. It is best to separate young males and females until they are a reasonable size, particularly in livebearers where a single insemination can fertilise several successive broods.
• Overbreeding. In nature, the frequency of ripening and spawning is controlled by the fluctuating seasonal food supply, which is likely to be less generous than in captivity. Aquarium fish sometimes ripen and breed more frequently than nature intended, and this can have undesirable side-effects such as stress (the breeding process imposes considerable physical demands) and retarded growth (especially in young females, see Precocious Breeding, above). The problem of overbreeding in egg-layers is best limited by restricting food intake, as separating males and females may sometimes lead to spawn binding in the latter.

CHAPTER 9

SHOWING FISH

1. Size and scope of shows
2. Classes and judging
3. Benching
4. Positive aspects of showing
5. Negative aspects of showing
6. A stress-free future for fish and fishkeeper?

Fish shows differ somewhat from shows for other types of animals, as fish rarely have pedigrees but are of unknown ancestry. In this respect, fish shows are comparable to pet classes usually included in shows aimed primarily at pedigree cats and dogs.

1. SIZE AND SCOPE OF SHOWS

Shows vary considerably in their size and scope, from very small local affairs at club meetings to huge international exhibitions. Some are entirely for the amateur aquarist, while others are largely for the benefit of professional breeders. Sometimes the large exhibitions include trade stands displaying and selling equipment, food, decor, etc; information stands where experts answer questions on aspects of the hobby; and, sometimes, demonstrations and lectures. The smaller shows are usually organised by local clubs, funded by 'benching fees' charged for each exhibit, and sometimes by a small charge to non-exhibitors wishing to view the fish. Large exhibitions also commonly charge an entrance fee, and are additionally funded by charges for stand space and by sponsorship for commercial interests.

2. CLASSES AND JUDGING

Because so many different species of tropical freshwater fish are kept in aquaria, it is not possible to have separate classes for every one. Some very popular species may have their own class, but most classes cover groups of fish, on the basis of taxonomic family (Chapter 2; Table 2) and sometimes also geography (e.g. 'African cichlids'). There are also 'breeders' classes', in which the exhibits are small groups of fish, from a single brood, which the aquarist has bred and reared himself; and classes for 'furnished aquaria', which enable the aquarist to demonstrate his skill at designing and setting up an attractive aquarium.

Fish are judged against a set of standards which cover the same elements – size, colour, finnage (the exact criteria vary internationally) – for their species or variety, rather than competing directly with each other. This is essential as, with so many species available, there may be only one individual of a species at the show. Points are awarded for each element of the standards, and the winner in each class is the fish with the most points. The standards for the species represent a huge volume of data that has been accumulated from a number of sources over the years. As new fish species are imported, new sets of standards have to be drawn up. One problem this presents is that aquarists sometimes enter fish for which no standards are yet available, and which thus cannot be judged. Likewise, fish whose identity (scientific name, see Chapter 2) is unknown cannot be evaluated.

3. BENCHING

Typically, fish are exhibited in small bare tanks set in rows on tables or special stands ('benches'), usually with just one fish per tank (except for a few classes, e.g. breeders', pairs). The aquarist must usually bring his own tanks and any equipment required, although it is usual for tanks to be unheated and unfiltered as many show tanks are too small to contain such equipment, and in any case there will not be sufficient power outlets at the venue for all the tanks. Aeration is, however, sometimes provided by the show organisers, as some fish cannot survive without an enhanced oxygen supply. Some aquarists bring their own water, but many use whatever tap water is available at the venue.

Once all the exhibits are benched (there is usually a deadline for this), then the exhibits are judged. Sometimes all exhibitors and spectators have to leave the room while judging is in progress. After judging, the fish are open to viewing until the end of the show, which may last from a couple of hours for small 'table shows' at club meetings to several days in the case of large exhibitions. Because of their duration, the latter do sometimes make electrical provision for heating and filtration equipment (provided by the exhibitor), assuming the tanks are large enough to contain such equipment.

Prizes vary from simple certificates ('cards') to trophies, and sometimes also include cash and goods. After the prize-giving, the exhibitors pack up their fish and equipment and return home.

4. POSITIVE ASPECTS OF SHOWING

Shows encourage aquarists to meet and communicate, which leads to an exchange of ideas, information, and tips, often beneficial to the maintenance of fish. Larger shows in particular enable aquarists to see fish which may rarely appear in the shops, to seek advice from experts on the identity of 'mystery' species (enabling the aquarist to provide the correct living conditions), or to ask about health and breeding problems.

The aquarist who shows his fish has an incentive to care properly for them, as only those in peak condition are worth showing. Breeders' classes are a particularly good test of an aquarist's abilities as a fishkeeper. To enter he must have bred the species exhibited and reared a set of young fish all of which are of good quality and all of the same quality – well matched in size, coloration, and finnage (apart from sexual differences). Such classes encourage the hobbyist to breed his fish rather than simply keeping them, enabling them to lead a more natural existence. In addition, the captive breeding of species which are not commercially bred helps to reduce pressures on wild populations; many species are spawned and reared for the first time by amateur aquarists.

5. NEGATIVE ASPECTS OF SHOWING

Showing, especially showing at a distance from home, involves numerous factors that may impair the fish's health and even endanger its life – many fish die at or after shows:
• Stress from transportation to and from the show.
• Stress from lack of any cover in the bare show tank.
• Stress from insufficient space in many show tanks, particularly where large fish are shown.
• Stress from a succession of people passing by, staring, pointing, taking photos, and tapping on the glass.
• Shock and stress from changes in water chemistry (Chapter 10) from home tank water to show tank water and back again.
• Possibility of copper poisoning if water from the hot water tap is used when setting up the show tank (to obviate the lack of heating in the latter).
• Possibility of chlorine or chloramine poisoning if no dechlorinator, or the wrong type, is used.
• Possibility of nitrate shock if tap water at the show is high in nitrate.
• Possibility of gas bubble disease if cold water is used and heated up in the tank.
• Chilling due to lack of heating.
• Likelihood of ammonia poisoning through lack of filtration.
• Possibility of hypoxia if aeration is absent or inadequate.
• Possibility of stress on reintroduction to the home tank – the fish may have lost their position in the aquarium pecking order.

There are also negative factors in the day-to-day life of many show fish. Some live a quite unnatural and stressful existence, kept alone in bare tanks so that no damage can occur to their scales and finnage. Very many are overfed in an attempt to achieve additional size, for which important points are awarded. Many fish seen at shows are obese, and this represents a serious danger to their long-term health.
(See Chapter 21 for further details of stress, shock and other problems listed above).

6. A STRESS-FREE FUTURE FOR FISH AND FISHKEEPER?

Given the increasing awareness of the fact that fish can suffer pain and stress, and that it is possible to be cruel to a fish, it will hopefully be only a matter of time before improvements are made to the current unacceptable situation as regards showing, which is born largely of ignorance. People who show fish are not monsters by and large, they are simply unaware of the suffering they are causing. Most people are genuinely distressed if one of their fish dies.

We would like to make the following constructive suggestions:
• Fish should be shown only in furnished aquaria with substrate, background, and other appropriate decor (Chapter 11). This would not only benefit the fish, but also demonstrate the attractiveness of a 'proper' aquarium to would-be aquarists visiting the show.
• Better still, fish should be shown in aquaria set up to simulate their natural biotope, and the entire display, rather than just the fish, judged. This would encourage aquarists to find out about the correct conditions for their fish. Additional points could be awarded for biotope-correct water parameters.
• All show aquaria should be of a size suitable for the occupants and have adequate heating, filtration and aeration.
• Where practicable, exhibitors should bring their own water to avoid subjecting the fish to any change. In case this is totally impracticable, the organisers should provide each exhibitor, several weeks in advance, with details of the composition of the show venue water, i.e. hardness, pH, nitrate level, type of dechlorinator required (chlorine or chloramine), and any other relevant information. The aquarist would then have the option of slowly adjusting his fish to the appropriate parameters at home, and/or bringing the necessary equipment/chemicals to adjust the show water for the fish.
• The organisers should routinely provide exhibitors with information on transporting fish, with special reference to stress minimisation (Chapter 6).
• All fish should be checked in by one or more expert aquarists, and any that are obviously stressed or otherwise unwell on arrival should be barred from the show.
• Obese fish should also be barred, or at least downpointed.
• A limit should be recommended as to how often an individual fish can be shown, to reduce undue stress.
• A fish health expert or vet should be on hand at the show to deal with emergencies.

The above ideas would involve radical changes to the entire show system as it currently stands, but would also lead to a huge reduction in suffering and deaths.

SECTION II
AQUARIUM MANAGEMENT

A well-planned and well-managed aquarium, attractive and natural-looking, with lively, unstressed, healthy fish, is an ornament to any home, and a constant source of interest and enjoyment to its owner and his household.

Unfortunately, many newcomers to the aquarium hobby, while hoping to achieve this ideal, make the basic mistake of assuming that setting up an aquarium is simply a case of filling a tank with water and adding fish. But with a little knowledge and understanding of the natural environment, plus careful planning, the goal can easily be attained.

As we have already seen in Section 1, the word 'fish' is a general term covering a huge group of creatures. They have certain basic features in common but have evolved an almost inconceivable diversity of size, form, and behaviour. Many of these variations on the basic theme have gradually developed as a response to the environments which fish occupy in nature, and these too are diverse.

It is readily apparent that mammals of different types require different types of environment. Some are bigger than others: we may keep a rabbit in a run on the front lawn, but we readily accept that a horse needs a larger area of grass. This size limitation applies equally to fish. It would be cruel to keep a horse in the garden, which would soon become a dung-strewn mud-patch where the animal would not have enough room to exercise its muscles at a gallop. Likewise, we must realise that keeping a large fish in too small an aquarium will have a very similar effect in terms of pollution and the lack of space to swim naturally. Indeed, some fish are really too large to be kept in domestic aquaria at all.

To continue the analogy: some mammals live among trees, some among rocks, some on open dusty plains, some on the Arctic tundra. Some even live in water all or much of the time. Tropical freshwater fish live in tiny streams and huge rivers, small pools and vast lakes, as well as other varying conditions. These waters may be shaded by forest trees or exposed to the full glare of the tropical sun. They may be still or turbulent. Beneath the water's surface, the habitat may be rocky, open sand or mud, densely vegetated, or filled with tangles of roots and fallen trees. Like the fish, the habitat is highly variable, and a single river or lake may offer a variety of different habitats and micro-habitats, occupied by different species of fish.

Then there are the invisible variations. Local pollution aside, the air we breathe is fairly uniform all over our planet, because the atmosphere is one continuous unit. River systems are separate units; each makes its individual one-way journey to the sea. Fresh water is not uniform; there is no pure H_2O in nature. Rivers are fed by rain, which dissolves atmospheric gases such as carbon dioxide on its way to the ground. En route to the sea they collect additional 'contaminants' (e.g. dissolved minerals and organic compounds) from the land across which they flow and from plants and animals living or dying in or close to their waters. The composition of the water in any particular river system will be subtly different to that in others because it is the sum of all the contaminants that river has absorbed; moreover, it often varies along the length of the main river or in its individual tributaries. Fish live in water and 'breathe' it, as we do air, but their biochemistry is commonly adjusted to the composition of the particular river system, or part of a river system, in which they originated. Putting them in water with a radically different composition can cause them to become unwell and perhaps die. Sometimes the effects can be as rapid as putting a freshwater fish into salt water, or vice versa.

Luckily for the aquarist, there are hardy fish which live in a variety of environments in nature or have been acclimatised to variable aquarium environments over generations of living and breeding in captivity. These may be loosely compared to dogs and cats, which have adapted to a quite unnatural environment in our homes – although their instincts remain basically unchanged. Nevertheless there are very many species that do require specific environmental conditions, and even the hardy types will often benefit from the 'back to nature' approach.

Thus to help the aquarist achieve his ideal, in this section we look at the various major features of the aquatic environment and the equipment, materials, and procedures involved in turning that 'tank filled with water' into an aquarium, an attractive underwater environment suited to its occupants.

CHAPTER 10

WATER

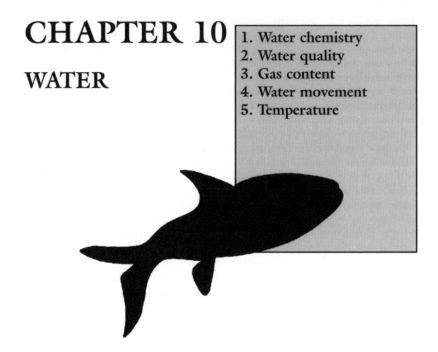

1. Water chemistry
2. Water quality
3. Gas content
4. Water movement
5. Temperature

The aquarium water is arguably the most important part of the fish's 'life-support system' in captivity. Pure water – the H_2O molecule – has the ability to carry many different gases, minerals, and organics in solution, and it is the nature and concentration of these contaminants (which are not necessarily harmful) in a natural body of water that determine the biochemical adaptations of the fish species found there. Some of these contaminants are found in all waters habitable by fish, and are essential to their life processes. The most obvious is dissolved oxygen, without which fish would be unable to breathe, but a supply of certain dissolved minerals is also essential. Put a fish into pure H_2O and it will quickly die. Fish may also be specifically adapted to other, physical rather than chemical, aspects of water – its temperature and movement. Hence, when setting up and maintaining an aquarium, a number of different aspects of water need to be taken into account:

• Its chemistry, usually understood, in the aquarium context, as simply its hardness and pH, although, strictly speaking, water chemistry encompasses the overall composition of the sample.
• Its quality, i.e. the measure of the harmful contaminants it contains.
• Its gas content (dissolved gases).
• Its movement.
• Its temperature.

1. WATER CHEMISTRY

HARDNESS
Most people will know whether their water is hard or soft from the effects it has in the home: hard water requires more soap to produce a lather and 'furs up' plumbing and kettles with deposits of (largely) calcium carbonate ($CaCO_3$). Hardness is the measure of the concentration of certain dissolved minerals, mainly salts of calcium (Ca) and magnesium (Mg). These will have entered the water in nature, as it flowed over or through rocks and soil containing the relevant minerals. In the same way, the aquarium water may be made harder by the presence of rocks and other decor containing the relevant soluble mineral salts. Water which contains little or no amounts of these salts is said to be soft.

Hardness versus mineral content
Hardness is an important consideration for the aquarist, but it is worth noting that it is a measure of only some soluble minerals. There are others which contribute to its total mineral content, but not to its hardness as defined above and measured by aquarium test kits. By the same token, although mineral-depleted water (minimal mineral content) is soft, soft water is not always mineral-depleted. It is important to bear this in mind, as some methods of softening water (see below) do not reduce mineral content, but convert salts that cause hardness to others that do not.

The distinction between hardness and mineral content may be relevant when dealing with some 'difficult' fish species with precise environmental requirements, for example some fish from parts of the Amazon system, where the water is not only soft but also extremely mineral-poor. When keeping 'hardy' fish, it is normally sufficient to consider hardness alone.

Measuring hardness and mineral content
Test kits for measuring water hardness are available from aquarium stores and can be used to test both the water supply and the aquarium water (e.g. to see if the decor has affected the hardness). Different brands of hardness-test kit sometimes use different scales of measurement (parts per million (PPM); English, French, German degrees); the aquarium literature may quote hardness according to any one of these systems, so it is important to establish which, and if necessary to convert the figure cited to that of the test kit used (see Table 5).

Aquarium test kits are not available for measuring mineral content. It may be possible to obtain an analysis of the local water supply from the water company, or by having a sample laboratory-tested. An indication of total mineral content can be obtained by measuring the ability of the water to conduct electricity, its conductivity. The higher the conductivity, the higher the mineral content. This will not, however, indicate what minerals are involved. Aquarists keeping fish for which mineral content is critical may wish to acquire a conductivity meter (from a laboratory equipment supplier); books which provide biotope data for aquarium fish commonly quote conductivity measurements (the equipment is easily portable when mounting an expedition to, for example, the depths of the Amazon rainforest, and its use is more practicable than bringing back perhaps hundreds of water samples for testing!).

> **Table 5 Hardness Units in terms of parts per million of dissolved calcium salts[*]**
>
> | | |
> |---|---|
> | 1 English (Clark) degree | = 14.3 ppm |
> | 1 German degree (dh)[**] | = 17.9 ppm |
> | 1 American degree | = 17.1 ppm |
> | 1 French degree (fh) | = 10.0 ppm |
>
> 1 ppm = 1 mg per litre
>
> [*] English, French, and American degrees of hardness are a measure of calcium carbonate ($CaCO_3$), while German degrees indicate calcium oxide (CaO) content.
> [**] Nominally 'dh' applies only to German degrees of hardness, but has been adopted into general use in recent years.

Softening and demineralising water

If the aquarist's water supply is hard or rich in mineral salts such that it is unsuitable for the fish he wishes to keep, a number of options are available:

• Dilution or replacement with soft or mineral-depleted water from an outside source, such as rain water, distilled water (from the pharmacist or a laboratory supplier), 'reverse osmosis water' (available from some aquarium stores). See also Table 6.

• Treatment with a reverse osmosis (RO) unit, which removes virtually all contaminants and is hence additionally useful if the quality (see below) of the domestic supply is also unsuitable for the fish.

• Treatment with an ion-exchange softening resin (use only resins sold for aquarium use). This will soften, but not demineralise, the water.

• Deionisation, using a combination of ion-exchange resins to demineralise the water.

• Boiling, which reduces hardness but not mineral content.

• Proprietary water softening chemicals (from the aquarium store), which irreversibly bind up the salts that cause hardness, effectively softening the water. These are a recent development and have not been available long enough to ascertain whether they carry any long-term disadvantages. It must be assumed that their effect is simply to soften the water, leaving its level of mineral content unchanged.

All these methods are normally applied to the water before it is added to the aquarium. Note that distilled and RO water are almost pure H_2O, and lack the dissolved oxygen fish require in order to breathe, as well as the minimum level of minerals essential for certain physiological processes. Hence these types of water must be well aerated before use, and if they are to be used 'neat', then the necessary minerals must be provided by adding a little mains supply water or remineralisation salts (available from aquatic stores).

pH

The pH of a liquid is the measure of its acidity or alkalinity. In general, the minerals that make water hard also make it alkaline, while organic materials (fish and plant wastes) and dissolved carbon dioxide have an acidifying effect.

The system used to express pH is used internationally, and hence pH measurements quoted in the aquarium literature can be regarded as universally applicable, unlike hardness measurements. pH is measured on a scale extending from 0 (extremely acid) to 14 (extremely alkaline); a measurement of 7 is neutral. The scale is logarithmic, such that each gradation represents a tenfold increase or decrease in pH. For example, pH 4 is 10 times more acid than pH 5, and 100 times more acid than pH 6. For aquarium purposes, pH is usually measured using test kits, less commonly with an electronic meter.

Most tropical freshwaters have a pH in the range 6 to 8, but a few are as acid as 4.5 or as alkaline as 9.5. Fish vary in their sensitivity to incorrect pH, and even hardy species may react badly if the acidity or alkalinity of the water is outside the range to which they are accustomed. Less hardy species often have a very narrow tolerance range (e.g. pH 6-6.5), and some may become stressed or even die if exposed to a pH on the wrong side of neutral. The latter are generally referred to as strictly acid water, or strictly alkaline water, fish.

Exposure to unsuitable pH may cause acidosis or alkalosis (Chapter 21, Section 1.1.1), and a sudden alteration in pH is likely to cause pH shock (*ibid.*, 1.1.3), even in hardy species. pH shock occurs not only where the pH of the aquarium has been altered too rapidly, but also where new fish have been introduced to water with a pH very different from that to which they are accustomed. In the longer term, incorrect pH can cause a gradual deterioration in a fish's health and compromise its immune response. Some species require the pH they would experience in nature in order to breed successfully.

Adjusting and buffering pH

The pH of the aquarium water may be adjusted as a one-off action, or buffered by including (in the decor or filter) materials which will help keep the pH stable. The most common type of buffering is the use of calcium carbonate to counteract the natural acidification caused by the organic byproducts (e.g. carbon dioxide) of fish and plant metabolic activity. This may be important where strictly alkaline water species are kept (to ensure pH does not dip below neutral); or where demineralised water is used (containing no alkalising mineral salts, it has no inherent buffering capacity) otherwise, dramatic acidity fluctuations may occur.

Proprietary chemical pH adjusters are available from aquatic stores; some include buffers to retain the pH, once adjusted, on the desired side of neutral, although this does not necessarily equate with the desired range. Some manufacturers do, however, offer a selection of adjusters designed to produce different pH ranges. Chemical pH adjusters should be used in strict accordance with the manufacturer's instructions, or the result may be a tankful of dead fish.

Even if he chooses to use a proprietary adjuster, the aquarist should appreciate the link between pH and mineral content, not least because fish from acid waters are generally (though not always) fish from mineral-depleted waters, while alkaline waters are normally mineral-rich. Using chemicals to adjust the pH does not always remedy the underlying cause: there is little point in trying to acidify hard water as its mineral content will simply buffer the pH back to neutral/alkaline, requiring further doses of chemical. But if the water is first wholly or partly demineralised, and the decor is 'hardness-free' (Chapter 11), acidification is simple, using peat as a filter medium (see below) or peat extract, i.e. a natural organic acidifier.

Equally, the pH of mineral-depleted water is best increased by the addition of suitable mineral salts – usually by using calciferous decor (Chapter 11). If this does not increase the pH to the desired level, bicarbonate of soda ($NaHCO_3$) can be used to achieve an additional (or faster) increase. The dosage must be worked out experimentally, dissolving a little in water and adding it to the aquarium. One level teaspoonful per 17 litres (4 gallons) is a good starting point.

To avoid pH shock, it is very important to make only small adjustments to pH (maximum 0.2-0.3 units per day, e.g. from 7.0 to 7.2 or 7.3) in any aquarium that contains fish. Adjustment by natural methods, such as by using peat (in filters) or calciferous decor, will normally satisfy this criterion.

2. WATER QUALITY

In aquarium circles, the term 'water quality' refers to the amount of pollutants (toxins and organic compounds) in the water, although, strictly speaking, water with incorrect chemistry and gas content (for the fish it contains) is also of inappropriate quality.

Pollutants may have a variety of origins. They may be present in some types of source water (Table 6), be derived from the aquarium decor/equipment, enter from the domestic environment, or be produced by the plants, fish, and other fauna of the aquarium. See also Chapter 21, section 2.0, for signs of poisoning and remedial action to be taken.

Table 6 Sources of Water for the Aquarium		
Water type	**Availability**	**Possible associated problems**
Domestic supply	On tap!	Chemistry may be unsuitable for fish kept. May contain chlorine/chloramine. May contain copper from plumbing, especially in soft water areas. May contain high levels of nitrate/phosphate from agricultural fertilisers or because recycled.
Rain water	Collected by aquarist	May be contaminated by roofing or guttering/pipework materials, or dirt/detritus on/in them. May be contaminated by the water container. May be contaminated by pollutants in atmosphere. Likely to be acid, possibly very acid ('acid rain').
Distilled water	Pharmacy, laboratory supplier	Pure, but requires oxygenation and remineralisation.
Reverse Osmosis water	Some aquarium stores	Pure, but requires oxygenation and remineralisation.

TAP WATER POLLUTANTS

Tap water for human use may nevertheless contain chemicals which are toxic to fish. The following are those most likely to be encountered:

• **Chlorine**. This gas is commonly added by water companies to disinfect the supply. High concentrations are apparent by the smell of the gas, familiar to many people from chlorinated swimming pools. It can be driven off by running the water hard into a bucket (but note, if the gas can still be smelt after this 'treatment', use another method), or by aerating the water in a bucket overnight; alternatively, a proprietary dechlorinator can be used.

• **Chloramine.** This chlorine/ammonia compound is used by some water companies instead of simple chlorine; this information can – and should – be obtained from the company concerned. Chloramine can be removed only by a dechlorinator that is designed to remove ammonia as well as chlorine. Not all are!

• **Copper.** This may enter the water in nature, from soil/rocks containing copper salts; or from the domestic plumbing, especially in soft water areas where the pipework does not develop a protective lining of calcium carbonate. Run the tap for a few minutes to clear water that has stood in the pipes, and never use water from the hot water cylinder. If the water is naturally contaminated, then treat with a proprietary copper remover (from the aquarium store), pass through a reverse osmosis unit, or use water from another source (Table 6).

• **Nitrate/phosphate.** Sometimes found in tap water which has been contaminated by agricultural fertilisers or sewage effluent and not adequately purified. Both can be removed by reverse osmosis; special nitrate-removing devices are available from aquarium stores. Alternatively, a different source of water can be used.

• **Pesticides.** These may be agricultural residues, or chemicals used by the water company to eliminate invertebrates living in the pipework. They can be removed by reverse osmosis, or a different source of water can be used.

Test kits for copper and nitrate are available. The aquarist should ask the water company to warn him when they plan to use pesticides in the water system, and seek their advice as to how long to wait before the water will again be safe for fish. Water companies will often also provide a printed analysis of the water supplied to the local area, which may be useful.

POLLUTION OF RAIN WATER

Using rain water may seem an ideal way to avoid problems of hardness and high pH, but is fraught with danger. Rain water tends always to be slightly acid, as it dissolves carbon dioxide from the atmosphere to form extremely dilute carbonic acid. In areas of high industrial pollution, however, it may become contaminated with sulphur compounds to form a dangerous strength of sulphuric acid (acid rain). Other poisonous contaminants may likewise be dissolved out of a polluted atmosphere. To some extent, this can be avoided by collecting only during a heavy rainstorm and after 30 minutes or so of downpour has washed the air clean.

Rain water may also be contaminated by the roof, guttering, and downpipe, or by dirt and debris (including leaves, birds' nests, drowned fledglings and insects, and so on). Unless the collecting/storing container is of non-toxic material, that too may cause contamination. At the very least, rain water should be strained immediately (or during collection) to remove debris, then stored in a non-toxic container and filtered over carbon before use.

CHEMICAL POLLUTION OF THE AQUARIUM WATER BY AQUARIUM HARDWARE

This generally results from the use of rocks or substrate containing toxic minerals; wooden items leaching tannins; pesticide or fertiliser residues on decor items; use of equipment not intended for aquarium use, particularly metal and/or plastic items placed in the aquarium; use of unsuitable glues, varnishes, and paints in the aquarium. See Chapters 11 and 13 for avoidance of this type of pollution.

POLLUTION ENTERING THE AQUARIUM FROM THE DOMESTIC ENVIRONMENT

Typical causes of this type of pollution, which usually results in rapid and fatal poisoning, are:

• Aerosol and other sprays, e.g. insecticides, furniture polish, houseplant fertilisers, domestic cleansers.

• Fumes from oil/paraffin heaters, paints, cigarettes.

ORGANIC WASTES GENERATED BY THE AQUARIUM FLORA AND FAUNA

All living things, whether animal or plant, produce organic wastes, either during their lives as products of their metabolic activity (excreta, carbon dioxide) and shedding of dead tissue (skin cells, leaves), or through decay of the entire organism after death. These residues are recycled in nature via biological processes, the most important being the nitrogen cycle, which also takes place in the aquarium.

The nitrogen cycle

An understanding of the nitrogen cycle, during which waste products are processed by certain types of bacteria, is vital to the successful maintenance of healthy fish. The basic features of the cycle, as they affect the aquarium, are shown in Fig. 1. It should be noted that the nitrogen cycle will take place in any aquarium which is biologically mature, and not just where biological filtration (see below) is in use. The bacteria involved will colonise surfaces in the aquarium as well as in a biological filter; what the filter does is to increase biological activity by offering additional, optimal (oxygen-rich) habitat for the essential bacteria to colonise.

Although ammonia and nitrite are highly toxic to fish, if the cycle is operating correctly then these toxins will be converted to relatively harmless nitrate before they can reach toxic levels. It must be stressed that the nitrogen cycle will not function in a newly set up aquarium until it and/or its biological filter has been properly matured hence no fish should be added until maturation is complete. A newly set up aquarium will lack the necessary bacterial populations involved in the nitrogen cycle. As a result, it will experience first a highly toxic ammonia surge, which will encourage the development of the bacteria that process ammonia to nitrite (also highly toxic) – leading to a nitrite surge! Finally, the bacteria that convert nitrite to relatively harmless nitrate will establish an adequate population and the aquarium will be safe for fish – but the entire process takes several weeks.

Moreover, although the bacterial population can quickly compensate for slight variations in workload (the amount of wastes to be processed), a sudden overload, caused by a dead fish or overfeeding for example, is liable to create a temporary surge in levels of ammonia and nitrite. Adding large numbers of new fish

The Nitrogen Cycle In The Aquarium

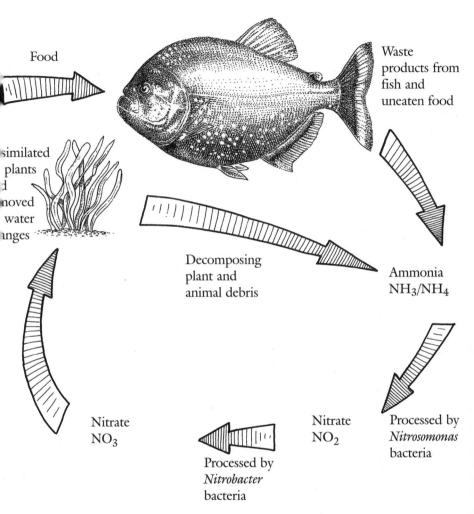

Food

Waste products from fish and uneaten food

similated plants d noved water anges

Decomposing plant and animal debris

Ammonia NH$_3$/NH$_4$

Nitrate NO$_3$

Nitrate NO$_2$

Processed by *Nitrobacter* bacteria

Processed by *Nitrosomonas* bacteria

simultaneously can also have this effect unless the aquarist takes the precaution of feeding only very lightly initially, gradually increasing the amount of food to normal levels over a period of a week or more, so that the beneficial bacteria have time to multiply in order to cope with the increased workload.

Test kits are available for measuring levels of ammonia, nitrite, and nitrate, and should form part of every aquarist's basic equipment. Even experts sometimes have problems with these organic products; having these test kits at hand means that the problem, usually evidenced by signs of ill health in the fish (Chapter 21, Sections 1.2.3, 1.2.8, 1.2.10), can be identified and remedied before lasting harm occurs.

PARTIAL WATER CHANGES

Aquaria often contain more fish and fewer plants than would a similar volume of water in nature, and there is no automatic renewal of aquarium water through rainfall and the flow of the river. So, although it is theoretically possible to achieve a balance whereby all nitrates deriving from fish waste products are used up by plants, in practice this is virtually impossible to achieve. Besides which, such an aquarium would of necessity contain very few fish, which is not the ideal scenario for the majority of aquarists. And some aquaria, may not contain plants at all.

What this means is that, unless the aquarist intervenes, levels of nitrate will creep up and slowly but surely cause health problems in at least some of the fish. If new fish are added to an aquarium in which nitrate levels are higher than those to which they are accustomed, then they may experience – and probably die from – nitrate shock (Chapter 21, section 1.2.9). High nitrate levels can also cause problems with algae and cyanobacteria ('blue-green algae') (Chapter 22).

We have seen earlier how nitrate can be removed from the source water using special equipment, but this is not the optimal method of removing it from the aquarium. Instead nitrate levels are best kept in check by regularly changing some of the aquarium water for new, removing nitrate and other undesirable contaminants (e.g. chlorine) before the new water is added. (Low concentrations of nitrate in the source water are acceptable, provided the level in the aquarium is kept within safe bounds.) Changing water also renews supplies of essential minerals, and the influx of new water generally causes increased activity in the fish.

The chemistry and temperature of the new water should be matched closely to those of the aquarium *before* it is used, to avoid any risk of pH shock, temperature shock (Chapter 21, section 1.4.2), and gas bubble disease (*ibid.*, 1.3.2).

The frequency and volume of water changes will vary from aquarium to aquarium, depending on a number of factors, chiefly the stocking density of the fish and plant populations vis-a-vis water volume, and the amount and type of food offered. No more than a third of the water should be changed routinely (emergencies, such as serious cases of poisoning, are a different matter). A good starting point is to change a fifth to a quarter of the water once per week, checking the nitrate level at this time. In some areas, especially during drought conditions, it may be advisable to check nitrate levels in tap water routinely before using it, in case of seasonal increases.

The mechanics of changing water are described in Chapter 15.

FILTRATION

Filtration is another important element in maintaining good water quality. Various types of aquarium filter are available (Chapter 13). Most consist of a container (the filter itself) which is filled with one or more special materials (filter media) which can be used to trap solids (mechanical filtration), provide a habitat for nitrogen cycle bacteria (biological filtration), and/or chemically alter the water chemistry or quality (chemical filtration). Virtually all aquarium filters and media act mechanically, and most are used biologically; chemical filtration requires special media, which can also act mechanically and biologically. Aquarium water is pumped through the filter so that the medium (or media) it contains can perform their various roles.

• **Mechanical filtration**. This is the simple collection of solid wastes (such as fish faeces, bits of dead leaf), removing them from the aquarium, and ensuring that it looks clean and the water is clear. It is vital to understand that the wastes nevertheless remain part of the aquarium system (because the aquarium water constantly circulates through the filter), and may still cause ammonia/nitrite/nitrate pollution. A filter full of uneaten food is just as dangerous as leaving that food to rot on the substrate, but many aquarists fail to appreciate this fact.

A filter can be used solely to trap wastes mechanically, but must then be cleaned out very regularly – as often as once per day, before the wastes can start to decompose and produce toxic ammonia. In addition, a mechanical filter will not have any effect on the constant ammonia output of the fish via their gills. For these reasons mechanical filtration is generally used in conjunction with biological filtration; i.e. the filter is left undisturbed so the nitrogen cycle can establish fully and process the accumulated solids, together with soluble wastes carried by the water.

• **Biological Filtration**. This is used to optimise the nitrogen cycle by providing a suitable habitat (the filter medium) for nitrifying bacteria, where they are provided with a constant supply of 'food' (wastes) and oxygen, by virtue of the flow of aquarium water through the filter. Any filter (mechanical and/or chemical) which is left running continuously and not cleaned out for a period of several weeks will develop the necessary bacterial population and become a biological filter.

Biological filters *must* be left undisturbed as much and for as long as possible. They should be run continuously – if they are switched off for more than an hour or so the nitrogen cycle bacteria will die through lack of oxygen, and the filter will need to be biologically matured again. Remember, this takes weeks, during which your fish are likely to die from ammonia and nitrite poisoning. From time to time, maintenance is necessary – such as when the filter starts to clog mechanically – but this must be undertaken with great care (P.141). Some types of medication will kill the filter bacteria with similar dire consequences – *always* check whether a medication is likely to have this effect before using it where biological filtration is present (See Chapters 24 and 27).

Very low pH can limit the efficiency of biological filtration; a pH of less than 6.5 is sometimes stated to be sub-optimal for the filter bacteria, but, in practice, biological filtration appears to function at much lower pH levels.

• **Chemical filtration**. This employs media which chemically alter the water and is used to improve water quality or alter water chemistry; it also acts mechanically, and, if left undisturbed, biologically. Chemical media include:
-- Carbon (activated carbon, activated charcoal), to remove dyes such as methylene blue, some other medications, discoloration from tannins (e.g. from peat), and some chemical pollutants.
-- Coral (crushed coral or coral sand), to raise/buffer pH.
-- Limestone (dolomite) chips, to raise/buffer pH.
-- Peat, to lower pH.
-- Zeolite (a natural ion-exchange resin), to remove ammonia.
  Note that zeolite should be used only as a short-term, emergency, measure (for example, to compensate for a temporary ammonia surge) and not as a substitute for the nitrogen cycle. It loses its efficacy after a short time, and could leave the fish

Tropical Fishlopaedia

exposed to lethal ammonia levels. Carbon also has a limited functional period and needs to be renewed regularly. However, it is preferable to remove pollutants from water *before* using it in the aquarium, so there is normally no need to use carbon on a permanent basis in the aquarium filter. Its most valuable function is its ability to remove some medications at the end of the treatment period; because of this ability it should, obviously, not be used during treatment. Peat also requires regular renewal; coral and limestone remain effective for very long periods.

3. GAS CONTENT

Water is composed of two gases, hydrogen and oxygen. It also has the ability to absorb free oxygen (oxygen which is not combined with hydrogen to form the water molecule, H_2O) and other gases, such as carbon dioxide, nitrogen, sulphur dioxide, ammonia, and chlorine. All of these may affect fish; ammonia, chlorine, and sulphur dioxide (in rain water) have already been discussed in this chapter. Excess nitrogen in the water may cause gas bubble disease (Chapter 21, section 1.3.2).

Fish, like humans, breathe in oxygen (free oxygen which they extract from the water) and expire carbon dioxide. Some fish species also have the ability to breathe atmospheric oxygen; these usually originate from waters which are, seasonally or permanently, oxygen-depleted (contain little dissolved oxygen).

Aquatic plants (including algae), like terrestrial ones, take in carbon dioxide during the day (or when the aquarium light is on), using the carbon it contains to create nutrients and releasing the spare oxygen into the water – under bright light, tiny bubbles of oxygen can been seen on their leaves; at night, however, they take in oxygen and give off carbon dioxide.

THE OXYGEN REQUIREMENTS OF FISH
Fish are not able to break the water molecule down into its component hydrogen and oxygen, so it is possible for a fish to suffocate if there is insufficient free oxygen in the water. This condition is called hypoxia, and is discussed in Chapter 21 (section 1.3.3). Fish which are receiving inadequate oxygen typically have a much increased gill rate, gasp, and hang at the surface where oxygen levels are higher.

The oxygen requirement of a particular fish species is generally a function of the oxygen content of its natural habitat. For example, fish from well-oxygenated biotopes, such as fast-flowing rivers or large lakes with waves, require more oxygen than those whose natural waters are slow-moving or virtually still.

Individual fish commonly have a higher than normal oxygen requirement if they are unwell, stressed, more active than usual (such as when breeding, or if chased), or if they are kept at a temperature higher than that which nature intended (see below). Equally, their requirement may be lower when they are inactive (e.g. diurnal species at night) or if the temperature is lower. That is not to say that lowering the temperature is an acceptable method of countering inadequate oxygen levels!

GAS EXCHANGE
Generally speaking, most of the free oxygen in water comes from the atmosphere, although during the daylight hours some may be contributed by plants (see below).

Water can absorb oxygen from the air only where the two elements meet – at the water's surface. Likewise, carbon dioxide can be given off into the atmosphere only at this interface. The larger the surface area of the water, the more oxygen it can absorb, and the more carbon dioxide it can discharge; this fact is very important in fishkeeping, as oxygen content influences the population of fish the aquarium can support (see below) and also the optimal tank shape (Chapter 13).

The process of absorbing oxygen and giving off carbon dioxide is called gas exchange. It is indeed an exchange to some extent, as the carbon dioxide content of the water does limit its oxygen absorption capability.

AERATION

Agitating the water's surface increases its effective surface area (a rippled surface has a greater area than a flat one), and hence its capacity for gas exchange. Circulating the water is also beneficial, as this carries water rich in carbon dioxide to the surface and carries newly-oxygenated water down to the bottom layers of the aquarium water. The processes of surface movement and water circulation are collectively termed 'aeration' by aquarists. The process can also be used to drive off other gases such as chlorine and nitrogen.

Aeration can be achieved using the filtration system, which should be arranged so as to create maximum circulation and, if appropriate, surface movement. This does *not* mean, however, that it is necessary to create a miniature maelstrom in the aquarium; simply that the filtration equipment appropriate (in terms of capacity and turnover) to the aquarium (Chapter 13) should be installed optimally. (See also Water Movement, below). Aeration can also be created using an airpump and diffuser (Chapter 13) to produce a stream of bubbles which again helps circulate the water and agitate its surface; contrary to popular belief, the bubbles of air do not themselves add any significant amount of oxygen to the water – it is their effect on circulation and surface gas exchange that is beneficial.

Aeration may be essential to provide adequate oxygen for fish from highly oxygenated waters. Aeration is also used by some aquarists to permit crowding the aquarium with more fish than its normal oxygen content is capable of supporting. This is all very well – apart from attendant problems like high levels of organic wastes – until the day the airpump breaks down. The aquarist maintaining species with high oxygen requirements usually keeps a spare airpump handy; the aquarist who foolishly overcrowds his aquarium often does not, and his fish die!

FACTORS AFFECTING OXYGEN CONTENT OF THE WATER

• **Temperature**. The oxygen content of water is affected by water temperature – the warmer the water, the lower its oxygen content, and *vice versa*. Increased temperature also accelerates the metabolic processes of fish, increasing their oxygen requirements at a time when oxygen content is lower. This can be countered by increasing aeration.

• **Plants**. Plants are often valued for their oxygen-producing ability, but it must be remembered that at night they use oxygen and produce carbon dioxide. Thus, although plants may help supply the oxygen requirements of the fish by day, at night all the aquarium life is competing for a reduced oxygen content, and heavily-planted aquaria may suffer oxygen depletion at this time.

• **CO_2 injection**. In recent years some aquarists have used this process, whereby carbon dioxide is added (from a gas cylinder) to the aquarium, in order to promote plant growth. CO_2 injection must be used with considerable care, if at all. Remember that high CO_2 levels may reduce the oxygen uptake of the water and lead to a risk of hypoxia in the fish, especially if the aquarium is crowded and/or the fish include species with a high oxygen requirement. Some aquarists try to get round this problem by using additional aeration, but, while this will certainly increase the oxygen content and benefit the fish, it will at the same time drive off the carbon dioxide, making the CO_2 injection a rather pointless exercise! CO_2 injection should always be turned off at night – when the plants do not need it.

• **Snails and other life forms**. A large population of snails may have a significant effect on aquarium oxygen levels. So too can bacteria; the use of oxygen by aerobic nitrogen-cycle bacteria is acceptable because of the considerable benefits they confer in return. If, however, the aquarium has an abnormally high organic loading, e.g. from regular overfeeding, the bacterial population will be higher, and consume more oxygen than it would if the fish were fed at the correct rate. Snails, of course, also increase the organic loading.

As with many aspects of aquarium maintenance, the trick is to achieve a sensible balance between the requirements of all the aquarium occupants.

4. WATER MOVEMENT

The waters in which tropical freshwater fish are found may vary considerably in their movement and turbulence, from slow-moving forest streams and still pools to torrential rapids and large freshwater lakes, some of which are effectively inland freshwater seas, with waves and surf (though deep-living fish from such waters may experience little turbulence away from the ever-moving surface). In general, water movement and oxygen requirement are linked (see above).

It must be accepted that fish from the two extremes are not normally compatible in the aquarium, as it is impossible to accommodate the needs of both as regards water movement. For example, the water movement required to supply the oxygen requirements of the rapids-dweller may cause considerable discomfort and stress to the fish whose laterally-compressed body shape and spreading finnage have evolved to allow it to sail slowly through the calm water of some forest pool. It may be buffeted by the current and unable to swim comfortably. Small fish likewise may find themselves unable to swim normally. This applies to fry of all species, even those of rheophilic (current-loving) and lacustrine (lake-dwelling) types, which in nature are commonly found in sheltered micro-habitats within the overall biotope. Such fish may find it difficult to obtain enough to eat, unable to swim fast enough to catch food whirling about in the current.

Fish which are continuously subjected to unnaturally (for their species) rapid water movement may quickly become badly stressed. In time – perhaps only a short time – this may have a harmful effect on their health. Undue turbulence may also adversely affect plant growth, particularly in association with undergravel filtration.

5. TEMPERATURE

As with other factors in the natural environment, tropical freshwater fish are adapted to life within a particular temperature range, which may vary greatly from species to species. Tropical water temperatures are highly variable. A sunlit stretch of stream may be considerably warmer, especially at midday, than a shady reach a short distance upstream. Temperature may also vary with depth. Of course, in such instances the resident fish have a choice, unlike in the aquarium. Water temperatures may also vary according to the time of the day, and seasonally – not necessarily because the local temperature has varied greatly, but because of an influx of cold water from heavy rain or melting snow in the mountains far upstream. On the other hand, the year-round and clock-round temperature in some large lakes remains fairly constant, except at the very surface, simply because it would take a very long period for such a vast volume of water to be affected significantly by any outside influence.

The existence of daily and seasonal variation in some natural waters permits a degree of latitude, as regards aquarium temperatures, in species from such waters. Others may be less tolerant. It must also be remembered that while some fish may be able to survive brief exposure to icy melt-water or to overheated and rapidly evaporating pools at the height of the dry season, they are not designed to withstand such temperatures all their lives. The important temperature is that at which the fish lives for most of its life, and suitable temperatures or temperature ranges are suggested for many species in the aquarium literature.

Tip: if dealing with a species for which you can find no suggested temperature (or other biotope data), look up that for other fish from the same biotope.

Only species with roughly similar temperature requirements should be kept together, and the normal operating temperature of the aquarium water should fall within the acceptable normal range for each species. Too low an operating temperature may render a fish lethargic and inactive, and can lead to serious ill health in the longer term. It will be unlikely to breed. Too high an operating temperature, however, will increase oxygen requirement and the additional workload for the gills may cause permanent damage; the fish may also become hyperactive, nervous, and stressed. Increasing the temperature of the aquarium water is sometimes used in the treatment of disease, but this should be regarded as simply a short-term measure.

In addition, a number of acute, sometimes fatal, health problems may result from exposure to incorrect temperature (Chapter 21, section 1.4).

It is not unknown for some people to keep their tropical fish at unnaturally low temperatures and low light levels (Chapter 12) in order to economise on electricity costs. This is totally unacceptable. If keeping fish properly is too expensive, then fish should not be kept at all!

CHAPTER 11

DECOR

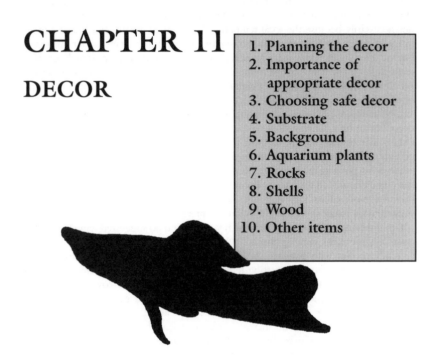

We have already seen, in the previous chapter, how an understanding of the various facets of water management is essential to providing the correct aquarium environment for ornamental fish. The same is true of the aquarium decor, the materials used to create suitable surroundings for the fish to live in. A fish's natural environment is the sum of the water and the cover – plants, rocks, tree roots and branches – it contains.

1. PLANNING THE DECOR

This involves establishing what decor is appropriate to the fish (by researching each species); choosing and acquiring suitable materials (see below); and designing the actual layout of the selected decor items (dealt with in Chapter 14, which also covers installation of the decor).

2. THE IMPORTANCE OF APPROPRIATE DECOR

In setting up his first aquarium, the novice commonly thinks only in terms of creating an underwater scene that will present a pleasing picture in the living room. The environmental needs of the fish are all too rarely taken into consideration.

Indeed, in recent years, there has been a horrifying tendency for some aquarists to attempt to colour-coordinate the aquarium with the domestic decor, encouraged by the availability of the 'raw materials' – gravel and plastic plants in all the colours of the rainbow, lumps of coloured glass, and so forth – in some aquarium stores.

Equally unnatural is the astonishing array of plastic trivia – mermaids, divers, shipwrecks, etc – which serve no useful purpose as far as the fish are concerned. Some of these items – psychedelic wheels, fibre-optic lights – may be positively frightening to many fish. Far too many people assume that because these items are available, they must be the right thing to put in an aquarium. On the contrary, their presence, and the absence of the correct decor for the fish concerned, can be positively harmful, causing stress (Chapter 21, section 1.5.2), one of the major causes of illness in aquarium fish.

In nature, the cover created by aquatic plants, terrestrial vegetation trailing in the water, rocks, roots, fallen trees, and so on, provides fish (and other aquatic creatures) with protection against the dangers that abound in most habitats. These may include larger fish as well as fish-eating birds, reptiles, and mammals. Even large fish are not immune from predation and may fall prey to herons, otters, crocodiles, humans etc.

Some fish gain a degree of protection by swimming in shoals, while some are able to swim fast or leap from the water to evade predation. But many rely entirely on the presence of cover for protection, and even those with other defence mechanisms commonly seek out cover when danger threatens.

The uninformed may argue that the aquarium is a safe environment, free of predators, and so it does not matter if the cover provided is unnatural, or worse still, the aquarium is left bare to make it easier to keep clean. But fear of predation is instinctive in small creatures. In nature, the momentary absence of any obvious threat does not mean that there is no danger lurking round the corner, or approaching in search of unwary prey. A fish without suitable decor to hide among may be a fish constantly in fear of its life.

Another specious argument often encountered is that if decor is provided, the fish will hide. Indeed, newly-introduced fish may initially hide all the time, recovering from the shock of being moved and evaluating their surroundings. After a while they will venture out, secure in the knowledge that they have somewhere safe to go if danger threatens. Without decor, however, they may try to hide behind equipment, huddle in corners, or rest motionless on the bottom, trying to make themselves as inconspicuous as possible. They are visible to their owner, certainly, but they are hardly an attractive sight. Such fish rarely live long, dying of starvation (too frightened to come out and feed), or diseases which their stress-compromised immune systems were unable to counter.

It is important not only that cover should be provided in the aquarium, but also that it should be appropriate cover for the fish concerned. Species which normally hide among plants will not recognise piles of rocks as a possible safe retreat. Likewise, rock-dwellers will not feel secure among plants – they need 'caves', suitably sized nooks and crannies in which to hide or breed. If both types of fish are present, then both types of cover are essential.

The general community, which commonly contains fish from a number of different habitats, will usually be decorated with a mixture of rocks, wood, and plants. The more specialised aquarist, however, may wish to simulate a particular biotope – perhaps a small stretch of slow-flowing rainforest stream or rock-strewn rapids, complete with a selection of fish appropriate to the chosen habitat. The general principles involved in the choice, acquisition, and preparation of decor remain the same in every case and are outlined in this chapter.

3. CHOOSING SAFE DECOR

The decor should not be harmful to the fish, that is, it should not poison the water, alter the water chemistry (unless that is the intention), or carry undue risk of causing injury. It is probably impossible to eliminate all risk of injury, but obviously dangerous decor such as razor-sharp edges, highly abrasive surfaces, or needle-pointed rocks, should be avoided. Some decor items contain interesting holes or cracks, and although these may look attractive, it is not unknown for some fish to try to swim into gaps which are too small, especially if frightened. 'See-through' holes are particularly dangerous as the fish may struggle to get through to the open space it can see beyond, and become inextricably stuck. Such dangers should always be considered when choosing and arranging decor.

4. SUBSTRATE

Many people think of the aquarium decoration simply as the plants and other items arranged around the tank, on or bedded in the substrate (the layer of material that is used to cover the bottom). But the substrate is itself an important part of the decor. Its primary purpose is to provide a natural floor to the fish's world – streams, pools, and lakes do not have bare glass bottoms. The coloration of many fish is designed to help them appear inconspicuous against the natural substrate when viewed from above, and against the light when viewed from below; this is why they are darker on their backs than on their undersides. As well as providing a base against which the fish will feel secure, the substrate also prevents stressful reflections from the lighting above. Some fish have an instinctive need to sift or dig substrate; some, for example a number of loaches, burrow into it to hide. It is also useful as a medium in which to root plants and embed rocks, to hold them firmly in place.

Gravel and sand are the substrates normally used for aquaria; pebbles, slate, and peat are sometimes used in specialised tanks. Mud, a common substrate in nature, is not used because of its effect on water clarity, and because it is impossible to clean!

Sand and gravel are available in various colours and grain sizes, and may or may not have an effect on water chemistry. A number of factors need to be taken into account when selecting a substrate for a particular aquarium and its intended inhabitants. Although fairly fine gravel (with a grain size of 3-5 mm) is commonly used for unspecialised general community tanks, it is unsuitable for some of the fish commonly housed in such aquaria, e.g. burrowing loaches, some fish that habitually rest on the bottom, and some bottom-feeders, especially those that probe the substrate or sift it through their gills. It is too coarse and may cause damage to mouths, skin, and gills. Such fish require a sand substrate.

Hence the substrate is an important element in every aquarium, and should be chosen with care. Factors to consider include:

• **Effect on water chemistry**. Many substrate materials contain calciferous (lime-rich) material and will increase hardness and pH. Some, for example, coral sand and dolomite chippings, are almost pure calcium carbonate and should be used only where high hardness and pH are required (and then only as 10-25 % of the total substrate). Unfortunately, some aquarists purchase these materials for a general community aquarium because they look nice!

'Hardness-free' substrate materials are available, but are usually a little more expensive than ordinary aquarium gravel. Not all hardness-free substrate materials are as inert as is claimed. They can be tested by adding a strong acid to a small sample, a task best undertaken by an experienced person such as a pharmacist or school chemistry teacher. If the material contains soluble minerals, it will fizz. Testing with weak acids such as lemon juice or vinegar, as sometimes advocated in the aquarium literature, cannot be relied upon.

• **Colour.** A dark substrate is preferable to a light-coloured one for freshwater tropical fish, whose natural waters may have an underlay of light-coloured sand or gravel, but which is often topped with leaf litter and other detritus, creating a darker effect. Fish will commonly endeavour to match their own colours to their surroundings for camouflage, and light-coloured substrates often mean 'washed-out' fish. Unfortunately, many aquarium substrate materials are very light in colour, and other considerations (such as the effect on water chemistry, texture) may necessitate using such material. In such cases, low-growing plants or a scattering of dark pebbles will help to break up the uniform pale effect.

Artificially-coloured substrate materials should be avoided, even if the colour is reasonably natural, because of the possibility of the dye proving toxic. Plastic-coated coloured gravels are intended to circumvent this problems, but the friction involved in washing gravel, or from digging and sifting by fish, may erode the plastic coating, exposing the dyed material to the water. Moreover, plastics tend to decompose or degenerate with time, and the process may be accelerated by acid water.

• **Texture.** Some materials are water-worn and smooth-edged, while others are coarse and may be razor-sharp. The latter may cause serious damage to fish that dig or sift, rest on, or burrow in, the substrate. Coral gravel is particularly dangerous.

• **Grain size.** A number of individual points must be taken into account as regards this factor:

− The larger the grain size, the larger the intervening spaces in which uneaten food may become trapped and rot.

− Burrowing and sifting species require a small grain size, ideally sand rather than gravel.

− Some species which dig as part of their breeding behaviour may fail to breed if the grain size is too large for their mouths.

− If undergravel filtration is used, the ideal grain size is 4-5 mm, which provides a large surface area for bacteria to colonise but does not clog easily. An alternative is to use a bottom layer of coarse gravel, topped by fine gravel or sand, the two layers separated by special plastic mesh ('gravel tidy') (from aquarium stores).

Often a compromise is needed in the choice of substrate; the prime consideration must be that it will not physically harm the fish (water chemistry, texture). Alternatively, the choice of fish can be modified to suit the available substrate.

The recommended depth of substrate is variable, depending on circumstances. Between 6-7.5 cm (2.5-3 in) is normally suggested where undergravel filtration is used, but 3-5 cm (1.25-2 in) is generally sufficient for growing most plants and supporting other decor.

ACQUIRING SUBSTRATE MATERIAL

Most aquarists purchase substrate material from the aquarium store; however, the available range may consist of just one type of natural gravel which may not be suitable for the purpose intended. It may be necessary to try other shops to find what is required. Aquarists confident of their geological knowledge may choose to collect their own gravel or sand, but this is not generally advisable. Garden centres are another possible source but, again, one that requires expert knowledge to identify what may or may not be suitable. Granite gravel (provided it really is granite) from garden centres is usually chemically safe (non-toxic) and inert (will not affect water chemistry), but may have sharp edges.

Aquarists requiring a sand substrate have used both swimming-pool filter sand and children's play sand without encountering problems; both are non-toxic and usually do not affect water chemistry.

PREPARING SUBSTRATE MATERIALS FOR USE

All substrate materials must be washed thoroughly before use. This can be done in a bucket, shaking or stirring and using repeated changes of water, or in a colander under a running tap. It is easier to wash a relatively small amount at a time. Each portion of substrate material must be washed until the water runs clear.

5. BACKGROUND

The aquarium background is another aspect of the decor that is often neglected by aquarists, who, if they use a background at all, commonly do so merely to hide the wall behind the tank and the cabling and pipes belonging to the aquarium equipment. The background should, however, be thought of as representing the bank of a river, pond, or lake, the area where most natural cover is found. Fish surprised by danger in open water will often head for the shelter of the bank. Hence, providing a background gives direction to the aquarium and its occupants, and adds to the fishes' sense of security. This can be especially important for surface-dwelling fish that live above the bulk of the other decor, and which, in the absence of a background, would find themselves exposed on all sides with no secure area. The background also provides a backdrop for the remaining decor.

Aquarists contemplating a freestanding aquarium (i.e. one that can be viewed from all sides), or one used as a room divider, should consider the stressful effects on the fish of the absence of a safe refuge at the rear of the tank, and of being exposed to view from all (or in the case of a room divider, both long) sides.

The background can be either internal or external – in the former case the materials used, including glues and paints, must be non-toxic and suitable for aquarium use. Internal backgrounds are sometimes sculpted from polystyrene foam or moulded in glass resin, or may consist simply of roofing slates (real slate, not synthetic) stood across the back of the tank.

The simplest form of external background is simply to paint the outside of the rear glass; the colour should be dark and subdued, like the river bank (e.g. black, brown, dark grey), not lurid red or yellow. Other possibilities are to stick suitably coloured paper, plastic, or carpet tiles to the glass. Cork tiles can be used to good effect.

OBTAINING BACKGROUNDS

Printed plastic background can be purchased, cut to length from a roll, in an aquarium store. Various designs are available for freshwater aquaria, depicting rocks, roots, plants, or combinations of these. Obviously, marine tank backgrounds (corals and sea anemones) are quite inappropriate! Glass resin backgrounds are commercially available in some countries, but are expensive. Tiles, paper and paint, for external backgrounds, are available from various sources, such as hardware stores, carpet suppliers, etc.

6. AQUARIUM PLANTS

A range of aquarium plants will be found in most aquatic stores, though the selection available may be limited or variable. Only some of these plants are likely to be true aquatics (live underwater all the time). Some may be 'marginal' plants, which in nature grow along the edges of streams and pools with only their roots and lower leaves/stems submerged. Some of these are not really suitable for aquaria. Some plants naturally grow underwater for part of the year, but are left high and dry when the water level drops during the dry season; in order to be long-lived such plants may require an emerse (out of water) period each year. Such plants may die back during their emerse period and not sprout again until the water level rises, or they may die back and then produce a quite different type of foliage. Some plants naturally float on the water's surface.

Regrettably some plants sold for aquarium use are not aquatic at all, but terrestrial (land) plants, which quickly die and may pollute the aquarium. Notable examples are *Dieffenbachia* (dumb cane), whose sap is poisonous and may kill the fish if the plant is damaged, and *Hemigraphis* species.

Aquatic plants come in different shapes and sizes: tall and slender, short and spreading, tall and spreading, and so on. Their leaves may spring direct from the crown of the rootstock or be arranged on stems. Some require specific water chemistry, some require brighter lighting than others, and temperature tolerance may also vary. It is usual to plant taller plants at the ends and rear of the aquarium, and shorter ones towards the front, so as to create a perspective.

Providing a catalogue of suitable plants is beyond the scope of this book, but Table 7 lists some popular types. Plant manuals are available (see Appendix A).

PLASTIC PLANTS

A wide selection of plastic plants is available, and some are extremely realistic. The unnaturally coloured types are best avoided. Only plastic plants intended for aquarium use should be purchased. Plastic plants have a number of advantages:
• They do not die (though in time plastic may disintegrate or degenerate).
• They are inedible.
• They do not mind being uprooted (by fish or aquarists rearranging the decor).
• They do not take over the aquarium.
• They can be scrubbed clean of algae if necessary.

Against these advantages, however, they cannot be propagated, they do not help remove nitrate, and real ones look infinitely nicer if grown well.

Table 7 Some Popular Aquarium Plants

Scientific name	Common Name	Brief details
Acorus variegatus	Variegated rush	Strictly a marginal and usually dies after a while under water.
Aponogeton spp.	–	Grown from corms. Long elegant leaves growing direct from corm. Dies back seasonally, sprouts again after rest period. May flower (above the water surface) and produce seeds from which new plants grow.
Barclaya longifolia	–	Corm-producing, long, pinkish-green, slightly undulating leaves. A lovely but fragile plant, which may flower and produce viable seed.
Cabomba spp.	–	Long stems with tiny leaflets. Requires regular pruning; grown from cuttings. Not easy plants to keep alive.
Ceratopteris thalictroides	Indian fern	Can be grown in substrate, but prefers to live floating. Fragile fern-like foliage. New plants grow from leaf edges.
Cryptocoryne spp.	Crypts	Many different species/sizes. Leaves grow from crown. Some species have an emerse period in nature and may die back seasonally in aquarium. Many species survive well at low light levels.
Echinodorus spp.	Swordplants	Various sizes. Crown-forming. Some have an emerse period in nature.
Hygrophila difformis	Water wisteria	Attractive plant with segmented leaves. Cultivated as for other *Hygrophila spp.*, below.
Hygrophila spp.	Willowleaf	Stemmed plants requiring regular pruning. Easily grown from cuttings Tough plant with strap-like leaves.
Microsorium pteropus	Java fern	Grows on rocks/wood rather than in substrate. Plantlets sprout from old or damaged leaves. Has a bitter taste which may deter herbivores.
Nymphaea spp.	Dwarf waterlilies	Buy only dwarf tropical forms! Grows from corms. Leaves can be allowed to grow to surface to form floating pads, or regularly removed to promote new underwater growth.
Pistia stratiotes	Water lettuce	Large floating plant, requires space above water's surface. Throws runners and young plants.

Riccia fluitans		Floating plant popular as a spawning medium for bubblenest-builders anabantoids.
Vallisneria spp.	Vallis	Long strap-like leaves growing from crown. Some types with twisted leaves. Propagates freely by runners.
Vesicularia dubayana	Java moss	Long strands forming a thick mass. Grows on rocks/wood or loose. Often used as spawning substrate in breeding tanks (Chapter 8).

ACQUIRING AQUARIUM PLANTS

Both live and plastic plants may be obtained from aquarium stores and other aquarists, or collected from the wild (if it is legal to do so). Whatever the source of plants, they may require disinfection or quarantine (Chapter 19). If they have been in contact with fish, they may harbour pathogens or parasites (Chapter 21), and wild-collected plants may also introduce pests such as snails (Chapter 22).

Many dealers keep plants in separate tanks to fish, or in special plant display units. Plants from the latter are generally pest- and disease-free, but it is not unknown for fish to be temporarily housed in 'plant-only' tanks in an emergency, and plants from such tanks often harbour snails.

Tropical aquatic plants, like tropical fish, tend to die very quickly if kept out of water or placed in cold water. They also require light, so they should not be purchased until the aquarium is set up, with its lighting in operation and the water warmed to the appropriate tropical temperature. They are normally packed in plastic bags to keep them moist, and in cold or very hot weather, or during long journeys, should be transported in insulated containers, just like fish (Chapter 6).

Planting the aquarium is dealt with in Chapter 14, and plant care in Chapter 15.

7. ROCKS

Most general community aquaria will contain a number of fish whose natural habitat includes some rocks and stones, and when keeping fish from naturally rocky habitats large amounts of 'rockwork' are an unconditional requirement.

Rocks, like substrate material, should not affect the water chemistry unless this is the aquarist's deliberate intention, and, obviously, they should not contain minerals that might prove toxic. It is also important to avoid rocks with sharp edges and points on which fish might injure themselves, especially if the aquarium is to house nervous species prone to panic dashes when frightened. If the rocks are to be used as spawning substrates, they should offer smooth surfaces at least in places. Crevice spawners will require crevices!

ACQUIRING ROCKS FOR THE AQUARIUM

Some aquarium stores offer a small range of rocks, typically tufa and slate, sometimes unsuitable slate (see Table 8). Aquarium stores sited in garden centres sometimes sell the rocks which are also for sale outside for horticultural use, which may not be suitable for aquaria and which are not always what they purport to be. The term 'granite' is sometimes applied, incorrectly, to any hard, heavy rock!

Table 8 Some Rocks Sometimes Used in Aquaria

Gneiss: A very hard metamorphic rock, often with a banded appearance, the bands being typically grey, grey-green, white, and sometimes pink. Usually fine-grained. Practically inert and a good all-purpose aquarium rock.

Granite: A hard igneous rock with a speckled grey/black/white appearance, much used for gravestones. There is also an orange-tinted variety. Practically inert, and an excellent all-purpose aquarium rock.

Limestone: A sedimentary rock consisting largely of calcium carbonate. Some limestones also contain magnesium salts. Limestones range from fine-grained and hard to coarse and crumbly. Usually greyish or whitish in colour. May contain fossils. Will increase/buffer hardness and pH.

Millstone grit: A very hard metamorphic rock, speckled greyish in colour. Practically inert, and suitable for general aquarium use.

Sandstone: A sedimentary rock composed of sand. Its composition, and hence its effect on water chemistry, may vary depending on the composition of the sand, and some sandstones may increase hardness and pH. Some are soft and crumbly and unsuitable for aquarium use.

Slate: A very hard metamorphic rock noted for its (usually dark) grey colour and laminated structure; it can easily be split into flat-sided, relatively thin, sheets or slabs. Some slates have intrusions of minerals between their layers, visible as coloured veins or as a coloured coating on the flat side(s) of the slate. Such slates are unsuitable for aquarium use, but pure slate, including old roofing slates, is an excellent, inert, rock.

Tufa: A very coarse and crumbly limestone. It is popular with aquarists keeping alkaline-water fish from rocky habitats, because it is porous and lightweight, and can be built into large structures supported by the back glass without overloading it. Totally useless as a spawning substrate because of its very rough surface.

The aquarist may therefore find it useful to consult a simple pictorial book on geology, which will also provide him with the scope to collect his own rocks if he wishes. Such a book will normally state the composition of the rocks pictured, so those containing calcium and magnesium salts can be avoided if appropriate. It may be helpful to know what sort of rocks are to be found in the locality, and to look specifically for those that are suitable. Water-worn rocks from the beach can make pleasing aquarium decorations.

A few dos and don'ts when selecting rocks:
• Don't collect rocks in areas where metal and/or mineral ores are mined/quarried. On the other hand, quarries producing stone used for buildings, gravestones, and sculpture are a good sign, as such stone needs to be even-textured and without extraneous (possibly toxic) minerals, although it may still affect hardness/pH. If asked politely, quarry staff may prove extremely helpful – they know all about rocks!
• Do avoid areas where rocks may be contaminated, e.g. with pesticides or radioactivity.
• Don't use rocks with metallic or rust-coloured veins or coatings, or

rocks containing coloured crystals. White or clear crystals or veins, however, are usually quartz, which is safe.

• Don't use soft or crumbly rocks (except tufa, in alkaline-water tanks).

• Do remember that light-coloured grey-white rocks may be limestones, and that sand-coloured/textured rocks are probably sandstones.

• Do look for rocks with a plain colour or regular speckling, and with an even texture.

• When selecting water-worn rocks, do look for a uniform surface without holes or cracks.

• Do remember that rocks containing fossils are commonly limestones.

• Do avoid brightly-coloured rocks (unless you know they are safe), as the colour may result from an undesirable mineral.

• Don't take rocks from walls, or denude the environment in one spot. Do ask permission if appropriate, and do try to leave no sign of your collecting activities and keep the countryside unspoiled.

In general, the plainer and less interesting-looking the rock, the more likely it is to be safe as regards toxicity, though it may still affect water chemistry. This can be checked using the 'acid test' mentioned in the section on substrate materials, above.

One final 'don't': *don't* be put off using rocks because their acquisition requires some effort. Once you have a safe rock, it will never break down or wear out, but will be a long-term asset to your hobby. If you do not feel confident to vet natural rocks, some aquarium stores stock artificial rocks (including so-called 'lava rock', which is man-made and not the same as volcanic lava), some of which look similar to the real thing, though the range of size and shape is limited, and they are quite expensive. But, again, they will last a lifetime.

PREPARING ROCKS FOR USE

All rocks should be thoroughly scrubbed in plain water (no soap or detergent) to remove dirt, moss, and lichens. Particular attention should be paid to any cracks and holes that may harbour dirt, insects etc. Rocks collected from natural waters are best dipped in boiling water to eliminate any aquatic life they may be harbouring, which may include pests (Chapter 22) as well as pathogens and parasites (Chapter 21, sections 3, 4, 5). Or they may be air-dried for a week or two.

8. SHELLS

Shells are not considered suitable decor for the general community, as they are composed of calcium carbonate and may thus affect hardness and pH. However, a few species of fish (mainly shell-dwelling cichlids from Lake Tanganyika) unconditionally require spiral shells as refuges and breeding sites. The shells of French edible snails (*escargots*), purchased from delicatessens or begged from French restaurants, are commonly used and are ideal for most species. Shells sold as domestic ornaments are also suitable provided they have not been dyed. Shells from the seashore must be boiled to sterilise them and all accessible surfaces scrubbed clean. Those which have obviously been empty for some time (water-worn) are preferable to those which may still contain residues of dead shellfish.

Obviously, whatever shells are chosen, they must be of a suitable size to accommodate the fish concerned.

9. WOOD

Wooden items can be extremely decorative, and wood is, of course, a commonplace form of cover in natural habitats. This does not mean that any piece of wood collected from the wild is suitable for aquarium use, even if it is found in a river or stream. The aquarium does not have the benefit of constantly renewed water to dilute and wash away any organic toxins leaching out of decaying wood. In the aquarium, such toxins can quickly build up to critical levels, and natural acids from wood can also cause a serious drop in pH. Normally only certain reasonably safe types of wood are used – bogwood, driftwood, cork bark, bamboo, and coconut shells. As these too may leach tannins and other substances into the aquarium water, they require careful selection and preparation before use (see below). They are generally used only in situations where any acidifying effect is unlikely to harm the fish, unless they have been varnished (see below) to prevent leaching. Unvarnished wood may also make the water tea-coloured; this is actually very natural for fish from many rainforest streams, but disliked by some aquarists. The colour can be removed by using carbon in the filter.

ACQUIRING WOODEN ITEMS FOR AQUARIA
• **Bogwood**, as the name suggests, is found in bogs and marshes, and is the remains of ancient trees which have been preserved by centuries of exposure to natural preservatives such as tannins, apparently solely for the benefit of aquarists! Suitable sources tend to be fiercely guarded by companies with 'mining rights', hence bogwood is usually purchased from the aquarium store rather than collected. It is expensive but lasts many years, and makes a most attractive and natural decor item.
• **Cork bark** is the bark of the cork oak tree (*Quercus suber*), and is available from some aquarium stores or florists/horticultural outlets. Again, collecting your own is not generally an option, and trees must never be vandalised.
• **Bamboo canes** are available from florists/horticultural outlets. Ensure they have not been treated with preservative or other chemicals. Use only new ones, not old beanpoles or plant sticks that may be contaminated with pesticides or fertilisers.
• **Driftwood** can be collected on the seashore. Only fully bleached (by exposure to the elements) and hard, solid pieces should be collected. Immersion in the sea will usually have removed most tannins, but driftwood may contain salt residues which are undesirable in the freshwater aquarium.
• **Simulated wooden items** for aquaria are also available, from aquarium stores, and some are extremely realistic and virtually indistinguishable from the real thing. They are expensive, but, like rocks, will last a lifetime.

PREPARING WOOD FOR AQUARIUM USE
All wooden items should be soaked (for weeks or months rather than days) to eliminate contaminants; the process can be hastened by boiling or using repeated changes of hot water. Any soft material should be scooped out or scraped away as much as possible.

Tip: if a coconut is hung out in the garden to feed the birds in winter, and left hanging there forgotten all summer, by autumn the shell will be nicely weathered.

Varnishing wood (with a waterproof non-toxic varnish) is often suggested as a quicker alternative solution to the problem of leaching. However, most wooden items have cracks and crannies which cannot be sealed effectively, so the slower method is safer. In addition, some fish (e.g. some catfish and cichlids of the *Uaru* genus) will rasp or gnaw on wood, and be poisoned by the varnish. This will occur even if the varnish is nominally safe, as this denotes only that it will not contaminate water in which it is immersed, and does not cover its effects when eaten!

10. OTHER ITEMS

Clay (earthenware) plant pots, plant-pot drainage saucers, and pipes, are often used to provide 'caves', and are often occupied in preference to more natural structures built of rock. If they are thought unsightly, they can be concealed under rocks or among plants. Pots can be placed on their sides, or a piece can be removed from the rim (the entrance) and the pot inverted. Drainage trays are usually inverted with an entrance in the rim. Clay items should be new, to avoid any danger of pesticide or fertiliser residues remaining in the porous clay despite thorough washing.

Plastic pots should not be used, as the plastic they are made from may be toxic. Plastic pipe intended for drinking-water supplies is suitable for aquarium use, but waste-water piping should be regarded as suspect.

CHAPTER 12

LIGHT

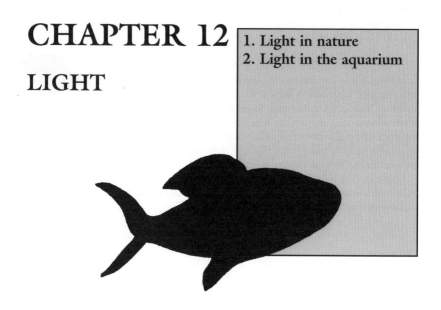

Light is the final environmental parameter that needs to be considered when setting up an aquarium. This chapter deals with the environmental aspects of lighting; lighting equipment is discussed in Chapter 13.

1. LIGHT IN NATURE

Light is, of course, a feature of the natural environment, and the daily alternation of light and darkness serves to regulate many of the activities of fish. Some species feed, breed, etc only during the daytime, so all such activity depends on the presence of light. Others are largely or exclusively nocturnal, and so the setting and rising of the sun signal the beginning and end of their active period and a number feed largely during the twilight periods at dawn and dusk. In the case of some species, seasonal changes in day length are a trigger for gonad development and reproduction.

Light also affects other aspects of the environment, such as the activity and location of living food items, and is particularly important to vegetation, which requires light in order to photosynthesise nutrients.

In the tropics, daylight lasts approximately 12-14 hours, with relatively little seasonal variation. Light intensity likewise varies little seasonally, as the sun is near the zenith all year round, but may be influenced by cloud cover. Thus light intensity

DECOR

Mary Bailey.

Without decor, fish will become stressed, having nowhere to bolt if danger looms. This flower pot acts as a great cave.

Make sure that decor items have no rough edges, and that they will not alter the water's chemistry, unless it is your intention to do so. Ensure they do not harbour any unwanted creatures or diseases before adding to your aquarium.

A collection of rocks and a piece of petrified wood (top left).

Cork bark.

Mopani wood.

River wood.

PLANTS

Keith Allison.

Sword plant (*Echinodorus major*).

Keith Allison.

Hygrophila
(*Hygrophila polysperma*).

Keith Allison.

Hair grass
(*Eleocharis*).

Keith Allison.

Java fern
(*Microsorium pteropus*).

Keith Allison.

Indian fern
(*Ceratopteris thalictroides*).

Mary Bailey.

Water lettuce (*Pistia stratiotes*).

HABITATS

Tropical fish come from a huge range of different habitats from around the world.

Small pool within a drying river bed (Trinidad, Caribbean), home to guppies and cichlids.

Peter Burgess.

Male (left) and female wild guppy.

Peter Burgess.

Peter Burgess.

Peter Burgess.

Rainforest river (Brunei, North Borneo). Home to a variety of fishes, including spiny eels, rasboras, barbs, and catfishes. Right: a rasbora photographed on site.

Mary Bailey.

Roman Sznober.

Typical sandy shoreline (Lake Malawi, East Africa), where you can find a variety of cichlid species.

Sand, the plant *Vallisneria ethiopica*, and an empty Lanistes snail shell is the natural environment for the fish of the Malawi shore.

Spring-fed
river
(Mexico),
inhabited by
livebearers,
cichlids, and
tetras.

Peter Burgess.

Astyanax tetra
found in the
environment above.

Peter Burgess.

Typical rocky shoreline (Lake Malawi, East Africa), largely populated by cichlid species.

Algae-covered rocks, the view below the water.

PLANTED AQUARIUMS

Keith Allison.

A planted aquarium, with the correct decor for the type of fish it contains, produces happy, healthy fish. Above: harlequin rasboras and rummy-nose tetras. Below: characins and catfish.

Peter Burgess.

is likely to be reduced during the rainy season in areas where this is a feature of the annual climatic cycle. Not all fish spend their daytime lives under brilliant illumination, however, as many aquatic habitats are shaded by overhanging trees and other terrestrial vegetation. Water clarity – or a lack of it – and depth will also affect light levels.

2. LIGHT IN THE AQUARIUM

In the aquarium, the main functions of the lighting are to encourage healthy plant growth, as well as to enable the aquarist to view the underwater scenery and its occupants. It should not, however, be forgotten that light is also important to the fish. In captivity, as in nature, it regulates their activity, and its intensity may affect their well-being – a point which few aquarists take into account. Incorrect lighting can also encourage the growth of various kinds of algae (Chapter 22).

The aquarium lighting should be switched on for 12-14 hours each day to simulate the natural photoperiod, and it is *not* acceptable to shorten this period in order to economise on electricity, even where plants are not being grown. Equally, it is wrong to extend the lighting period in order to try to promote plant growth. Both diurnal and nocturnal species require the appropriate periods of light and darkness in order to regulate their circadian rhythms, and may otherwise suffer stress, as well as behavioural and even physiological changes (for example, atrophy of the gonads).

Providing the appropriate light intensity can present problems. Aquatic plants generally require fairly strong light in order to thrive, yet many of the fish kept in planted aquaria originate from shaded waters. All too often the needs of the plants are placed first, and the fish obliged to endure a level of lighting which they may find uncomfortable, and hence stressful. From the aquarist's viewpoint, they may show rather pallid, 'washed-out' coloration instead of their natural vivid colours. They may also hide when the tank is lit – the very time when he would like to be able to watch them swimming around.

The problem of over-bright illumination has been exacerbated since the advent of tanks with a depth in excess of the once-standard 30 or 38 cm (12 or 15 in). Nowadays, tanks are commonly 60 cm (24 in) deep, and a greater light intensity is required to promote growth in plants growing on the bottom, especially low-growing types that cannot extend their leaves up to the more brightly-lit upper levels. But the problem of excessive light intensity is also commonplace in unplanted aquaria, where bright light is unnecessary as well as undesirable. In short, the lighting in many aquaria is far too bright for its occupants, who all too often do not have the option of seeking a shady area (under cover or in deep water) as they would in the wild.

If plants are absent, then the solution is to reduce the amount of lighting (wattage, not the illuminated period). As a general rule, 8-10 watts of lighting per 30 cm (12 in) of aquarium length will illuminate the aquarium adequately for viewing purposes and not stress most fish (albino varieties may, however, require dimmer lighting – see Chapter 21, section 5.2). This lighting level equates with a single fluorescent tube running the length of the tank. Many plants will do reasonably or very well at this light level, unless the tank is very deep.

If plants requiring brighter light are to be grown, or the aquarium is deep, then a compromise must be achieved (the fishes' well-being, however, must never be compromised!). There are a number of possible options:

• Keep only fish that come from shallow, brightly-lit waters, and install lighting to suit the plants.

• Grow only plants that will tolerate the relatively low light levels required by many fish.

• Grow plants whose leaves grow up to the surface, or float on it (including floating plants), so the fish can swim in the shade underneath. This requires that the tank be set up and planted, and the plants allowed to root and grow to provide the necessary shade, *before* the fish are added. This may involve waiting a couple of months before fish can be introduced, but will benefit both plants and fish in the long run; the plants will be well-rooted before the fish come along to disturb them. Because there will be no fish waste products to feed the plants, artificial fertilisation (Chapter 15) will be necessary during this initial period.

• Grow plants with leaves at or near the surface in some parts of the tank, and have open spaces for low-growing plants elsewhere, so the fish have a choice. This is not feasible in small aquaria, as the amounts of shaded and open swimming space would be too restricted.

• Illuminate only part of the aquarium, or have brighter lighting in one area (where the plants are grown), again so the fish have a choice of environment. This option is feasible only in larger aquaria, but can look very effective, especially if the dark area is decorated with bogwood so as to resemble a root tangle in the naturally darker bank zone.

The imaginative or inventive aquarist may, of course, think of other options to those listed.

DAWN AND DUSK

Although the sun rises and sets fairly rapidly in the tropics, there is still an appreciable twilight period at both ends of the day; the sun does not come on or go off suddenly like the aquarium lighting! Sudden changes from light to total darkness, and *vice versa*, can throw both diurnal and nocturnal fish into confusion and panic. This leads to stressed and nervous fish.

In addition, most nocturnal fish retire to a safe or shaded place during the day, and many diurnal species do so at nightfall. Nocturnal species can at least see in the light and find their way 'home', but some diurnal fish seem unable to find their way around in the dark, and may be left stranded, exposed to nocturnal dangers and hence frightened, if plunged into sudden darkness. Some parental fish, such as cichlids, need a twilight period in which to round up their fry into a safe place for the night; in their case nocturnal predation may be a real rather than an imagined hazard, as the fry may be eaten by nocturnal tankmates if not shepherded to a place of relative safety.

Dawn and dusk can be simulated by the simple expedient of turning the room light on 10-20 minutes before the aquarium lighting, and off 10-20 minutes after 'lights out' in the tank. It does not matter if the dawn/dusk period is longer, for example, if the family do not wish to sit in darkness for the rest of the evening! Artificial twilight may not be necessary all year round, of course, if the room is lit by the real sun before and/or after the aquarium lighting period.

The observant aquarist will note how some fish quickly learn that they have a quarter of an hour to put their affairs in order at the end of their active period, and it is particularly entertaining to watch breeding cichlids start rounding up their family as soon as the tank light goes out.

NATURAL VERSUS ARTIFICIAL LIGHTING

Most aquaria are illuminated by electric lighting. An aquarium lit by natural light (by standing it close to a window or in a conservatory) can look enchanting, and the colours of the fish superb, but there are disadvantages:

• In temperate zones, both the photoperiod and the light intensity are likely to be unsuitable for tropical fish and plants for a major part of the year; the days will be the wrong length and the light often too dim.

• The sun may not necessarily be shining at the time when the aquarist wishes to view the aquarium, often in the evening.

• During hot, sunny weather, sunlight may cause serious overheating of the aquarium, which can be fatal to the fish; this is almost inevitable in an unshaded conservatory.

• Direct sunlight tends to encourage rampant algal growth.

• The aquarium must be left without a hood in order to admit light from above, and this negates the advantages and purposes of using a hood (Chapter 13). If light is instead admitted via the rear glass, then the tank must be left without a background, which is equally undesirable. The rear glass will quickly become coated in algae, which will cut out the light. Moreover, light entering from the side, rather than from above, is unnatural and therefore possibly stressful.

If these problems can be countered effectively (by using supplementary electric lighting or drawing the curtains, whenever necessary), then there is no radical objection to natural light – after all, it is natural!

CHAPTER 13

EQUIPMENT

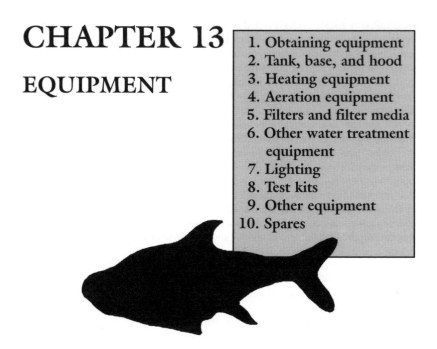

In this chapter we summarise the equipment required for the normal maintenance of tropical freshwater fish, as well as items which may prove useful for some applications. (See also Chapter 24).

In recent years, the variety of aquarium equipment available has increased exponentially, such that the beginner may find himself utterly confused as to what is necessary and what is not. He may pause to wonder how aquarists managed to keep fish at all when there was no such 'essential' gadgetry to help them! In fact, they managed quite nicely by understanding and applying the principles of water management described in Chapter 10. All too often nowadays the aquarist buys the largest and most powerful filter he can afford, thinking it must be the best, but without any understanding of how it works – mechanically, chemically, biologically – or any thought for its suitability for his aquarium and its occupants.

The same "it's available so I must need it" philosophy is generally applied to other equipment as well, such that we find aquarists with mineral-poor and contaminant-free tap water using reverse osmosis units; heating small tanks with high-wattage heaters; or trying to keep their fish healthy with ozonisers or UV sterilisers. Meanwhile they commonly neglect to acquire relatively cheap but quite essential items such as water test kits, a selection of nets, and an aquarium manual (such as this one!) explaining what they do and do not need.

116

The catalogue of equipment below explains briefly the function and uses of various items of equipment. What it cannot do, because of the sheer diversity of products available, is to offer an evaluation of the efficiency and function of every single model of filter, heater, and so on.

It must be stressed that all equipment used for fishkeeping must be designed for that purpose. Ancillary equipment, such as buckets, should be made of materials that will not react with the aquarium water or poison/harm the fish in any other way. In particular, plastic items should be chosen with care, using only those intended for aquarium or food use (see also Chapter 21, section 1.2, Poisoning).

1. OBTAINING EQUIPMENT

A limited amount of aquarium equipment may be found in most general pet stores and small aquatic outlets, but to find an extensive range it will normally be necessary to visit one of the larger aquarium stores. Prices for the same item may vary considerably from outlet to outlet, so it can be worth shopping around. It may also be worth considering mail order once you have decided what specific item/model you require. Large mail order businesses usually offer a huge selection and a 24-48 hour service is common. They normally advertise in aquarium magazines.

Some items, while available by mail order, are generally best purchased locally – these include large and/or breakable items such as tanks, stands, hoods, and fluorescent tubes. Equipment which is required urgently will also have to be purchased locally. It is also worthwhile considering the goodwill factor if you regularly patronise a particular store where you receive good service and honest, valuable advice. You may find these dry up if the staff realise you are using them as an equipment evaluation and advisory service and then buying elsewhere.

Provided you are intending to buy from the store, do not be afraid to ask for a demonstration of any piece of equipment, either to evaluate its performance or so you will know how to use it!

NEW OR SECOND-HAND?
Setting up an aquarium for the first time is an expensive business, and the aquarist may be tempted to save money by purchasing second-hand. There are a number of very good reasons not to do so:
• 'Complete set-ups', as commonly offered for sale in the small classified advertisements of the local newspaper, generally come complete with someone else's choice of fish. The owner may be selling because he has been having insoluble problems (e.g. disease, fish incompatibility), which you will inherit. The tank must be 'broken down' (emptied of fish, water, decor, and equipment) in order to move it, and, once set up again, will require a minimum of two to three weeks to mature before it is safe for fish. Meanwhile you already have the fish...
• Second-hand tanks, equipment and decor may harbour infectious diseases, parasites, and other unwanted pests (Chapter 22) such as snails and *Hydra*.
• Second-hand tanks may have scratched viewing glasses.
• Second-hand electrical equipment may be unsafe, or at the end of its useful life. It will probably be out of its guarantee period, and in any case guarantees are commonly not transferable to a second-hand purchaser.
• Second-hand decor may be unsuitable for the fish you wish to keep.

• Defective new equipment will generally be exchanged by the supplier, regardless of any manufacturer guarantee, as a token of goodwill (or legal requirement in some countries). The vendor of second-hand goods is unlikely to be so accommodating.

The experienced aquarist, with experience of sterilising equipment and decor, may nevertheless sometimes decide to buy second-hand equipment. But second-hand electrical equipment is best avoided under all circumstances, and the beginner is strongly recommended to invest exclusively in new equipment.

2. TANK, BASE, AND HOOD

These three items are discussed together because it is necessary for them to have the same width and length, and hence they are commonly bought together as a unit. This does not mean that the aquarist has to buy the tank, hood, and stand assembled together in the shop for display purposes. Most shops stock a variety of 'separates' in various sizes, from which the aquarist can make his selection.

THE TANK

Tanks are nowadays normally made of panes of glass joined together with silicon sealant ('all-glass tanks'), or may be one-piece acrylic mouldings. Small tanks are sometimes made of other clear plastics. Plastics have the advantage of being relatively unbreakable, but scratch more easily than glass and may distort the view of their contents. They may also melt if in contact with a high-wattage heater.

It is important to consider what fish are to be kept before purchasing the tank, to ensure the latter is suitable for its occupants *when they are fully grown*.

Stocking density is normally calculated in terms of fish length (excluding the tail) relative to water surface area (roughly equivalent to oxygen requirement vis-a-vis the area available for gas exchange). The usual formula for tropical freshwater fish is 2.5 cm (1 in) of fish per 64 sq cm (10 sq in) of surface area. Remember that some fish have space requirements based on different criteria (e.g. territory); any such special needs will normally be found in the literature on each species.

Tank size may be limited by the space available, and also by access (width of doorways, corners to be negotiated), as well as by cost. The weight of a tank, when filled with water, can be considerable (see box) and this too may be a limiting factor if the floor is unable to bear the heavy load represented by a large aquarium (professional advice may be needed to evaluate this). Generally speaking, however, a medium to large tank (90 cm/36 in or more in length) is easier to keep biologically stable, and will, of course, accommodate more (cm/inches of) fish.

Calculating the weight of water in the aquarium

- Metric: multiply aquarium length x width x depth, in centimetres, to give the volume in cubic centimetres (cc). Divide this value by 1,000 to convert to litres. 1 litre weighs 1 kilogram.
- Imperial: multiply aquarium length x width x height in inches to give the volume in cubic inches (in^3). Divide this value by 277.36 to convert to imperial gallons. 1 gallon weighs 10 pounds.

Tank shape is also important. Fish normally swim horizontally rather than vertically, hence the traditional horizontal-rectangular aquarium remains that most suited to the needs of fish. Tall thin 'towers' offer relatively little surface area and swimming space, and are really no more than high-rise versions of the goldfish bowl, now universally condemned as cruel. The value of the aquarium as a room decoration should be a function not of its shape, but of the attractive underwater scene, with healthy plants and fish, that it contains.

Plastic tanks are factory-manufactured, as are many glass tanks. However, many dealers may be able to supply quality glass tanks manufactured locally to order (and to customised size/shape) and these may be cheaper because there are no overheads (such as transportation costs). It is advisable to check that the glass used is new (rather than recycled shop windows – look for scratches), of the appropriate thickness, and that the top edges are properly reinforced with bracing bars (compare with a factory-made tank). Factory-made tanks often have a plastic frame which is commonly purely decorative (concealing the joins).

THE BASE
The aquarium base may take several forms:
• A purpose-built cabinet, usually made of wood, complete with a cupboard underneath for external equipment and storage. Probably the most attractive option for the living room, but also the most expensive. Check that the materials and construction are able to withstand moisture and carry the weight of the filled aquarium (see above and box).
• A welded tubular metal stand, usually painted or plastic-coated in black or white.
• A solid piece of furniture or built-in feature (shelf/cupboard), which must be strong enough to take the weight of the tank and water. If in doubt, seek professional advice.
• The floor; not ideal from a viewing point of view.
• Impoverished aquarists have been known to improvise very adequate bases from stacks of concrete blocks or bricks topped with a thick solid board, sometimes concealing their handiwork with a curtain.

The base should have a solid flat surface on which to place the aquarium. Cabinets usually have a suitable surface built-in, but metal stands and some built-in features (e.g. stone fireplace surrounds) will need to be topped with a 'baseboard'. This is a piece of exterior or marine grade plywood, at least 1.25 cm (0.5 in) thick and cut to the correct size, and obtainable from a timber merchant or home-improvement store. Do not use interior grade ply, chipboard, or blockboard, all of which may disintegrate and rot if (as is almost inevitable) they get wet.

In addition, the bottom of the aquarium should be protected by a piece of polystyrene foam ('styrofoam') of similar thickness, and with the same dimensions as the tank bottom. This will absorb any unevenness in the base – without this precaution the tank bottom may crack! Styrofoam sheet can also be obtained from home-improvement stores or builders' merchants.

THE HOOD
The hood is used to keep the fish in the aquarium – without it, some fish may jump, or even, in the case of some groups (Clariidae, Channidae), climb, out! It also prevents pets, children, and dirt from getting in. It houses the light tube(s) (see

below), and sometimes has a rear compartment for other external electrical equipment (however, this is best sited away from the aquarium and any danger of contact with the water and should not be a major consideration when choosing a hood). Aquarium cabinets have an integral hood.

Most hoods have a flap for access. Check that the knob is a sensible size and shape, such that it will not slip from the (possibly damp) fingers, letting the flap down with a loud bang to terrify the fish.

The hood should be supplied with built-in cover glasses or plastic condensation trays, which are used to minimise evaporation and to ensure that the air space above the water's surface remains at water temperature. This is important when keeping gouramis and other fish that have accessory respiratory organs enabling them to breathe atmospheric air. Check that cover glasses/condensation trays provide access to the interior of the aquarium, as otherwise the hood will have to be removed every time you want to feed the fish or change the water.

Some types of lighting require that the aquarium is operated without a hood. Banks of aquaria in fish-houses are also normally hood-free. Cover glasses should nevertheless be used, and must then also serve to keep fish in and dirt etc, out.

3. HEATING EQUIPMENT

The heating equipment consists of the heater, which warms the water; the thermostat, which regulates the water temperature by switching the electrical supply to the heater on/off; and the thermometer.

Nowadays the most commonly used form of heating is the combined heater and thermostat unit ('heater/stat') which is immersed in the aquarium, but 'separates' of various types are also available. The advantages of using separate heaters and thermostats, as opposed to heater/stats, are flexibility as regards type of heating and wattages, and that it is not necessary to throw away a perfectly good thermostat when the generally much shorter-lived heater element fails. Heater/stats are more convenient, requiring at most the addition of a suitable plug in order to install them. Separates need to be connected, a task requiring electrical knowledge. However, a recent welcome development is modular heating, where different or replacement heaters can be attached to thermostats using pre-fitted plug/socket connectors.

Heaters come in a variety of wattages. It is important that the total wattage is adequate for the size of aquarium at the time when room temperature is at its lowest (and hence aquarium heat loss greatest), for example on a cold winter's night when the room heating is off. The wattage required must be discussed with the supplier, as it is impossible to lay down hard-and-fast criteria for every situation.

The wise aquarist will split the desired wattage between two heaters, so that if one fails, the tank will not be left completely unheated. (This is, however, impracticable in small aquaria). Two heater/stats used in tandem confer the additional advantage that if one thermostat fails 'on', the other will remain off, and reduce the likelihood of serious overheating.

THERMOSTATS

Aquarium thermostats normally have a limited temperature range corresponding to that generally required by tropical fish. The operating temperature is set using a control knob or screw, and sometimes there is a temperature indicator scale (of variable accuracy), otherwise trial and error is required. Most 'stats' (including those in heater/stats) have an indicator light which comes on when current is flowing to the heater; however, some indicators are illuminated permanently to show current is reaching the unit. In at least one currently available model of heater/stat the light comes on when the heater is off.

Two basic types of thermostat are available:

• **Mechanical thermostats**, employing a bimetallic strip. Separate internal (submerged) thermostats of this type were once commonplace, and are still available though not popular. Most heater/stats use this type of thermostat. External mechanical thermostats are also available, and sense the aquarium temperature by contact with the glass.

• **Electronic thermostats.** These are usually considerably more expensive, and in most cases are installed outside the aquarium with a temperature probe installed in the water. They are accurate, reliable, and long-lived, with the reservation that a small percentage do not work properly from the start, or fail within a short period (usually days). It is thus a good idea to 'run them in' on an aquarium that does not contain fish or plants.

External thermostats have the advantage of easy access for adjustment; however this is also a disadvantage as they are easily adjusted by unauthorised fingers.

HEATERS

Three main types are available:

• **Tubular immersion heaters**, consisting of a wire element on a ceramic core and enclosed in a tube, which is sealed with a rubber plug from which the electrical lead protrudes. Easily replaced without much disturbance to the aquarium.

• **Heating mats**, which are sited beneath the aquarium such that the warmth rises through the bottom glass. These are said to benefit plants by warming their roots (a luxury which, however, plants do not enjoy in nature!) but a major disadvantage is that they cannot be replaced without 'breaking down' the aquarium. They are, however, generally much longer-lasting than tubular immersion heaters.

• **Heating cables.** These are similar to greenhouse soil-warming cables and are buried in the substrate. Like heating mats, they are said to benefit plants; they are somewhat easier to replace but still involve much disruption. Easily damaged by heavy decor items, such as large rocks.

HEATER/STATS

These are usually a combination of a bimetallic strip thermostat and a tubular immersion heater, all enclosed in a single tube, which is immersed in the aquarium. Because heat rises, this type of heater/stat should not be positioned vertically or the thermostat may switch off prematurely; instead the unit needs to be positioned horizontally or at an angle.

Some electronic external thermostats have a factory-fitted integral heater which is submerged in the aquarium, and hence are also sometimes described as heater/stats.

THERMOFILTERS

External canister filters (see below) with an integral heater/thermostat unit which heats the water as it passes through the filter. Although this may sound like a good idea, these units are expensive, and if filter flow is slowed by clogging, then the

121

aquarium may become chilled. Also, it may be considered unwise to have the entire 'life-support system' of the aquarium dependent on one electrical unit and one fuse.

THERMOMETERS

Most aquarium thermometers are either conventional tubular types, fixed inside the aquarium, or liquid crystal display (LCD) strips which are fixed to the outside of the glass. The former have a tendency to detach themselves (or be detached by inquisitive fish), but can be moved from tank to tank; LCD strips cease to work if removed from the aquarium glass. Plastic tubular thermometers are preferable to glass ones, which are easily broken and may contaminate the aquarium with mercury or alcohol.

Digital thermometers are a relatively recent innovation, some with alarms that are activated by the temperature dropping or rising outside specified bounds. Although more expensive than simple thermometers, some are now quite reasonably priced.

The degree of accuracy of aquarium thermometers is notoriously variable. It is sensible to use two and take a consensus reading, or, ideally, check accuracy against a laboratory or other accurate thermometer and adjust subsequent aquarium thermometer readings accordingly.

HEATER HOLDERS AND HEATER GUARDS

• **Heater holders** are intended to attach immersion heaters and heater/stats to the aquarium glass. Unfortunately, the plastic suckers provided for this purpose are normally reluctant to stay in place. Provided the aquarist is aware of this problem, they can be stuck in place with silicon sealant before the aquarium is filled.

• **Heater guards** are used to protect glass heaters from accidental knocks, to prevent contact with the aquarium glass/plastic (to avoid cracking/melting), and to prevent fish from burning themselves (Chapter 21, section 1.6.1). They may be fitted with suckers so as to serve as heater holders as well.

4. AERATION EQUIPMENT

This is used to pump air through the aquarium to circulate the water and improve gas exchange at the surface. Contrary to popular belief, the air bubbles have very little direct effect on the dissolved oxygen content of the aquarium. As the stream of bubbles rises through the water, it draws water with it; this phenomenon is known as the 'airlift principle' and is used not only to create circulation, but also to 'power' some types of filter, which themselves help circulate the water.

• **Airpumps** are electrically powered devices which generally work by vibrating a rubber diaphragm inside the pump to produce a current of air. They are also known as vibrator pumps. Piston-operated pumps are also available. Neither type is submersible. Airpumps are highly variable in terms of output and it is important to choose one suited to actual air requirements. A small cheap pump will be adequate for basic aeration in a small tank, but a large, powerful model may be required to power multiple filter outlets. One airpump can serve several tanks if desired, provided it is sufficiently powerful. It is worth buying an airpump even if it is not immediately required, as a source of air will probably be needed sooner or later, whether it be for hatching brine shrimp, additional emergency aeration, or powering a small filter in the quarantine tank.

• **Airline** is narrow gauge plastic or silicone tubing used to convey air from the pump to the aquarium.

• **Non-return valves** are installed in the airline between pump and water to protect the pump against water siphoning back up the tube if the electrical supply to the pump is interrupted.

• **Gang valves** are used to split the air supply between a number of outlets in the aquarium, and to regulate the supply to each outlet. Fitted out of the water.

• **T-pieces** are used to split the air supply; in two, without any regulation.

• **Clamps** are often used in conjunction with T-pieces to provide the regulation element, and can also be used to reduce the supply to a single outlet. However the increased back-pressure may rupture the pump diaphragm, so if the pump is producing more air than required, it is better to split the supply and bleed off excess air into the atmosphere, using a gang valve or a T-piece/clamp combination.

• **Diffusers** are used underwater to break up (diffuse) the air from the pump into thousands of tiny bubbles. They may be made of wood, plastic, or a stone-like composite, and are commonly known as airstones, whatever their construction.

In addition a number of air-operated 'toys' are available: opening and closing clams, divers that travel up and down, and so forth. Some of these items may cause considerable fear and stress in fish, and are best avoided. Although they provide aeration, they serve no useful purpose not fulfilled by a simple airstone.

5. FILTERS AND FILTER MEDIA

The principles of filtration were dealt with in Chapter 10 to which the reader should refer.

Filters are powered either by electric pumps or by air, using the airlift principle (see above). The latter type is considerably cheaper than the former.

Most newcomers to the aquarium hobby tend grossly to overestimate the amount of filtration required to maintain good water quality. Old-timers from the days when few people could afford a motorised filter, however, will be aware that 'primitive' air-driven filtration is perfectly capable of biologically processing a remarkably high waste output. Where such systems may sometimes (but by no means always) prove inadequate is in mechanically collecting all the solid wastes and keeping the water clear.

Filter capacity is evaluated in terms of two factors – volume (of media) and turnover (the rate at which water is pumped through the filter). Motorised filters commonly have a stated turnover rate, e.g. 300 litres per hour (lph). It is very important to select a filter suited to the aquarium in question, as regards the size of tank (amount of water to be filtered), loading (amount of wastes to be processed), and the water movement preferences of the occupants. The biggest and most powerful filter available (or affordable) is not necessarily the most appropriate for all applications. Excess media capacity will do no harm, but excessive turnover may cause the fish considerable discomfort and stress. If the turnover rate is too high, they may find it difficult to swim against the current; small fish, especially fry, may be sucked into the filter and die. A 300-lph filter will process the water in a 600-litre aquarium once every two hours, but will take only ten minutes to filter a 50-litre tank – from the fish's point of view, a bit like living in a washing machine.

Inadequate turnover, on the other hand, may mean cloudy water, and insufficient media capacity can lead to rapid clogging and the need for over-frequent maintenance (Chapter 15). Reduced biological efficiency may occur as a result of the repeated disruption of the bacterial population of the filter.

It is a positive advantage to have a filter with a variable flow rate (all air-driven filters can be regulated by varying the air input; some, but not all, motorised filters have a flow rate regulator). Such a filter is versatile and can be used for different tanks and different types of fish, if the aquarist's interest develops or changes.

FILTERS

The following are the types of filters most likely to be encountered commercially:

• **Box, external**. A rectangular plastic box, sometimes with a number of chambers, that hangs on the outside of the aquarium, and may be motorised (electric) or air-powered. No longer popular in Europe, but much used in the USA, where highly sophisticated motorised models are available. Water may be siphoned from the aquarium and pumped back after passing through the media, or pumped from the aquarium and allowed to run back via a lip that overhangs the tank rim.

• **Box, internal**. A small plastic container, typically cube-shaped, triangular, or an upright cylinder, in each case air-powered. Water usually passes in through the perforated top, down through the filter medium, and up and out via a vertical tube. Formerly very popular when the only alternatives were primitive, leak-prone external boxes or expensive motorised external canister filters, but now largely superseded by other types. Still useful for small tanks and for additional or short-term chemical filtration.

• **Canister, external**. An upright cylindrical (or occasionally box-shaped) container for filter media, topped by an electric pump. Water is siphoned from the aquarium via flexible plastic piping and pumped back after passing through the media. Separate internal 'baskets' may be provided for separate media. A 'spray bar', a rigid plastic tube with perforations, is sometimes attached to the outlet to diffuse the returned water, and can be operated both above and below the surface. External canister filters are available in various canister sizes and with various turnover rates, which can be regulated in some models. Efficiency and reliability are also variable. External canisters are not normally appropriate for small tanks.

• **Canister, internal**. A plastic canister with perforated (inlet slots) sides, containing filter media (usually one or more plastic foam cartridges), and topped by an electric pump. The entire unit is submersible. Various sizes available, some with flow regulators. Should not be used in breeding tanks as fry are easily sucked in.

• **Powerhead**. An electric pump designed to fit on to the canister of an internal canister filter or the uplift of an undergravel filter. Some types have a variable flow rate. Most are far too powerful for use in small tanks.

• **Protein skimmer**. This piece of equipment uses a process known as 'air-stripping' whereby proteins and other pollutants stick to air bubbles and are carried to the top of the unit, where they are collected in a removable cup. The process works best in salt water; freshwater models are inefficient and confer no real benefit.

• **Sponge**. Air-powered sponge filters have typically superseded internal box filters as the filter of choice for the small aquarium. They consist of a perforated plastic tube on to which are fitted one or more plastic foam cartridges. Air is passed through the tube drawing water with it, such that waste-bearing water is in turn drawn through the sponge and into the tube. Many aquarists keep a sponge filter operating, and hence biologically mature, in a corner of the main aquarium, for use in the quarantine or breeding tank when required.

• **Trickle**. Trickle filters consist of one or more perforated trays of media stacked above the aquarium. Water is sprayed (typically by the spraybar return from an external canister) on to the medium in the top tray of the stack, and then trickles through to the lower trays and eventually into the aquarium. The advantage of this type of filter is the high level of oxygenation permitting optimal biological activity.

A single trickle tray can be a useful method of diffusing the return from an external canister filter, reducing turbulence in the aquarium, and is an excellent way of ensuring a high oxygen content.

• **Undergravel (UG)**. This consists of a perforated plastic plate which is placed on the tank bottom, underneath the substrate. The filter plate is fitted with one or more uplift tubes which extend above the substrate, usually terminating at or near the water's surface. The substrate acts as the filter medium (the 'filter bed'). For optimum efficiency the filter bed should be 6-7.5 cm (2.5-3.0 in) deep and have a grain size of 4-5 mm.

UG filters can be run in 'conventional flow' or 'reverse flow' mode. In the former, water is drawn down through the gravel and up the uplift tube; in reverse flow, water is pumped down the tube and rises through the substrate. Conventional flow is powered by air or powerheads, or occasionally by an external canister whose inlet pipe is placed in the uplift. Reverse flow is powered by a powerhead operating in reverse mode (not all models can do this), or by an external canister whose outlet pipe is placed down the uplift. Conventional flow has the advantage that the 'inlet' is the entire surface of the substrate, so all solids are captured and processed, but this eventually leads to clogging of the substrate with inert residues (not harmful wastes as many aquarists assume). With reverse flow operated by a canister filter, solids are mechanically extracted in the canister and the substrate acts chiefly as a biological filter, although in all probability most biological filtration takes place in the canister, where the wastes are broken down. It is difficult to see any potential advantage to powerhead-operated reverse flow.

It is a serious mistake to run UG with a very rapid throughput. This is likely to result in particles being sucked through the filter bed and up the uplifts (conventional flow), or blasted out of the substrate (reverse flow).

FILTER MEDIA

Except where otherwise stated, the following media can be used in any type of 'container filter' (canister, box, trickle tray) that does not require a specific type or form (e.g. cartridge) of medium.

• **Calcium carbonate**. Used in the form of coral sand, coral gravel (crushed coral), or limestone chips, as a chemical medium to harden water and increase/buffer pH. Can also act mechanically and biologically. Such media should be rinsed free of fine particles before use. Can be washed and re-used.

• **Carbon**. Used as a chemical medium to remove some medications (especially dyes, such as methylene blue) and dissolved heavy metals. Contrary to popular belief, it does not remove nitrogen cycle products, i.e. ammonia, nitrite, and nitrate. Can also act mechanically and biologically. Carbon works by adsorption (collection of contaminants on its surfaces). The amount it can adsorb is limited, so it needs to be replaced regularly. Activated carbon is charcoal that has been specially treated to increase its porosity (and hence its total surface area) and thereby its capacity for adsorption. Carbon should be rinsed free of fine particles before use.

• **Ceramics.** A number of ceramic shapes, commonly hollow tubes, are available as coarse filter media. They act mechanically and biologically, and are usually used as the first medium in a sequence, as they do not clog easily and hence permit water flow. Can be washed and re-used.

• **Floss (filter wool).** Spun nylon, nowadays often regarded as old-fashioned, but still a cheap and very efficient mechanical and biological filter medium. Can be rinsed and re-used many times.

• **Foam.** Another cheap and very efficient mechanical and biological medium, usually supplied as cartridges for specific filters. Can be rinsed and re-used many times, but eventually needs replacement when it loses its resilience. It is vital to use *only* special filter foam; other types may be toxic to fish.

• **Gravel.** Any type of aquarium gravel (not sand, which clogs too easily), washed well before use, can be used as a simple mechanical and biological medium. May also act chemically unless 'hardness-free'. Can be washed and re-used indefinitely.

• **Peat.** Normally used as a chemical medium, to lower pH. Can also act mechanically and biologically. Stains water tea-coloured (natural for many acid-water fish). Peat should be used only in a nylon bag (a nylon stocking is ideal) as otherwise it is likely to escape into the aquarium. The bag of peat should be rinsed free of tiny particles before use. Special aquarium peat is available, but additive-free horticultural moss (not sedge) peat is an acceptable and far cheaper alternative.

• **Sintered glass.** Glass that has been specially treated to make it highly porous, such that it offers a huge surface area for bacteria to colonise. It is thus a very efficient biological medium. Used mechanically it soon clogs, so a layer of, for example, floss or foam should be used to remove the bulk of solids from the water before it reaches the glass. Expensive, but because of its high biological capacity a relatively small amount is the equivalent of much larger quantities of floss, foam, gravel, etc.

• **Zeolite.** A naturally-occurring ion-exchange resin which neutralises ammonia and is used primarily as a chemical medium. Can also act mechanically and biologically. Has a limited capacity but can be regenerated by soaking for 24 hours in a strong salt solution (rinse the zeolite in fresh water before re-use). Zeolite should *not* be used as a routine substitute for biological filtration (should it become 'exhausted' the aquarium would suffer an ammonia crisis). It is useful for dealing with temporary ammonia problems; for hospital tanks where the medication used is harmful to biological filtration; and in transportation containers, to prevent fish from being poisoned by their own wastes during long journeys.

6. OTHER WATER TREATMENT EQUIPMENT

• **Ion-exchange (IEX) unit.** These utilise ion-exchange resins to chemically alter some water parameters, and are normally used to condition tap water before it is added to the aquarium. Ion exchange can be used to soften or deionise water or to remove nitrate. Different resins/units are required for the different processes (e.g. water must be treated twice to remove hardness and nitrate). The aquarist needs an ion-exchange unit *only* if his water actually requires this type of pre-treatment. If multiple processing (e.g. hardness and nitrate removal) is required, reverse osmosis (see below) may be a better option.

• **Ozoniser**. Used to eliminate free-living pathogens in the aquarium water, usually in marine aquaria. Rarely used for freshwater aquaria.
• **Reverse osmosis unit (RO)**. The reverse osmosis process removes all impurities from water, leaving virtually pure H_2O. RO is used primarily to demineralise tap water for use with fish which require mineral-depleted conditions as well as to remove nitrate and other contaminants. The units are expensive and should be purchased only where tap water actually requires this type of treatment.
• **Ultraviolet steriliser**. Used to eliminate free-living pathogens in the water, usually in marine aquaria. Not normally necessary for domestic freshwater aquaria.

7. LIGHTING

Fluorescent lighting, consisting of one or more fluorescent tubes, each of which requires a control unit, is the most commonly used type of aquarium illumination. Some control units operate two tubes. Each tube is normally installed lengthwise inside the hood, and is generally about 15 cm (6 in) shorter than the aquarium length.

Only control units specifically designed for aquarium use should be used, as these have built-in safety features for damp conditions (they should never come into contact with the aquarium water), for example damp-proof plastic 'cups' on the ends of the tube leads, to keep condensation out of the connectors. These cups vary in diameter, so it is important to obtain a tube of the correct size.

A variety of special – and generally expensive – tubes are available, producing light in different areas of the spectrum for various purposes. Generally speaking, however, a cheap tube from the hardware store is perfectly adequate.

Pendant lamps and **spotlamps** are also available, but require that the aquarium be operated without a hood. They are more commonly used for marine aquaria or for large 'built-in' set-ups where the space above the aquarium is enclosed.

Spotlights can sometimes be fitted inside aquarium cabinets, and can be used to illuminate some parts of the aquarium, leaving others 'in shade', for a natural effect.

8. TEST KITS

Test kits can be obtained from aquarium stores to monitor various aspects of water chemistry and quality. Various brands, sometimes using different testing methods, are available. Test kits commonly consist of one or more bottles of liquid chemical reagent(s) and a testing vial, which is used to hold a sample of the water to be tested. The reagent(s) is/are added to the sample according to the instructions, which must be followed exactly to obtain an accurate result. Other test kits utilise reagents in powder or tablet form, or test papers that are dipped in a water sample. In most cases a colour reference chart is supplied; the reading is taken from the chart colour which best matches the sample or test paper.

Some test kits are more accurate than others. In some the colour gradations may be difficult to differentiate – avoid those with colour charts where all the shades are very similar. Some have a very limited shelf life, notably nitrate test kits – if one of these gives a zero reading (theoretically impossible in water containing living creatures), then suspect that it is no longer effective.

Warning: some of the chemicals used in test kits are toxic to fish, other animals, and humans. They should be stored and handled as detailed in Chapter 26.

Test kits are available for measuring levels of the following in the aquarium water:
* Ammonia
* Copper
* Hardness
* Nitrate
* Carbon Dioxide
* Chlorine
* Nitrite
* pH

Ammonia, nitrite, nitrate, and pH kits are essential, plus hardness in the case of some fish. The others are needed only if a problem is suspected.

9. OTHER EQUIPMENT

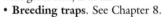

* **Algae removers** (magnets, scrubbers, scrapers) are used to keep the viewing glass clear of algae. Some metal-bladed scrapers can slice through the silicon sealant holding the all-glass aquarium together, and must be used with great care, if at all.
* **Breeding traps**. See Chapter 8.
* **Buckets**. Indispensable for various purposes. Standard plastic buckets are not food-grade plastic, but can be used for disposal of waste water. For water to be added to the aquarium use brewing bins, large food storage boxes, recycled ice-cream containers, etc.
* **Gravel cleaner**. Used to 'hoover' the substrate. Good for clearing up loose detritus (which can, however, be removed with a simple siphon, from the surface of the substrate. Also useful for cleaning clogged substrates, but should not be used for this purpose during regular weekly maintenance as this will disturb the biological function of the aquarium.
* **Isolation tank**. An extra small plastic tank for use when one or more fish need to be kept in isolation, e.g. for medication (Chapter 24), quarantine (Chapter 19), or breeding (Chapter 8). This tank can be set up, when required, on any flat surface capable of taking its weight, and does not require a special base. It should, however, have a hood or cover glass, and will require its own heating and aeration. It may or may not require a filter, depending on the use to which it is put at any given time; a sponge filter is normally used.
* **Nets**. Two nets are required to catch fish, using a pincer movement. Chasing with a single net is stressful for the fish. Very small nets are useless, even for catching small fish; 10 x 15 cm (4 x 6 in) is the minimum sensible size. Obviously, larger nets are required for large fish. Most nets are made of nylon mesh; special close-weave nets are required for fish that erect their spines when threatened (e.g. catfish), and can become entangled in ordinary nets. Check the texture of the net – coarse material can damage a fish's skin.
* **Silicon sealant** has a multitude of uses for repairing, waterproofing, and improvising equipment. Use only that intended for aquarium use – domestic silicon sealants (e.g. for double-glazing) may contain toxic fungicide and colorants.
* **Siphon tube**. Used to remove water from the aquarium during partial water changes. Any piece of non-toxic plastic tubing can be used (a diameter of about 1-1.25 cm/0.5 in is required). Aquarium stores sell siphons with an integral 'starter', avoiding the risk of a mouthful of tank water when sucking the tube to start the siphon.
* **Tank divider**. Used to divide an aquarium into compartments – for example to

separate fish that keep fighting, to provide peace and quiet for a sick fish, or to ensure privacy for breeding stock. Normally employed as a temporary measure pending a more permanent solution to the problem. Dividers can be purchased, or a suitably-sized piece of glass or clear plastic can be used. Plastic condensation trays can be cut down to make excellent dividers.

• **Water treatments**, e.g. dechlorinators, copper removers, and other detoxifiers; pH adjusters; mineral salts; plant fertilisers; 'tonics'; and so on. Some of these are genuinely useful and necessary, others are of dubious value or can be substituted by mechanical treatments/natural methods. It is essential to understand that the existence of a chemical treatment does not mean it is actually required in all cases (if any at all!). Far too many aquarists believe, or are led to believe, that their fish cannot survive or be healthy without the use of these water treatments. Yet fish were being kept and bred long before most of these potions were devised, and survive perfectly well without them in the wild!

Subjecting fish to a mixture of chemicals can be extremely harmful (Chapter 21, section 1.2). If water treatments are to be used, select those required from the range produced by a single manufacturer, as these are formulated to be safe when used together (unless otherwise stated). Using treatments from different manufacturers may result in undesirable chemical reactions and poisoned fish.

10. SPARES

It is advisable to keep a small supply of spares in case of equipment failure when the aquatic store is closed:

• Heater or heater/stat.
• Airpump diaphragm.
• Airline and valves.
• Any other essential item that is found to require regular replacement.
• Any item difficult to obtain, such as special light tubes/bulbs.
• Silicon sealant, which can be used to mend or temporarily waterproof many items.

CHAPTER 14

SETTING UP
AN AQUARIUM

In the preceding chapters of this section we have looked at the different components of the aquarium – water, light, decor, and the equipment used to run the fish 'life-support system'. It remains to consider how they may be assembled into a single unit, installed in the home.

Every aquarium is unique. There are so many possible variations – tank size, selection of fish, choice and arrangement of decor items, choice of equipment – that no book can hope to cover every eventuality, only to offer guidelines on setting-up and to warn of possible problem areas.

1. PLANNING AND PREPARATION

Planning is one of the major keys to success. Before you buy a single piece of equipment you should have considered all the points shown in Table 1.

It is a very good idea to draw up a plan of everything that has to be done, both in advance and on the day; this can be based on the suggestions given below. The more that can be arranged or done in advance, the better, so as to ensure that plenty of time is available on 'setting-up day'; not just for the planned work, but for any unforeseen hitches that may occur despite your careful planning.

SITING THE AQUARIUM

The following points should be taken into account when deciding where to site the aquarium:

• Which room? Most people prefer to have their aquarium in the living room, so they can watch their fish during their leisure hours. However, other considerations – including other points in this list, and the value of the carpet (accidents do occasionally happen where water is being moved around) – may dictate an alternative site.

• Desired tank size vis-a-vis available space.

• Access, when considering a large aquarium. Will it be possible to manipulate the tank through doorways and round corners, or through a window, to the chosen site?

• Strength of wooden flooring. Large tanks filled with water may weigh a ton or more. Professional advice may be required. The orientation of the aquarium relative to the joists of wooden floors is very important. Except when dealing with relatively small aquaria, the long dimension of the tank should run at 90 degrees to the direction of the joists, so that the load is distributed across as many as possible. (The joists run at 90 degrees to the floorboards, or along the rows of nails securing sheets of flooring board). The aquarium should be sited against a wall, where the joists are supported by the latter and their load-bearing capacity is greatest.

• Electricity supply. Ideally, the aquarium should be sited close to an electrical socket. If this is not possible, remember that an electric extension cable should always be clipped securely in place (e.g. to the skirting) rather than left loose. It must always follow the edge of the room, and never take a short-cut across or under the carpet.

• Water supply and disposal. Obviously there will not usually be a water supply in the room where the aquarium is to stand. But think very hard before siting even a small tank in, for example, an attic bedroom when the only water supply (and disposal point) is on the ground floor.

• Viewing convenience. It should be possible to view the aquarium without having to move the furniture around. The aquarium should also be at a comfortable viewing height from the planned viewing position (e.g. aquarist's armchair).

• Disturbance. Some fish do not like continuous disturbance, such as from people passing by. Equally, some fish may become shy and frightened of people if they are shut away in a room where no-one goes. A site in a regularly-used room, but away from normal walkways, will suit most fish. Children and animals must be trained to leave the fish alone, or be excluded from the room except under supervision.

• Risk of damage. Do not site the aquarium where a piece of furniture, such as a chair, might inadvertently be pushed against – and possibly through – the glass.

• Risk of poisoning by fumes, aerosol sprays, etc. (See Chapter 21, section 1.2.1.)

• Other room features. Aquaria should not be sited against radiators or too close to any room heater, because of a risk of overheating. Siting the aquarium close to a window exposed to prolonged or midday sunshine may also cause overheating and possibly problems with algae.

This may sound daunting, but remember that millions of people have faced the same problem and solved it, though some of the above points were learned from their mistakes!

OUTSIDE HELP

You may need professional help or advice, or extra muscle power:

• Builder to advise on strength of flooring. Such advice should be sought at an early

stage when you have a provisional idea of the desired tank size and its possible siting.
• Electrician to assist with wiring. Unless you are a competent electrician, you should arrange to have the work done by a professional. You do not want to risk losing your fish through electrical failure, electrocuting yourself or anyone else, or burning the house down as a result of an electrical fault. You will need to book a suitable person in advance, and discuss your requirements with him. (See also below and pp134-136).
• Assistance with transporting the tank, carrying it into the house, and putting it in place. Tanks more than 75 cm (36 in) in length require at least two people to carry them, because of their bulk as well as their weight. Some smaller tanks may require two people to move them.

A van or large car may be needed, although some shops will deliver large tanks and even carry them in. An assistant may still be needed to lift the tank into position if it requires any preliminary work, e.g. fitting an external background (see below).

TOOLS AND EQUIPMENT

It is a good idea to think beforehand about what tools, etc, you will need when setting up. It can be inconvenient and cause an annoying delay if you have to go out and buy essential bits and pieces halfway through the setting-up process.
Examples of tools and equipment likely to be required:
• Spirit level for checking the tank is level, and packing pieces (for the stand/cabinet legs) in case adjustment is necessary.
• Glue, adhesive tape, paint, paintbrush, scissors, craft knife, or anything else needed for fitting the chosen background.
• Electrical equipment: suitable screwdriver, wire-strippers, plugs, fuses, cable clips, insulation tape, electrical cable. You will also need either a cable tidy (from the aquarium store) or a four-gang multi-socket (electrical or hardware store), unless you have several wall sockets available at the tank site. Both pieces of equipment can be used to enable all the aquarium electrical devices to be operated from a single plug at the electrical socket. A multi-socket is preferable to a cable tidy, because each electrical circuit – heating, filtration, airpump, lighting – can have its own plug, fitted with a fuse of suitable rating, and can thus be disconnected if necessary. By contrast, all the equipment has to be wired into a cable tidy, and although some circuits are switched, it is not possible, for example, to take the filter to the sink for cleaning without either unwiring it from the cable tidy, or taking along all the other equipment as well! The combination of water and electricity can be particularly hazardous, so a residual current device should be fitted at the mains outlet as a safety precaution. If you are employing a professional electrician, he will probably supply all or some of these electrical bits and pieces – discuss this with him in advance.

If you do not understand anything in the paragraph above, you definitely need to employ a professional electrician!

SHOPPING FOR EQUIPMENT AND DECOR

You should not leave this until setting-up day. The tank and stand should always be ordered in advance unless the tank is small and a standard size, and thus likely to be kept in stock. Even so, it is wise to make sure. Expect to have to pay at least a deposit on the tank when you order it, and probably the full price if it is a non-standard size or shape.

Decide in advance on the type and amount of heating, lighting, and filtration equipment, and discuss with your dealer the actual models, wattages, and so on, that you will require for the tank you are ordering. Although considerations of storage space may mean delaying collection/delivery of a large tank and stand until the day, the remainder of the aquarium equipment is neither particularly heavy nor bulky, and can be purchased in advance, then stored somewhere in the house until required. Alternatively, it can be chosen and paid for, and collected/delivered with the tank and stand.

Rocks, gravel, and wood can be stored in the garage, shed, or even the garden, provided contamination with pesticides/fertilisers is avoided. Wood should, in any case, be purchased well in advance so it can be made safe for use. Live plants, of course, must not be purchased until the aquarium is up and running, and fish must wait until the aquarium is biologically mature. A lot of time can be saved on the day by washing rocks and substrate beforehand. Once clean, these items must, of course, be stored so that they stay that way.

Remember to obtain in advance items not usually available from the aquarium store, e.g. the baseboard and styrofoam padding. Use double-sided adhesive tape to stick the styrofoam to the board, and have it ready, styrofoam side up, when the tank arrives, as then the tank can be set down safely on this base. The whole can then be lifted on to the stand or other base in due course. It will be easier to lift if you rest it on two or more pieces of timber, say 5 x 5 cm (2 x 2 in) and as long as the board is wide. If you want to install the baseboard separately and then the tank, the latter can instead be temporarily set down on these timbers, which should be smooth and free of nails or screws or any projections that might damage the tank. Never put the tank down on the floor – a small stone, from the tread of someone's shoe, can split the bottom of an all-glass tank.

If you are collecting the tank, you can take the board/styrofoam assembly with you to protect the tank bottom in the car/van. During transit all the tank glasses should be protected against knocks (blankets or duvets are ideal) and the tank should be firmly strapped or otherwise held in place.

A properly manufactured aquarium should have no sharp edges, but glass is always dangerous to handle, and if the worst happens, and the aquarium is broken during transportation or handling, then you do not want to add injury to the catalogue of disaster. When moving the tank, those involved should wear stout trousers and long sleeves of thick material no matter how hot the weather, as well as stout shoes and leather gloves (leather gardening gloves are ideal).

PLANNING THE INTERNAL LAYOUT
Some aquarists like to prepare a rough or detailed plan of the decor, while others prefer to design as they go along, placing rocks and wood experimentally to gauge the effect. Either method is perfectly acceptable. The positioning of in-tank equipment must also be taken into account; decor can be used to conceal some items of equipment, but accessibility (for maintenance, adjustment) must be considered as well. It is thus advisable to draw up a plan of where each piece of internal equipment is to be sited, and then design the decor accordingly.

PREPARING THE WATER
If the aquarium water will require time-consuming adjustments to its chemistry or quality, e.g. using reverse osmosis or ion-exchange equipment, then this should be done a day or two before setting-up day.

CLEARING THE DECKS

Unless you are installing only a very small aquarium, make sure you have room to manoeuvre on setting-up day. Move furniture and other obstructions away from the site and the access route.

Arrange that all members of the household not involved, especially children and pets, are kept well out of the way. You will not want an audience or interference, and a dog or cat running between the legs of those carrying a heavy tank can cause a nasty accident.

Protect expensive floor coverings, preferably with polythene sheets (or newspapers and old sheets) as spillages are possible. This precaution should extend to the route the tank will follow through the house to the site if outdoor shoes are likely to be dirty. It will not be practicable to stop on the doorstep and change footwear!

2. SETTING UP THE AQUARIUM

As mentioned at the beginning of this chapter, the diversity of possible combinations of equipment and decor items is such that, of necessity, we can merely offer a roughly sequential list of tips. The aquarist is advised to make a sequential list of all the operations to be undertaken for the specific equipment he has chosen – and follow it. The manufacturer's instructions must be followed when installing each item of equipment.

• If there is no electrical socket close to the tank and an extension electrical lead is needed, then install this before positioning the stand, so it can easily be clipped to the skirting.

• Position the stand and ensure that it is level before placing the aquarium on it. If adjustment is required, then use stout (e.g. hardwood, metal, or exterior grade plywood) packing pieces.

• Fit any external background to the tank before lifting the latter into place. This will be far easier than trying to work between tank and wall.

• Remember that, as their name suggests, under-tank heating mats go under the tank, between it and the styrofoam cushion.

• Likewise, undergravel (UG) filter plates go beneath the substrate, and their uplift pipes should be fitted before any substrate is added, to stop the latter from getting under the plates.

• Fit any internal background that extends beneath the surface of the substrate, again before adding the latter.

• If building elaborate rockwork, the foundation rocks should be placed on the aquarium bottom or UG plates before any substrate is added. If UG is not to be used, it is a good idea to protect the aquarium bottom against rock damage by lining it with a piece of styrofoam (UG plates provide similar protection).

• Add the substrate.

• If using an electric gang socket, fit plugs to electrical equipment, ensuring they have appropriately rated fuses. Connect any separate heaters and thermostats. (If you have hired an electrician, he can be doing this while you are installing background, substrate, and so on). *Do not* plug anything in at this stage.

• Fit airline to any air-powered internal equipment. There is no need to connect the free ends to valves and airpump at this stage, but it is much easier to attach airline to equipment before it is installed in the tank. Estimate the lengths needed, and be generous – airline is cheap and it is better to waste a few pence cutting it a bit too long than to have to fit a new length because it was too short.

• Install hard (non-living) decor items, heaters and thermostats, internal filters. Rocks should be bedded in the gravel or rest securely on the foundation rocks if you are erecting a large and complex structure. Rockwork should be stable – i.e. constructed so that no rock can slip sideways out of place and through the glass, or bring the entire edifice tumbling down. Some aquarists use silicon sealant to glue rocks together, but this means it is impossible to remove a rock or two if this proves necessary (e.g. to catch a fish).

Tip: the plastic suckers provided for attaching heater holders, some filters, and external filter pipes to the aquarium glass are usually reluctant to stay in place. Use silicon sealant to glue them to the glass. Although silicon sealant takes 24 hours to set completely, it forms a waterproof skin within about 30 minutes. Have a tea-break or lunch! (Of course, if the tank arrived before setting-up day you can stick suckers in place in advance. However, this then commits you to a particular position, which may not be convenient when you arrange the decor.)

• The aquarium can now be filled with water. Because no fish are present, it is not necessary to warm or dechlorinate the water at the setting-up stage, or to adjust its pH, but any other water treatments (e.g. demineralisation, nitrate removal) should be performed before the water is added to the aquarium. To avoid disturbing the substrate and other decor, pour the water into a dish (which must be free of detergent residues) or on to a flat rock placed on the substrate.

• Fit any external canister filter(s).

• Fit cover glasses if these are not integral with the hood.

• Feed the tube leads from the fluorescent control unit(s) into the hood compartment that is to hold the tube(s), and attach to the tube(s). This is easiest if done before clipping the tube(s) into place – the next step. Hoods commonly have a rear compartment to house control units and airpumps, with ready-cut slots for leads. However, while it may be easiest to keep electrical equipment in the hood compartment, it is safer to hang it on the wall behind the aquarium, where it cannot accidentally fall into the water or get splashed. Nevertheless, the compartment is a useful place to put the control unit(s) temporarily until the hood is in position, so that they are not suspended from the hood when it is lifted into place.

• Locate the airpump, and connect airlines to it.

• Fit the thermometer.

• Lift the hood into place and locate the lighting control units and airpump on the wall if appropriate.

• At this stage *either*:

– wire up the multi-socket (unless you have bought one with a lead and plug fitted) and plug in all devices

or

– wire all devices into the cable tidy, which will need to be fitted with a lead and plug. The electrical system can now be plugged into the socket, via the residual current device, and switched on. If any device is not working, then first check if it needs to be switched on individually (built-in switch (light units, some airpumps) or cable tidy switch). If you have filled the aquarium with cold water as suggested, then the heating should come on automatically – check the thermostat indicator light(s). If the aquarium was filled with warm water, then the thermostat(s) may not switch on at this juncture. If you need to handle, remove, or adjust any piece of equipment, switch off the electricity supply to the aquarium first.

PLANTING

When the aquarium has warmed up to operating temperature (overnight) it is time to buy and add any live plants required.

Live plants do not take well to being repeatedly planted and uprooted, so it is important to decide where each is to be planted in advance. It is normal to plant taller plants at the rear and ends of the aquarium and shorter ones towards the front. Allow those with spreading leaves sufficient space to grow, even though this may mean the planting looking a little sparse initially. A degree of imagination is required to envisage the ultimate effect when they have rooted and grown.

If you are on a budget, buy one or two stemmed plants that are easily rooted from cuttings (Table 7, Chapter 11) and cut them into pieces about 10 cm (4 in) long – this way you will get three or four plants for the price of one. It is worth doing this anyway, as they will usually root and grow quickly. If you plant the whole purchased stem, which may in any case be 'leggy', then you will be pruning it back soon afterwards. If you use short cuttings, pinch out the tips of long shoots to produce a bushy, attractive plant rather than a single long stem. Cuttings can simply be pushed into the substrate. Horticultural rooting compound must never be used – it is poisonous!

Plants with crowns must be planted with care, with the crown above the surface of the substrate, otherwise the plant will probably die, and certainly not thrive. Corms/bulbs (e.g. waterlilies, *Aponogeton* and *Barclaya* species) should be planted, the right way up, just below the surface of the substrate.

At this time, the aquarium will not contain any nutrients for the plants, so you will need to use an aquarium plant fertiliser. Once the system is matured and contains fish, then artificial fertiliser should not be needed.

3. MATURING THE AQUARIUM

At this stage you will probably be disappointed with the appearance of your aquarium if this is the first one you have set up. It will probably look rather stark: no algae on the rocks; plants looking straggly and sparse (if you have planted to allow for growth); water probably slightly cloudy (it is impossible to get substrate material perfectly clean), and maybe with scum on the surface. And, of course, no fish.

It usually takes some two to four weeks for a tropical freshwater tank and its biological filter to mature, that is, to develop an adequate population of the nitrifying bacteria involved in the nitrogen cycle (Chapter 10). During this maturation period, ammonia and nitrite will peak at dangerous levels, and no fish should be present until these potentially lethal stages are over. Far too many new aquarists allow their enthusiasm to run away with them and add fish too soon, and then have to watch as their new pets fall ill, and usually die, from new tank syndrome (Chapter 21, section 1.2.7).

Small numbers of the necessary bacteria will usually be present even in a newly set-up aquarium, but it is also possible to add a 'bacterial starter', which can be purchased (from the aquarium store) or take the form of a couple of handfuls of substrate from another aquarium (as long as there is no risk of this affecting water chemistry or introducing disease). As there will be no fish wastes for the bacteria to process, they must be fed during the maturation process; again special proprietary products are available, but simply adding a small pinch of flake or granular food each day will have the desired effect. You may read elsewhere that one or two hardy fish, such as guppies (*Poecilia reticulata*) can be used to mature the aquarium with their wastes, but this is cruel; at best this treatment will cause the fish suffering, and they may well die.

During the maturation period you should monitor ammonia and nitrite daily. You will find that first the ammonia, then the nitrite, level will reach a peak (in the 'dangerous to fish' range indicated by the test kit, – this is why no fish should be present!) and then drop away to safe levels. Only when both toxins have peaked and returned to zero is it safe to add fish.

Nowadays products are available that claim to make an aquarium safe for fish immediately, or within a day or two. But it is far safer to use the natural method – if the instant product fails to work (perhaps because it is past its effective 'life'), then the fish will probably die. And there are other advantages to a lengthy maturation period:

• It allows the water to clear of any suspended matter and the bacterial bloom that commonly occurs during the first day or two after a new aquarium is set up.

• It gives the plants an opportunity to root and start growing before they are disturbed in any way by fish.

• It allows water chemistry and temperature to be monitored, and adjusted if necessary.

• It allows the aquarist to monitor hardness and pH for any desirable or undesirable effects from the decor (in both cases usually an increase due to the presence of calcium carbonate).

• It enables the aquarist to make sure all the equipment is working correctly and to replace any that is not.

• It will teach him the essential quality of patience!

4. INTRODUCING THE FISH

Even when the tank and its filtration system are mature, the bacterial population will still be limited, and unable to cope immediately with the load imposed by a tankful of fish on normal rations. It needs to take up the loading gradually. Hence it is normally suggested that the fish should be added a few at a time, over a period of weeks. This not always possible, however – for example if a single large fish is to be kept, or territorial fish likely to attack subsequent new arrivals. In such cases, the only option is to add all the fish, but feed them very lightly initially, gradually increasing their rations until the optimal level is reached. The bacteria are then able to increase their population in line with the slow increase in wastes.

If fish are introduced in batches, then subsequent batches must be quarantined (Chapter 19) to avoid the risk of introducing disease among the already-established, healthy fish.

Tip: If you plan to keep one or two territorial fish (e.g. cichlids) and are introducing your fish in small batches, leave the territorial fish until the final batch. That way they will not harass new fish intruding on their territory.

Purchasing and transporting fish, and the precautions to be taken as regards their physical introduction to the aquarium, are dealt with in Section 1, Chapter 6.

CHAPTER 15

AQUARIUM MAINTENANCE

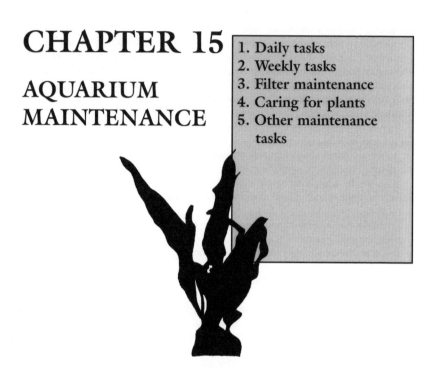

1. Daily tasks
2. Weekly tasks
3. Filter maintenance
4. Caring for plants
5. Other maintenance tasks

Once the aquarium is up and running and fish have been added, routine maintenance is needed to keep everything running smoothly, with the fish in good health and the aquarium looking its best.

Each aquarium will have its own particular maintenance schedule depending on its size, occupants, equipment, and decor (e.g. whether it has live plants). The following are simply suggestions and guidelines – for example, we have suggested water-changing as a weekly activity, but some aquaria may require fewer partial changes, some may require more. The aquarist must devise a schedule suited to the needs of each of his aquaria, based partly on our suggestions, partly on what is found to be necessary and desirable.

Generally speaking, maintenance will require about ten minutes daily, and a one- or two-hour session weekly, with extra time needed for irregular tasks when these become necessary, or if anything goes wrong (Chapter 16).

Remember always to turn off the electricity to the aquarium before working on it *and* to turn it back on again afterwards!

1. DAILY TASKS

These will consist largely of feeding the fish (Chapter 7); making sure that all are present, behaving normally, and in good health (Chapter 18); and checking that all the equipment – heating, filtration, aeration, lighting – is working correctly. Ideally, such checks will be made twice per day.

It is not normally necessary to check water chemistry and quality parameters daily unless slow adjustments are being made (such as to pH), there is a known problem to be monitored (fluctuating pH, measurable ammonia/nitrite), or a possible problem is suspected.

CHECKING THE FISH
The best time to check the fish is at feeding time, when most will come out to feed if they are not already out and about. Nocturnal species may need to be checked after lights out. Most secretive fish will have normal, individual hiding-places, so get to know where these are. If any fish appears unwell or is behaving strangely, attempt to identify the cause (Chapters 5, 20), and take any appropriate action; if the cause cannot be established, keep the fish under close observation.

If any fish has died, remove the corpse immediately and dispose of it safely (Chapter 25).

CHECKING EQUIPMENT
Equipment checks can be made either at feeding time or when the lighting is switched on and off: the temperature should be within the set range, water flowing through the filter, air coming from the airpump, and the lighting working.

If multiple heating devices are in use, it is worth checking that all are working; if one of a pair of heater/stats has failed, the other may keep the aquarium at the right temperature – unless it too fails. It is better to identify and replace failed heating equipment before the aquarium is left completely without functional heating. If the thermostat indicator light indicates that the heater is on, then it should be possible to see convection currents in the water just above an immersion heater. Alternatively, switch the electricity off and feel the heater (with care – it may be very hot!) to see if it is warm. Under-tank heating mats, and cable heaters buried in the substrate, can be checked only by monitoring tank temperature.

If the filter output is inadequate, the media may be clogged (see Filter Maintenance, below).

2. WEEKLY TASKS

Weekly maintenance consists largely of replacing a portion of the aquarium water with fresh, of checking water parameters (pH, ammonia, nitrite, nitrate), and general tidying: siphoning off any detritus ('mulm') that has not been collected by the filter, cleaning algae from the viewing glass(es), and tidying the plants (see Caring for Plants, below).

WATER CHANGING
The size and frequency of water changes varies from aquarium to aquarium, and needs to be established with reference to nitrate levels. A good starting point is 25% weekly, but if nitrate levels start to creep up the schedule may need to be amended. However, if the nitrate increase is slow, a single extra water change from time to time is usually sufficient. Except in emergencies, such as poisoning (Chapter

21, section 1.2), no more than a third of the aquarium water should be changed at one time.

Water changes are effected by siphoning off the requisite amount of water and replacing it with fresh, dechlorinated, water whose chemistry and temperature should be a close match with those of the aquarium water. Water is usually taken from the bottom of the aquarium, so that any mulm can be siphoned off at the same time. Be careful not to siphon off small fish! Some siphon tubes have guards to prevent this, or a piece of nylon net (e.g. net curtain, or from an old aquarium net) can be used, held in place with a rubber band.

When adding the new water, avoid disturbing the fish and decor by either siphoning the water from a bucket placed on the hood, or pouring the new water over your free hand.

Substrate cleaning

Some aquarists like to use a gravel cleaner when siphoning off water during water changes. These devices can be used simply to remove loose mulm from the surface of the substrate, or to turn the substrate over and extract any solids accumulated there. This may sound a good idea, but bear in mind that regular disturbance of the substrate with one of these devices will affect the biological processing of wastes that takes place on the surface of the substrate (as well as in the filter). The efficiency of undergravel filtration may be seriously compromised by regular disturbance of the filter bed. Disturbance of the substrate in unfiltered aquaria may cause serious ammonia and nitrite problems as the bulk of 'nitrogen cycle bacteria' will be found coating the grains in the surface layer of the substrate, where the oxygen they require is available. Bury this surface layer by gravel cleaning, and most of the useful bacteria will be eliminated as there will be insufficient oxygen for them in the lower layers.

Provided the substrate is not too large-grained, then unprocessed faeces and uneaten food will not penetrate to its lower layers; the 'dirt' found in the substrate of a healthy aquarium is normally simply inert residue from bacterial processing. Substrates may nevertheless occasionally need thorough cleaning if they clog with these residues; when this is necessary, then temporarily reduce fish waste output rate (and hence bacteria workload) by reducing feeding (see also biological filter maintenance, below); avoid cleaning the gravel and the biological filter at the same time.

ALGAE REMOVAL

A number of devices (algae magnets, algae scrapers) can be purchased for this task. Care is required when using some types of metal-bladed scraper as these can slice through the silicon sealant at the angles of the aquarium, with dire consequences. Although this may not result in an immediate leak, it will reduce the strength of the glass-to-glass join, such that the aquarium must be stripped down, resealed, and set up again from scratch. Plastic-bladed scrapers are safer!

Visible and invisible wastes

Points which many aquarists fail to appreciate:

• The aquarium water passes continuously through the filter, so the aquarium and the filter are one system, even if the filter is external to the aquarium. Thus, removing solid wastes with a filter does not remove them from the aquarium system, any more than sweeping dirt under a mat removes it from the house.

• Solid wastes are not directly harmful; the invisible (dissolved in the aquarium water) products of the breakdown of wastes may be harmful if allowed to accumulate to toxic levels. In a biologically mature aquarium system the nitrogen cycle and water changes prevent fish from being poisoned by the products of their own wastes (ammonia, nitrite, nitrate).

• The solid residues of bacterial activity (the accumulated fine 'dirt' in a biological filter) are inert and harmless.

• Fish continuously excrete invisible, highly toxic, ammonia as well as visible faeces, so simply removing solids will not eliminate the need to process fish wastes.

• The presence of solid wastes in the aquarium is not a disaster, provided the aquarium system is biologically mature. Wastes are broken down by nitrogen cycle bacteria in the mature aquarium as well as in the filter. And the invisible products of that breakdown will be passing through the filter, even if the latter is not collecting the solids. Faeces are unsightly and may transmit any infectious disease present, but their presence is not directly harmful to fish.

• On the other hand, it is possible – and frequently happens – that an aquarium may look spotless and have crystal-clear water, but have a lethally high level of invisible ammonia or nitrite if it lacks sufficient nitrogen cycle activity to process these invisible toxins. This often happens where aquarists keep fish in bare, unfiltered, tanks and siphon off solids in the misguided belief that this provides optimum cleanliness, but can be a problem in any aquarium. Undesirably high levels of nitrate, resulting from inadequate water changes, can also occur in spotless aquaria.

3. FILTER MAINTENANCE

The filter maintenance schedule will depend on the type of filtration (mechanical, chemical, biological – Chapter 10), the type and model of filter, and the type(s) of medium used. The manufacturers' instructions may offer guidance. Some media, such as filter floss and filter foam, can be cleaned (though ultimately they will need replacing); some (e.g. zeolite) can be regenerated; some (usually chemical media such as peat or carbon) may need to be replaced regularly.

• **Mechanical filters**, i.e. those used solely to trap solids, with no biological action, need to be cleaned out regularly, possibly as often as daily, before the solids are broken down into toxic products such as ammonia.

• **Chemical filters** may require renewal of the media; media that require only very occasional renewal (for example, limestone chippings) may occasionally require rinsing to remove any solids that have been trapped, if filter flow rate is being impeded by clogging.

• **Biological filters** should be left undisturbed as much as possible. Only part of the biological filter medium should ever be cleaned or replaced at any one time; one-third of the total should be the normal maximum. If the filter is cleaned out completely, or all the media replaced, the aquarium will be left without effective biological filtration for days, possibly weeks, while the bacteria regenerate their numbers in cleaned media, or colonise new. As a result the tank may suffer high ammonia and nitrite levels and fish deaths are likely. Cleaning of media should consist solely of gentle rinsing in a bucket of aquarium water. The chlorine in tap water is bactericidal, and very hot water will also kill the beneficial filter bacteria.

The highly inadvisable practice of regularly 'hoovering' undergravel filter beds will also result in the loss of large numbers of useful bacteria.

If a biological filter causes problems by regular clogging, it may be possible to trap the bulk of solids mechanically, for example with a layer of filter floss or sponge which is then cleaned regularly, leaving the biological part of the filter untouched. If the aquarium has two or more biological filters, a sensible approach is to clean them in rotation.

Whenever the biological filtration requires maintenance, reduce the loading (fish wastes) while the bacteria (re)colonise the cleaned or replaced medium; reduce feeding 24 hours before filter maintenance and gradually increase back to normal levels over a three-to six-day period afterwards.

It is wise to monitor ammonia levels in the aquarium on a daily basis for a few days after biological filter maintenance.

Any biological filter should be maintained and returned to service as quickly as possible, as the beneficial bacteria may die if deprived of the flow of oxygenated water for more than an hour or so.

• **Combination filters** (those where various media are used mechanically, chemically, and/or biologically), may need attention to their media at different intervals. For example, a filter may contain a layer of floss to trap solids (mechanical), a bag of peat to acidify the water (chemical), and gravel to act biologically, with the water passing through the media in that order. The floss will clog quickly and perhaps need washing every week; the peat will probably need to be renewed every two or three weeks; one-third of the gravel may be washed at most every six weeks, less frequently, if possible. If the biological medium needs attention more frequently, then the media capacity of the filter is probably inadequate for the aquarium. In some cases, this may mean simply that the aquarium is overpopulated and/or the fish overfed, rather than having anything to do with aquarium size *per se*.

4. CARING FOR PLANTS

Aquarium plants, like house or garden plants, need regular attention. Dead leaves need to be removed, some require pruning, and artificial fertiliser may be required if the fish wastes are not generating sufficient nitrate.

Some aquarists have aquatic green fingers, some do not! Equally, some plants seem to 'like' some aquaria, others do not. This is sometimes due to water chemistry or lighting preferences, but sometimes is apparently inexplicable. If you find you cannot grow a particular plant species at all, or in a particular aquarium, do not despair. Try other species and you will probably find a number that do well.

PRUNING AND THINNING

Those plants that have leaves arranged on stems, e.g. *Hygrophila* spp., generally have a continuous upward urge, and will commonly grow up to the surface and above or along it. The lower growths then often become relatively or completely leafless, and hence unattractive. Such plants need to be cut back hard so they can sprout again, this time with several shoots sprouting from the leaf axils below the cut. If the growing tips of these shoots are pinched out, they too will branch, producing an attractive bushy plant instead of a single long, leggy stem. Prunings can be used as cuttings to produce new plants to fill any gaps to decorate other aquaria, or be given to aquarist friends.

Some plants (e.g. *Vallisneria* spp.) reproduce by runners, and can quickly choke an aquarium with rampant greenery. These may need to be thinned out regularly, and again the young plants can be used elsewhere or given away.

FERTILISATION

Think long and hard before using artificial fertilisers. Plants utilise nitrate produced from fish wastes as their 'food'. Yet even in planted aquaria, much of the effort involved in fishkeeping is aimed at removing excess nitrate via water changes. Most aquaria have a higher fish-to-plant ratio than an equivalent volume of natural water, and most aquarium fish generate more wastes than their wild cousins, because of their generous diet. So do you really want – or need – to put nitrate into your aquarium in the form of artificial fertiliser?

If your plants are not thriving, but your water has measurable nitrate present, then the problem is probably nothing to do with lack of nutrients. If artificial fertiliser is to be used, preference should be given to the pelleted slow-release type placed in the substrate near the roots, rather than adding fertiliser directly to the water.

Carbon dioxide fertilisation and its inherent dangers are dealt with in Chapter 10.

5. OTHER MAINTENANCE TASKS

COMPENSATING FOR EVAPORATION

A properly covered aquarium will not normally suffer excessive evaporation, which can, however, be a problem with open-topped aquaria. If the aquarium water level drops through evaporation, it will need to be refilled ('topped up'), using properly matched water, as during water changes.

Because only pure water evaporates, leaving behind the minerals it contains, topping-up (unless with mineral-free – such as distilled, RO – water) may cause a probably undesirable increase in mineral content. The need for topping-up can be avoided by preventing evaporation, by using cover glasses or a tight-fitting hood.

MAINTAINING THE LIGHTING

The light output of fluorescent tubes diminishes with time, and aquarists growing plants often choose to replace them regularly, say every six months, instead of waiting until they cease to work at all.

If the light fails to come on, this does not always mean the tube has failed. The control unit consists of two parts: the 'choke' and the 'starter'. The latter takes the form of a small sealed cylinder (often white plastic) which plugs into the unit, often so that only its circular end is visible. Starters do not last forever and, without a functional starter, the tube will not light when the unit is switched on. A tube at the end of its life usually flickers for some days (or weeks) before failing completely. If the tube takes a long time to come on, or will not come on properly, then the problem may be either the tube or the starter; if a previously healthy tube suddenly fails to come on, the problem is most likely the starter. A new starter, of appropriate rating, can be obtained from electrical, and most hardware, stores.

MAINTAINING THE AERATION EQUIPMENT
• Vibrator airpumps, and sometimes non-return valves, contain air filters which require cleaning or renewal from time to time.
• Both may also contain rubber valves which perish in time and need to be replaced. New 'valve blocks' can be purchased for airpumps, while non-return valves are normally replaced completely.
• Diffusers often clog – sometimes with bacteria, and, in hard water, with calcium carbonate – and require replacement.
• Piston airpumps require regular oiling and periodic factory servicing – see manufacturer's instructions regarding both points.
• Airline eventually becomes hard, inflexible, and sometimes brittle, particularly where it has been immersed in water. If this is a problem, replace or cut back.

COOLING IN HOT WEATHER
In some countries aquaria may overheat during periods of hot weather, especially if exposed to direct sunlight. If possible, cut out the sunlight (curtains, blinds) before overheating occurs. An overheated aquarium can be cooled by performing a water change, refilling with cooler water – slowly, so as to avoid too rapid a change in aquarium temperature. Alternatively, plastic bags filled with cold water or ice cubes can be suspended in the tank to act as coolers.

CHAPTER 16

AQUARIUM CRISES
(What if my aquarium...?)

From time to time every aquarist is confronted by a situation which might be described as an emergency, or at least a crisis. This chapter covers a few of the most common such crises, as well as a number of other problems affecting the aquarium as a whole, utilising the What if...? format also used for problems involving fish behaviour and fish health in Chapters 5 and 20, respectively.

1. What if my aquarium leaks?

This problem can take two forms: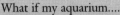

• Damage to, or failure of, the silicon sealant joints. Some metal-bladed algae-removers can slice through silicon sealant; the joint may have been less than perfect when the tank was manufactured; or the sealant may be degenerating through age (suspect this in tanks ten or more years old).

• Cracking of the glass.

The action to be taken will depend on the severity and location of the problem.

• Slight leaks from small faults in the silicon sealant can often be remedied by applying extra silicon to the outside of the tank where it is leaking. Lower the water level below the leak if possible, but in any case, lower the water level as this will reduce pressure and hence water flow through the leak, making it easier to seal. Clean the outside of the glass immediately around the leak with a piece of tissue moistened with white spirit, dab away any water with a clean tissue, and apply a blob of silicon quickly before more water escapes and wets the glass.

• If the tank is leaking badly from its bottom half, the fish may need to be evacuated as for What if no. 2, What if my aquarium breaks?, as that may be the sequel.

• If the tank is leaking badly from a silicon joint or horizontal crack in its upper half, then lower the water level below the leak, ensuring heaters and thermostats remain below water level. UG uplift pipes may need to be cut shorter; some internal power filters can, if necessary, be laid on their sides. The tank can be run like this while a new tank is obtained and set up.

• If the tank has a vertical or diagonal crack in its upper half, proceed as for the previous point, but bear in mind that fish evacuation may become necessary if the crack spreads downwards. Lower the water level as far as practicable to reduce pressure on the glass. Wipe the glass around the crack (inside and outside the tank) clean and dry with a clean detergent-free cloth, then apply silicon sealant along the crack – again inside and outside the aquarium. A glass patch, or bar, siliconed to the outside of the glass, across the crack, will strengthen the temporary mend.

TIP

It is possible to dismantle all-glass tanks and reassemble them, either to renew ageing silicon or to replace a broken pane, but if this is done professionally, the cost is likely to be at least as high as that of a new tank, because of the labour involved in the dismantling, cleaning, and reassembling of the glass.

If the problem is the result of algae-scraper damage to the internal sealant, the tank can easily be re-sealed and some aquarists feel competent to do this themselves.

---

2. What if my aquarium breaks?

This is every aquarist's nightmare. If you are lucky, you may be there and able to rescue the fish.

Before you do anything else, switch off the power to the tank, even if fish are flapping around on the carpet, and put on shoes capable of protecting your feet against broken glass. You will be no use to the fish if you are in Accident and Emergency, and an extra minute on the floor will not make much difference.

If you have another operational tank available, and its water chemistry is not too different to that of the broken aquarium, then siphon off a bucket of its water, pick the fish up and rinse off dirt in the bucket before placing them in the aquarium.

If you do not have another tank, or the water chemistry is totally wrong, try to salvage a bucket or two of water from the broken tank, and put the fish in it. Ideally, rinse them in one bucketful then transfer to another. Rescue the airpump and aerate the water. Phone anyone you can think of who might be able to help you with temporary accommodation for the fish, including local dealers.

If there is no other option, rinse the bathtub thoroughly, half-fill with cold water, add dechlorinator and adjust pH to that required. Pour in boiling water to bring the water up to the approximate operating temperature. Install heaters, filtration and aeration. If you have been using UG filters, beg, borrow, steal, or buy an external power filter and fill it with gravel (mature filter medium) from the broken tank.

If the disaster occurs in your absence, you may return to find only corpses. It is still worth picking the fish up and putting them in well-aerated water to see if any recover. Again, switch off the aquarium electricity supply first – the equipment may be ruined but it may still be 'live'.

> **TIP**
>
> A fish box, if clean and undamaged (i.e. does not leak) can be used as a temporary small aquarium. Note that styrofoam may melt if in contact with an aquarium heater (a heater guard should prevent this). Fish boxes are easily broken, so must be treated with care if used in this way. If possible, use one with a cardboard outer for protection.

> **TIP**
>
> Fortunately, the nightmare does not become reality for all aquarists. It is, however, a good idea to insure against the damage to carpets and furniture that may be caused by such an accident. It may also be possible to insure the tank against accidental breakage (i.e. if something hits and breaks the glass) or vandalism (e.g. by burglars), but not against failure of the silicon sealant. Insurance of fish against loss through this type of accident is possible, but normally only by special arrangement rather than a standard policy – and at a price.

3. What if my aquarium heating has failed?

This problem can take two forms:
• The heating has failed 'off' (usually because the heater element has burnt out, sometimes because the thermostat is defective) and the tank temperature has dropped (or is dropping) to room temperature.
• The heating has failed 'on', usually because the thermostat is defective and the tank temperature has risen (or is rising) dangerously.
In both cases the defective equipment must be replaced. A sticking thermostat may sometimes unstick, but should not be trusted. Next time, you might not discover the problem in time...

The wise aquarist always keeps a spare heater/stat for emergencies when the aquarium store is closed; the foolish aquarist must improvise. The aquarium can be kept at the appropriate temperature by raising room temperature to aquarium temperature, or by standing/floating containers (e.g. plastic drink bottles or plastic bags, respectively) of hot water in the aquarium as heaters. The hot water must be renewed periodically.

Fish that are chilled or overheated need to be brought back to normal temperature with care; this topic is dealt with in Chapter 21, section 1.4.1.

4. What if my aquarium power filter has broken down?

If you use a power filter, it is as well to be prepared for this emergency. There are a number of options, depending on circumstances. Remember you have only a couple of hours to effect a repair or replacement before the filter bacteria start dying.
• If the aquarium store is open, obtain and fit the necessary spare part. If you do not know what is wrong, take the filter with you to the store. If it is irreparable, or the

---

TIP

It is sensible to split the required heater wattage between two heaters: if one fails, the tank will not be left completely unheated. (This is, however, impracticable in small aquaria). Two heater/stats used in tandem confer the additional advantage that if one thermostat fails 'on', the other will remain off, and reduce the likelihood of serious overheating. Monitoring tank temperature twice daily, and checking regularly that heating equipment is working properly, will usually obviate heating failure disasters. An electronic thermometer with a built-in alarm is another useful safeguard.

---

part needs to be ordered, buy a replacement filter and transfer the biologically mature media into it. If you buy the same model as before, you can use the defunct one for spares, unless you want to repair it (a spare for future emergencies).

• If the aquarium store is closed, but you have another tank up and running, then move the fish to it, provided the water chemistry is a reasonable match, there is room for them, and there will be no conflict with fish already housed there (a divider could be used to solve this problem). If the other tank is too small, consider moving its occupants and filter to the problem aquarium if it is large enough. To avoid problems caused by tank overcrowding and filter overloading, do not feed the fish, or feed only very lightly.

• If the aquarium store is closed, but you have a couple of air-driven box filters and an air supply, then fill the box filters with media from the defunct filter, or with zeolite (to remove ammonia). Do not feed the fish, or feed only lightly.

• If the aquarium store is closed and you have no box filters available, phone your fishkeeping friends to see if any can lend you a filter. This could be a mature biological filter, a power filter into which you can put your mature media, or a couple of plastic box filters. Alternatively, see if anyone can accommodate your fish until the filter is repaired/replaced and the aquarium safe for them again. Borrowing equipment or boarding out fish runs a risk of introducing any disease present in your friend's aquarium, but is usually a safer option than ammonia poisoning.

• If all else fails, reduce rising ammonia levels by changing up to 30% of the water several times per day (and night) until you have functional biological filtration again. Do not feed the fish at all.

5. What if my aquarium air supply fails?

This will usually mean that the airline has become disconnected at some point, or that the diaphragm in the vibrator pump has split. A spare diaphragm should *always* be kept in stock and replaced as soon as it is used.

If the pump motor has failed, a new pump must be purchased. If the filtration is air-driven, then this must be as a matter of urgency; otherwise it may be possible to arrange the filtration so as to increase aeration (if necessary – i.e. fish showing signs of hypoxia, Chapter 21, section 1.3.3). For example, you can use a spray bar with an external filter (many come provided with one; if not, any perforated tube will do, even the flexible return pipe, duly drilled); or you can raise an internal filter so its outlet is at the surface.

An emergency air supply can be contrived in a number of ways (if the filtration is air-powered):

• Inflate an airbed, car tyre inner tube, or similar, and use this as an air reservoir, bleeding air slowly using a clamp to regulate the flow. If no clamp is available, improvise with a clothes peg, twisted wire, or similar.
• Use an airbed/tyre pump to pump air through the system for five minutes every hour (day and night).

> **TIP**
> A battery-operated airpump is a useful investment, not only for airpump failure, but also in the event of power failure.

6. What if my aquarium has no electricity?

First check to see if the rest of the house has electricity. If so, the fuse may have blown in the multi-socket or in the plug at the wall socket. Someone may have switched off the socket or unplugged the aquarium supply. The fuse for the electrical circuit may have blown in the fuse box.

If the house has no electricity, first check the circuit-breaker (if fitted, this is usually close to the fuse box where the power enters the house). If this is in the 'on' position, then the problem is with the electrical supply to the house.

The blowing of a fuse or the tripping of a circuit-breaker may be simply 'one of those things', rectifiable by replacing the fuse or resetting the circuit-breaker. But it may mean there is a short circuit in the domestic or aquarium wiring. Unless you are competent to deal with this type of problem, call an electrician immediately. You cannot afford to wait long as your tank may be cooling already, and your filter bacteria will start dying within an hour or so.

If the problem is a power outage (power cut), call the electricity company immediately to report it – never assume they know! If they are already aware of the problem, ask for an estimate of the duration of the outage. If it is likely to be more than an hour or two, or they do not know, then action is necessary:

• Heating
Assuming the ambient temperature is cooler than desired tank temperature, you will need to prevent heat loss and/or improvise a way of warming the water.
– If the room heating does not depend on electricity, try to raise the room temperature to the required tank temperature.
– If you cannot raise room temperature, cover the aquarium with items such as duvets, sleeping bags, blankets, and so on, to prevent heat loss. Most heat loss will be upwards (heat rises) so pay special attention to the top of the tank – if you have any styrofoam (e.g. fish box lids) put this on top of the hood under the blankets etc. Improvise heating as for What if no. 3, What if my aquarium heating has failed?.
• Filtration and aeration.
Aeration and air-driven filtration can be dealt with as for What if no. 5, What if my aquarium air supply fails?.

Power filtration presents greater problems. What if no 4, What if my aquarium power filter has broken down? may suggest possibilities, e.g. alternative air-powered filtration. Allowing oxygenated water from the tank to run through an external canister (if the filter outlet pipe is put in a bucket below filter level this will happen by siphonage) once per hour may help keep the bacteria alive. Insert an airline into the canister of internal power filters to oxygenate them. Even though the aquarium may be left unfiltered, it will help to have a functional biological filter when the power resumes. Do not feed the fish during the outage; monitor ammonia levels during the first few ensuing days. If necessary, refer to What if no.7, What if my aquarium has a serious problem with ammonia, nitrite, or other poisoning?.

Do not be afraid to keep phoning the electricity company for progress reports. Having some idea of the likely length of the outage will enable you to, for example, organise help so you can get some sleep if the power is likely to be off for long.

TIP
If you have several aquaria and your area is subject to regular outages, buying a petrol-driven generator may be a sensible option. If you have only one or two tanks, a battery-operated airpump and air-powered filtration may be a better option than power filters.

---

7. What if my aquarium has a serious problem with ammonia, nitrite, or other poisoning?
See Chapter 21, section 1.2, for the remedial action necessary.

8. What if my aquarium is overgrown with algae?
See Chapter 22: Algae and Cyanobacteria.

9. What if my aquarium has been invaded by strange creepy-crawlies?
A number of aquatic creatures sometimes establish themselves in the aquarium. Most are harmless to fish, but their presence may indicate an underlying hygiene problem, and some may be carriers of diseases. See Chapter 22, Aquarium Pests.

10. What if my aquarium water is cloudy or a 'funny' colour?
Clouding or colouring of the aquarium water is not a disease in itself, but it, or its underlying causes, can lead to serious health problems in the resident fish.

The aquarium water may become cloudy or coloured for a number of reasons:
• Bacterial bloom (proliferation of bacteria in the water). This is usually seen only in newly set up aquaria and can be expected to dissipate naturally during the maturation period. It is highly unlikely that a bacterial bloom will occur in an established aquarium; such an event would be indicative of such atrocious organic pollution that in all probability the fish would already be dead. Any survivors of such a catastrophe should be moved to alternative accommodation while the aquarium is cleaned out and set up again from scratch (and properly matured).
• Incorrect use of chemical pH adjusters – i.e. failure to follow the manufacturer's instructions, in particular if the chemicals are added to the aquarium neat instead of pre-diluted. This sometimes results in the coating of decor and clouding of the water with a whitish precipitate. If this distresses the fish, reaccommodate them immediately as in cases of acute poisoning (Chapter 21, section 1.2.1).
• A bloom of unicellular algae ('green water', see Chapter 22), often associated with over-bright lighting and high nitrate levels, and hence possibly indicative of underlying problems with equipment, diet, or maintenance.
• Wooden decor items, filtration through peat, and use of peat extract may all stain the water tea-coloured. This is usually harmless (unless accompanied by poisoning

or undesirable changes in pH) and actually typical of the natural environment of some fish (and hence desirable as long as the water remains perfectly clear).

• Some medications (e.g. Acriflavin and Methylene blue) may also stain the water. Many types of staining can be remedied by filtration over activated carbon, but this will also negate the chemical effects of some water-staining medications.

• Suspended material in the water. This may stem from any of a number of causes:

– Dirt from improperly cleaned substrate or other decor. The debris will settle or be filtered out during that essential maturation period before fish are added.

– Material which has accumulated in the substrate over a period of time, and has been subsequently stirred up (accidentally by the aquarist during maintenance, or deliberately by digging/sifting fish). If the aquarium filtration is adequate, it will soon clear up the mess.

– Overpowered undergravel filters sometimes draw/push (reverse flow) detritus right through the substrate and spew it out into the water.

– Inadequate filtration – i.e. filter not trapping detritus.

– Particles of food escaping from the gills of feeding fish. This problem is common with some types of (usually large) fish and some foods. The particles usually settle out quickly into the substrate or are picked up by the filter, but may cause an organic overload leading to problems with ammonia (Chapter 21, section 1.2.3), nitrite (*ibid*, 1.2.10), and/or nitrate (*ibid*, 1.2.8), or encourage the proliferation of some aquarium pests (Chapter 22).

– Foods which disintegrate or release particles before ingestion by the fish. Such foods may include mammal meat (coagulating blood), poor-quality dried foods, and frozen foods that have not been defrosted and strained. Again, there is a risk of organic pollution.

– Tiny particles of substrate. Coral sand is the commonest offender, and its sharp particles can irritate (evidenced by scratching) and damage delicate gill tissue.

TIP

With some of these problems, the time lapse between cause and visible effect is short (seconds, hours, or a few days), such that the connection is generally obvious. What many aquarists fail to realise is that, while cloudy or discoloured water is not normally harmful *per se*, its underlying causes may have other, invisible, harmful effects. If the fish are unwell, they assume that remedying the visible problem is sufficient response, and are mystified when the fish remain ill or die. It is thus essential to monitor the water for other problems, both at the time of the visible pollution and for a week or two subsequently, and to bear in mind that any fish health problem over the next few weeks can perhaps be traced back to this earlier event.

---

11. What if my aquarium water has scum on its surface?

This was a problem which commonly beset aquarists in the past, when aquaria were filtered by air-driven box filters, or run on a balanced basis (few fish, many plants) such that a filter was deemed unnecessary. Now that almost every aquarist uses a powerful motorised filtration system regardless of whether it is necessary or desirable, scum is rarely seen. This is a pity as its presence or absence (because there is none, rather than because the filter has dissipated it) is a useful indicator regarding the health of the aquarium.

The cause of a layer of scum should be identified and eliminated, as scum may inhibit the vital gas exchange that takes place at the air/water interface, ensuring the oxygen supply of the aquarium occupants.

• Scum on the surface of newly set up aquaria may be caused by bacterial activity or floating particles of dirt (from the substrate, which can never be washed perfectly clean). It normally dissipates within a few days, during the maturation period.

• Oily scum on the surface of a mature aquarium may be a function of the food offered. Although the scum is unlikely to harm the fish, it may indicate that the food is unsuitable.

• Oily scum may indicate contamination by fumes if the room is heated by a self-contained oil or paraffin heater. This should be cause for concern, as such fumes may cause poisoning (Chapter 21, section 1.2.1). If alternative room heating is impracticable, then the aquarium hood should be tight-fitting to prevent direct ingress of fumes, and the air-pump (if used) should be sited in an unpolluted area, or the air pumped through a water-filled pre-filter (see below).

See also What if no. 10, What if my aquarium water is cloudy or a 'funny' colour?

Home-made pre-filter for removing pollutants from the air supply.

The air bubbles through the water, which traps the pollutants.

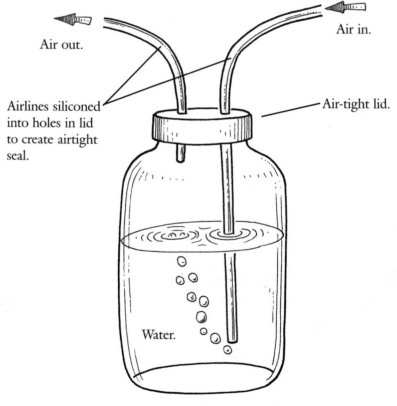

Air out.

Air in.

Airlines siliconed into holes in lid to create airtight seal.

Air-tight lid.

Water.

12. What if my aquarium has to be left while I go on holiday?
Unless you have an aquarist friend prepared to perform routine maintenance (e.g. water changes) in your absence, then your aquarium must make do without for as long as you are away. Ensure water quality is optimal before you depart, if necessary making additional partial water changes to lower nitrate to minimal levels. Perform filter maintenance if this is due (or will be before you return). Check that all equipment is working properly. This final 'servicing' of the aquarium should take place two or three days before you leave, so you can make sure all is working correctly and that water parameters are optimal before you go.

If you are going to be absent for more than a week, the fish must be put on greatly reduced rations to ensure water quality does not degenerate in the absence of the usual water changes. Reduce feeding to holiday levels (see below) at the time of the final water change – it is a serious mistake to feed the fish heavily for the last few days because they are going to go short. The extra food will not give the fish 'reserves' to see them through, but it will lead to an increase in nitrate and deterioration in water quality – the last thing you want at this stage!

If possible, arrange for someone to come in each day to check that the aquarium temperature is in the correct range, that the aeration and filter(s) are working, and that the fish appear to be in good health. This person can also feed the fish at whatever interval you decide is necessary. If the 'minder' is not a fishkeeper, they should be provided with the telephone number of someone who is prepared to come over and sort out any problem that may occur. You should leave a selection of spares (e.g. heater/stat, airpump diaphragm, light tube) and some money to buy anything else that may be needed (or come to an arrangement with your dealer whereby he will allow credit to your minder on your behalf).

As far as feeding is concerned, fish are generally very easy to cater for during holidays. Healthy adult fish can safely be left for a week without food. For longer periods, arrangements should be made for someone to come in occasionally. If the minder is not an experienced fishkeeper, there is a genuine risk that he may overfeed. One way to avoid this is to provide measured portions of food, with instructions to feed one portion each day (or some other suitable time interval). The individual portions can be stored in small airtight containers, such as 35mm photographic film canisters.

Fry or very young fish should not be left without food for long periods of time; they do require regular feeding else they may starve. For this reason, it is wise to avoid attempting to spawn fish prior to taking a vacation.

TIP
Holiday feeder blocks are available commercially. These consist of dried food in a plaster of Paris (gypsum = hydrated calcium sulphate) base, which dissolves slowly to release the food particles. These blocks are unsuitable for aquaria containing acid-water fish (such as Amazonian species) because they increase pH. In any case, it is better to arrange for regulated amounts of food to be fed at regulated intervals. Holiday blocks can, however, be useful if your fish have inconsiderately produced fry just before your holiday!

13. What if my aquarium is in a room that needs decorating?
Decorating the room can present various problems. From the domestic viewpoint, it may be impossible to get at the wall behind the tank or to take up the carpet if required, while the fish may be poisoned (Chapter 21, section 1.2) by fumes, dust, and other fall-out getting into their tank. The general disturbance in the room, plus vibrations from hammers, sanders, etc, may be extremely stressful, and there is also the risk of damage to the tank.

Various options are available:

• Move the aquarium to another room, well away from fumes and other hazards. Switch off the aquarium, and siphon off about two-thirds of the water, saving it in suitable containers (buckets, brewing bins). Next, catch the fish and place in one or more of the buckets/bins. Remove all decor (if the tank, with substrate, can be carried, it is best to leave the substrate untouched; this is essential if UG filters are used, unless an alternative filter has been matured for temporary use). Carry the tank, on its baseboard, to the alternative site; either move the base as well, or site the tank on a suitable area of floor, still on its baseboard. Set the tank up again, using the old water and topping up with suitably prepared new water. To minimise stress, the whole operation should be carried out as quickly as possible – plan it in advance. Keep intervening doors shut during the decorating so that fumes cannot penetrate to the new site. When the decorating is over, the move must, of course, be made in reverse.

• Set up another tank, with minimal but adequate decor, in another room and mature it, then move the fish to it during the decorating. The main tank must be broken down and moved away from the fumes, etc, or sealed up as described below.

• Ask a friend, or your dealer, to accommodate the fish for the necessary period. Ensure they will be able to provide the correct water chemistry, or else slowly adjust the chemistry of your tank water to match theirs, over a period of weeks. Remember: there is a risk of the fish contracting disease in someone else's tank. Again, the main tank must be moved away from the fumes, etc, or sealed up as described below.

• Seal the top of the tank with several layers of clingfilm (plastic food wrap), ensuring a tight seal round cables and airlines, etc. Switch off the lights first, and leave them off, so the heat from them does not overheat the tank or melt the plastic film. Move airpumps to another, fume-free, room (extra airline will be needed for this) to avoid pumping contaminated air into the aquarium. As the aquarium is sealed, it will have to rely entirely on aeration for its oxygen supply; at the same time, it must be fitted with an air outlet to relieve the pressure from the air constantly pumped in. This should be a piece of plastic tubing (airline will do) opening into the airspace above the aquarium water – if it enters the water, then water will escape rather than air! This air outlet should be fitted before the tank is sealed, and should also extend away from the fumes. Under normal circumstances, the pressure of escaping air should prevent fumes from entering, but if the electricity has to be switched off at any stage, a contamination problem could then occur. Cover the tank with a layer of blankets or similar to protect against knocks.

A tank can be sealed up like this with or without fish present; obviously, if fish are present, the time the tank can be left sealed will be limited to a few days. If decorating is likely to take weeks, the fish must be housed elsewhere. If the fish are left in the aquarium, they must be regularly monitored, in particular for signs of poisoning. Plants must also be taken into consideration – they will not survive for weeks without light. The aquarium must be kept running even if the fish are moved, in order to maintain biological activity (if the electricity supply in the room is likely to be cut off for more than an hour or two, then make sure you have a suitable extension lead to provide a power supply from another room). The room must be completely free of fumes before the tank is unsealed again.

SECTION III
THE FISH IN HEALTH AND ILLNESS

The control and treatment of disease in tropical aquarium fish differs markedly from that in most other pets and domesticated animals. Because fish live in water rather than air, a visit to the veterinarian is not simply a matter of taking the animal on a lead or in a basket – its environment has to be taken, too.

Fish are not used to being handled regularly, so being packed up and transported to the vet can be extremely stressful, and lead to further deterioration in the patient's health, perhaps even its demise. Further handling at the veterinary surgery may exacerbate this problem. At the same time, the cost of a home visit by the vet is likely to be regarded as prohibitively expensive, vis-a-vis the monetary value of the fish. Indeed, many aquarists regard any kind of veterinary treatment for fish as unjustifiable on a cost basis. For these reasons, actual veterinary treatment of fish is the exception rather than the norm. As a consequence, very few veterinarians have much, if any, experience of diagnosis and treatment of fish diseases. This task instead falls largely on the aquarist himself, perhaps in consultation with a professional fish health consultant (Chapter 23), or with other, usually more experienced, aquarists.

Another significant difference between aquarium fish and other pets is that the limited volume of their environment renders them extremely vulnerable to disease problems. The air that we – and our dogs, cats, budgerigars, etc – breathe in our homes is subject to constant renewal from the atmosphere of our planet. If the house becomes stuffy, we can open windows and let in fresh air. Not so in the case of our fish, which are confined to a very limited volume of easily polluted water. And environmental troubles are the root cause of, or a contributory factor in, the bulk of fish health problems.

Not only that, but many pathogens or parasites that may invade this tiny underwater world will quickly infect all its residents, much as colds and childhood diseases run through a class of schoolchildren. Aquarium fish are typically kept in crowded conditions compared to those in the wild, so proliferating parasites will be virtually assured of locating a host; and, unlike in larger, natural bodies of water, the same small number of fish will be attacked each time. Thus, while a wild fish may quite normally carry a few parasites that do it little or no harm, the aquarium fish can easily and quickly incur a lethal burden.

If we also consider that disease diagnosis (Chapter 20) is not always easy, and that permanent or terminal harm may have occurred before the problem can be diagnosed and rectified, then it should be obvious that avoidance of environmental problems and other diseases must be a paramount consideration.

It has to be said that the 'do-it-yourself' approach to fish treatment is far from ideal, as few aquarists, at least as beginners, have any knowledge of how to spot, diagnose, and treat any illness that may occur in their fish, and are faced with a steep, and often painful, upward learning curve. Even the experienced aquarist may find himself confronted with a problem he has not previously encountered and which he is at a loss to diagnose and treat. In addition, the external features of the fish quickly become familiar to the newcomer to the hobby, but its internal structure and functions remain a mystery to the majority of even advanced aquarists. The aim of this section is, therefore, to provide both novice and advanced fishkeepers with all the information they are likely to require on the subject of fish health.

CHAPTER 17

ANATOMY AND PHYSIOLOGY

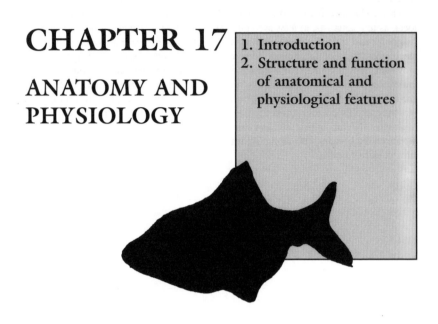

1. INTRODUCTION

Fish are a specialised group of aquatic vertebrates which first appeared on earth about 450 million years ago, long before the reign of the dinosaurs. From these primitive ancestors, fish evolved and diversified, and today they have successfully colonised virtually every major aquatic habitat on the planet. Given their long evolutionary history, it is hardly surprising that fish have undergone various anatomical and physiological adaptations to colonise, survive, and reproduce in widely differing aquatic environments. Our present-day fish can be found in environments as diverse as jungle streams, cold Antarctic waters, the pitch-black depths of the oceanic abyss, subterranean caves, and high-altitude Andean lakes. Even water itself is not always a boundary, for some fish are able to live for periods on land and can even move across the land or climb emerse plant stems and rock walls. Others are capable of brief flight by propelling themselves into the air and gliding for some distance above the water's surface, aided by their rapidly beating pectoral fins.

Fish are the most numerous of all the living vertebrate groups, with approximately 24,600 extant species (in about 480 families) having been scientifically documented. (By way of comparison, there are only about 23,500 species of land vertebrates – i.e.

amphibians, reptiles, birds and mammals.) Every year, a number of new species of fish are discovered, and the true world total may be as high as 40,000 species. Approximately 40% of all fish inhabit fresh waters (although freshwater habitats comprise only 0.01% of the earth's total water volume), with rich assemblages in tropical regions such as the River Amazon basin, which is home to around 1,500 species.

When asked to describe or draw a fish, most people conjure up the general body shape represented by the goldfish, trout, minnow, and other familiar species. However, a tour around any aquarium shop will reveal numerous anatomical variations on this basic plan. It is not just shape which varies between species or groups, but also aspects of anatomy and physiology. Fish are such a diverse group that there is no precise and simple definition of what actually constitutes a 'fish'. It is a remarkable fact that some lineages of fish are more closely related to humans than they are to other fish!

In addition to variations in shape and structure, fish also span a wide range of sizes, ranging from the great whale shark (*Rhincodon typus*) which can reach almost 15 metres (50 feet) in length, to the tiny Philippine goby (*Pandaka pygmaea*) which grows to only 0.8 cm ($^1/_3$ in). A considerable size diversity is also seen among those species sold for tropical freshwater aquaria. Many aquarium fish, such as the tetras and the barbs, reach only 2-3 cm (1-1$^1/_4$ in), their diminutive size and colourful markings contributing to their popularity among aquarists. At the other extreme, species such as the pacu (*Colossoma* spp.), red-tailed catfish (*Phractocephalus hemioliopterus*), and giant gourami (*Osphronemus goramy*) are also encountered in the aquarium hobby, but these can exceed 60-90 cm (24-36 in) in length, often to the surprise and dismay of their owners, who are ultimately faced with the formidable task of re-housing such monsters. The size potential of a particular species should be one of the major considerations when selecting stock for the aquarium, as discussed earlier in this book.

2. STRUCTURE AND FUNCTION OF ANATOMICAL AND PHYSIOLOGICAL FEATURES

Virtually all the fish encountered in tropical freshwater aquaria are teleosts (division Teleostei*), the major group of bony fish within the class Actinopterygii. Exceptions are the lungfish (infraclass Dipnoi*) which are occasionally seen for sale, and the freshwater stingrays (relatives of the sharks, subclass Elasmobranchii*) in which cartilage instead of bone is used to support the body tissues. Certain anatomical and physiological features are common to most teleost fish, and these are outlined below, along with examples of the many variations. Most of the fish cited in this chapter are tropical freshwater species, and many of them are available in the aquarium hobby.

BODY SHAPE
The typical fish shape can be represented by a barb, but while many fish species follow this basic body pattern, numerous others exhibit variations, which may be

---

There is as yet no universal agreement among ichthyologists regarding the taxonomic structure of the major fish groups. The reader may therefore encounter slightly different taxonomic categories and designations in other works on fish. See also Chapter 2.

extreme. For example, the South American angelfish (*Pterophyllum* spp.) and freshwater hatchetfish (e.g. *Gasteropelecus* spp.) are highly compressed laterally, whereas the freshwater stingrays (e.g. *Potamotrygon* spp.) and frog-mouth catfish (*Chaca* spp.) are compressed dorso-ventrally. Others are snake-like in shape, examples being the reedfish (*Erpetoichthys calabaricus*) and khuli loaches (*Acanthopthalmus* spp.). And some can assume an almost spherical appearance, such as the freshwater pufferfish (e.g. *Tetraodon* spp.), which are able to inflate with water if threatened by predators.

BASIC BODY STRUCTURE

The body of a fish can conveniently be divided into three sections: head, trunk and tail. As already mentioned, the vast majority of freshwater aquarium fish possess skeletons composed of true bone, in contrast to the cartilaginous skeletons of the more primitive elasmobranchs (sharks, rays, and relatives).

A fish's skeleton basically comprises the skull, vertebrae (composing the spine), ribs and fin rays. The skeleton functions as a solid frame which supports the soft organs, musculature, and other tissues. The musculature is arranged in a series of blocks known as myotomes which are able to flex from side to side, producing a wave-like motion which propels the fish forward. Most of the major organs of fish – heart, liver, kidneys, spleen, and gut – are also found in mammals, although their form and function may be modified to varying extents. Some of the other organs of fish relate to the animal's aquatic lifestyle, notably the gills and swimbladder. These various organs and their functions will be discussed in greater detail later.

GETTING AROUND: THE LOCOMOTORY SYSTEM

Water is approximately 800 times denser than air, and thus movement through it requires greater effort. In the case of most fish species, propulsion through water is achieved largely with the aid of the flexing body muscles and the caudal fin, with fine manoeuvring and slow movements being under the control of the other fins. Many species possess an internal gas-filled organ, known as the swimbladder (or airbladder), which helps them achieve neutral buoyancy, while the mucus coating of the skin reduces drag. Swimming speeds vary considerably between species and may be a function of the type of habitat they frequent, as well as other factors such as feeding habits and the need to avoid predation. In general, mid-water riverine fish are more agile and streamlined and hence potentially much faster than those which inhabit sluggish streams and static-water pools.

The fins play a key role in locomotion. A typical teleost fin consists of soft and/or hard rays (spines or spinous rays) which support a thin, often translucent, tissue, the fin membrane. The basic arrangement is seven fins, of which three are unpaired (the so-called median fins), namely the dorsal, anal, and caudal (tail). The other four fins are arranged in two pairs: the pectorals and pelvics (ventrals), these being used primarily for steering.

Many fish possess more than the standard seven fins, whereas others have fewer. For example, many characins (e.g. tetras) and most catfish possess an eighth fin, known as the adipose, which is situated posterior to the dorsal. It is so called because it contains fatty tissue. In some of the smaller tetras the adipose is tiny and transparent and hence difficult to see, whereas in certain catfish (e.g. *Synodontis* spp. and *Auchenoglanis* spp.) it is very large and pigmented.

Basic Anatomical Features of a Fish

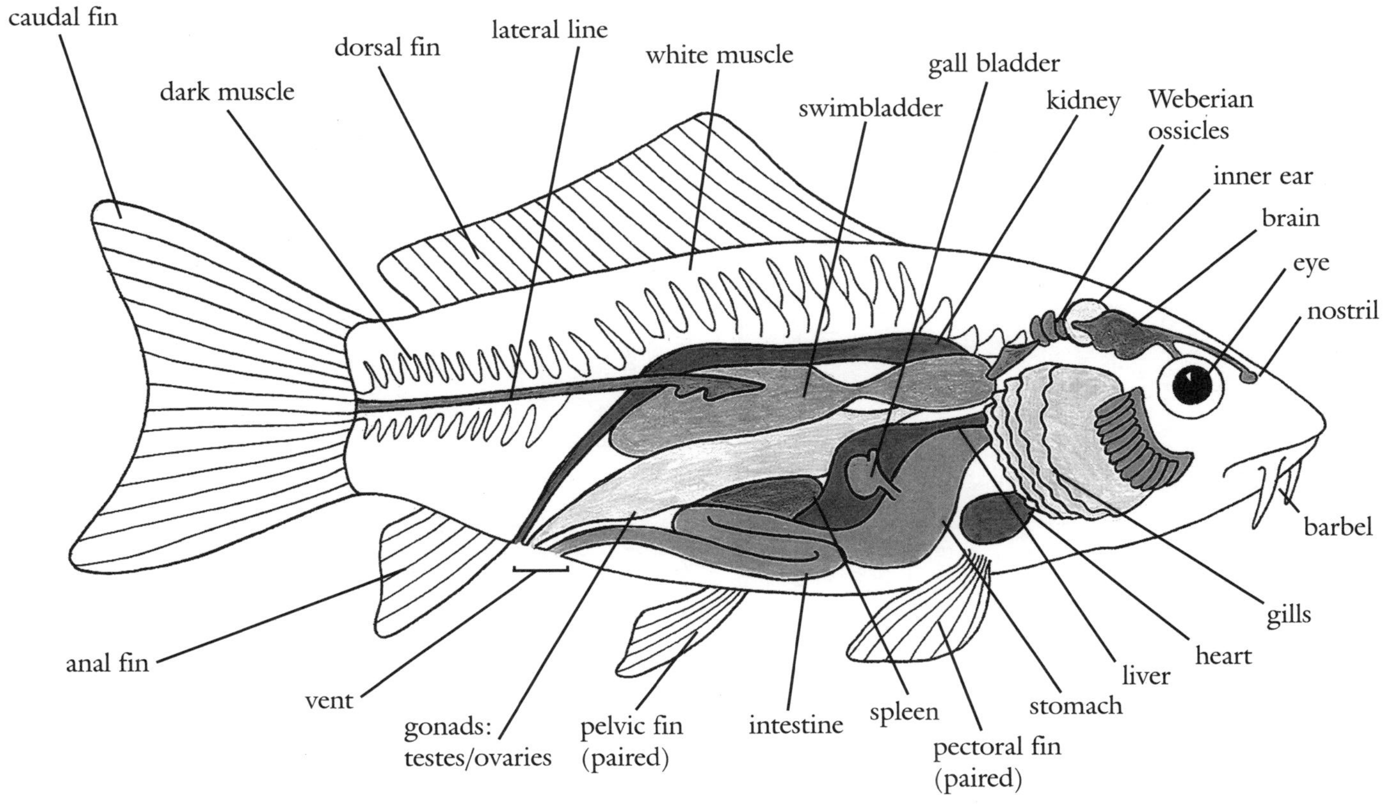

barbel

nostril

eye

brain

inner ear

Weberian ossicles

kidney

gall bladder

swimbladder

white muscle

lateral line

dorsal fin

dark muscle

caudal fin

gills

heart

liver

stomach

pectoral fin (paired)

spleen

intestine

pelvic fin (paired)

gonads: testes/ovaries

vent

anal fin

There can be considerable interspecific variation in the finnage, and this is often of taxonomic significance (in differentiating families, genera, and species). For example, the dorsal commonly varies in terms of its size, position along the back, and fin-ray structure. Some groups of fish possess two dorsals, aquarium examples being the gobies, mudskippers, glassfish (family Ambassidae), and rainbowfish. However, some glass catfish (*Kryptopterus* spp.) and knife fish (e.g. family Gymnotidae) have none. In the snakeheads (*Channa* spp.) and *Clarias* catfish, the dorsal is ribbon-shaped and extends over two-thirds of the fish's length, while in the spiny eels (family Mastacembelidae) it is represented by a row of isolated spines. The cyprinids (family Cyprinidae – carp, barbs, and their relatives) have soft-rayed dorsal fins whereas those of cichlids include both soft and spiny rays.

In addition to their locomotory function, the fins of some fish may also be used for one or more of the following purposes:

• Communication – for example, folding the fins may denote submission.

• Defence – erecting the fins helps make the fish look larger, and the spines of some fish are formidable defensive weapons.

• Courtship and mating – extending and quivering the finnage in front of a potential or actual breeding partner. The males of some cichlids use their tails to fan sperm into breeding caves which they themselves are too large to enter. In the poeciliid livebearers, such as the popular guppies and swordtails, part of the male's anal fin is modified into a tube-shaped organ, called a gonopodium, which is used for inseminating the female.

• Movement over land – as in the case of amphibious species such as the climbing perch (*Anabas testudineus*) and mudskippers (*Periophthalmus* spp.).

Several popular aquarium species have been selectively bred over many generations to achieve longer fins or unusual fin shapes. Species available as long-finned varieties include the White Cloud Mountain minnow (*Tanichthys albonubes*), the zebra danio (*Brachydanio rerio*), the rosy barb (*Puntius conchonius*), and various species of livebearers (family Poeciliidae). In other 'man-made' varieties the shape of the caudal fin has been modified through selective breeding. Nowhere is this more striking among tropical fish than in the various cultivated strains of the guppy (*Poecilia reticulata*).

A COAT OF MANY FUNCTIONS: THE SKIN

The skin of fish is basically divided into two layers, the outer epidermis and the inner dermis. The skin serves many functions: it helps protect the internal organs from abrasions and other physical damage, and it acts as a waterproof membrane which separates the internal body fluids from the external environment. Without such an impermeable layer, the fish's internal salt balance would be diluted by an influx of fresh water from the environment. (The ability of fish to maintain a constant salt balance, known as osmoregulation, is discussed below).

The skin also serves as a first line of defence against pathogens. Apart from providing a physical barrier to pathogen invasion, the skin is covered in a sticky mucus which is continuously secreted by special epidermal cells. This mucus layer, which comprises proteins, glycoproteins, proteoglycans, and other chemicals, is able to entrap and immobilise small pathogens such as bacteria. The mucus itself also contains an armoury of antimicrobial chemicals and cells which can kill or neutralise viruses, bacteria, and certain protozoan parasites. Mucus also reduces drag in the water and thereby improves swimming efficiency. The body mucus of a few cichlids, notably discus (*Symphysodon* spp.) and some loricariid catfish, serves as a source of food for their fry. In addition to its nutritional value, there is some evidence that the mucus produced by brooding discus also contains immunoglobulins which may help protect the fry against infections. If this is confirmed, then the skin mucus of discus may have a similar role to that of colostrum ('first milk') in mammals.

Scales and scutes
The scales are anchored in the dermis. They are hard but flexible structures, and are essentially calcified plates which have a protective function. Much of the body is covered by scales, and in some species the scalation may also extend on to the head and/or parts of the fins. In others the scales are so tiny that the fish appears scaleless. However, only a few fish (such as the silurid catfish, family Siluridae) are genuinely without scales and are hence sometimes referred to as 'naked'. If a scale happens to be dislodged, perhaps through injury, it will normally be replaced.

There are two basic scale forms in teleost fish. Cycloid scales are smooth and round, and are common in fish with soft-rayed fins. Ctenoid scales are spinous and comb-like. Both scale types may be found occurring together on some species.

Catfish do not possess scales. Instead, either they are 'naked' or, in the case of the doradids (family Doradidae) and some others, they possess thick, heavy, bony plates termed 'scutes'. In the large doradid *Pseudodoras niger*, the scutes are visibly armed with sharp spines which serve in a defensive role against predators. Care must be taken when handling such fish, as the scutes can easily lacerate the hands.

Skin colour
Many tropical fish are brightly coloured, and their coloration is due largely to the presence of pigment cells (chromatophores) which lie within the dermal layer of the skin. Several types of chromatophores exist, the best known being the melanophores, which contain brown-black pigment; others include xanthophores (yellow pigment) and erythrophores (red-orange pigment). Contraction or dispersion of the pigment within the cell (in response to neural or hormonal signals) causes the colour to pale or intensify, respectively.

In general, fish which are stressed or kept under bright lighting may develop pallor, whereas certain diseases or traumas can cause them to become abnormally dark. Cichlid fish are noted for their ability to alter their overall body colour and markings as a way of communicating with other fish, and, in the case of some species, as a means of signalling to their young.

In addition to chromatophores, fish also possess a layer of cells known as iridocytes which function mainly to reflect light. Iridocytes are composed of a reflective material (guanin) and impart the silvery appearance to the belly region of many fish.

Some fish lack pigment due to genetic aberration and are referred to as albinos. In the wild, albinos tend not to survive as their pale bodies are more easily detected by predators, but in captivity these mutants often fare as well as their normal-coloured counterparts. Several popular aquarium species are commercially produced in an albino form, examples being the bronze catfish (*Corydoras aeneus*), the tiger barb (*Barbus tetrazona*), and the swordtail (*Xiphophorus helleri*). At the other extreme, some fish exhibit abnormal (for the species) amounts of dark pigment (melanism), and this trait has also been exploited and developed by commercial breeders, resulting in popular varieties, such as the black lace angelfish. Leucistic (white, but possessing pigment), xanthic (yellow pigment predominant), and erythric (red-orange) forms also occur.

KEEPING AFLOAT: THE SWIMBLADDER

Fish are slightly denser than the surrounding water and would sink to the substrate without some form of 'lift' mechanism. Most fish are able to achieve neutral buoyancy at various water depths by virtue of an internal gas-filled organ known as the swimbladder (also called the gas bladder or airbladder). In most fish the swimbladder is a relatively large organ, comprising up to 7% of the total body volume in freshwater species, and appears white to semi-translucent and shiny. It typically comprises a single chamber, but may be two-chambered in the carps. The bladder wall is thin and flexible, enabling it to expand or contract in response to endocrine and neural control, and these variations in its gas volume enable the fish to maintain the desired neutral buoyancy. In most teleost fish the swimbladder is an isolated structure with no ducts to the external environment through which gas can be exchanged; instead, gas absorption and secretion occurs via the blood system, mediated through a network of capillaries in the swimbladder wall.

Not all fish possess a functional swimbladder. In some groups which spend most of their time in contact with the substrate, such as the gobies, there is no need for neutral buoyancy, such that the swimbladder has become redundant and is either atrophied or absent altogether.

Some fish are able to receive or emit sounds via their swimbladder, which functions as a resonator or vibrator.

MAINTAINING THE SALT BALANCE: THE OSMOREGULATORY SYSTEM

The body fluids of fish contain various salts which must be kept within narrow concentration limits so that the animal can metabolise effectively. In the case of freshwater fish, the internal fluids contain higher quantities of salts than the surrounding water (the reverse is true for marine fish which are less salty than the sea). If fish were completely watertight, they could maintain their internal salt/water balance without expending energy. However, fish are 'leaky', in that water and salts can cross the thin epithelial surfaces, notably those of the gills. Water enters through the gills of freshwater fish by a process of osmosis, and salts are lost via the gills through simple diffusion. Fish must therefore expend energy to counteract these forces, which they do by a process known as osmoregulation.

Osmoregulation in freshwater fish is achieved by a combination of physiological processes which take place principally in the kidneys and gills. The kidneys function to eliminate excess amounts of water from the body, and this is achieved by special tubular structures within the kidney tissue which filter water out of the blood and pass it into the urinary bladder to be vented as urine. (The urinary bladder, which is not present in all groups of fish, should not be confused with the swimbladder.) Weight for weight, freshwater fish produce around 10 times as much urine as marine fish (and, similarly, around 10-20 times as much urine as land animals).

In addition to coping with an excess influx of water, fish must also conserve their body salts. A proportion of the salts in the urine is reabsorbed within the kidney before the urine is vented, and special cells in the gills, known as chloride cells, also help maintain the salt differential by actively taking up salts (as ions) directly from the water. This energy-consuming salt-uptake system is known as an ion pump, and the process works in both directions, with unwanted ions (such as ammonium ions, NH_4^+) being exchanged for beneficial ions such as sodium (Na^+). For this reason, fish should never be kept in totally demineralised water (e.g. reverse osmosis water or distilled water), since such an environment will lack essential ions.

PROCESSING THE FOOD: THE DIGESTIVE SYSTEM

The digestive system comprises the digestive tract (mouth, stomach, intestine) plus associated organs, notably the pancreas, liver, and gall bladder. A series of physical, chemical, and enzymatic processes enable food items to be broken down into proteins, carbohydrates, and lipids, and finally into their molecular constituents, namely amino acids, sugars, and fatty acids, respectively. These food molecules are sufficiently small to be absorbed (or actively taken up) across the gut wall and into the blood, where they are circulated to the various tissues and storage organs, ready to be used for growth and metabolism.

Mouth, lips and teeth

The mouth, lips, and teeth are used for sucking, grazing, probing, tearing, or impaling food items. The actual techniques employed vary according to the fish species. Some cichlids, for example, have evolved highly-specialised techniques and associated apparatus to enable them to exploit often quite bizarre food sources. Many (but not all) specialised feeders can, however, alter their feeding style to exploit more generalised food sources when available, and non-specialists switch their mode of feeding routinely depending on what food is available. Thus, for example, we may find the same species picking invertebrates from a substrate or snapping up zooplankton in the water column.

Food items, once taken into the mouth, are generally swallowed whole, although some fish are able to use their teeth to grate, crush, or grind the food into more easily swallowed pieces. Sometimes separate sets of teeth are used for the acquisition and processing of the food, for example cichlids use their maxillary (jaw) teeth to seize or bite off items of food, and additional teeth on the lower pharyngeal bone (pharyngeal teeth), to process them. In contrast to mammals, very few fish are capable of a sideways chewing action. Fish do not possess salivary glands and there appear to be no digestive enzymes in the mucus of their mouths.

The shape and orientation of the mouth usually reflect the fish's feeding behaviour. Many bottom-dwelling species, such as the loaches, some catfish (such as *Corydoras*), and freshwater stingrays, possess underslung mouths which are adapted for taking food items (e.g. worms, aquatic insect larvae) from the substrate. By contrast, surface-dwelling fish, such as some killifish and poeciliid livebearers, have upturned mouths which are able to snap up mosquito larvae and terrestrial insects which have fallen on to the water's surface. In between are mid-water species whose mouths tend to be forward-pointing. There are, of course, many exceptions.

The lips may be specially modified for food acquisition. For example, certain bottom-dwelling species, such as *plecostomus*-type catfish (family Loricariidae) have greatly enlarged lips which serve both as attachment organs (enabling the fish to maintain position in fast-flowing waters or on vertical surfaces), and for grazing on algae and other microbial life which coats the substrate and other submerged objects.

As well as its role in the feeding process, the mouth may also be used for other purposes, such as fighting (exemplified by jaw-locking in anabantids, and cichlids), for attack/defence, for brooding eggs and fry (various groups) and for digging (notoriously in cichlids and gobies).

The teeth

Most teleost fish possess teeth, although their position in the mouth varies according to the taxonomic group of fish. In the case of characoids (tetras and their relatives), for example, the teeth are set in the jaw. The piranha, a large characoid, is famous for its razor-sharp teeth which can be seen protruding over the lips even when the fish's mouth is closed. The teeth of cyprinids, on the other hand, are located in the throat and are known as pharyngeal teeth. Cichlid fish possess both maxillary and pharyngeal teeth, whereas in many catfish the teeth are situated on the roof of the mouth and are termed 'vomerine' or 'palatal' teeth, depending on their exact location (on the vomer or the palate).

In a few species the tongue may be equipped with teeth, as occurs in the osteoglossids (family Osteoglossidae), a very old group which includes the arawanas and relatives. In fact, these fish are commonly known as 'bonytongues' (the meaning of osteoglossid) because of this unusual anatomical feature. Another unusual form of dentition occurs in the pufferfish (family Tetraodontidae), in which the teeth are fused to form a pair of beak-like plates used for crushing hard-shelled prey such as aquatic snails. The puffer's teeth continue to grow throughout life and are kept in check by constant wear. In most fish, however, the teeth are routinely replaced.

Even within a particular taxonomic group there may be considerable variation between species in terms of the shape, number, size, and arrangement of the teeth, reflecting different feeding strategies and preferred food items. Such diversity in dentition has been well documented in the case of the cichlid fish inhabiting the great lakes of East Africa, and is regarded by many systematicists as an important character in differentiating these, as well as other, taxa.

The intestinal tract

Food taken into the mouth passes into the chamber of the pharynx (which, as mentioned above, in some species harbours teeth) and then down a short oesophagus before entering the stomach or intestine.

The presence or absence of a stomach is generally a function of the species' diet. Some herbivores, such as the cyprinids, do not possess a true stomach and are termed 'agastric'. In some fish the stomach may be quite simple in form, but in the case of large predators it is sac-shaped and distensible to accommodate and digest large food items such as whole fish. Digestion of food items within the stomach is aided by enzymes such as pepsin and trypsin, and by hydrochloric acid (the stomach fluids of fish may be very acid, with a pH below 2.0 in some cases).

From the stomach (where present) the food enters the intestine where further digestion takes place. The small organ known as the gall bladder stores green-yellow bile fluid (produced by the liver) which is periodically emptied into the gut where it emulsifies lipids to aid their digestion. Pancreatic enzymes are also emptied into the intestine where they help digest carbohydrates. The intestine is the major site where nutrients are taken across the gut wall and into the blood.

The total length of the intestinal tract also reflects the fish's main diet, typically being long in omnivores and herbivores but comparatively short in carnivores. The time taken for a meal to pass through the digestive system varies according to the species and other factors (such as size of meal, water temperature), and ranges from just a few hours to almost a week (sometimes more!) in some carnivorous species.

Any undigested food is vented through the anus as faeces, along with significant quantities of urine. The faeces, which may vary in colour and consistency according to the recent diet, contain undigested proteins, carbohydrates, and lipids, together with cellular material from the fish itself.

BREATHING UNDERWATER: THE RESPIRATORY SYSTEM

Fish, in common with other animals, must obtain oxygen from their environment in order to live. The uptake of oxygen and the elimination of carbon dioxide as a waste product is known as respiration. This gaseous exchange occurs in fish and land vertebrates; however the organs of respiration differ between these two animal groups. In terrestrial animals, such as mammals and birds, gaseous exchange occurs in the lungs, whereas the analogous organs in most fish species are the gills, which have to be far more efficient than the lungs of land animals since water contains only 2-3% of the amount of free oxygen present in the air.

Fish possess two sets of gills, one on each side of the body, posterior to the head. These delicate organs are protected by hard plates, known as gill covers or opercula (singular = operculum). Each set of gills is a complex structure comprising four bony arches, each supporting two rows of feather-shaped gill filaments known as primary lamellae. Each primary lamella is in turn covered with tiny plates (secondary lamellae) which are supplied with narrow blood capillaries. It is across the thin membranes of the secondary lamellae that the exchange of gases occurs between the blood and the external environment. The blood within the secondary lamellae flows in the opposite direction to the water passing over the lamellar surfaces, resulting in a high diffusion gradient of oxygen and carbon dioxide between the two fluids. This 'counter-current' system greatly increases the efficiency of gaseous exchange.

Most fish have actively to pump water across their gills in order to achieve adequate gaseous exchange. Given that water is around 800 times denser than air, a fish has to expend more energy during respiration than does a land animal. The water-pumping action involves a sequence of events: the fish opens its mouth so that water is drawn into the buccal cavity; the mouth is then closed and muscular contraction forces the water across the gills and out through the opercula. The net result is a steady flow of water across the gills.

The level of respiratory activity in fish can be roughly gauged by the gill beat rate (also known as opercular beat rate or simply 'respiratory rate'). The respiratory rate increases in response to heightened activity, fright, or certain water conditions, notably rising temperature, which exerts a dual effect as regards increasing the fish's respiratory rate: firstly, the dissolved oxygen concentration falls with increasing temperature; and secondly, the fish's metabolic rate, and hence oxygen requirement, increases with temperature. Environmental- or pathogen-induced gill damage also leads to increased respiratory activity as the fish struggles to obtain sufficient oxygen across the damaged gill surfaces.

Considering that the oxygen content of air is more than 30 times that of water, it may seem surprising that fish can die of oxygen starvation when held out of water. The reason for this apparent anomaly is that the gill lamellae collapse when the fish is out of water, such that the surface area available for gaseous exchange becomes greatly reduced. Furthermore, if the gills become dry as a result of prolonged exposure to air, then gaseous exchange will stop completely and the fish will die. The duration of survival in air varies considerably between fish species, but, as a general rule, fish should not be held out of water for more than a minute or two.

Accessory breathing

Some fish are able to remain out of water for extensive periods without harm, or to survive in poorly oxygenated waters. These fish have special accessory breathing organs which enable them to extract atmospheric oxygen by gulping in air. Well-known aquarium examples are the gouramis (various genera) and fighting fish (*Betta* spp.) of the family Belontidae, many of which occur naturally in poorly oxygenated pools; these fish, and a number of close relatives, are sometimes known as 'labyrinth fish' because they possess an accessory respiratory apparatus known as the labyrinth. This structure, which comprises a series of folds containing a rich blood supply, connects with an air-filled pharyngeal chamber. Organs with a similar function are found in certain catfish which are able to survive the low-oxygen conditions prevalent in pools that are drying up, and in fish that are able to migrate over land, a well-known example being the *Clarias* catfish.

Some other catfish (e.g. *Corydoras* spp.) and loaches (family Cobitidae) are able to absorb atmospheric oxygen directly across the walls of their highly-vascularised intestines. In the aquarium these normally bottom-dwelling fish may be seen periodically to visit the water's surface and gulp air – this is quite normal behaviour and does not necessarily imply that the aquarium water is low in oxygen.

PUMPING BLOOD: THE CIRCULATORY SYSTEM

The main function of the circulatory system is to supply the various organs and tissues with oxygen and nutrients, and to remove the waste products of metabolism. The circulatory system essentially comprises a heart and a network of arteries, veins, and fine capillaries. The heart, which acts as a pump, is situated close to the gills and is composed of four chambers: the sinus venosus, atrium, ventricle, and conus (bulbus) arteriosus. Of these, the atrium and ventricle are the largest components, such that the organ is sometimes described as being only two-chambered.

The total blood volume of a fish is approximately 5% of its body weight. The blood itself consists of a fluid known as plasma which carries soluble substances, such as nutrients, as well as specialised red and white blood cells. The function of the red blood cells (erythrocytes) is to carry oxygen from the gills to the tissues. Each oxygen molecule attaches to the haemoglobin, a pigment which is present in erythrocytes and gives them their red colour. Functionally, the erythrocytes of fish are similar to those of mammals but differ in that they possess a nucleus. The white blood cells, comprising lymphocytes and other types, are involved in immunity (discussed below). In addition to oxygen/nutrient transportation and immune function, the blood is also the route by which hormones reach their target organs.

Fish also posses a lymphatic system which circulates around the so-called white muscles (used for short bursts of activity). The lymph fluid, which is about four times the volume of the blood, is similar in composition to the blood plasma but does not contain red blood cells.

FISH HAVE BRAINS: THE NERVOUS SYSTEM

The nervous system comprises the brain and its associated spinal cord and nerve network. A major function of the brain is to receive, interpret, and respond to electrical signals from the various sensory organs, such as the eyes, taste buds, auditory and tactile organs. The brain itself is composed basically of three segments: the forebrain, midbrain, and hindbrain. Each segment deals with specific sensory inputs; for example the hindbrain is linked to gustatory (taste) receptors.

IN TOUCH WITH THEIR ENVIRONMENT: THE SENSORY SYSTEM

Although intimately linked to the brain and nervous system, the sensory system is often, as here, considered separately, in part because of the sheer complexity and variety of fish sense organs, some of which have no counterpart in land vertebrates. The sensory system supplies the brain with data regarding external stimuli, enabling the fish to perceive, interpret, and respond to its surroundings.

The eyes

Fish eyes are structurally similar to those of mammals, and most teleost fish are able to see in colour. Unlike mammals, however, fish are not able to bend their necks in order to look from side to side, and so their eyes are specially adapted to achieve a wide field of vision. Many predatory fish, such as pike (*Esox* spp.), rely on acute binocular vision to stalk and capture their prey. For many fish, however, sight is not quite as important as it is for higher vertebrates, because fish are able to use other senses to help them feed and navigate through the water (thus loss of one or both eyes is not usually a reason for euthanasia). This is particularly true of nocturnal species, such as many catfish, which rely primarily on special taste organs to detect food items during their nocturnal forays.

A small number of fish species live partly or totally in caves and have no need for sight, such that their eyes are either absent or greatly atrophied. One well-known aquarium example is the blind cave tetra (*Astyanax fasciatus mexicanus*), which is not only eyeless but has also lost the need for pigmentation. There is also a blind cave form of the *sphenops* molly (*Poecilia sphenops*), recorded from southern Mexico, and several other groups of fish are also represented by blind cave-dwelling species, including cyprinids, catfish, gobies, and eels.

The acoustico-lateralis system

Fish are capable of detecting vibrations through the water even though they do not appear to have ears. In fact, fish do possess ears, but they are totally internal and without the external auricles possessed by mammals. The fish's ears are equipped with sensitive cells (hair cells) which act as vibration detectors, and semi-circular canals for sensing gravity and balance, just as in the higher vertebrates.

A further component of the acoustico-lateralis system is the lateral line system, which consists of a series of canals that run just beneath the fish's skin and connect with the external environment via a number of tiny pores. This system has no counterpart in land vertebrates. A number of small canals are concentrated on the head region and a main canal extends along each side of the body as far as the caudal peduncle. The route of this elongate canal can be visibly detected on the body surface as a groove, known as the lateral line. In some groups, such as cichlids and anabantids, it is split into two or three sections. In common with the ears, these canals contain sensitive hair cells for detecting vibrations in the water. The acoustico-lateralis system thus enables the fish to detect even small vibrations caused by nearby moving objects, such as other fish. Some fish utilise this capability to locate prey items, such as small invertebrates concealed in the substrate.

Long-distance taste and smell

Taste (gustatory) and smell (olfactory) senses are found in fish as in other vertebrates.

In terrestrial vertebrates, the taste buds are restricted to the tongue, whereas in fish they may occur on any part of the body. Studies on the North American bullhead catfish, (*Ictalurus nebulosus*), have revealed high concentrations of taste buds on the barbels, indicating the important sensory function of these appendages (see below). Many fish are able to 'taste the water' and can sense the concentration and types of food molecules in the surrounding water. This enables them to track down a potential meal by navigating along the concentration gradient of food molecules emanating from the source. In fact, the bullhead catfish has been shown to be capable of detecting food as far as five metres away, even in complete darkness.

Fish are also able to use their olfactory sense to locate distant food, the olfactory chambers being associated with the nares (pronounced 'nar-rays'), = nostrils. As the fish swims, water is pushed across the nares and over the olfactory detectors. In some fish, the water is actively pumped across the detectors. In addition to food location, fish also use their olfactory sense to detect molecules emitted by other fish. These molecular cues are sometimes used for reproductive purposes, or to alert the fish to the nearby presence of predators.

Barbels

These organs, known commonly as 'whiskers' in catfish, are generally associated with nocturnal fish or those which inhabit murky waters. As mentioned earlier, the barbels are richly supplied with taste buds, and they also possess tactile function, enabling the fish to locate food by taste and touch, rather than having to rely on visual senses. Among aquarium fish, barbels are found on the loaches, catfish, and some groups of cyprinids. In some catfish and a few cyprinids (e.g. the flying barbs, *Esomus* spp.) the barbels are very long.

Electric organs

The elephantnose fish (mormyrids, family Mormyridae), the South American and African knifefishes (various families), along with a few freshwater eels and catfish, possess electric organs which can generate low or high frequency pulses as a means of communication or for locating food. This remarkable adaptation enables such fish to inhabit muddy waters where eyesight alone would be of little use. A popular aquarium example is the African mormyrid *Gnathonemus petersi*. A small number of species have powerful electrical organs capable of producing a high-voltage discharge, used for defence and to stun prey, an example being the African electric eel (*Electrophorus electricus*) which can generate an incredible 500 volts.

COMBATING DISEASE: THE IMMUNE SYSTEM

Fish are vulnerable to a variety of infectious diseases caused by viruses, bacteria, fungi, protozoa, and parasitic worms and crustaceans (Chapter 21). The aquatic environment is particularly suited to the survival of many of the smaller pathogens, notably the bacteria and protozoa, which would otherwise desiccate and die in air. In order to ward off diseases, fish possess a battery of defence mechanisms which include specialised defence cells, antibodies, and antimicrobial substances. The immune systems of fish (and higher vertebrates) can be conveniently divided into innate immunity (non-specific immunity) and acquired (specific) immunity.

Innate immunity
Innate immunity is the more primitive of the two systems, but often forms the first line of defence against pathogens. It can take the form of a simple physical barrier to pathogen invasion, such as is afforded by the skin and skin mucus, the latter being capable of entrapping and immobilising bacteria. In addition, there are chemical barriers to infection, such as the acid produced by the stomach, and specialised proteins with antimicrobial activity, examples being C-reactive protein (possessing antibacterial and anti-fungal properties) and interferon (antiviral). Cellular defences take the form of primitive white blood cells, known as phagocytes, which patrol the blood and tissues in search of invading pathogens which they attack and engulf.

Acquired immunity
This is a more specialised form of defence with two key features:
1) The ability to distinguish between various pathogens.
2) The capacity for 'memory'.
  Upon exposure to a particular pathogen, various immune cells are stimulated into action to eliminate the invader. Should the same type of pathogen ever happen to invade the fish on a subsequent occasion, then the acquired immune system is already primed for combat and the pathogen is dealt with more effectively and more swiftly. The memory ability lies with a particular group of white blood cells known as lymphocytes. When activated by contact with a pathogen, these lymphocytes interact with other immune cells and trigger additional defence systems into action. One group of lymphocytes is able to synthesise special protein molecules, known as antibodies, which can inactivate viruses and help destroy larger pathogens and parasites. In addition to their presence within the blood plasma, these antibodies may also be found in the skin mucus and other body secretions.
  The ability of fish to develop acquired immunity suggests that it might be possible to produce vaccines against various fish diseases, just as we have done for humans.

Lymphoid function
Fish possess a number of lymphoid organs and tissues which are involved in the production and storage of white blood cells. Lymphoid function is associated with the thymus, spleen, kidneys, and liver. There is evidence to suggest that the intestines of fish may also possess regions of lymphoid tissue.

HORMONE MESSENGERS: THE ENDOCRINE SYSTEM
The endocrine system secretes special protein molecules known as hormones, which regulate and synchronise key physiological processes, such as reproduction and osmoregulation. Hormones function as chemical messengers which travel via the blood until they reach their respective target organs. Several of the fish's organs and

glands possess endocrine function, including the thymus, pineal gland, and interrenal gland. The endocrine function is largely under the control of the pituitary gland, which is linked to the forebrain. This neural-hormonal network enables the fish to respond physiologically to sensory cues within its environment. For example, when a fish catches sight of a predator, its eyes will convert the visual cue into electrical signals which travel via optic nerves to the brain where they are processed. From here, electrical signals trigger the production of stress hormones, such as adrenalin, which travel to their various target organs and systems. The overall effect of the stress hormones is to channel large amounts of energy into locomotory activity, enabling the fish quickly to flee from the threat.

THE NEXT GENERATION: REPRODUCTIVE STRATEGIES

The majority of teleost species are egg-layers (oviparous), with fertilisation being external, i.e. taking place after the eggs have been laid by the female (although in some maternal mouthbrooding species, fertilisation takes place after the eggs have been collected into the mouth of the female, and might thus be classed as internal).

On the other hand, more than 500 species of fish are viviparous (livebearers), practising internal fertilisation (discussed below) and producing fully-formed young which may be immediately able to swim and feed. Many popular species of aquarium fish, such as guppies, mollies, platies, and swordtails, are livebearers, and part of their aquarium appeal relates to their reproductive habits: these fish readily breed in captivity and provide the aquarist with the thrill of watching the female give birth to fully-developed babies which are generally easy to rear.

There are many variations on these two basic reproductive styles. For example, a few species are self-fertilising ('hermaphrodites').

The fish's gonads (reproductive organs) are generally paired structures, comprising testes in the male and ovaries in the female. The size of the gonads varies between species, but is often quite large, particularly in the case of the ovaries which may account for more than 50% of the female fish's body weight. The size and state of maturation of the gonads may be influenced by environmental factors such as variations in water temperature and/or photoperiod (increasing or decreasing amounts of daylight), although these factors are more significant in the case of temperate fish. The influence of environmental conditions on gonad maturation and spawning ensures that reproduction occurs during optimal conditions for survival of the offspring, for example to coincide with a plentiful food supply for the fry.

Most teleost fish exist as two sexes – males and females – though some species are able to transform from one sex to another. In the case of livebearing fish, it is usually easy to tell the sexes apart. In poeciliids (guppies, swordtails, mollies, and relatives) the sexually mature male has a modified anal fin, known as a gonopodium, used to transmit sperm into the female. During mating the male swims beside the female and his tube-shaped gonopodium is swung forward in order to pass sperm into her genital tract. Female poeciliids are able to store sperm such that a single mating can give rise to several broods of young. In other livebearers, such as the Mexican goodeids, the anal fin of the male is slightly notched rather than tubular.

In the case of egg-laying fish, it can be far more difficult to tell the sexes apart. There may be a size disparity between mature males and females, and often the males (sometimes the females) are more brightly coloured. The length of fins, especially the dorsal and anal, is sometimes greater in the males of certain species, for instance some cichlids as well as gouramis and gobies. Another clue to sex is that mature female egg-layers may have larger bellies than males, due to their enlarged ovaries. Needless to say, there are many exceptions, and in some species it is impossible to tell the sexes apart on the basis of external features alone.

In general, egg-laying species are much more fecund than livebearers, such a difference being necessary to compensate for the low survival rate of eggs and fry compared to that of live young, which are better equipped to avoid predation. There are exceptions, however. Certain groups of egg-laying fish, notably the cichlids and anabantids, exhibit parental care which greatly improves the fry survival rate, and hence their clutch size is generally smaller (proportional to their own size) than that of many other fish groups. Another reproductive behaviour which limits clutch size is mouthbrooding, in which either the male or female parent (sometimes both) incubates the eggs and fry within its buccal cavity. This habit, which is practised by some species of cichlids, anabantoids, and catfish, obviously imposes physical constraints on the size of brood which can be reared.

CHAPTER 18

THE HEALTHY FISH

1. Appearance
2. Behaviour

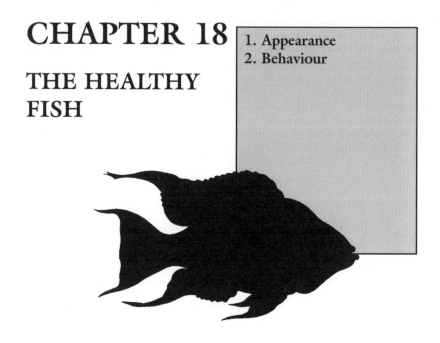

In order to recognise signs of illness in fish, it is important to be familiar with the signs of a healthy individual.

As we have already seen, there are many different types of tropical aquarium fish, in terms of external appearance, requirements, and behaviour. This means that qualifying signs of health – and illness – is not as straightforward as in most other pets. If, for example, a dog or horse lies down most of the time, and walks with difficulty and unevenly when it does get up, then it is obvious that something is wrong. But there are fish for whom it is quite normal to rest on the bottom, sometimes even lying on one side; and when they do move, they do so in a series of rather ungainly hops. Yet if this behaviour were seen in fish that normally swim around in mid-water, it would be considered a serious sign of ill health. Again, most fish swim the right way up, and any deviation from this normal position is cause for concern. But a few species swim upside-down – or head-down – for much of the time, as part of their normal behaviour.

Changes in the fish's external appearance may likewise signify illness in some species, but in others they are a perfectly normal occurrence. For example, the sudden appearance of white spots signifies disease in most fish – but a few species develop such spots quite normally at breeding time. The list of examples is practically endless, because for almost every sign of possible ill health – e.g. changing colour, folding or

174

twitching fins, swimming on the spot, developing an abnormal mucus coating – there will be a species that does this routinely, whether it be on a day-to-day or seasonal basis. Table 9 shows some of the more commonly encountered changes in appearance and 'alarming' behaviour that are in fact quite normal for the fish concerned.

Note: grouped by family, in the order used in Table 3 (Chapter 3). Most fish can be expected to exhibit strange behaviour at spawning time, though the degree of 'abnormality' is highly variable.

Table 9 Some Fish that Exhibit 'Abnormal' Features as Normal

Family	Species	Common name	Behaviour
Lebiasinidae	*Copeina arnoldi*	Splash tetra	Jumping from water (to spawn)
Anostomidae	*Anostomus* spp.	Headstanders	Swimming head-down
Cyprinidae	Various	Barbs and others	White spots (tubercles) on/near head of male when breeding
Cobitidae	*Botia* spp.	Loaches	Resting on bottom, lying on side
	Some species	Loaches	Taking air at surface
Gymnotidae (and related families)	Various	Knifefishes	Able to swim backwards
Many siluriform families	Various	Catfish	Resting on bottom
Clariidae	*Clarias* spp.	Walking catfish	Resting on side on bottom, taking air at surface
Mochokidae	*Synodontis* spp.	Upside-down catfish	Swimming upside-down
Doradidae	Various	Talking catfish	Making clicking and other noises
Callichthyidae	*Corydoras* spp. *inter alia*	Corys, mailed catfish	Taking air at surface
Cyprinodontidae	Several genera	Annual killifish	Death at about 9-15 months old
Cichlidae	Most	Cichlids	Changing colour, quivering, hiding
	Many	Cichlids	Males develop hump on head when breeding/adult

	Several genera	Rapids cichlids	Resting on bottom or decor
	Spathodus, Eretmodus, Tanganicodus	Goby cichlids	Tanganyika – bottom or decor
	Julidochromis spp.	Julies	Swimming upside-down, on side, backwards
	Symphysodon and Uaru spp.	Discus, uaru	Increased mucus when breeding
	Mouthbrooding species	Mouthbrooders	'Swollen' mouth (when brooding)
Eleotridae	Various	Sleeper gobies	Resting on bottom
Gobiidae	Various	Gobies	Resting on bottom
Belontidae	Various	Gouramis	Males blow bubbles at surface when breeding
Mastacembelidae	Mastacembelus spp.	Spiny eels	Resting on bottom, burrowing into substrate with head protruding
Tetraodontidae	Tetraodon spp.	Puffers	Inflating body when frightened

The solution to this problem is for the aquarist to familiarise himself with what is normal for the species – sometimes the individual – concerned. This can be achieved in part by personal observation. When fish are purchased they will generally be selected from a group offered for sale, and the bulk, if not all, should be behaving in a similar fashion. The behaviour in the shop can be regarded as normal. When introduced to their new home, they may disappear into the plants or rockwork to recover from the upset of being moved, and to get their bearings; they may change colour to some degree to fit in with their new surroundings; but eventually they should look and act much as they did in the shop. Subsequent observation of each fish will enable the aquarist to establish the norm for that particular individual.

In addition, normal fish behaviour is rarely uniform under all circumstances. Most fish behave quite differently when they breed, sometimes with significant changes in coloration. Some fish change colour and shape as they grow from juvenile to sexually mature adult. This – especially the often sudden changes associated with the onset of breeding activity – can cause great alarm in the owner. So by far the best approach is to use the aquarium literature to learn at an early stage what is to be expected of each and every species kept. Ideally this research should take place before the fish is purchased, as some of the surprises may be unwelcome ones! (Chapter 1). General guidelines to major groups of fish have been provided in Chapter 3, but for details of individual species the best source of information is one of the large catalogues of fish species available (Appendix B), or if the aquarist decides to specialise in a particular group such as catfish, killifish, or cichlids, the appropriate specialist literature can be consulted.

From the above it should be obvious that it is impossible to provide a definitive catalogue of signs of health in fish. It is, however, possible to list aspects of appearance and behaviour for which the aquarist should be familiar with the norm and with normal variations, and which he should monitor regularly for any warning signs. Equally, he should take these indicators into consideration when purchasing new fish. These same features will be found again in Chapter 20, where deviations from species norm are used to help identify possible associated health problems.

1. APPEARANCE

• **Body**. The shape should be normal for the species, not distorted (i.e. possibly deformed). The fish should not be too thin or too fat, and its body should not be swollen, evenly or asymmetrically (lopsided bulge or lump); except that, if it is a female, remember that a swollen abdomen may simply be full of eggs, or fry in the case of livebearers.

• **Coloration and markings**. These are fairly static in many species, but may be highly variable in others, where they may be used to communicate mood, as well as sexual and/or social status, to other fish of the same and other species. Some fish may change colour dramatically within seconds. In all species, continuous unusual colour (especially plain dark or faded), coupled with unusual behaviour, may be suspect, indicating that the fish is diseased or stressed. In some species, where colour indicates status within a group, then it is important to identify the lowest-status individual, which is the one most likely to be stressed, and keep it under close surveillance.

• **Eyes** – one feature which can be used as a positive indicator of good health in most species. The eyes should both be the same size, clear (not cloudy), and not protrude beyond species norm. They should be alert and responsive to external stimuli, not rigidly staring into space.

• **Fins** – shape, length, condition. The fins should not be split or have frayed edges, and there should be no unusual areas of colour (e.g. abnormal light edges, red streaks) or other abnormal features.

• **Gills**. Both opercula (gill covers) should be intact and cover the gill filaments, which should be visible only as the gill cover opens when the fish 'breathes'. The gill filaments should be bright red, and should not be swollen and preventing the gill cover from closing properly.

• **Head**. This should be laterally symmetric, usually (but not always) with a symmetric colour pattern.

• **Mouth**. Except in a very few species, this should be symmetric, and will generally repeatedly open and close slightly in time with the opening and closing of the gill covers. In most species, the mouth should not be held permanently open. Some lip distortion or damage is permissible, especially in fish that use their mouths to wrestle or dig, but there should be no signs of infection. If the fish has barbels, these should be undamaged; they are normally present in pairs, and those of each pair should be of equal size, shape, and length.

177

• **Scales**. There should be no patches of damaged or missing scales, and the scales should lie flat to the body, not protrude.

• **Sensory pores**. The sensory pores on the head and in the lateral line should be small and round. Enlarged or infected (inflamed, pus-filled) pores may signify disease.

• **Size**. The size of a young fish, relative to its age, is highly variable depending on the conditions under which it has been kept and the diet it has been fed. If it is smaller than its siblings, it may be stunted (this also applies to smaller-than-normal adults which have stopped growing). If young fish stop growing or their growth rate slows, this may be a sign of environmental or other health problems.

• **Skin**. There should be no injuries, unusual spots, patches, or lumps. The mucus coating should be uniform and normally invisible. Check for visible parasites (See Chapter 21).

2. BEHAVIOUR

• **Activity level**. The fish should swim around at its normal speed, not dash about abnormally or 'swim on the spot'. It should not hide if it would normally be in the open, nor should it hang in a corner or lie on the bottom.

• **Appetite**. The fish should feed normally, i.e. exhibit species-normal activity at feeding time and accept foods which it is known normally to enjoy.

   Tip: when buying fish, ask to see the fish feed if there are any slight doubts regarding their health.

• **Fin carriage**. The fins should be carried and moved in the manner normal for the species. Permanently clamped or erected fins may denote a problem, as may twitching.

• **Respiratory rate**. This should be relaxed, not laboured, with the gills opening slowly, slightly, and regularly at each beat. Increased gill rate, coupled with gasping, is a sign of 'respiratory distress', i.e. that the fish is having to breathe faster than normal to obtain its oxygen requirement. This may be the result of unusual exertion (itself sometimes a warning sign), or be indicative of environmental or physiological problems.

• **Swimming position** – horizontal, at an angle, right-way-up or upside-down, resting on bottom, etc, depending on species norm. Remember that some fish may adopt a different angle when feeding to that used when swimming from place to place, or when spawning/brood-guarding.

• **Tank level occupied** – bottom, middle, top, or combination. The level occupied should be normal for the species, but may vary at breeding time – for example, top-dwelling killifish sometimes spawn in the substrate.

• **Unusual behaviour**. Certain types of behaviour are normally a sign of a problem. These include: making coughing, choking, or yawning motions; scratching; shimmying; loss of swimming and/or buoyancy control (somersaulting, rolling, floating upwards or sinking downwards). Jumping is a perfectly normal escape response in nature, but may indicate a problem in captivity where the fish should normally neither want nor need to escape.

CHAPTER 19

PREVENTION OF DISEASE

1. **The prevention of different types of disease**
2. **Methods of avoiding the introduction of infectious diseases and parasites**
3. **Prophylaxis**

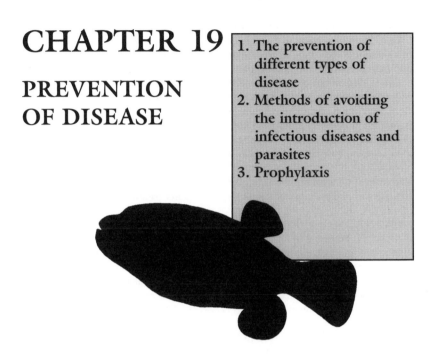

Prevention of disease is paramount. Obviously it is impossible to avoid disease totally, but with a little care and attention to detail the aquarist can minimise the likelihood of his fish becoming unwell. This will not only save lives in many instances, but also avoid the difficulties often inherent in the diagnosis and treatment of fish diseases, and the accompanying distress for aquarists when their pets are unwell.

1. THE PREVENTION OF DIFFERENT TYPES OF DISEASE

The following four subsections discuss groups of diseases defined in Chapter 21, and should be read in conjunction with the introductions to the relevant sections of that chapter. In addition, notes on the prevention of specific diseases are provided under each separate entry in Chapter 20.

PREVENTION OF ENVIRONMENTAL DISEASES AND PROBLEMS
(Chapter 21, Section 1.0)
Many environmental problems can be avoided simply by good husbandry: by providing an environment suited to the aquarium occupants (Chapters 10-12), maintenance of good water quality and general aquarium hygiene (Chapters 10

and 15), and by keeping only fish that are compatible with one another in all respects (Chapter 1). Would-be aquarists who are not prepared to go to the trouble involved should, quite simply, abandon all ideas of keeping fish. Provided the aquarium is properly thought out and set up in the first place, however, maintaining optimal conditions should normally be simply a matter of routine maintenance (Chapter 15) and common sense, e.g. in not overfeeding and/or overcrowding.

In addition, it is essential to avoid sudden environmental changes (such as when fish are introduced to the aquarium, or during partial water changes) which can be extremely dangerous and often lethal.

It is impossible to overstate the importance of observation in preventing environmental disasters in the aquarium: not just regular checks on equipment but close observation of the fish, who themselves can provide an excellent early warning system for developing problems. Clamped fins, increased respiratory rate, yawning or coughing, shimmying, or scratching (Chapter 20) may be transitory reactions to some temporary irritation or exertion. They could also be the first sign of something more serious. It is certainly worth an additional check a little later to see if behaviour has returned to normal. Several fish behaving abnormally should ring warning bells straightaway and prompt immediate checks on water parameters.

PREVENTION OF DIETARY DISORDERS
(Chapter 21, Section 2.0)
This is largely a matter of feeding the fish the correct amounts of suitable foods at appropriate times (Chapter 7). As with prevention of environmental problems, observation is important – no fish should be neglected to the point where it becomes seriously obese or emaciated. These developing problems should be identified and remedied at an early stage.

PREVENTION OF PATHOGENIC AND PARASITIC DISEASES
(Chapter 21, Sections 3.0 and 4.0)
For the purposes of considering prevention, the bulk of pathogens and parasites can be loosely divided into three groups:
• Opportunistic pathogens/parasites (i.e. those which are commonly present in aquaria but harmless under normal circumstances).
• Virulent pathogens/parasites (those which are not normally present and, if accidentally introduced, can cause a disease epidemic).
• Multi-host parasites (those which may occasionally be present in aquaria but are either non-infectious or unable to complete their full life cycle under aquarium conditions owing to their need for one or more 'non-aquarium' hosts to complete their life cycle).

Prevention varies between the groups; but note that encouraging a healthy immune system, by providing optimal conditions and ensuring minimal stress, will better enable the fish to ward off or deal with infectious diseases.

Opportunistic pathogens and parasites
Any established aquarium will be home to a variety of organisms which are potentially pathogenic to fish. These organisms may be present in one or more locations in the aquarium: freely in the water; in the substrate; on aquatic plants; in/on the fish. Despite their presence, they may not necessarily pose an immediate

threat to healthy fish, perhaps because they are unable to attack healthy tissue, or because their numbers are kept in check by the fish's immune system. They may, however, multiply and cause disease if the fish's health or immunity is compromised by traumas such as injury, chronic stress, and, perhaps most commonly, by adverse water conditions (Chapter 21, sections 1.6.1, 1.5.2, 1.1-1.3, respectively). Such pathogens and parasites are sometimes termed 'opportunistic'.

Prevention should be by maintaining optimum environmental conditions and by avoiding stress (Chapter 21, 1.5.2). A healthy environment with minimal stress will enable the fish's immune system to work effectively in warding off opportunistic pathogens or parasites. In some cases proliferation of the potential pathogen will be actively suppressed by maintaining good aquarium hygiene and water quality. In addition, **quarantine** (see below) will largely avoid the introduction of opportunistic pathogens and parasites not already present in the aquarium, thereby further reducing the likelihood of disease.

Virulent pathogens and parasites
These organisms are highly dangerous in that they are capable of causing disease in previously healthy fish. Many species of pathogens, and some species of parasites, exist as various strains, some strains being more virulent than others.

The term 'virulent' is used loosely in this context as regards parasites, whose effect on fish is commonly far more serious under aquarium conditions than in the wild. This is largely a function of the high fish population density relative to the small volume of water in the aquarium, such that the fish are repeatedly exposed to large numbers of infective stages, and can quickly acquire a very heavy and potentially lethal parasite burden. In nature this is very unlikely to happen.

Diseases and parasites of this type are normally introduced to an aquarium via newly-purchased fish, but can also be transmitted by equipment, live foods (and the water in which they have been transported), plants and other decor items, which have been in contact with infected fish or their environment. Their introduction should be avoided by **Inspection** (see below) of any potential source of disease, **Quarantine** (see below), or **Disinfection** (see below). These methods can also be used to avoid transmission of disease from an infected to an uninfected aquarium. Alternatively, sources of infection (including second-hand equipment) can simply be avoided.

Multi-host parasites
Some of these utilise not only a fish, but also another aquatic organism (such as a snail or a crustacean) in their life cycle. The introduction of such hosts may cause a parasite problem if an infested host organism (usually an aquatic invertebrate) releases the next stage of the parasite life cycle into the aquarium, leading to infestation of the fish. In practice, this very rarely happens. Prevention may be possible by quarantine (see below) in the case of snails, otherwise avoidance of potential intermediate hosts is the only guaranteed method.

PREVENTION OF GENETIC DISEASES AND DISORDERS
It is not possible entirely to prevent genetic disorders, but the risk can be minimised by selecting only top-quality, apparently healthy, fish as breeding stock (see Chapter 8) and by avoiding inbreeding (mating closely related fish).

2. METHODS OF AVOIDING THE INTRODUCTION
OF INFECTIOUS DISEASES AND PARASITES

INSPECTION

Many problems can be avoided by careful inspection of potential fish purchases. *Never* buy a fish that is clearly unhealthy. It is equally unwise to buy a fish that looks healthy but has unhealthy tankmates. If the vendor has many unhealthy fish, it may be safer to acquire fish elsewhere. Disease can easily be transferred from tank to tank unless strict precautions are taken (see Quarantine, below).

Aquatic plants, whether purchased or collected, should be inspected for snails and other undesirable stowaways such as leeches and their cocoons (Chapter 21, 4.2.6). The same applies to rocks taken from natural waters. Pond-dwelling live foods, such as *Daphnia*, should be tipped into a shallow pan and checked carefully for undesirables. Always strain such live foods and never add the accompanying water to the tank – it may contain eggs or minute larval forms of parasites.

QUARANTINE

Quarantine, along with good husbandry, is one of the aquarist's most important weapons against disease. Yet, regrettably, a very large number of fishkeepers ignore these two essentials, whether through ignorance, complacency, or simply a 'don't care' attitude. Unfortunately, many aquarists learn to appreciate the value of quarantine only after having introduced some deadly disease via newly-acquired fish.

The quarantining of newly-purchased fish involves housing them in a separate aquarium (the quarantine tank) for a period of several weeks (three to four weeks is generally recommended), during which the majority of seriously infectious diseases will manifest, if present. Except when the very first fish are introduced to a newly set up (and matured) aquarium, quarantine is essential to avoid the risk of introducing pathogens and parasites to the established community of fish.

During the quarantine period, no fish, equipment, plants or other decor, or anything else in (or which has been in) the quarantine tank should be allowed to come into contact with any other aquarium (or pond), until it is reasonably certain that the occupants are disease-free (i.e. they either have not developed disease, or have been successfully medicated). It is important to be aware that disease can be transmitted via human hands, so the quarantine tank should be dealt with last in the feeding and maintenance schedules, and the hands washed thoroughly afterwards.

As well as guarding against the introduction of disease, the quarantine period can also be used, if necessary, to adjust water chemistry gradually from that in which the fish has previously been kept to that in its future home. Equally important, it allows the new fish to recover from the stress of netting, packing, and transportation (Chapter 6) before encountering its new tankmates and finding its place (geographically and socially) in the main aquarium.

Quarantine has other uses, too. Many pathogens and parasites likely to be introduced via plants and decor will die without a host fish within a variable period of time, so quarantining plants for three to four weeks will help reduce any likelihood of disease transmission.

It is advisable to quarantine snails for three to four weeks in case they are harbouring fish parasites, although this is by no means foolproof as some of the worm diseases carried by snails may remain viable within the mollusc's tissues for weeks or months. Snail quarantine should be necessary only for wild snails, which may include some unusual purchased types as well as those from native waters.

The quarantine tank should be of adequate size for its occupants, and provided with a thin layer of substrate, suitable biological filter, heating, lighting, and adequate decor to make the fish feel at home. Use plastic plants (as any medication necessary may be harmful to live plants), and bear in mind that some drugs may eliminate the biological function of the filter. Unless the quarantine tank is kept set up all the time, the biological filter must be matured before the tank is used. Many aquarists keep a small air-powered sponge or box filter running in a corner of their main aquarium, for transfer to the quarantine tank when required.

If, despite all precautions, the main aquarium becomes infected with any infectious disease or parasite, then it too must be placed in quarantine; that is to say, there should be no contact between it (and its contents) and other aquaria (or ponds) until the problem has been remedied. It is, of course, totally unethical to sell, or even give away, any fish or item of equipment that may be infected with a disease.

DISINFECTION

Disinfection involves the immersion of any (possibly) infected item in hot (or boiling) water or a solution of an aquarium disinfectant. It should be used only to remove micro-organisms from decor and equipment, never from fish.

The method of disinfection should be appropriate to the item to be disinfected. For example, rocks are fairly indestructible, but some (e.g. plastic) items of equipment are not. It may sometimes be necessary instead to discard and replace possibly infected items, either because disinfection will destroy them, or because the pathogen may be resistant to any form of disinfection.

3. PROPHYLAXIS

This is the term applied to the use of medication or other forms of treatment to prevent disease. Except where there is danger of secondary infection of an injury (see below), it is not usually desirable to use prophylactic treatment on tropical freshwater fish and aquaria. The aquarist should *never* subject his fish to medication 'just in case' they might be infected with pathogens and/or parasites. Many medications are toxic to fish to various degrees, and should be used only when it is necessary to treat a particular disease diagnosed as actually affecting the fish.

Equally, it is neither necessary nor desirable routinely to dose the aquarium with drugs, or to use other control methods such as ultraviolet irradiation or ozone to eliminate opportunistic pathogens which are not normally harmful to healthy fish (see Opportunistic pathogens/parasites, above).

Prophylactic treatment may, however, be desirable where a fish has sustained skin damage, in order to prevent secondary bacterial/fungal infection of the damaged tissue, and/or osmotic stress.

CHAPTER 20

SIGNS OF ILLNESS
(What if my fish...?)

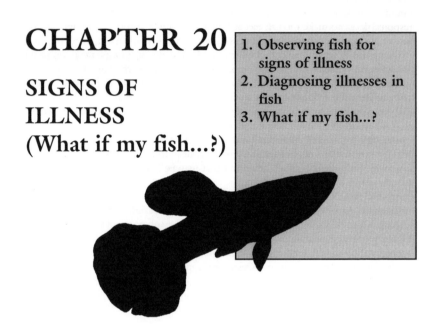

Early recognition and treatment of illness is important, not only to minimise suffering, but also because treatment is more likely to be effective. Many aquarium fish are small, not particularly robust creatures whose likelihood of survival will be appreciably diminished unless the problem is spotted, identified, and treated promptly. The object of this chapter is to enable the aquarist to recognise signs of suffering and illness in his fish, and, hopefully, to diagnose and treat the cause.

As we have already seen, veterinary treatment is the exception rather than the rule where fish are concerned. Nevertheless, the aquarist should carefully note down the signs of the illness, and record water parameters at the time the signs are first noticed. He should also keep a record of the disease, the diagnosis, the medications used (with dosages and dates) and their effect, if any. This information, together with details of the tank, its equipment, decor, and other occupants, may prove invaluable should it prove necessary to seek outside advice/assistance (Chapter 23), or if the problem recurs at a later date.

1. OBSERVING FISH FOR SIGNS OF ILLNESS
The responsible aquarist will have familiarised himself with the normal appearance, habits and behaviour of his fish from background reading before purchase and by

subsequent personal observation (Chapter 18). This will enable him quickly to spot any changes that may indicate the onset of illness.

Any changes in behaviour or appearance should be regarded as a cause for immediate concern unless these can be attributed to normal behaviour – for example, courtship behaviour and related changes in coloration. Again, the responsible aquarist who has researched his fish properly will be in a better position to recognise and identify these changes for what they are.

The circumstances in which a fish becomes unwell may be just as useful in making a diagnosis as the actual signs exhibited by the sick fish. If illness is suspected, then water parameters (chemistry and quality) should be checked immediately. Many cases of illness in fish are directly attributable to environmental factors, which may also be a contributory cause in many pathogenic and parasitic infections. It is a mistake automatically to assume that illness is caused by some infective agent and can be cured only by the use of chemical medications.

The behaviour of the other fish vis-a-vis the sick individual(s) should also be observed. Stress (Chapter 21, section 1.5.2) is one of the commonest illnesses in fish, predisposing them to disease, and can result from aggression as well as from other environmental problems.

Transportation (Chapter 6) and changes in surroundings/companions are highly stressful, and fish can be expected to show signs of shock or stress after such trauma. Unless the problem is due to a concomitant change in water parameters, then no action is required except to minimise further stress.

If the problem remains a mystery, the aquarist should not be afraid to seek immediate advice from an expert – another aquarist, a dealer, or a fish-health consultant (Chapter 23). Delay may result in the death of the fish.

2. DIAGNOSING ILLNESSES IN FISH

The changes in appearance and/or behaviour exhibited by a sick fish are termed the **signs** of the illness. Many of these are **non-specific**, that is to say, they are simply signs that the fish is ill, and they are not necessarily symptomatic of any specific illness. Table 10 lists a number of such non-specific signs, while Table 11 catalogues signs that the fish may be experiencing some form of skin/gill irritation, again from some unspecified cause.

Table 10 Non-specific Signs of Illness in Fish
Note: these signs may appear singly or in any combination. They are significant *only* if they represent a deviation from the norm.   • Loss of or reduction in appetite   • Abnormal behaviour of any type   • Changes in coloration   • Clamped fins   • Hiding   • Lethargy   • Respiratory distress   • Abnormal swimming   Fish exhibiting any of these signs should be kept under close observation for additional signs of a specific problem. Levels of nitrogenous wastes, and other water parameters (such as temperature, pH), should be checked.

Table 11 Non-specific Signs of Irritation in Fish

These signs may appear singly or in combination, and may denote irritation of the skin and/or gills, commonly from adverse water conditions or, less frequently, from skin/gill parasites. Note, however, that fish, like people, often suffer a momentary 'itch'; it is only repeated signs of irritation that are cause for concern.

- Clamped fins
- Coughing
- Darting/dashing
- Fin twitching
- Head shaking
- Jumping
- Respiratory distress (gasping, increased gill rate)
- Scratching and flashing
- Shimmying (usually while stationary)
- Yawning

Unless there are also specific signs of parasite infestation (e.g. tiny white spots, visible parasites), then levels of nitrogenous wastes, together with other water parameters, should be checked and ruled out as causes of the irritation.

Diagnosis of a specific illness is commonly a process of deduction, using a combination of the signs exhibited by the fish, data and observations regarding environmental factors, and the history of the fish, the aquarium, and its other occupants. For example, if one or more fish become ill, with non-specific signs, after living in the aquarium for several months, and no new fish, plants, or other decor items have been added recently, then the illness is probably the result of deterioration in water quality. If the circumstances are the same, except that all the fish are ill and a flowerpot from the garden has just been added, then the fish are probably being poisoned by pesticide residues from the flowerpot. If, instead of a flowerpot, the introduction is a new fish, there is a possibility that the problem is pathogens or parasites. Each case requires different treatment. Yet, in each case, the signs exhibited by the fish may be broadly similar.

It must be accepted that it is not always possible to diagnose a specific illness. In such situations, the course of action will depend on the circumstances. It must be stressed that there is no point in trying to treat an undiagnosed disease by random application of chemical medications in the hope of hitting on the right one. Many medications are ichthyotoxic to some extent and may even exacerbate some problems. Using a combination of chemicals (this includes using different medications in succession without eliminating the previous treatment by partial water changes) is a very effective method of killing fish through poisoning.

If diagnosis on the basis of signs proves impossible, then it may be necessary to submit samples for laboratory testing. Possible tests include detailed analysis of water samples (useful if poisoning is suspected but the cause is not apparent) and post-mortem examination. In both instances, the tests will normally have to be arranged via, or on the advice of, a vet or fish-health consultant (Chapter 23). Whether the effort and expense are justified may depend on the circumstances.

If just one fish is unwell, it may be that it has a non-infective, non-environmental, disease, such as a tumour or simply old age. Provided no other fish shows signs of illness and environmental conditions appear to be optimal, the appropriate action is normally to do nothing; but observe carefully for any additional clues that may appear. If the fish dies, a post-mortem may be considered out of interest rather than necessity. If, on the other hand, several or all the fish become ill within a short period of time, or a succession of individuals fall sick with the same signs, and no diagnosis proves possible, then water analysis and/or post-morten should be seriously considered.

There are, however, exceptions to the 'do nothing' rule. If the fish is being harassed by tankmates, is unable to compete for food, or is otherwise stressed by the company of other fish, then it should be removed to the peace and quiet of the hospital tank; but because such a move is itself stressful, it should be undertaken only where necessary. Moveover prompt isolation is the wisest course if the sick fish is a new purchase, perhaps preventing the spread of an infectious disease.

3. WHAT IF MY FISH...?

This section uses a 'What if' question and answer format to help the aquarist decide whether his fish are ill, and to match the various signs of possible illness with the diseases catalogued in Chapter 21. Each disease or condition is identified by name and by its section reference number (e.g. stress, 1.5.2) in that chapter.

Use Table 13 (P.189), to identify the relevant 'What if...?' number.

> **History tips**
> 'History tips' are highlighted throughout this chapter. These detail information which may be helpful in arriving at the correct diagnosis, whether this task is attempted by the aquarist himself or outside advice is sought. These tips relate to specific data which may be relevant to the problem in question; general information regarding the aquarium – its water, equipment, decor and occupants – is likely to be invaluable in most cases.

HEAD

1. What if my fish 'coughs'?
2. What if my fish vomits?
3. What if my fish 'yawns'?
4. What if my fish appears to be choking?
5. What if my fish won't eat?
6. What if my fish is blind?
7. What if my fish has a bulging eye?
8. What if my fish seems to be staring fixedly?
9. What if my fish can't shut its mouth?
10. What if my fish shakes its head?

GILLS

32. What if my fish is gasping for breath?
41. What if my fish twitches its fins?
42. What if my fish is breathing faster than usual?

FINS

39. What if my fish has fins which are frayed and ragged?
40. What if my fish clamps its fins?

BREEDING/FAECES

35. What if my fish jumps?
36. What if my fish has eggs which don't hatch?
37. What if my fish is producing abnormal droppings?
36. What if my fish has eggs which don't hatch?
37. What if my fish is producing abnormal droppings?
38. What if my fish has worms hanging out of its 'bottom'?

WHOLE FISH (body, head, fins)

11. What if my fish has 'worms' or other creatures attached to it?
12. What if my fish has spots?
13. What if my fish has lumps on it?
14. What if my fish is too thin?
15. What if my fish is stunted?
16. What if my fish changes colour?
17. What if my fish has what looks like cotton wool (cotton) on it?
18. What if my fish has holes?
19. What if my fish appears to be coated in slimy mucus?
20. What if my fish has bubbles on it or in its faeces?
21. What is my fish develops a distorted shape?
22. What if my fish has scales which stick out?
23. What if my fish swells up?

BEHAVIOUR

24. What if my fish has lost some scales?
25. What if my fish seems to be trying to get out through the front glass?
26. What if my fish is less active than usual?
27. What if my fish hangs at the surface?
28. What if my fish swims at an odd angle?
29. What if my fish rests on the bottom?
30. What if my fish keep dashing and darting around the aquarium?
31. What if my fish keeps scratching?
32. What if my fish is gasping for breath?
33. What if my fish hides?
34. What if my fish 'shimmies'?
43. What if my fish has gills which look abnormal?

Table 12 List of Problems Discussed in Chapter 20

1. What if my fish 'coughs'?
2. What if my fish vomits?
3. What if my fish 'yawns'?
4. What if my fish appears to be choking?
5. What if my fish appears to be blind?
6. What if my fish won't eat?
7. What it my fish has a bulging eye?
8. What if my fish seems to be staring fixedly?
9. What if my fish can't shut its mouth?
10. What if my fish shakes its head?
11. What if my fish has 'worms' or other creatures attached to it?
12. What if my fish has spots?
13. What if my fish has lumps on it?
14. What if my fish is too thin?
15. What if my fish is stunted?
16. What if my fish changes colour?
17. What if my fish has what looks like cotton wool (cotton) on it?
18. What if my fish has holes?
19. What if my fish appears to be coated in slimy mucus?
20. What if my fish has bubbles on it or in its faeces?
21. What is my fish develops a distorted shape?
22. What if my fish has scales which stick out?
23. What if my fish swells up?
24. What if my fish has lost some scales?
25. What if my fish seems to be trying to get out through the front glass?
26. What if my fish is less active than usual?
27. What if my fish hangs at the surface?
28. What if my fish swims at an odd angle?
29. What if my fish rests on the bottom?
30. What if my fish keep dashing and darting around the aquarium?
31. What if my fish keeps scratching?
32. What if my fish is gasping for breath?
33. What if my fish hides?
34. What if my fish 'shimmies'?
35. What if my fish jumps?
36. What if my fish has eggs which don't hatch?
37. What if my fish is producing abnormal droppings?
38. What if my fish has worms hanging out of its 'bottom'?
39. What if my fish has fins which are frayed and ragged?
40. What if my fish clamps its fins?
41. What if my fish twitches its fins?
42. What if my fish is breathing faster than usual?
43. What if my fish has gills which look abnormal?
44. What if my fish has jumped out of the tank?

1. WHAT IF MY FISH 'COUGHS'?

A fish which makes coughing motions is usually experiencing some sort of irritation of the mouth/gullet/gill area. Coughing may also occur in fish recovering from anaesthesia. The occasional isolated cough is no cause for concern, but if any fish coughs regularly or repeatedly, this may be a sign of a health problem. Causes may be:

• **Environmental**, e.g. Poisoning (1.2), (including by ammonia (1.2.3), nitrite (1.2.10), nitrate (1.2.8, 1.2.9), chlorine/chloramine (1.2.5); excessive carbon dioxide (1.3.1)); incorrect pH (1.1.1, 1.1.3); insufficient oxygen in the water (1.3.3); suspended material in the water (cloudy water, see Chapter 15, What if no.10)

What if my aquarium water is cloudy or a 'funny' colour?.

• **Pathogenic**, e.g. gill rot (3.3.5), fungal attack of gill tissue (3.3.3).

• **Parasitic**, e.g. whitespot (4.1.23), velvet disease (4.1.22), skin slime disease (4.1.18), gill parasites (4.2.8, 4.2.9.), skin flukes (4.2.11), larval stages of some other parasites (4.2.5, 4.2.1).

• **Mechanical damage** to gill tissue, e.g. where bottom-sifting species have been kept over a sharp substrate.

See also What if no.4, What if my fish appears to be choking?

> **History Tip**
> Coughing may accompany any of the possible causes listed. It may also continue for some time after the cause has been rectified, until any tissue damage has healed. Although the aquarist should remain vigilant, coughing does not necessarily imply further problems in these circumstances.

2. WHAT IF MY FISH VOMITS?

Some fish are known occasionally to vomit back their meal. This may be the result of incorrect diet, or stress (1.5.2). It may also be a means of eliminating toxins or unpalatable/indigestible material ingested with, or as part of, the meal. Sometimes a fish may take in and immediately eject any food which it deems unpalatable or finds unfamiliar.

Repeated vomiting or spitting out of food may indicate digestive problems (2.0) – possibly inflammation caused by bacterial infection (3.2), or a blockage (constipation (2.1), tumour (6.7), or an item of equipment or decor lodged anywhere in the digestive tract – including the gullet, see also What if no.4, What if my fish appears to be choking?).

3. WHAT IF MY FISH 'YAWNS'?

Little is known about this behaviour, but in some cases it appears to be a response to poor water quality, so check ammonia, nitrite, and nitrate levels. Commonly only one or two fish yawn, sporadically, sometimes while shimmying. Both yawning and shimmying are often early warning signs of deteriorating environmental conditions.

Other factors which should be considered are oxygen depletion (1.3.3) and/or raised carbon dioxide levels (1.3.1); incorrect pH (1.1.1); chemical poisoning (1.2), including chlorine/chloramine (1.2.5).

Even if no environmental cause can be found, a partial water change will commonly rectify the problem. Failing which, there is a slight possibility that the yawning may be associated with gill disease/parasitisation (e.g. 3.3.2, 4.2.8, 4.2.9).

4. WHAT IF MY FISH APPEARS TO BE CHOKING?

It probably is! Especially if it has just been feeding or using its mouth to dig in the substrate. The problem usually occurs where the gravel is too large for the species concerned to dig safely, or where the food particle size is too large for the fish in question. Many fish swallow their food whole, and will instinctively grab the largest piece of food they can in the often highly competitive aquarium environment where the form of the food is different to that of the natural diet. Choking is also sometimes seen in fish recovering from anaesthesia.

Choking caused by gravel often requires immediate remedial action. The fish should be netted and the gravel carefully removed with forceps, if possible – otherwise veterinary intervention will be required. If the problem is caused by food, it will often resolve itself – the fish will either eject the food or, eventually, get it down. If not, then again it must be removed. Such traumas are best avoided by providing suitably-sized substrate and appropriate foods (Chapter 7).

See also What if no.1, What if my fish 'coughs'?

5. WHAT IF MY FISH APPEARS TO BE BLIND?

Blindness may affect one or both eyes, and be permanent (loss/atrophy of the eye, permanent opacity of the pupil) or temporary (many cases of cloudy eye, (6.2)).

Partial or complete blindness in fish is generally not as debilitating as it is for higher vertebrates; even in cases of complete blindness, euthanasia is not normally necessary as the fish can use other senses (see Chapter 17) to find its way around and locate food (unless it hunts solely by sight, as is common with pursuit predators). Indeed, some fish are naturally blind. If, however, a blind fish finds it difficult to compete in the community aquarium, it should be housed in its own aquarium or one shared with slow-moving peaceful fish.

The following are some of the possible causes of blindness and/or cloudy eye:
• Injury (1.6.1) resulting from aggression, collision with decor, or clumsy handling.
• Genetic mutation (5.0).
• Eye fluke (*Diplostomum*) (4.2.5).
• Nutritional deficiency (2.5).
• Bacterial infection (3.2).
• Fungus infection (3.3).
• Chlorine damage (usually very temporary) (1.2.5).
• Gas bubble disease (1.3.2).
• Pop-eye (exophthalmia) (6.5).
• Old age.

History tip

Eye clouding is commonly a sign of an underlying general disorder. For example, poor water quality or pathogenic illness may impair the fish's immune response such that the delicate eyes become susceptible to attack by opportunistic pathogens (bacteria and fungi). It is important to identify, and if possible remedy, the underlying problem in such cases; the eye condition will then commonly clear up without any need for specific medication.

6. WHAT IF MY FISH WON'T EAT?

Whether or not loss of appetite is a cause for concern will depend on the circumstances:

• It is quite normal for a newly-introduced fish to show no interest in food for a period (hours or days) because of the stress involved in transportation and adjusting to new surroundings. Such fish may also be reluctant to feed if the type of food is unfamiliar, and this may also apply to established fish if a strange food is offered. This problem usually resolves itself when the fish become hungrier, but, in the meantime, uneaten food must be scrupulously removed to prevent pollution.

• Some fish require special foods and will reject alternatives offered. Some piscivores, for example, may refuse to eat anything but live fish, at least initially.

• Mouthbrooding species commonly cease feeding during the brooding period.

• Otherwise, reluctance to feed in established fish may be a sign of a health problem. Water chemistry and quality tests should be made and any problem rectified (1.1.1, 1.2.3, 1.2.8, 1.2.10), and the fish observed for additional signs of illness.

• If the fish takes a normally accepted food into its mouth and spits it out again, the problem may be obstruction of the gullet (lumps of food, gravel, pieces of equipment, or a tumour (6.7)). The fish should be netted and the gullet inspected. Soft or smooth items can sometimes be removed by the aquarist with long forceps, but veterinary assistance may be required, and should always be sought if the obstruction is sharp (e.g. some types of gravel) or angular (e.g. airline valves).

• Sudden loss of appetite plus absence of faeces may denote constipation (2.1).

A few days without food will not generally cause any harm, except in the case of young fry, which can quickly starve to death.

History tip

Both acute and chronic stress (1.5.2) can lead to loss of appetite. This may occur if, for example, the affected fish has recently been subject to aggression (acute stress), or has a history of nervousness and reluctance to compete at feeding time (chronic stress). The chronic stress situation should never be allowed to arise, and acute stress should be dealt with speedily.

---

7. WHAT IT MY FISH HAS A BULGING EYE?

This is the condition known as pop-eye (6.5) or exophthalmia, and it may affect both eyes. A bulging eye is a cause for concern and requires urgent attention as otherwise it may literally pop out of its socket and be lost.

Exophthalmia is a common sign of a number of environmental and pathogenic diseases (see 6.5).

History tip

If the cause of pop-eye is environmental, it is common for only a single, susceptible species (or even just one individual) to be affected – *at first*. An environmental cause should thus not be ruled out simply because the problem is specific to one or a few fish. If the problem is not identified and rectified, other fish may soon succumb to this and/or other manifestations of the underlying cause.

FISH VARIETIES

The 'red zebra' (*Metriaclima estherae*).

Neolamprologus tretocephalus.

Arawana (*Osteoglossum bicirrhosum*).

Steel-blue killifish *(Aphyosemion gardneri)*.

Clown loach (*Botia macracantha*).

Green terror (*Aequidens rivulatus*).

Gar fish (*Ctenolucius hujeta*).

Nimbochromis fuscotaeniatus.

Red-bellied piranha (*Serrasalmus nattereri*).

Neolamprologus buescheri.

Red-tailed black shark (*Epalzeorhynchus bicolor*).

Metynnis luna.

Borelli's dwarf cichlid (*Apistogramma borellii*).

Angel fish (*Pterophyllum scalare*).

Peter Burgess.

Hart's rivulus (*Rivulus hartii*).

Keith Allison.

Plecostomus (*Hypostomus plecostomus*).

8. WHAT IF MY FISH SEEMS TO BE STARING FIXEDLY?

Fish do not have eyelids, so their eyes are constantly open – in that sense it is normal for them to stare. Normally, however, the eyes are responsive to visual stimuli, and the fish moves either its eyes (in species where the eyes are mobile) or itself to look at whatever catches its attention.

A fish that is unwell for any reason commonly develops a fixed stare and seems less alert and interested in its surroundings than normal. If, however, a fish's eyes have a glazed look and lose their mobility, as if staring into the distance without seeing, and it does not respond to visual (or other) stimuli, then there may be a serious and acute problem:

• Poisoning (1.2.1), including ammonia (1.2.3) and nitrite (1.2.11) poisoning, as well as that caused by extraneous toxins such as pesticides and domestic chemicals.
• Extreme hypoxia (1.3.3), including that resulting from diseases or parasites that damage the gills and affect oxygen uptake.
• Severe chilling (1.4.1), – the metabolic rate is slowed and the fish barely conscious.
• Severe shock (1.5.1).

> **History tip**
> In the case of shock or chilling, the fish is likely to rest on the bottom, possibly on its side, and the gill rate is likely to be abnormally slow. The fish may also rest on the bottom in cases of hypoxia and poisoning, but may equally dash or swim around in an uncontrolled manner, or swim on the spot (ammonia/nitrite poisoning): in all these cases the gill rate is likely to be accelerated.

9. WHAT IF MY FISH CAN'T SHUT ITS MOUTH?

This situation requires prompt attention as it normally means the fish cannot feed. This is one of the rare situations where a trip to the vet may be the only answer.

• There may be something stuck in the mouth – a stone, lump of food, or piece of equipment. It may be possible for the aquarist to remove the item, but if there is any risk of damage, the vet must be consulted.
• The lower jaw (maxilla) may be dislocated. The vet may be able to relocate it in medium to large fish, but small ones will probably have to be euthanased to prevent death by slow starvation.
• The mouth cavity, or opening, may be obstructed by a tumour (6.7) or *Lymphocystis* cysts (3.1.1). Surgery may be possible, otherwise euthanasia.
• In pufferfish (Tetraodontidae) the problem may be overgrown teeth, which can be trimmed by the vet. The teeth of puffers are fused and very strong, to enable them to crush open the snails which are their natural diet. The problem should ideally be avoided by feeding them snails in captivity.
See also What if no. 32, What if my fish is gasping?

> **History tip**
> Bottom-feeders and fish which use their mouths for digging are those most likely to pick up stones and stray pieces of equipment such as suckers, clips, airstones, and the like. Jaw dislocation is usually seen in cichlids and results from their habit of jaw-locking during battles and courtship. Experienced aquarists with a penchant for large cichlids may find it worthwhile to take jaw-relocation lessons from the vet!

10. WHAT IF MY FISH SHAKES ITS HEAD?

This behaviour normally takes place while the fish is 'swimming on the spot' and is commonly accompanied by shimmying and yawning. The head movement sometimes continues along the body in an overall sinuous movement. Usually seen in association with raised nitrate levels (1.2.8) or suspended matter in the water (see Chapter 16, What if no.10, What if my aquarium water is cloudy or a 'funny' colour?), and indicative of slight irritation.

11. WHAT IF MY FISH HAS 'WORMS' OR OTHER CREATURES ATTACHED TO IT?

These will be large parasites (4.2), visible to the naked eye as individual creatures. It is usually easy to identify the individual type:

• A Y-shaped elongate parasite, attached to the fish at the foot of the Y, is an anchor worm (*Lernaea*) (4.2.1).
• A roughly circular, semi-transparent parasite with visible dark eyes, lying almost flush with the skin/fin, is a fish louse (*Argulus*) (4.2.7).
• Brownish worms protruding from the anus are *Camallanus* (4.2.3), an endoparasitic roundworm (nematode worm) (4.2.10).
• A worm-like parasite, usually attached at both ends to the fish, or moving across the fish in a looping manner, is a fish leech (*Piscicola*) (4.2.6).
• Whitish 'maggots' on the gills are gill maggots (*Ergasilus*) (4.2.9) – the 'maggots' are actually the egg pouches of the female parasite.

See also Chapter 15, What if no.9, What if my aquarium has been invaded by strange 'creepy-crawlies'?

History tip

Because these parasites are so visible they are rarely seen on fish offered for sale, having been eradicated before the fish reach the retail outlet. (Fish with visible parasites should not be purchased – or, indeed, offered for sale.) Thus the presence of any of these parasites in the domestic aquarium is more likely to be traceable to the use of wild-collected live foods or decor items. Even so, they are rarely seen.

---

12. WHAT IF MY FISH HAS SPOTS?

First of all, make sure the spots or blotches are not simply part of the fish's normal coloration repertoire. Sometimes such markings are present in only one sex, or develop only as the fish matures or during periods of sexual activity. There are, however, many abnormal spots that can affect fish. So many, that we have grouped them by colour for easier reference, starting with light-coloured spots, which include the type most likely to be encountered: whitespot.

White or light-coloured spots:
• Pinhead-sized white spots on head, body, and fins are most likely to be whitespot (4.1.23). Less probable possibilities are newly-developing *Lymphocystis* (3.1.3) cysts, or, far less probably, *Apiosoma* (4.1.1).
• Tiny off-white spots on the fins are commonly tiny injuries, but may sometimes look like whitespot. Newly-purchased fish exhibiting such spots should be kept under observation.

• Whitish spots, which on closer inspection can be seen to be tiny tufts protruding from under the edges of scales, may be due to systemic fungus (3.3, 3.3.8).
• Small whitish tufts, especially on hard tissues (fins, gill-covers) may be *Epistylis* (4.1.5).
• Small whitish patches in poeciliids may signify guppy disease (4.1.6).
• Whitish circles may be wounds caused by leeches (4.2.6).
• A white spot obscuring the lens of the eye may be caused by eye fluke (4.2.5). See also cloudy eye (6.2), and What if no.5, What if my fish is blind?
• Grey-white patches under the skin, usually in tetras (but possibly some other fish), may indicate neon tetra disease (4.1.13).
• Greyish or whitish patches are most likely to be mucus hyperproduction (see What if no.19, What if my fish appears to be coated in slimy mucus?).
• Grey spots/patches on the skin of angelfish (*Pterophyllum* spp.) may be caused by *Meterosporis* (4.1.8).
Note: at spawning time the males of some cyprinids (e.g. barbs) may develop white spots (tubercles) around the gills/head and sometimes the base of the pectorals. These are quite normal and not a cause for concern.

Black or dark-coloured spots:
• Black spots on the body/fins are usually black spot disease (4.2.2).
• Black/dark spots or patches round the mouths of East African cichlids are usually 'black chin' (1.2.4).
• Dark/discoloured patches on the body may be superficial injuries (1.6.1), including burns.

Red spots:
• Red spots on the skin may be wounds caused by large ectoparasites (4.2) or subcutaneous haemorrhages – perhaps caused by systemic infection (3.1, 3.2).
• Red spots/streaks on the fins (fin congestion) are often a sign of impending fin rot (3.2.2).

Other-coloured spots:
• Very tiny yellow-green spots, sometimes in huge numbers so that the fish appears to be coated in the colour, are a sign of velvet disease (4.1.22).
• Tumours (6.7) may initially appear spot-like. They can be any size or colour, and anywhere on the body.

See also What if no.13, What if my fish has lumps on it?

> **History tip**
> In diagnosing the cause of one of the many different types of white/light spots, it is especially important to take into account the circumstances (new or established fish); other signs (present or not – for example, fish with whitespot scratch, fish with cauliflower disease do not); the fish species (cichlids and killifish, for example, don't get guppy or neon tetra disease!); the progress and infectivity of the disease (rapid in whitespot, far less so in others). These distinctions are discussed in the relevant sections of Chapter 21.

13. WHAT IF MY FISH HAS LUMPS ON IT?

Lumps, growths, or swellings on the body surface come in all kinds
of shapes, sizes, and colours, with an equivalent range of causes:

• Raised lumps ('lesions') may occur as a result of some bacterial infections (3.2) such as fish tuberculosis (3.2.3). These lumps may have a pale to white necrotic region (sometimes with an ulcerated pit) and a reddened haemorrhagic region.
• Digestive blockage (including constipation (2.1)), occasionally causes a laterally asymmetric bulge, usually on one side of the abdomen.
• An internal tumour (6.7) can cause a similar bulge, while an external one can appear virtually anywhere on the head and/or body. External tumours may be the same colour as the surrounding skin or sometimes black (melanoma). They vary greatly in size and shape, and may appear singly or in numbers.
• Fish pox (3.1.2) initially produces greyish or whitish patches resembling mucus hyperproduction; these are soft when new, but hard and waxy in time. This condition is very rare in tropical fish.
• Encysted helminth ('worm') larvae (4.0, 4.2.2) beneath the skin may look like smallish growths on the body. There may be just one or several, and they may appear pale to dark grey when the fish is light-coloured.
• Whitish growths, often forming grape- or cauliflower-like clusters, particularly noticeable on the fins, are cauliflower disease (3.1.1).
    See also What if no.12, What if my fish has spots?

Note: some fish (notably some cichlids) develop large fatty lumps (nuchal humps) on the top of the head when adult, especially in males. Sometimes these humps are permanent, sometimes they become smaller, or virtually disappear, when the fish is not breeding. Ripe female fish may naturally have one ovary more developed than the other, producing an asymmetric swelling of the body.

> **History tip**
> Tumours are more likely to occur in older fish. To differentiate between a bulge caused by an internal tumour and one resulting from digestive blockage, consider whether the fish is producing faeces, and whether it is eating (both are unlikely in the case of such a severe blockage). A bulge caused by an internal tumour is also likely to be slower in developing.

14. WHAT IF MY FISH IS TOO THIN?

Weight loss and emaciation may result from a number of different causes:
• The direct pathogenic effects of a disease. Examples are:

– Pathogenic, usually systemic, infection with bacteria (3.2) or fungus (3.3) (uncommon). Fish tuberculosis (3.2.3) is particularly likely to cause emaciation.
– Endoparasitic protozoan infection, e.g. neon tetra disease (4.1.13) (in tetras and some cyprinids); hole-in-head disease (4.1.10) (in cichlids); *Heterosporis* (4.1.8) (in angelfish (*Pterophyllum* spp)).
• The side-effects of almost any illness, i.e. the fish does not eat because it is unwell, and gradually becomes emaciated.
• Heavy infestation with endoparasitic worms (4.2.3, 4.2.4, 4.2.10, 4.2.12, 4.2.13)

may cause emaciation (owing to the parasites feeding on the host's food), but, at the same time, the abdomen may be distended by the sheer bulk of the worms in the gut. Some worms may also affect nutrient uptake by the fish, by damaging the lining of its gut.
• Incorrect diet or long-term shortfall in food intake (2.0, 2.4) (see also Chapter 7).
• Species which do not feed during brood care (e.g. mouthbrooding species) may become very emaciated.
• Spawning parturition may cause a sudden reduction in the girth of the female. See also What if no.6, What if my fish won't eat?

> **History tip**
> 'Too thin' is a relative term – most fish that have lived for any time in a domestic aquarium are rather fatter than Nature intended. The fact that a fish is slender and has a flat abdominal profile does not necessarily mean it is unhealthy in any way, and should not deter the aquarist from making a purchase. Genuine emaciation (concave abdominal profile) is another matter entirely, indicating genuine ill health and serious undernourishment. If, however, an established fish loses weight/bulk (unless its diet/food intake has been deliberately modified because it is too fat, or it has spawned/given birth/mouthbrooded), then there is cause for concern.

15. WHAT IF MY FISH IS STUNTED?
Stunting, whether permanent (the fish does not reach normal full size) or temporary (the fish grows slowly, or stops growing for a while), is a fairly common problem. Some types of stunting (e.g. genetic defect) are irremediable, others may respond to amelioration of the underlying problem. The sooner the latter is remedied, the better the chance of avoiding permanent stunting. Possible causes of stunting include:
• Genetic defect (5.0), sometimes associated with inbreeding. Incurable.
• Poor/incorrect diet (1.2.2, 2.4, 2.5), or inadequate feeding (2.4).
See also Chapter 7.
• Lack of appetite – see What if no.6, What if my fish won't eat?
• Direct biochemical effects of adverse water conditions (1.1, 1.2, 1.3).
• Direct result of pathogenic disease (3.0).
• Direct result of some parasitic infections, for example, leeches (4.2.6), and intestinal worms (4.2.10, 4.2.12, 4.2.13).
• Inadequate living space – tank too small for the specific fish, or tank overcrowded.
• Growth-inhibiting hormones. Research has shown that in a small number of species (but further research may reveal far more), the dominant (largest) individual in a brood produces growth-inhibiting hormones, preventing further growth by potentially competing siblings in the immediate vicinity (anywhere in even the largest domestic aquarium may be classed as the immediate vicinity!).
• Over-breeding. This affects chiefly female fish, who divert a considerable amount of their nutrient intake into the production of eggs/fry. Mouthbrooder females may be dramatically affected by their refusal of food during the brooding period. Males of bi-parental or paternal mouthbrooding species may also be affected. Other types of parental care may also affect the guarding parent(s), who often cannot guard eggs/fry and hunt for food simultaneously.

History tip
Remember that in some species one sex may, quite normally, be larger in eventual size than the other; in other species differential growth may be regulated by other factors. This dimorphism commonly manifests at an early stage, and may become more pronounced with time as the larger fish are better able to compete for the available food. The smaller fish, meanwhile, may become stressed, lose appetite, and grow even more slowly. Ultimately the large may cannibalise the small. Hence, juveniles of some species need to be regularly 'size-sorted' into batches which are grown on separately. It is also important to remember the possibility of early-manifesting sexual dimorphism of size when culling a brood. While culling obvious runts is good practice, if all culling is on a size basis, the aquarist may end up with all one sex.

---

16. WHAT IF MY FISH CHANGES COLOUR?

Changes in the coloration of a fish may sometimes be indicative of changes in its health or in its status in the aquarium (which may affect its health). Fish which become noticeably darker (or, sometimes, lighter) may be suffering from stress or disease. Abnormally bright coloration may occasionally denote a problem.

Unexpected or abnormal colour changes should always be regarded as suspicious if accompanied by other generalised signs of possible illness.

The following colour changes may be indicative of particular problems:

• A fish which has become blind may take on overall permanent dark coloration, perhaps because the fish perceives its environment to be uniformly dark and therefore endeavours to match it (camouflage).

• Abnormally dark coloration is a very common sign of stress (1.5.2), but may also be seen during many other diseases. It may reflect physiological changes, or represent an attempt by the sick fish to render itself inconspicuous (a natural defence against predation and confrontation).

• A laterally asymmetric dark area, commonly on one side of the head, may signify localised nerve damage inhibiting control of the melanophores. Possible causes are a burn or injury (1.6.1), localised bacterial infection (3.2) (e.g. an abscess), or a tumour (6.7). Permanent damage may result in permanent discoloration.

• Dark/discoloured patches may be the result of burns or other superficial injuries (1.6.1), such as bruising.

• Black patches which expand with time (days/weeks) may be melanomas (6.7).

• In cichlids, dark areas around the mouth may be black chin (1.2.5).

• In characins (and less commonly in some cyprinids), fading of the normal colour, sometimes accompanied by whitish/greyish patches under the skin, is a sign of neon tetra disease (4.1.13).

• Abnormally pale coloration may denote, *inter alia*, fish tuberculosis (3.2.3); shock (1.5.1); osmotic stress (1.1.2, 1.6.2).

• A grey appearance (all over or in patches) may be mucus hyperproduction, which is a response to irritation by various adverse environmental conditions (1.0) and/or parasites (4.0). Alternatively, it may be skin slime disease (4.1.18).

• A yellowish cast may be velvet disease (4.1.22).

• Reddened areas can be the result of ectoparasite damage (4.1); injury (1.6.1);

irritation caused by acidosis/alkalosis (1.1.1) or ammonia (1.2.3); inflammation and/or haemorrhaging as a result of a systemic bacterial (3.2) or viral (3.1) infection; vitamin C deficiency (2.5).

• Extensive pale red coloration of the abdomen is associated with dropsy (6.3) and some other systemic bacterial (3.2) or viral (3.1) infections.

• Discoloration of the fins (including the tail) – lightened, grey-white, ragged edges, with or without reddening through inflammation; and/or red streaking of the affected fin(s) – may denote fin rot (3.2.2).

• Heightened or otherwise abnormal coloration may be a sign of damage to the central nervous system with resulting loss of control of the chromatophores. Possible causes are hypoxia (1.3.3); poisoning (1.2.1); acidosis/alkalosis (1.1.1); injury (1.6.1); or tumour (6.7).

> **History tip**
> In order to evaluate the significance of colour changes, it is essential to be aware of the normal variations exhibited by the type of fish concerned. In many fish, coloration is relatively static, such that any significant change should immediately be cause for concern. Some fish, however, change colour in the course of their development from juvenile to adult, while others utilise colour variation for communication, to indicate *inter alia* mood, status, sexual status, and courtship display. The aquarium decor and lighting may play a part, as some fish become darker or paler according to their surroundings.

17. WHAT IF MY FISH HAS WHAT LOOKS LIKE COTTON WOOL (COTTON) ON IT?

Cotton-wool-like growths are most usually fungus (cotton wool disease) (3.3.3). Similar growths are produced by the bacterial disease known as mouth fungus (Columnaris) (3.2.4), which commonly affects the mouth area, but can also attack other parts of the body as well as the fins and gills.

18. WHAT IF MY FISH HAS HOLES?

Apart from the mouth, gill slits, and anus, fish have a number of other perfectly normal apertures: the nostrils (on the snout – some types of fish have a single pair, others two pairs), and the sensory pores, (a scattering of tiny holes on the head; and one or more rows along either side of the body, sometimes extending on to the tail).
Problem holes:

• In cichlids, the sensory pores on the head and in the lateral line (rarely) may become enlarged and infected during hole-in-head disease (4.1.10).

• If, however, there is no sign of pus, enlarged or eroded sensory pores in cichlids may be simply a function of old age and are not known to be harmful.

• Holes in the fins or body are usually injuries (1.6.1); holes in the body may also be wounds left by ectoparasites such as anchor worm (4.2.1), leeches (4.2.6), or fish lice (4.2.7).

> **History tip**
> Cichlid-keepers who have never seen hole-in-head disease, but are aware of the threat it represents to their 'loved ones', tend to become quite paranoid and imagine that the nostrils and healthy sensory pores are the first signs of the dreaded illness. To avoid unnecessary distress to the aquarist and pointless medication of healthy fish, it is strongly suggested that any new cichlid-keeper, worried about the disease, should ask someone more expert to point out and identify the normal holes on cichlid heads, for reference!

19. WHAT IF MY FISH APPEARS TO BE COATED IN SLIMY MUCUS?

It is! The external surfaces of fish are protected by a mucus coating, which is normally barely visible, if at all. Under certain circumstances, however, the fish may produce more mucus than normal so that the fish looks greyish and slimy; this is called mucus hyperproduction. It is a very common sign that the fish's skin is being affected by an irritant, which may be connected with water chemistry (1.1), water quality (1.2), or parasites (4. 0). The condition is so characteristic of one type of parasitic protozoan infection that it is called skin slime disease (4.1.18). Overdosing with, or other misuse (e.g. mixtures) of, chemical medications can also irritate the skin and lead to mucus hyperproduction.

> **History tip**
> Mucus hyperproduction caused by an irritant is almost invariably accompanied, or preceded, by other signs of irritation, e.g. scratching and flashing. A small number of fish, however, most notably discus (*Symphysodon* spp.) and *Uaru* cichlids, produce large quantities of additional mucus as a first food for their fry, which 'glance' (graze) on their parents' flanks and fins.
>   Interestingly, both *Symphysodon* and *Uaru* sometimes slough body mucus, apparently as a reaction to stress (1.5.2) (especially that caused by transportation), incorrect environmental (water) conditions, or a change (often only minor) in water parameters. The process looks horrendous, but apparently the situation is not serious, as the fish shows no other signs of distress. In neither situation (feeding fry or mucus sloughing) are there normally any accompanying signs of irritation.

20. WHAT IF MY FISH HAS BUBBLES ON IT OR IN ITS FAECES?

Bubbles in the faeces may indicate a digestive disorder (2.0). This is normally a short-term phenomenon, in individual fish, which clears up very quickly, but if it occurs whenever a particular food is used, then it may be better to eliminate that food from the diet of affected fish.

Bubbles on the fish (commonly also on the tank glasses and decor), usually following a partial water change using cold water, may indicate a risk of gas bubble disease (1.3.2).

21. WHAT IS MY FISH DEVELOPS A DISTORTED SHAPE?

• Some fish have skeletal deformities as a result of genetic mutation (5.3) and this is not always initially apparent if the deformity is slight.

• Such deformities may also occur as a result of injury (1.6.1); fish tuberculosis (3.2.3) and some other pathogenic diseases (3.0); some endoparasite infestations (4.2.13, 4.2.10, 4.1.13); adverse water conditions (particularly in young, growing fish); and vitamin deficiency (2.5).
• A tumour (6.7) may cause a fish to appear deformed (relatively uncommon).
• Undernourishment can cause concavity of the abdominal profile, and overfeeding on an unsuitable diet may lead to obesity (2.3) – perhaps the most commonly seen type of body distortion.
• Some fish change shape as they grow, e.g. discus (*Symphysodon* spp.), and some develop what look like deformities as part of their 'breeding dress'. Notable among the latter is the so-called 'nuchal hump', a fatty gibbosity of the forehead region seen in adult or breeding males (less commonly females) of some cichlid species.
See also What if no.23, What if my fish swells up?

History tip
If we leave aside obesity, body distortion in adult fish is most likely to occur as the result of pathogenic or parasitic disease. This may also be the case with young, growing fish, but in such cases water quality and dietary deficiency may equally be involved. If either of the last two problems occurs where a brood is being grown on, all fish are likely to be affected more or less equally.

22. WHAT IF MY FISH HAS SCALES WHICH STICK OUT?
This phenomenon is commonly seen in conjunction with abdominal swelling caused by dropsy (6.3). See also What if no.23, What if my fish swells up?

23. WHAT IF MY FISH SWELLS UP?
There are several possible reasons for a fish having an abnormally swollen body or swollen belly region:
• Dropsy (6.3) (swelling commonly accompanied by protruding scales, giving the fish a pine-cone like appearance).
• Malawi bloat (6.4) (East African mouthbrooding cichlids only).
• Females that are gravid or ripe with eggs may have distended bellies.
• The fish has just eaten a large meal. Certain carnivorous and predatory fish consume large items of food which may last them for several days, during which the belly slowly reduces to 'normal' size and shape. Fish which are continuous feeders should not be fed quantities large enough to produce this effect, otherwise digestive disorders (2.0) are likely to result in the short or long term.
• Deformity (5.3). Certain species have been selectively bred to create 'fancy' varieties, some of which have distended or abnormally rounded bodies.
• Tapeworms (4.2.13). The distension is often laterally asymmetric and may cause lopsided swimming.
• An internal tumour (6.7) may cause body distension and give rise to dropsy-like symptoms. Unlike dropsy, however, the condition may be laterally asymmetric.
• Obesity (2.3), usually resulting from long-term unsuitable diet.
• Vibriosis (3.2.11) (rare).
See also What if no.21, What if my fish develops a distorted shape?

> **History tip**
> If the distension arises gradually often almost unnoticeably over time, then it is likely to be obesity in most cases, or possibly tapeworms or a tumour (the latter particularly in old(er) fish). Sudden distension is more likely to be pathogenic or environmental (dropsy, Malawi bloat, *Vibrio*). Note that gas production by bacterial fermentation can cause distension after death; such distension of the corpse cannot be taken as an indication of the cause of death.

24. WHAT IF MY FISH HAS LOST SOME SCALES?

This can easily happen. Even a minor injury of this type can develop a secondary bacterial (3.2) or fungal (3.3.3) infection, so the fish should be kept under observation. The loss of large numbers of scales may indicate a risk of osmotic stress (1.6.2). Normally scales regenerate in time. Causes of scale loss include:

• Collision with a hard object during flight (see What if nos.30, 35, What if my fish keep dashing and darting around the aquarium?, What if my fish jumps).
• Scratching against decor (see What if no.31, What if my fish keeps scratching?).
• Knocked/pulled off during an attack/figh/spawning activity.
• Knocked/pulled/scraped off by clumsy netting or other handling.
• Eaten by a scale-eating fish.
• Lost through skin damage caused by some diseases, e.g. ulceration (3.2.9), skin slime disease (4.1.18).

> **History tip**
> Although scale loss may seem, and often is, trivial, it is essential to identify the cause, in case there is any repetition. Regular panic-stricken flight may lead to serious injury and stress; bullying and/or fighting likewise. The accidental introduction of a scale-eating fish can have a devastating effect in the confines of an aquarium, where the same small group of victims provide the lepidophage's food supply. Hence scale loss should always be regarded as a potential warning sign of a more serious problem.

25. WHAT IF MY FISH SEEMS TO BE TRYING TO GET OUT THROUGH THE FRONT GLASS?

This is a common escape response, often seen in newly-introduced fish, and sometimes in established fish that are severely stressed, (e.g. trying desperately to get away from an aggressor or ardent suitor).

In some, often (but not always) large territorial fish this behaviour is territorial defence against anyone near the tank. The fish may charge and bite at the glass. The behaviour is likely to be even more violent if the fish is guarding fry. It is inadvisable to put a hand into the tank in the latter circumstances!

Swimming up and down the front glass is often a reaction to the presence of the owner, and translates, roughly, as 'Feed me!'. This is very appealing and can encourage overfeeding, so remember the dangers of pollution (1.2) and obesity (2.3).

26. WHAT IF MY FISH IS LESS ACTIVE THAN USUAL?

As ever, it is important to be aware of what is usual for the species (for example, nocturnal species may appear lethargic by day, and *vice versa*), and some species are rarely active at all! If, however, a fish becomes less active than its norm, this is usually an early, but non-specific, sign of illness. Lethargy commonly increases as the illness worsens, and decreases as the fish recovers.

> **History tip**
> Recently-introduced fish are commonly inactive for a while as a result of shock and stress (1.5). Provided the fish is left in peace, it will usually quickly start to recover. Fish may become progressively less active in old age.

27. WHAT IF MY FISH HANGS AT THE SURFACE?

Hanging head-up at the surface is commonly a sign of hypoxia (1.3.3). Similar behaviour is sometimes seen in (bottom-dwelling) fish, typically cichlids, attempting to evade an aggressor by retreating to the upper levels.

> **History tip**
> The victim of aggression is just as likely to have an increased respiratory rate (through stress (1.5.2) and exertion) as the fish suffering from hypoxia as a result of insufficient oxygen in the water or impaired oxygen uptake (e.g. through gill damage). However, the victim of aggression will tend to make for the corners and edges of the aquarium, where it feels a little more secure, while the hypoxic fish may move slowly around the surface. The bullied fish is also likely to show signs of injury, in particular a frayed tail.

28. WHAT IF MY FISH SWIMS AT AN ODD ANGLE?

Assuming this is abnormal behaviour for the fish concerned, there may be several causes:

• Loss of buoyancy or buoyancy control is usually the result of swimbladder dysfunction. The fish may swim head- or tail-down, partially or wholly on one side, or even upside-down. The problem may be indicative of injury (1.6.1) to, or bacterial infection (3.2) of, the swimbladder. Swimbladder dysfunction may also occur in the later stages of some illnesses (e.g. dropsy (6.3), Malawi bloat (6.4), fatty liver (2.2), obesity (2.3)), or may be a genetic problem (5.0). Loss of buoyancy control may also result from disruption of the central nervous system as the result of other illness, for example hypoxia (1.3.3), poisoning (1.2), or brain tumour (6.7). If the fish is obviously suffering (its swimming is severely impeded, for example) and it has shown no signs of recovery after two or three days, then euthanasia (Chapter 25) is the only humane solution.

• Swimming head-down may be indicative of a stone, piece of equipment, or large tumour (6.7) in the mouth or gullet. The fish should be netted and the mouth/gullet inspected. Soft or smooth foreign objects can sometimes be removed with forceps, otherwise veterinary assistance may be required.

• Fish may swim head-up or head-down in corners or behind items of decor in an attempt to avoid aggression. If the aquarium is observed, it will normally be noted that one unaffected fish is clearly in command of the aquarium and chases any of the affected fish that dares to emerge from its retreat. The stress experienced by the victims is a serious threat to their health, and the situation must be quickly remedied, often by removing the aggressive fish.

• Swimming head-down or head-up, on encountering a higher-status fish, indicates deference/submission.

• Swimming head-down may denote stress (1.5.2) from various causes.

• Long-finned 'fancy' varieties of fish sometimes swim slightly head-up (or, more accurately, tail-down) as a result of the weight of their finnage.

• Fish suffering from hypoxia (1.3.3) often swim or hang head-up near the surface, where the oxygen content of the water is greater.

History tip

If a fish with swimbladder dysfunction has recently been bullied, handled, involved in a fight, or engaged in courtship activity, then the problem is probably due to injury to the swimbladder.

---

29. WHAT IF MY FISH RESTS ON THE BOTTOM?

For some fish, e.g. catfish and loaches, resting on the bottom, or even lying on one side, is quite normal; some diurnally active fish, e.g. many cichlids, usually rest on the bottom when it is dark.

Where resting on the bottom is abnormal behaviour for the fish, it is often accompanied by respiratory distress (gasping and increased respiratory rate). Any of the following may be the cause:

• Shock (1.5.1), including temperature shock (1.4.2), nitrate shock (1.2.9), pH shock (1.1.3), osmotic shock (1.1.2).

• Acidosis or alkalosis (1.1.1).

• Swimbladder dysfunction. The problem may denote injury (1.6.1) to, and/or bacterial infection (3.2) of, the swimbladder. Swimbladder dysfunction may also occur in some illnesses (such as dropsy (6.3), Malawi bloat (6.4), fatty liver (2.2), obesity (2.3)), or may be a genetic problem (5.0). If the fish is obviously suffering (swimming severely impeded) and shows no signs of recovery after two or three days, then euthanasia (Chapter 25) is the only humane solution.

• Exhaustion, which may itself be due to a number of causes, including aggression, courtship/spawning, hypoxia (1.3.3), overheating (1.4.1).

• Chilling (1.4.1), leading to severe slowing of the metabolic rate.

• Severe stress (1.5.2).

• Impending death (from any cause).

• In fry that have used up their yolk sac, resting on the bottom and moving with jerky hops may be 'bellysliding' (5.1), a genetic disorder.

History tip

The circumstances in which fish rest on the bottom are critical in diagnosing the cause of the problem. In newly-introduced fish, the most likely cause is shock or stress. If all or many of the fish are affected, then the problem is usually environmental – shock caused by a sudden change in water conditions (e.g. following a partial water change), overheating, chilling, hypoxia. If a single, established fish is involved, which has recently been bullied, handled, involved in a fight, or engaged in courtship activity, then the problem is probably due to injury to the swimbladder, exhaustion, or stress.

30. WHAT IF MY FISH KEEP DASHING AND DARTING AROUND THE AQUARIUM?

This is a cause for concern only if it is abnormal behaviour for the species.

• Abnormal short darting movements are sometimes associated with poisoning (1.2.1); acidosis or alkalosis (1.1.1); whitespot (4.1.23); and irritation from ectoparasites (4.2). Such behaviour is sometimes also seen in cases of osmotic stress (1.1.2, 1.6.2).

• A nervous fish may dart from cover to take food or when disturbed; dash for cover when it feels threatened (e.g. when a human approaches the tank, or when the tank light is turned on); or, if it has no personal safe retreat, dash as quickly as possible from place to place to evade potential or actual danger. Each behaviour is indicative of stress (1.5.2) and the cause(s) should be identified and rectified.

• A fish may dart or dash in pursuit of another (territorial or courtship behaviour). There is usually no reason to worry about the fish doing the dashing, but the situation should be monitored carefully as there may be a risk of stress (1.5.2) and/or a collision injury (1.6.1) in the fish pursued.

> **History tip**
> Newly-introduced fish may be very unsettled initially and dash around whenever anyone approaches the aquarium. Apart from avoiding sudden movements near the aquarium, and monitoring for injury, no action is required. If most of the established occupants of an aquarium start darting/dashing, suspect a serious environmental or parasitic problem. If just one or two established fish exhibit atypical darting, suspect changes in the social hierarchy or the onset of breeding activity.

31. WHAT IF MY FISH KEEPS SCRATCHING?

Scratching is invariably a sign of some kind of irritation. It is sometimes also described as 'flashing', which, strictly speaking, should be used only where the fish turns on its side and scratches. Occasional scratching is no reason for alarm, but when one or more fish are observed repeatedly to scratch, this may be indicative of:

• Irritation proceeding from poor water quality (1.2), including suspended matter in the water. (See Chapter 16, What if no.10, What if my aquarium water is cloudy or a 'funny' colour).

• Infection with skin or gill parasites (4.0), including whitespot (4.1.23).

> **History tip**
> Most cases of scratching are caused by environmental problems or whitespot (4.1.23), the latter rapidly becoming obvious by the appearance of the characteristic spots. Unless there is good reason to suspect parasitic infestation (i.e. new fish have recently been introduced), then always suspect water quality in the first instance. Even if new fish have been introduced, it is still worth checking water quality before reaching for the parasite treatment.

32. WHAT IF MY FISH IS GASPING FOR BREATH?

• Gasping at the surface is normally a sign of hypoxia (1.3.3), with the origin of the latter usually environmental (i.e. insufficient oxygen content

in the water), rather than physiological (including physiological hypoxia caused by gill parasites damage). The fish are seeking out the area where oxygen content is highest.
• Gasping away from the surface (typically resting on the bottom) also denotes ill-health (but without indicating any specific cause), and includes cases of hypoxia where the fish is too weak and exhausted to remain at the surface.

History tip

In both cases the respiratory (gill) rate is likely to increase greatly. If not, the fish is more likely to be simply hanging at the surface (see What if no.27, What if my fish hangs at the surface?) or resting on the bottom (see What if no.29, What if my fish rests on the bottom?). Alternatively, the fish may simply be unable to close its mouth (see What if no.9, What if my fish can't shut its mouth?). This may affect the gill rate, depending on whether the passage of water through the mouth/gills is impeded.

---

33. WHAT IF MY FISH HIDES?

Hiding is quite normal behaviour for some species. In nature, most of our aquarium fish are on the menu of their larger cousins and other predators, so hiding is an instinctive method of self-preservation. If the appropriate type of hiding place is provided for a fish, it will generally feel secure and may become rather bolder and more outgoing than is natural once it realises it is unlikely to be eaten (assuming the aquarist has been careful about mixing only compatible fish!).

Nocturnal fish can be expected to hide, or at least remain inactive in some quiet spot during the day. Newly-introduced fish will commonly hide for a while until they have recovered from the stress of transportation and familiarised themselves with their new surroundings. Some livebearer females hide when about to give birth, and some species that practise parental care of eggs/fry may choose a private and secluded corner to do so.

Nevertheless there are circumstances in which hiding may be cause for concern, i.e. if it is abnormal behaviour for the species or for the individual, or if it cannot otherwise be attributed to any of the reasons listed above. Abnormal behaviour of this type indicates that the fish is stressed, even if it is not actually unwell. If the situation is not rectified, the stress may cause serious health problems.
• A fish may hide because it is the victim of aggression.
• A fish may hide because it fears it may be the victim of aggression, or may be eaten. This sometimes happens if fish of excessively disparate sizes are mixed, even if the larger individuals are peaceful herbivores. Being instinctively aware that larger fish may be a threat, the smaller fish will take cover.
• A similar situation may arise if fish with disparate swimming habits are mixed. Fish that rush around the aquarium, may be extremely unsettling companions. The rapid movement may signify the threat of aggression or predation to some other fish, and simple fear of a collision may also be stressful.
• A fish may hide if the lighting is too bright (Chapter 12), or may shelter behind decor items to escape from over-strong filter currents.
• Shoaling species may be nervous and hide if kept singly or in too small a group – lacking the natural protection of the shoal, they seek alternative protection.
• Fish may hide if they are unwell – probably an instinctive reaction, to avoid predation and other 'trouble', while unable to take normal evasive action.

34. WHAT IF MY FISH 'SHIMMIES'?

This is the term used to describe the flexing of a fish's body from side to side while it remains stationary, swimming 'on the spot'. It is a sign of irritation and is often seen in association with other such signs, especially head shaking and yawning. It may be almost continuous or interspersed with normal activity. Almost all known causes are environmental:

• A change in water chemistry (1.1).
• Poor water quality, including very high nitrite (1.2.10) levels and other types of poisoning (1.2.1). Even if measurable pollutants are within safe bounds, a partial water change commonly solves the problem.
• Suspended matter in the water causing skin/gill irritation (see Chapter 16, What if no.10, What if my aquarium water is cloudy or a 'funny' colour?).
• Chilling (1.4.1).
• *Flexibacter* (3.2.4) infection, especially in poeciliid fish.

35. WHAT IF MY FISH JUMPS?

Jumping is an escape response, as is 'pancaking', where laterally compressed fish skim along the surface on their sides. In the aquarium, where there tends to be less open space than in the wild (not to mention glass walls and a cover blocking the escape route), both may lead to serious injury. If regular, such behaviour should be investigated and the cause(s) remedied. It may be provoked by, *inter alia*:

• Aggression or fear of aggression (including fear of predation).
• Panic (e.g. induced by an external stimulus such as a sudden or unusual movement near the tank, or the appearance of a hand or net in the tank); or by too sudden illumination of the aquarium. Fish newly introduced to an aquarium also often jump.
• Poisoning (1.2) – the fish is trying to get away from the toxin, which may include chlorine/chloramine (1.2.5) and a number of medications (Chapter 27).
• Acidosis or alkalosis (1.1.1).
• Irritation caused by ectoparasites (4.0); again an escape reaction.

• Feeding or breeding behaviour.

See also What if no.30, What if my fish keep dashing and darting around the aquarium?

> **History tip**
>
> Jumping and pancaking are highly instinctive escape reactions in some species. The cause of this behaviour in the aquarium is often obvious because of the immediacy of their reaction to the stimulus. If such fish jump for no apparent reason, or if normally non-jumping species start to jump, then poisoning, pH problems, or parasites should be suspected.

36. WHAT IF MY FISH HAS EGGS WHICH DON'T HATCH?

Eggs may fail to hatch because they have not been fertilised (no male present; sterility (6.6)), or, if they are covered in a fluffy whitish, growth, because of attack by egg fungus (3.3.4).

> **History tip**
>
> Female fish may lay eggs even if no male is present. In some cichlid species, it is quite common for two females to 'pair' if there is no male, and to go through all the motions of spawning. There is, of course, no sperm, and the eggs do not hatch.

37. WHAT IF MY FISH IS PRODUCING ABNORMAL DROPPINGS?

The colour and consistency of fish faeces vary according to the diet, and to some extent the species of fish involved. Normal faeces are usually brownish or greenish and of a regular diameter typical for the fish concerned. They commonly break off soon after emerging from the vent, although sometimes an inch or two may be extruded before dropping off.

Abnormal faeces should be regarded as suspicious, particularly if persistent.

• White, stringy faeces are characteristic of *Hexamita* (4.1.9) or *Capillaria* (4.2.4).
• Faeces with alternating dark and light segments may denote *Capillaria* (4.2.4).
• Gas bubbles in the faeces may indicate a digestive or dietary problem (2.0).
• Irregularly-formed faeces may also indicate a digestive or dietary problem (2.0).
• Absence of faeces for any appreciable period may signify constipation (2.1), and will, of course, also occur if the fish is not feeding (See What if no.6, What if my fish won't eat?).

> **History tip**
>
> The colour and consistency of the faeces are normally related to the colour and texture of the food recently eaten. Thus a herbivore which has been eating green vegetable foods should produce green faeces, and, because of the roughage content, these may also be bulkier than those resulting from flake food. Fish which have eaten earthworms often produce rather irregularly-shaped faeces because the worm and its stomach contents represent a mixed, non-uniform, diet. If variation in the faeces can be related to variation in the diet, there is no cause for concern. If unsure, try the suspected food again to see if it has the same effect!

38 WHAT IF MY FISH HAS WORMS HANGING OUT OF ITS 'BOTTOM'?
This is a diagnostic sign of infestation with *Camallanus* worms (4.2.3).

39 WHAT IF MY FISH HAS FINS WHICH ARE FRAYED AND RAGGED?
The technical term for this is 'fin erosion'. The edges of the fins may turn pale
and start to rot away, and/or the fins may be split. If neglected, it may develop
into fin rot (3.2.2), a bacterial disease that can have fatal consequences in extreme
cases. The following are possible causes, the first two being the most common:
• Poor water quality (1.2).
• Damage caused by other fish (aggression, courtship, etc).
• Damage caused by ectoparasite infestation, e.g. skin flukes (4.2.11), whitespot,
(4.1.23), and the protozoans causing skin slime disease (4.1.18).
• Damage caused by clumsy handling.
• Vitamin deficiency (2.5).

History tip
If fin damage is a widespread and repeated problem, try to identify the
culprit(s). Often this/these will be the only fish with undamaged finnage. Fin
damage is particularly associated with some types of fish or individual species:
cichlids are notorious for damaging each other's fins during territorial
squabbles and courtship, while tiger barbs (*Barbus tetrazona*) are notorious fin-
nippers, especially if kept singly. Common victims are fish with long and/or
flowing finnage, e.g. angelfish (*Pterophyllum* spp.), gouramis, and Siamese
fighting fish (*Betta splendens*).

---

40. WHAT IF MY FISH CLAMPS ITS FINS?
Clamping of the fins, where the fish folds the dorsal, anal, ventral, and
pectoral fins close to its body, and does not spread its tail properly, is
one of the earliest signs that something is amiss. This behaviour may be
the result of adverse water conditions (1.1, 1.2, 1.3), stress (1.5.2), or almost
any disease. Clamped fins are commonly seen in conjunction with other signs of
illness or irritation (Tables 11 and 12).
    Temporary clamping of one or more fins is usually a sign of transient irritation and
not a cause for concern. Fin-clamping is sometimes also a behaviour used to
communicate mood/status (e.g. deference to a higher-status fish during an
encounter), and the fins may be folded if the fish accelerates across the aquarium,
e.g. in pursuit of another fish or to feed.

History tip
If all or most of the fish have clamped fins, the problem is likely to be one of
water conditions or a highly infectious disease such as whitespot (4.1.23) or a
fluke outbreak (4.2.8, 4.2.11), especially if scratching is also observed.
However, such a disease outbreak is unlikely unless new fish have very recently
been introduced. If a single fish is involved, which has recently been bullied,
involved in a fight or courtship activity, or handled/transported, then stress
and/or shock (1.5.1) are more likely causes.

---

41. WHAT IF MY FISH TWITCHES ITS FINS?

This is generally a sign of irritation, caused by poor water quality (1.2), whitespot (4.1.23), or ectoparasitic infestations (4.0). However, occasional transitory fin-twitching may simply be due to a passing irritation (i.e. an 'itch').
See also What if no.40, What if my fish clamps its fins?.

42. WHAT IF MY FISH IS BREATHING FASTER THAN USUAL?

Increased gill rate is almost always a sign that something is amiss, and often one of the earliest signs of an impending serious problem. It is a sign of hypoxia (1.3.3), i.e. it indicates that the fish cannot obtain the oxygen it requires by breathing at the normal rate. This may indicate a problem with the oxygen content of the aquarium, or that the fish is finding it more difficult than usual to take up oxygen (for example, because of gill damage), or because the fish needs more oxygen than normal (e.g. due to heightened activity), or a combination of these factors.

Fish exhibiting an increased respiratory rate should be kept under careful observation until the cause can be established (and remedied) or the gill rate returns to normal. Levels of ammonia, nitrite, and nitrate should be checked, as these are commonly at the root of the problem.

See also What if nos.32, 27, What if my fish is gasping for breath? and What if my fish is hanging at the surface? respectively.

> **History tip**
> If the fish has been more active than normal, this may explain the increased gill rate; for example, spawning commonly involves unusual activity levels and hence increased gill rate. Competition at feeding time can have a similar effect. These activities are not normally a cause for concern provided the gill rate quickly returns to normal. But if the increased respiration is because of chasing, this may signify a problem requiring intervention.

43. WHAT IF MY FISH HAS GILLS WHICH LOOK ABNORMAL?

Normal gills are red in colour. This can be difficult to see when the fish is in good health as the operculum will open only slightly and slowly with each respiratory beat. Thus, if the aquarist is aware of a change in the gills, this may itself indicate a clearly visible abnormality, or that the fish has been netted and the gills inspected because other signs point to a possible gill problem. The following are the abnormalities most likely to be seen in either situation:
Discoloration:
• Pale colour: anaemia (6.1).
• Dark or grey spots: iron deposition during acidosis (1.1.1).
• Grey-white mucus coating, perhaps trailing from gill slit: reaction to irritation by gill parasites (4.2.8, 4.2.9); poisoning (1.2); acidosis or alkalosis (1.1.1); suspended matter (see Chapter 16, What if no.10, What if my aquarium water is cloudy or a 'funny' colour?)
• Mottled dark red and light: gill rot (branchiomycosis) (3.3.5).
• Brownish: nitrite poisoning (1.2.10).
Swollen, gill cover constantly expanded (increased respiratory effort):
• Gill damage or irritation from parasites (4.0); poisoning (1.2); acidosis or

alkalosis (1.1.1); suspended matter (see Chapter 15, What if no.10, What if my aquarium water is cloudy or a 'funny' colour?); sifting sharp substrate material.

• Exertion resulting from evading aggression, reproductive activity (courtship, spawning, mouthbrooding), and from panic-stimulated flight.

• Respiratory difficulties caused by obstruction of the mouth/gullet (see also What if no.4, What if my fish appears to be choking? and no.9 What if my fish can't shut its mouth?).

Erosion (rotting away) of gill filaments:
Gill rot (3.3.5), bacterial infection (3.2).

Worm-like parasites, visible to the naked eye:
Gill maggots (*Ergasilus*) (4.2.9).

Gas bubbles on gill filaments:
Gas bubble disease (1.3.2).

Gill cover (operculum) wholly or partly missing:
• Genetic deformity (5.3).
• Injury (1.6.1) (rare).

History tip
Temporary flaring of the gills is part of the courtship/defensive/aggressive display of some fish, most notably the firemouth cichlid (*Thorichthys meeki*). Note that an apparent abnormality of one gill (especially in inactive stationary fish) may be due simply to environmental factors such as exposure to the current of water from the filter. The fish can be expected to 'recover' when it changes position.

---

44. WHAT IF MY FISH HAS JUMPED OUT OF THE TANK?
This should be avoided by keeping the aquarium tightly covered, but accidents do happen. Some fish (notoriously killifish) seem able to find the tiniest aperture, some may make a bid for freedom when the cover is removed for maintenance, and some may jump out of the net.

• If the fish has not been out of the water for long, it should be gently rinsed of dirt and fluff (in a bucket of aquarium water), any superficial injuries treated with a topical antiseptic (Chapter 27), and returned to the aquarium. This will avoid the additional trauma of a move to a strange isolation tank. In many cases, the fish will look a trifle 'tatty' for a while, but should recover without further treatment.

• If the fish has remained out of water for some time (several minutes, even an hour or more) it can sometimes be revived in a well-aerated hospital tank. Holding the fish gently underwater above an airstone will help flush its gills of floor dust and dried mucus. Again, skin abrasions should be treated topically with antiseptic. The fish should be kept in the isolation tank for at least a few days to recover from stress (1.5.2) and hypoxia (1.3.3) associated with its experience.

• If more serious visible injuries have occurred, hospitalisation should follow even a brief extra-aquarium excursion and steps be taken to avoid osmotic stress (1.6.2).

• In all cases the fish should be monitored for secondary bacterial (3.2) and/or fungal (3.3) infections.

• If the fish has suffered internal injuries, euthanasia (Chapter 25) may be necessary if it shows no signs of improvement after a couple of days.

CHAPTER 21

DISEASES AFFECTING TROPICAL AQUARIUM FISH

1. Environmental diseases
2. Dietary problems
3. Pathogenic diseases
4. Parasites
5. Genetic diseases and disorders
6. Diseases with more than one possible cause

Disease is herein defined as any health problem – infectious or non-infectious. Infectious diseases are those that can be transmitted from one individual to another and are caused by agents known as pathogens (viruses, bacteria, fungi; section 3.0, below) and parasites (section 4.0). Non-infectious diseases are those which arise through some physiological or genetic malfunction in the individual (e.g. tumours, many deformities, organ failure) or are caused by environmental or dietary problems.

Although most aquarists tend to assume that any health problem in their fish must be caused by a pathogen or parasite, in fact the vast majority of aquarium illnesses are environmental in origin, requiring rectification of living conditions rather than recourse to drugs and other chemicals. (Even when an infectious disease is found to be affecting the fish, it may have been triggered or exacerbated by adverse environmental conditions.) To further emphasise this vital point, environmental diseases are dealt with first in this chapter.

Table 13 Index of Diseases Covered in Chapter 21.

1.0	**Environmental diseases**
1.1	**Conditions caused by incorrect water chemistry**
1.1.1.	Acidosis and alkalosis
1.1.2	Osmotic stress and osmotic shock
1.1.3	pH shock
1.2	**Poisoning and other water quality problems**
1.2.1	Poisoning (general)
1.2.2	Aflatoxin poisoning
1.2.3	Ammonia poisoning
1.2.4	Black chin
1.2.5	Chlorine and chloramine poisoning
1.2.6	Metal poisoning
1.2.7	New tank syndrome
1.2.8	Nitrate poisoning
1.2.9	Nitrate shock
1.2.10	Nitrite poisoning
1.3	**Problems associated with the levels of atmospheric gases in the aquarium**
1.3.1	Carbon dioxide (CO_2) problems
1.3.2	Gas bubble disease
1.3.3	Hypoxia (oxygen starvation)
1.4	**Problems associated with temperature**
1.4.1	Chilling and overheating
1.4.2	Temperature shock
1.5	**Shock and stress**
1.5.1	Shock
1.5.2	Stress
1.6	**Accidents, injuries and associated problems**
1.6.1	Accidents and injuries
1.6.2	Osmotic stress
2.0	**Dietary problems**
2.1	Constipation
2.2	Fatty liver (fatty degeneration of the liver)
2.3	Obesity
2.4	Undernourishment and malnutrition
2.5	Vitamin deficiency
3.0	**Pathogenic diseases**
3.1	**Viruses and viral diseases**
3.1.1	Cauliflower disease (lymphocystis disease)
3.1.2	Fish pox (carp pox)
3.1.3	*Lymphocystis*
3.2	**Bacteria and bacterial diseases**
3.2.1	*Aeromonas*
3.2.2	Fin rot (including tail rot)
3.2.3	Fish tuberculosis (fish TB, mycobacteriosis)
3.2.4	*Flexibacter* (synonyms *Chondrococcus, Myxobacteria*)
3.2.5	Mouth fungus
3.2.6	*Mycobacterium*

3.2.7	*Nocardia*
3.2.8	*Pseudomonas*
3.2.9	Ulcers
3.2.10	*Vibrio*
3.2.11	Vibriosis
3.3	**Fungus and fungal infections**
3.3.1	*Achyla*
3.3.2	*Branchiomyces*
3.3.3	Cotton wool disease
3.3.4	Egg fungus
3.3.5	Gill rot (branchiomycosis)
3.3.6	*Ichthyophonus*
3.3.7	*Saprolegnia*
3.3.8	Systemic fungal infections
4.0	**Parasites**
4.1	**Protozoan parasites**
4.1.1	*Apiosoma*
4.1.2	*Chilodonella*
4.1.3	*Costia*
4.1.4	*Cyclochaeta*
4.1.5	*Epistylis*
4.1.6	Guppy disease
4.1.7	Head and lateral line erosion
4.1.8	*Heterosporis*
4.1.9	*Hexamita*
4.1.10	Hole-in-head disease (hexamitiasis)
4.1.11	*Ichthyobodo*
4.1.12	*Ichthyophthirius*
4.1.13	Neon tetra disease
4.1.14	*Octomitus*
4.1.15	*Piscinoodinium*
4.1.16	*Pleistophora*
4.1.17	*Spironucleus*
4.1.18	Skin slime disease (costiasis)
4.1.19	*Tetrahymena*
4.1.20	*Trichodina*
4.1.21	Trypanosome infection
4.1.22	Velvet disease
4.1.23	Whitespot
4.2	**Other parasites**
4.2.1	Anchor worm (*Lernaea*)
4.2.2	Black spot
4.2.3	*Camallanus*
4.2.4	*Capillaria*
4.2.5	Eye fluke (*Diplostomum*)
4.2.6	Fish leech (*Piscicola*)
4.2.7	Fish louse (*Argulus*)
4.2.8	Gill flukes (*Dactylogyrus*)

1.0 ENVIRONMENTAL DISEASES

Environmental diseases are, as the term implies, those caused by aspects of the fish's surroundings, including water chemistry and quality, decor and tankmates, and other potential stressors. Environmental diseases are, of course, not infectious.

For ease of reference, environmental diseases have been grouped into the following categories: Conditions caused by incorrect water chemistry (1.1); Poisoning and other water quality problems (1.2); Problems associated with the levels of atmospheric gases in the aquarium (1.3); Problems associated with temperature (1.4); Shock and stress (1.5); and Accidents, injuries, and associated problems (1.6).

1.1 CONDITIONS CAUSED BY INCORRECT WATER CHEMISTRY

A number of fish health problems are caused by incorrect water chemistry – either as a result of long-term exposure to incorrect conditions, or following a sudden dramatic change in water chemistry.

1.1.1 ACIDOSIS AND ALKALOSIS
A condition where the pH of the aquarium water lies below (acidosis) or above (alkalosis) the optimum pH range of the species affected. This disease will not necessarily involve all the aquarium occupants, since different species vary greatly in their pH tolerance range. Both conditions may be **acute**, where the pH shift is rapid, or **chronic**, where the change takes place slowly over a period of time. The acidity or alkalinity irritates the fish's external surfaces (including the gills) and may also cause adverse physiological changes.

Alkalosis is less common than acidosis, as the dissolved minerals causing alkalinity also help to stabilise pH, and the metabolic processes of the fish have a constant acidifying effect which counteracts any tendency to excess alkalinity. It should also be noted that any ammonia (1.2.3) in the water will be considerably more toxic at high pH levels, whereas any heavy metal contaminants (1.2.6) in the aquarium will be more toxic at low pH.

Signs:

• Acute acidosis/alkalosis: Excitable behaviour, rapid darting movements, jumping, often followed rapidly by death.

• Chronic acidosis/alkalosis: Signs are less obvious, but may include gasping and coughing, mucus hyperproduction, and reddened skin resulting from irritation by the acidity/alkalinity. Osmoregulatory problems caused by chronic alkalosis may lead to swelling of the abdomen (see also Dropsy, 6.3).

As the signs are very similar for both acidosis and alkalosis, and for certain other conditions, a pH test may be required for confirmation. In the case of acidosis, dark grey marks (iron deposits) may appear on the gills if the pH falls below 5.

Cause: A pH outside the tolerance range of the species affected. The critical level will vary considerably from species to species. The physiological tolerance range of a species broadly reflects the pH conditions encountered in its natural habitat.

• Acidosis: Some fish from naturally alkaline waters may be unable to survive any degree of acidity for long, while those from neutral or slightly acid conditions may survive - but not necessarily thrive at – a pH of 5 or less. Sudden drops in pH usually occur only in mineral-depleted water with little or no buffering capacity such that the pH may be unstable. Slow decreases in pH are generally the result of gradual acidification of the water caused by acidic byproducts of the nitrogen cycle. Chronic acidosis also sometimes occurs where, through ignorance or lack of attention to detail, fish are kept long term at a lower-than-natural pH.

High levels of carbon dioxide can lower pH, as can occur in heavily-planted aquaria during the night when photosynthesis ceases and the plants release CO_2. The use of CO_2 injection to encourage plant growth may also cause a pH drop.

• Alkalosis: In the case of some acid-water species, exposure to moderately alkaline conditions (say, pH 7.3-8.0) may cause alkalosis, while those from neutral or slightly alkaline waters may not be affected until the pH reaches 10-11. Acute alkalosis is likely only if fish are moved from one tank to another without due regard for differences in pH, or following overdose with alkaline pH adjusters. Chronic alkalosis may occur where, through ignorance or negligence, fish are kept at a higher-than-natural pH; where evaporation is regularly replaced with mineral-rich water; or where soluble minerals are continuously dissolving from decor items (e.g. limestone rocks).

Prevention: Acidosis and alkalosis can be prevented by selecting fish species which are compatible with the pH of the aquarium, or by modifying the pH to suit the proposed occupants, which must themselves be pH-compatible. Select decor which will not adversely affect the water chemistry desired (Chapter 11). Check pH regularly to detect early signs of acidification by organics, or alkalinification by calciferous decor. Improve husbandry (Chapter 15) if necessary. In mineral-depleted water ('soft-water aquaria'), provide an alkaline buffer (to prevent pH instability and avoid pH collapse) in the form of some calciferous material (e.g. a bag of limestone chips suspended in the aquarium or placed in the filter). The actual amount of buffering material required may need to be established by trial and error.

Treatment: Correct the pH level. This can be achieved using an appropriate proprietary pH buffer. Sodium bicarbonate ($NaHCO_3$) can also be used to increase pH. Partial water changes, using water with a pH closer to neutral (e.g. many tap water supplies), can be used for slow adjustment. This is the method of choice for chronic pH problems, as partial water changes will reduce the underlying excess organic wastes or high mineral content normally at the root of chronic acidosis and alkalosis, respectively.

• Acute acidosis/alkalosis: survival of sudden and extreme changes in pH is unlikely unless the pH is immediately returned to the normal level; gradual adjustment would leave the fish exposed to the harmful effects of the incorrect pH for too long. Acute acidosis and alkalosis are, however, commonly fatal even if fast remedial action is taken. Thus it is important to identify the cause of the problem and take steps to prevent any repetition.

• Chronic acidosis/alkalosis: slowly adjust the pH to within the optimal range for the fish being kept. The rate of change should not exceed 0.3 pH units per day, so as to allow the fish to adjust gradually.

Comment: There is a possibility of infection accompanying/following acidosis or alkalosis, resulting from stress-induced immunosuppression, (especially if the problem is chronic) and pH-damaged gill and skin membranes may be vulnerable to secondary infections (3.2, 3.3).

1.1.2 OSMOTIC STRESS AND OSMOTIC SHOCK

Osmotic stress may arise when the fish's osmoregulatory system is compromised by incorrect water chemistry. It can also occur as a result of extensive skin permeability arising from injury or disease (dealt with under 1.6, below).

Osmoregulation is the process by which fish maintain the appropriate salt/water balance in their bodies in order to provide optimal conditions for various physiological and biochemical processes (see Chapter 17). The osmoregulatory system of any species will have been evolved to maintain this balance vis-a-vis the water chemistry of its natural environment. If the system is overburdened by prolonged exposure to incorrect conditions (osmotic stress), or sudden exposure to a dramatic change in water chemistry (osmotic shock), then the fish may be physiologically unable to cope. Chronic osmotic stress may eventually lead to death, and osmotic shock can be quickly fatal. (See also Shock, 1.5.1).

Osmoregulatory problems may be responsible for some cases of the condition known as Malawi bloat (6.4), which commonly affects Rift Valley cichlids.

Signs: The fish may exhibit typical signs of Stress (1.5.2), such as abnormally light or dark coloration, unusual behaviour (lethargy or hyperactivity), clamped fins, increased respiratory rate, and in severe cases there may even be loss of balance.

Causes:

• Osmotic stress: exposure to water which is either unnaturally mineral-rich or unnaturally mineral-depleted for the species concerned. Osmotic stress is usually more serious when species from naturally mineral-rich waters are kept under extremely mineral-depleted water conditions, such that the osmotic difference between the fish and its environment is significantly increased. Such species may have less efficient osmoregulatory systems than those that are physiologically adapted to live in mineral-poor waters, and thus be unable to cope with the resulting osmoregulatory overload. Nevertheless, osmotic stress can also occur when fish from mineral-poor waters are kept in very hard water.

• Osmotic shock: sudden changes in concentrations of dissolved salts, e.g. if a fish is moved from mineral-depleted to mineral-rich water (or *vice versa*) without gradual acclimatisation. This commonly leads to death within 24-72 hours and is a frequent cause of fatalities in fish newly-purchased by ignorant or uncaring aquarists. Exposure to high concentration salt baths (e.g. as a treatment for external parasites) may also cause extreme osmotic shock; any fish exhibiting an adverse reaction to such treatment should be returned to fresh water immediately.

Prevention: Fish, especially wild-caught stocks and those captive-bred for only a couple of generations, should be maintained in water with a mineral content similar to that encountered in the natural habitat (bearing in mind that hardness and mineral content are not always synonymous, Chapter 10).

Fish should *never* be subjected to sudden changes in water chemistry.

Treatment: Adjust the mineral content of the water to the level appropriate to the species concerned.

In cases of osmotic shock the adjustment should be total and immediate. Obviously affected newly-purchased fish can be moved to another aquarium with correct water chemistry (e.g. the quarantine tank, where they should be anyway!) rather than altering the water chemistry in the main aquarium (which might cause osmotic shock in established fish). The water in the quarantine tank can then be adjusted gradually to that of the main aquarium over a period of 2-3 weeks, and the new fish then transferred to their permanent home.

In the case of osmotic stress, the concentration of dissolved salts should be rectified gradually over a period of 1-2 weeks, to avoid osmotic shock.

Comment: The presence of ammonia (1.2.3) in the aquarium may also have adverse effects on osmoregulation.

1.1.3 pH SHOCK
Shock (1.5.1) caused by a sudden change in pH, usually when a fish is transferred from one tank to another without water chemistry parameters being checked/adjusted in advance. Overdosing with pH adjusters can also cause pH shock.

Signs: In the case of extreme changes in pH, the fish may exhibit typical signs of shock, lying on the bottom, sometimes on its side or even upside-down. Commonly, however, no signs are seen until 24 hours or longer after introduction, by which time irreversible damage has normally occurred. The fish are often found dead at 'lights on' on the second or third day.

Prevention: Always check that pH is a reasonable match (no more than 0.5 pH units), before moving fish between tanks. In the case of newly-purchased fish, the quarantine period can be used to make any pH changes required, gradually.

Treatment: As for acute acidosis or alkalosis, as appropriate (1.1.1).

1.2 POISONING AND OTHER WATER QUALITY PROBLEMS

This section covers not only poisoning caused by obvious toxins such as pesticides and domestic chemicals, but also that resulting from metabolic byproducts such as ammonia and nitrite, and from toxic substances inadvertently introduced via tap water, e.g. chlorine and chloramine.

1.2.1 POISONING (GENERAL)

Poisoning is a common problem in aquaria, and a frequent cause of illness, and sometimes death. It may be acute or chronic, depending on the ichthyotoxicity of the causative agent, its concentration, and exposure time. Some substances are highly toxic in even small amounts, while others are less toxic and have an acute effect only if present at high concentrations. Some poisons may be present at low levels but slowly accumulate in the tissues of the fish, causing chronic illness. Acute poisoning (sometimes called toxic shock) is generally obvious, with fish dying in a short space of time, but chronic poisoning may go unnoticed, manifesting only as general malaise, impaired immune response, and occasional unexplained deaths.

Poisons may be absorbed via the digestive system or the gills, and corrosive poisons may affect the skin.

Signs:

• Acute poisoning: gasping, at the surface or lying on the substrate; shimmying, or, in very severe cases, uncoordinated or uncontrolled swimming (often with loss of stability); sometimes heightened coloration; glazed-looking, immobile eyes. Normally, most or all fish will be affected, with numerous deaths over a short period. Similar signs may, however, be attributable to other causes, for example severe Hypoxia (1.3.3). Specific diagnosis can often be confirmed by circumstances, i.e. the existence of a potential cause of toxicity. For example, if fish suddenly become ill after a water change, then, provided the new water was a good match as regards hardness, pH, and temperature, suspect contaminated tap water; or following introduction of new decor, suspect toxicity from that source.

• Chronic poisoning: signs are typically non-specific and develop over a period of time, and could equally denote many other problems. They include: loss of appetite, increased respiratory rate, flashing, shimmying and/or swimming on the spot, glazed staring eyes, increased susceptibility to infections such as Fungus (3.3), Fin rot (3.2.2), and Skin slime disease (4.1.18). Commonly, not all fish will be affected equally, and deaths, if any, occur only sporadically.

Cause: Numerous substances are toxic to fish. Some – ammonia, nitrite, and nitrate – are naturally-occurring byproducts of the nitrogen cycle (nitrogenous wastes), produced in the aquarium. Others may derive from the water supply, e.g. chlorine, chloramine, and insecticides, used to eliminate bacteria and invertebrates from drinking water supplies. Toxic metals such as lead and copper may also be present in some tap water. Many medications can be ichthyotoxic under certain circumstances (for example overdoses, mixtures, susceptible species) – see also Chapter 24.

Unsuitable decor (Chapter 11) and equipment items (Chapter 13) are a common cause of toxicity:

• Metals may form toxic salts when used in, or to contain, salt or acid water.

• Rocks may contain toxic minerals.

• Stones or flowerpots from the garden may be contaminated with horticultural chemicals.

• Many plastics leach toxins when immersed in water – only those intended for aquarium or food use should be used.

• Paints, varnishes, glues, and dyes, unless intended for aquarium use.

• Varnished bogwood may poison wood-gnawing species such as some catfish and *Uaru* cichlids.

• Unsuitable plants – including some sold for aquarium use, e.g. *Dieffenbachia.*

• Poorly stored fish foods can occasionally lead to Aflatoxin poisoning (1.2.2).

In addition, various extraneous toxins may be unwittingly or carelessly introduced by the aquarist or his family:

• Paint or chemical fumes, tobacco smoke, domestic insecticides (fly spray), aerosol polishes, can all enter the water at its surface or via the airpump.

• Aluminium or other metal saucepans can contaminate peat extract made in them.

• Soaps, detergents, and other substances can be introduced on equipment, decor, and hands.

The above lists should not be considered exhaustive, but are simply catalogues of common causes of toxicity.

Prevention: Avoid problems with nitrogenous wastes by good husbandry (Chapter 15). If necessary, treat tap water before use. Never overdose with medication, and never mix medications (do not use more than one at a time, unless instructed to do so by a vet or fish health specialist). Exercise extreme care regarding items used in, near, or in any association with the aquarium. Before putting anything into the aquarium (including one's hands), pause to consider whether there is any possibility of introducing toxins.

Treatment:

• Acute poisoning: if possible, move all fish to alternative, unpolluted, quarters. Otherwise remove the source of contamination (if known, or feasible) and make repeated large water changes until the signs are alleviated, even if this means an effective total change of water.

• Chronic poisoning: identify and remove the source of toxicity, and make a series of 25-30% water changes, at the rate of one per day over the next few days, to reduce toxin levels. Normal water changes will then gradually eliminate any residues. However, there is no treatment for problems caused by toxins that may have accumulated in the fish's tissues, and such fish may remain unhealthy and die prematurely. Nevertheless remedying the cause will safeguard new introductions from a similar fate. In cases of poisoning by nitrogenous wastes, improve husbandry and consider other possible underlying causes, such as overcrowding.

Comment: It is advisable to monitor for secondary infections (3.2, 3.3) in fish which have been exposed to poisons. Euthanasia (Chapter 25) may be necessary if there are permanent after-effects, causing suffering.

In view of the frequency of poisoning as a source of illness and death in aquarium fish, a number of types are dealt with in more detail below.

1.2.2 AFLATOXIN POISONING

Aflatoxins are toxic substances produced by certain types of moulds which sometimes colonise dried fish foods stored under warm damp conditions. Aflatoxin poisoning is uncommon, but possible where bulk food supplies are purchased and kept, after opening, in a fish-house or other unsuitable environment.

Signs: Poor growth, anaemia, general poor health, occasionally death, in fish that have been fed suspect or obviously mouldy dry foods.

Cause: Feeding with aflatoxin-contaminated dried food.

Prevention: Store foods in a dry place. Discard any dry food that shows signs of dampness or deterioration.

Treatment: None.

1.2.3 AMMONIA POISONING

Ammonia is an end-product of protein metabolism, and in fish is excreted mainly via the gills. It is also produced during the nitrogen cycle. In the closed system of the aquarium, it may attain toxic levels unless removed by efficient chemical or biological filtration.

Signs: Increased gill rate and gasping; mucus hyperproduction; reddening of the skin (haemorrhage from capillaries); hyperactivity and excitability; erratic swimming and twitching.

Cause: High levels of free ammonia in the water, caused by overcrowding, overfeeding, other sources of waste matter (dead plants, fish, snails, etc), inadequate or failed biological filtration, or a combination of any of these factors. Fish packed for transportation, especially if overcrowded and/or heavily fed beforehand, may be particularly vulnerable. Hospital tanks, where biological filtration is incompatible with the chosen medication, may also experience problems.

Prevention: Good husbandry and efficient biological filtration. Zeolite (an ammonia-removing mineral) can be used in fish bags and hospital tank filters, but is not recommended as a routine substitute for proper biological filtration.

Treatment: As for acute Poisoning (1.2.1). Low levels of ammonia can be remedied with zeolite (as a temporary measure, pending identification and rectification of the basic cause of the problem) or by use of an additional or replacement biological filter, previously matured in another aquarium.

1.2.4 BLACK CHIN

An apparently environmentally-induced skin condition in cichlids, particularly those from the lakes of the East African Rift Valley.

Signs: Small grey-black irregular spots or patches, initially on the lower jaw region, in severe cases spreading along the underside of the head to the pelvic fins such that the entire lower head and chest exhibit a mottled grey-black appearance.

Cause: Not clinically investigated, but apparently related to high Nitrate (1.2.8) levels. Susceptible species generally originate from virtually nitrate-free water.

Prevention: The condition rarely, if ever, occurs in water with a nitrate level of <25ppm.

Treatment: Improve water quality by one or more additional partial water changes, using water free of, or low in, nitrate. The condition usually disappears in days.

1.2.5 CHLORINE AND CHLORAMINE POISONING

Chlorine and chloramine (a chlorine/ammonia compound) are added to domestic water supplies as disinfectants. Both are highly ichthyotoxic, the more so with decreasing pH and increasing temperature. Their effect may be acute, with all fish affected immediately; or chronic, manifesting as long-term general ill health. Chlorine levels of 0.2 to 0.3 mg/litre are sufficient to cause acute poisoning.

Signs:

• Acute toxicity: following the addition of fresh tap water to the aquarium, fish may exhibit an escape reaction, darting around, in severe cases leaping from the water; trembling, sometimes a change in pigmentation and altered coloration; increased respiratory rate and other signs of Hypoxia (1.3.3). Repeated exposure may result in lethargy and exhaustion, and is often fatal due to respiratory failure.

• Chronic toxicity (resulting from repeated exposure): no specific signs.

Prevention: Tap water should always be dechlorinated mechanically or chemically, *before* coming into contact with fish. Test kits are available for measuring levels of chlorine and chloramine in mains water.

Treatment: Ideally, immediately transfer the fish to an uncontaminated aquarium. Alternatively, as a strictly emergency measure, add sufficient dechlorinator to the aquarium to treat its entire volume, and ensure the chemical is well dispersed. If chloramine is present, ensure the dechlorinator is one that neutralises this chemical. Increase aeration to help drive off the chlorine and to relieve hypoxia.

Comment: There is no excuse for chlorine/chloramine poisoning.

1.2.6 METAL POISONING

Iron, lead, and copper are the most common causes of metal poisoning. Water chemistry influences the type of metallic salts produced. In particular, the calcium level in the water may reduce the toxicity of several metals, and low pH may increase toxicity. In consequence, several heavy metals are more toxic in soft acid waters, i.e. those with a low pH and low calcium hardness. Toxicity levels may also be a function of the mixture (if any) of metals involved. Susceptibility to metal poisoning varies between species and even individuals.

Signs: As for general Poisoning (1.2.1).

Causes:
• Metallic salts in tap water, derived from natural water sources.
• Metals dissolved from pipework and water tanks, especially hot-water systems in soft acid water areas (no calcium carbonate deposit forming a barrier between metal and water, and acid water more likely to react with metals).
• Unsuitable equipment, including metal-framed tanks containing salt water and metal hoods subject to constant splashing with salt or acid water (violent filtration/aeration and no cover glasses).
• Copper medications.
• Metal ores in rocks.

Prevention: Metal salts can be removed by reverse osmosis or rendered harmless by some proprietary water conditioners. Avoid using water from copper hot water cylinders, especially in soft water areas. Run the cold water tap for a few minutes before drawing water for aquarium use, to run off water that has stood in the pipes. Use only equipment suitable for the aquarium water and avoid misuse of copper-based medications.

Treatment: As for general Poisoning (1.2.1). Proprietary metal-chelating solutions may alleviate the problem in the short term. Remedy cause.

Comment: Test kits are available for monitoring copper (and certain other metals).

1.2.7 NEW TANK SYNDROME

Acute poisoning by Ammonia (1.2.3) and/or Nitrite (1.2.10) in newly set up aquaria to which fish have been added before the nitrogen cycle is established in the tank/filtration system. A similar problem may result from the total replacement or incorrect cleaning of the biological filter medium, or from the destruction of nitrifying bacteria by chemicals (e.g. medications).

Signs: As for acute ammonia and nitrite poisoning, in recently set up, inadequately matured, aquaria.

Prevention: The aquarium should be properly matured and no fish added until ammonia and nitrite have peaked and returned to zero. Biological filters should be properly maintained and never exposed to chemicals that may harm filter bacteria.

Treatment: Ideally, move the fish to a biologically mature aquarium. If this is not feasible, there are a number of alternatives which should alleviate the toxicity:

• Frequent partial water changes, if necessary as much as 50% twice daily, to lower ammonia (and/or nitrite) levels.

• Zeolite can be used (in a filter) to reduce ammonia to safe levels.

• A biologically mature filter (borrowed from another tank, or aquarist) will generally reduce the toxicity to safe levels within 24 hours.

Comment: Given a little patience, new tank syndrome is easily avoided. Ignorance is no excuse, and, in the view of the authors, no penalty is too dire for dealers who sell tank, equipment, and fish together at the same time.

1.2.8 NITRATE POISONING

Nitrate (NO_3) is the final product of the nitrogen cycle. Nitrate is far less toxic to fish than other nitrogen cycle products. In fact, although it is nitrate that is measured by aquarists, and assumed to be the cause of any problems occurring at high nitrate levels, it is possible that other toxic waste products, which accumulate in parallel with nitrate (but are not measured), may be the actual cause of any illness that occurs. A high nitrate level can, nevertheless, be regarded as an indication of poor water quality and of the need for remedial action, hence we refer here to nitrate levels and nitrate toxicity in line with normal aquarium hobby practice. It should, however, be borne in mind that some methods of reducing nitrates (water changes, reverse osmosis) will reduce concentrations of other chemicals as well, but few data are available as regards the effect of other methods of nitrate removal (such as resins) on other chemicals.

Some species can survive very high nitrate levels (although this does not mean they should be exposed to such concentrations), while others may be affected by a comparatively small amount of nitrate pollution. A level of 50 mg/litre is generally regarded as the maximum acceptable for keeping nitrate-tolerant species; however the aquarist should aim for a value below 25mg/litre, with much lower levels required for many species, particularly those from naturally nitrate-poor waters (especially wild-caught stocks).

Nitrate normally has a chronic rather than an acute effect, although sudden exposure to a much higher concentration than normal commonly induces Nitrate shock (1.2.9), which may perhaps be regarded as acute nitrate poisoning. Long-term exposure to excessive (for the species) levels of nitrate may cause poor growth, chronic Stress (1.5.2), general ill health, reluctance to breed. It may increase susceptibility to other diseases – particularly Fin rot (3.2.2), Malawi bloat (6.4) and Cloudy eye (6.2). It also appears to be the cause of Black chin disease (1.2.4).

Signs: No specific signs, but those of chronic general Poisoning (1.2.1) may be seen. Poor coloration, scratching, loss of appetite and gradual emaciation, increased gill rate, clamped fins, 'yawning', and lethargy are all commonplace. Rampant algal growth is usually a sign of high nitrate concentrations in the aquarium.

Causes: Poor husbandry, notably overfeeding and/or overcrowding coupled with inadequate regular partial water changes. In some countries, the water supply may be the source of the high nitrate level, owing to contamination with agricultural fertilisers and/or organic wastes. Some aquarium plant fertilisers may cause a sudden dramatic increase in nitrate levels.

Prevention: Nitrate should be measured routinely in the aquarium to ensure that it is kept within safe levels. Good husbandry, avoidance of overstocking, sensible feeding, and regular partial water changes, should avoid high nitrate problems. As a general rule, changing 25-30% of the aquarium water every 1-2 weeks should be sufficient. If nitrate remains a problem, check to see whether the problem lies at the source, e.g. tap water. Nitrate can be eliminated from tap water using reverse osmosis or nitrate-removing ion-exchange resins. Assuming the source is not the cause, then the problem is probably due to overcrowding and/or overfeeding, which should be rectified. Avoid fertilisers with undesirable side-effects.

It should *never* be necessary to use nitrate removal devices/chemicals on a properly-run aquarium.

Treatment: Rectify the underlying causes of the high nitrate level, and the fish generally recover quickly.

Comment: Test kits for measuring nitrate levels sometimes have a limited 'shelf life' and lose their sensitivity, giving a zero reading. However, a nitrate value of zero is at best unlikely, and probably impossible, in a system containing any form of life.

1.2.9 NITRATE SHOCK

Shock (1.5.1) caused by sudden exposure to high levels of Nitrate (1.2.8), normally upon introduction to a poorly-maintained aquarium where nitrate levels have gradually risen, usually over a long period of time, as a result of inadequate partial water changes. The resident fish may appear healthy because they have adjusted gradually to the rising nitrate level.

Whether 'nitrate shock' is due to high nitrate alone, or to the combined toxic effects of other accumulated waste chemicals, is not clear (see 1.2.8, above).

Signs: Typically the fish become ill, sometimes with signs of acute Poisoning (1.2.1), 24-72 hours after introduction. They are often found dead, with no previous sign of illness, at 'lights on' of the second or third day in their new home. Suspect nitrate shock if a high nitrate reading (say, above 25 mg/litre) is obtained.

Prevention: High nitrate levels should be avoided (see 1.2.8) for the sake of the health of all the fish. Nevertheless, always check nitrate levels in a tank to which new fish are to be introduced, and take remedial action if necessary. New fish should never be introduced to aquaria with high nitrate levels.

Treatment: In the event that the aquarist quickly realises his error, e.g. by checking the nitrate level as an afterthought soon after introducing the fish, then a large water change or removal to a low-nitrate aquarium should help. In many cases, however, irreversible damage or death occurs before any signs of a problem become apparent.

Comment: The dealer who sold the ill-fated new fish is usually unjustly blamed for selling poor-quality stock. In fact his only 'fault' is in keeping his fish in far better quality water than many aquarists!

1.2.10 NITRITE POISONING

Nitrite (NO_2) is formed during the nitrogen cycle, being the breakdown product of ammonia. Nitrite is toxic to fish, but far less so than ammonia.

Nitrite harms fish by affecting their respiration: it enters the blood via the gills, where it causes the haemoglobin (the pigment in red blood cells which transports oxygen) to be oxidised into methaemoglobin which is an inefficient oxygen-carrier.

High nitrite levels may cause some of the symptoms associated with acute Poisoning (1.2.1) and death by Hypoxia (1.3.3). Long-term exposure to slightly elevated nitrite levels, although relatively uncommon, will cause general ill health and immunosuppression, as with other types of chronic poisoning.

Signs: Indications of acute nitrite poisoning include increased gill rate and gasping at the surface, flashing, and shimmying, the last of these particularly in small fish. In addition, the gill tissues may become violet to brown instead of their normal healthy bright red. Death may follow within hours or days, depending on species tolerance. Fry are generally very susceptible.

Cause: High levels of nitrite in the water, causes as for Ammonia poisoning (1.2.3).

Prevention: Good husbandry and efficient biological filtration. Nitrite levels should be maintained at zero (i.e. undetectable by the test kit).

Treatment:
• As for acute Poisoning (1.2.1), with removal to an unaffected aquarium the treatment of choice.
• Alternatively, if the species present are salt-tolerant, adding 1g of common salt (sodium chloride) per 10 litres of aquarium water significantly reduces nitrite toxicity (see Chapter 27, Environmental Treatments).
• A further option is to use a mature filter from another aquarium (if available), which will generally reduce nitrite levels to near-zero within 24-48 hours.
• The underlying cause of the problem must be identified and rectified.

Comment: Test kits are available for measuring nitrite levels.

1.3 PROBLEMS ASSOCIATED WITH THE LEVELS OF ATMOSPHERIC GASES IN THE AQUARIUM
See Chapter 10.

1.3.1 CARBON DIOXIDE (CO_2) PROBLEMS
• CO_2 may be a contributory factor in cases of acidosis (1.1.1).
• High levels of free CO_2 may cause hypoxia (1.3.3) in aquarium fish, particularly species evolved for life in turbulent, well-oxygenated, waters.
• Long-term exposure to unnaturally high (for the species) but sub-lethal CO_2 levels may cause damage to the kidneys as a result of calcium deposition.
• High CO_2 levels may also reduce ability to cope with other Stress (1.5.2).
• Too low a level of CO_2 (less than 1 mg/litre) can cause hyperventilation in fry, and can be lethal.

Interspecific variation exists as regards tolerance of high CO_2 levels; some species can gradually adapt to increased concentrations as long as these are not too high.

Signs: Increased respiratory rate; loss of appetite; in the longer term, reduced growth rate in young fish. (But note, all these signs may be caused by other problems.)

Causes: A high level of carbon dioxide in the aquarium water affects the fish's ability to transport oxygen to its tissues and thus may cause hypoxia. Hypoxia caused by high CO_2 levels is most likely to occur during transportation (Chapter 6) and in heavily-stocked tanks where carbon dioxide produced during fish respiration can reach critical levels (around 25mg/litre). Critical levels of carbon dioxide may be lower for some sensitive species, and the fish's tolerance may be reduced if the dissolved oxygen level is low.

Prevention: Adequate water circulation and surface movement (filtration/aeration) will ensure CO_2 is dispelled into the atmosphere. Because plants produce CO_2 in darkness, heavily-planted aquaria should be adequately aerated. CO_2 injection (for improving plant growth) should be used with caution.

Avoid overcrowding aquaria, packing too many fish per bag, and putting too large a fish in too small a bag. Use oxygen in bags for long journeys, or pack fish in lidded buckets which can periodically be opened to refresh their air content.

Treatment:
• Increase aeration and improve water circulation.
• Allow newly-arrived fishes showing signs of respiratory distress to recover in well-oxygenated and stress-free conditions, e.g. the privacy of the quarantine tank. Avoid violent aeration or circulation during the recovery period, as this may increase stress in the circumstances. Provided the water is well oxygenated and low in CO_2 before the fish are added, normal aeration should suffice.
• An apparently asphyxiated fish can sometimes be revived by holding it gently in a horizontal position in the aquarium, and moving it slowly backwards and forwards to cause water to pass into the mouth and out across the gills. As soon as the fish starts breathing independently, it should be released, to avoid further stress.

Comment: Carbon dioxide test kits for aquaria are available, but there is normally no need to monitor this gas, except where CO_2 injection is used.

1.3.2 GAS BUBBLE DISEASE

Gas bubble disease results from gas (usually nitrogen) supersaturation of the aquarium water and is analogous to the 'bends' in human divers.

Signs: Lethargy, usually with no other signs of disease; microscopical examination of the gills may reveal small bubbles on the gill filaments. If there are gas bubbles on the glass and other surfaces in the aquarium and the fish appear unwell, then suspect gas bubble disease. In acute cases the fish may have bubbles adhering to their external surfaces. Death may ensue, and sub-lethal exposure can result in brain damage. In the case of breeding and rearing aquaria, affected eggs and fry may become buoyant, and fry yolk-sacs visibly distended with gas.

Cause: Gas (chiefly nitrogen) supersaturation of the water, usually occurring when cold gas-rich, water is heated quickly – as the temperature rises, its capacity for carrying gases decreases, leading to supersaturation and the formation of bubbles (the same phenomenon can be seen in saucepans of cold water put on to heat).

Gas supersaturation commonly occurs where freshly-drawn (and hence likely to be gas-rich) cold water has been used to fill a newly set up aquarium and rapidly heated to operating temperature; or if cold, or rapidly warmed, water is used to refill after a large partial change. Fish exposed to such conditions breathe in the excess concentrations of gas which may subsequently come out of solution in the blood and cause gas embolism (the obstruction of blood vessels by gas bubbles).

It is possible, but unlikely, that the use of high-turnover powerheads, with venturis, in too small an aquarium might also cause gas supersaturation. Sensible use of appropriate equipment will avoid any chance of this.

Prevention: Freshly-drawn cold water should be warmed and aerated (to drive off excess gases) before being used for water changes. Fish should not be placed in a newly set up aquarium until it is biologically mature, by which time excess gases will have dissipated naturally.

Treatment: Move the fish to another, problem-free, aquarium; otherwise drive off the excess gas by aerating vigorously or otherwise agitating the water.

Comment: Specialised (and expensive) equipment is needed to measure nitrogen levels in water, but the 'finger test' can be used to test for gas supersaturation: if numerous bubbles form on a dry finger immersed in the aquarium (for about a minute), there may be a supersaturation problem. This test can also be used for checking recently-drawn water before it is added to the aquarium.

1.3.3 HYPOXIA (OXYGEN STARVATION)

A condition, often fatal, where insufficient oxygen reaches the fish's tissues. The cause may be physiological (in most cases the result of gill damage limiting oxygen uptake) or environmental (insufficient oxygen in the water); however, gill damage is itself commonly caused by adverse environmental factors.

Oxygen requirements vary from species to species, generally as a function of their natural environment. For example, fish from well-oxygenated waters are generally less able to withstand low oxygen levels in the aquarium than those from naturally low-oxygen habitats. Such fish may prove vulnerable to fatal hypoxia simply because a seasonal rise in aquarium temperature (i.e. during very hot weather) reduces the oxygen-carrying capacity of the water while increasing their oxygen demand.

Demand may also depend on activity levels, hence fish which are the object of continual aggression from tankmates may be unable to take up sufficient oxygen for their increased metabolic requirement (for flight), even though aquarium oxygen levels are nominally adequate for their normal needs.

Fish packed for transportation (Chapter 6) are particularly vulnerable to hypoxia because of the small (easily polluted) volume of water and limited oxygen supply in the bag. The risk is greater if water temperature increases during transportation (hence insulated packaging is required even in hot climates).

Signs: Increased respiratory rate, and hanging or swimming near the surface (in species where this is abnormal) where oxygen content is generally higher. In severe cases, respiration may become extremely laboured, with the mouth gaping and gills swollen, and the fish commonly rests on the bottom, in evident distress. Swimming co-ordination may be impaired. Sometimes heightened coloration and glazed immobile eyes. Note: some of the clinical signs are similar to those of acute Poisoning (1.2.1) and certain gill infections (which commonly cause hypoxia).

Causes:

• Environmental hypoxia (i.e. that caused by insufficient oxygen in the water):

– Increased temperature (climatic, thermostat failure) without a compensatory increase in aeration.

– Aeration/surface turbulence inadequate to provide sufficiently high oxygen levels for the species kept.

– Failure of the aeration system in situations where this is essential to the provision of adequate oxygen for the aquarium residents. Such failure may include equipment breakdown, power outage, or turning off the aeration (for example at night to reduce noise, or to save money!).

– Bacterial bloom caused by organic pollution (poor maintenance, overfeeding); the bacteria use part of the available oxygen supply, reducing that available for the fish.

– Some disease remedies (including formalin, phenoxyethanol) can reduce the level of dissolved oxygen.

– Excessive requirement due to abnormal metabolic demands, e.g. as a result of spawning activity, fighting, or flight (from an aggressor, or in panic at extra-aquarium stimuli – such as children constantly tapping the glass or running past). Female mouthbrooding cichlids often have an increased oxygen requirement due to the need to oxygenate the eggs in the mouth.

– Any combination of these factors.

• Physiological hypoxia resulting from environmental factors:

– Gill damage caused by: Acidosis or alkalosis (1.1.1); some types of Poisoning (1.2.1) (such as by Ammonia (1.2.3), Chlorine (1.2.5), and/or some chemical treatments); or mechanically (for example by sharp substrate being ingested and passed out through the gills in bottom-sifters).

– Nitrite (1.2.10) damage to the red blood cells, which convey oxygen around the body, and the inhibitory effects of nitrite on haemoglobin function.

– Excessively high levels of Carbon dioxide (1.3.1) in the water may inhibit oxygen transportation to the tissues.

• Physiological hypoxia resulting from infectious diseases:

– Gill damage caused by pathogen attack (i.e. by gill parasites or by bacterial, fungal, and protozoan infections affecting the gills – see 3.2, 3.3, 4.1, 4.2).

Prevention: Proper research into the specific oxygen requirements of species kept, coupled with avoidance of the causative factors listed above. Awareness of the particular vulnerability to hypoxia of some species in certain situations, e.g. rheophiles and other species from turbulent water in hot weather. Prompt diagnosis and treatment of pathogenic conditions likely to cause gill damage.

Prevention is paramount – environmental hypoxia can be rapidly fatal, while physiological hypoxia can cause permanent debility.

Treatment:

• Whatever the cause, aerate the aquarium vigorously to raise oxygen levels.

• A partial water change may also be considered where the cause is environmental.

• In emergencies, use hydrogen peroxide (Table 22) to bring about a rapid increase in oxygen levels.

• Fish whose gills have been damaged may require a permanently higher oxygen level in the aquarium than would normally be expected for the species concerned.

Comment: Dissolved oxygen levels can be measured using a test kit or electronic meter. This can only be done at home, since the sample tested should be freshly taken from the aquarium to ensure an accurate reading.

1.4 PROBLEMS ASSOCIATED WITH TEMPERATURE

It should be self-evident that tropical fish require tropical temperatures. However, this general designation – tropical temperatures – encompasses a range of more than 14 degrees on the Celsius scale (25 degrees on the Fahrenheit), although most species will survive reasonably well in the range 22-26 °C (72-80 °F).

Nevertheless, an unsuitable temperature over a long period may cause Stress (1.5.2). Too high a temperature may result in Hypoxia (1.3.3), as can exposure to extremely cold temperatures which may cause coma. More acute problems are Chilling and overheating (1.4.1), and Temperature shock (1.4.2).

1.4.1 CHILLING AND OVERHEATING

The water temperature gradually drops or rises, respectively, to levels outside the normal tolerance of the species concerned.

Signs:
• Chilling: lethargy, resting on the bottom. On checking, water temperature is too low. Death may occur if the fish remains chilled for too long.
• Overheating: increased respiratory rate, often gasping, with swollen flared gills; hanging near the surface where oxygen levels are higher; eventually exhaustion, resting on the bottom, and death from Hypoxia (1.3.3). On checking, water temperature is too high.

Cause: heating equipment failure – burnt-out heater in the case of chilling, jammed thermostat in either case. Chilling may also occur as a result of power outages, inadequate heater wattage (may be critical on cold winter nights when the room heating is off) at shows (where tanks are often unheated); during transportation in cold weather. Conversely, overheating can be a problem during transportation where ambient temperatures are high. Occasionally aquaria may also overheat during very hot weather, or if exposed to direct sunlight. Some forms of aquarium lighting can overheat the aquarium water if incorrectly positioned. Siting the aquarium too close to a heat source (e.g. a radiator) may cause problems.

Prevention: Use two independent heater/thermostats per aquarium, with a combined wattage appropriate to tank size; if one fails 'off', the other should maintain adequate warmth; if one fails 'on', the other will remain off such that serious overheating is less likely, or will take longer to occur. Avoid placing the aquarium next to hot-spots such as radiators or fires. Extra heater wattage may be required if the tropical aquarium is sited in a potentially cold room, such as an unheated conservatory during winter.

Aquaria at risk of over-/under-heating can be fitted with a battery-operated digital thermometer (ensure it has a waterproof probe) which constantly displays temperature and emits an audible alarm when the water temperature goes above or below pre-set limits.

Adequate insulation during transportation; transport fish at night in hot climates.

During heatwaves the aquarium can be kept from overheating by performing small (to avoid temperature shock) partial water changes, topping up with cooler water. Alternatively, bags of cold wate or ice can be floated in the aquarium (after first removing sufficient water to accommodate them); the bags can be refilled as necessary for as long as the problem lasts, avoiding the need to dechlorinate and match water chemistry (except when the tank is eventually topped up).

Special aquarium cooling units are available for use in hot climates.

Treatment: Defective equipment should, obviously, be replaced.
• Chilling: Chilled fish should be warmed up slowly (e.g. by replacing and using the aquarium heating after a failure, or, in the case of chilling during transportation, by lowering the quarantine tank temperature to that in the bags and then slowly increasing it to optimum), to avoid Temperature shock (1.4.2).
• Overheating: Serious overheating is more likely to cause rapid death. Because of the varied temperature tolerance of different species, it is impossible to quote a critical upper temperature value which is applicable in every case – the aquarist must exercise his judgement as to the severity of the crisis depending on the degree to which the fish are affected. If the fish are obviously severely distressed (hanging at

the surface or lying on the bottom, gasping) then immediate remedial action is necessary. A partial water change should be made, refilling with cold water to reduce the temperature rapidly to a safer level. Provided the fish then show signs of recovery, the temperature can subsequently be allowed to drop naturally to normal. Otherwise, a further partial water change should be considered. Aeration should be increased – to improve dissolved oxygen levels – until the temperature has returned to normal. Even with remedial action, seriously overheated fish may nevertheless die, or suffer serious after-effects (e.g. gill damage, permanent respiratory problems, brain damage) requiring euthanasia (Chapter 25).

Comment: Use of twin heating circuits will not be an effective safeguard unless both are regularly checked as functioning correctly!

1.4.2 TEMPERATURE SHOCK

Shock (1.5.1) caused by a sudden change in water temperature. The degree of change tolerated varies with species. Fry are particularly sensitive. In general, a sudden drop in temperature is more likely to cause shock than a sudden rise.

Signs: As for Chilling and overheating (1.4.1), but with rapid and immediate onset.

Cause: Usually failure to match the temperature of new water to that of the aquarium during a partial water change, or when fish are introduced to the aquarium without temperatures being first equalised (Chapter 6). Can also occur during transportation of fish (Chapter 6) if uninsulated transport bags are exposed to extremes of ambient temperature.

Prevention: Avoid the causes!

Treatment: Should never be necessary, but if an error does occur, return the fish to their previous water temperature as quickly as possible. If the problem results from a water change, then normal tank temperature should be a known quantity, and a further partial change, using warmer or cooler water, as appropriate, will rectify the situation. If the shock results from failure to equalise temperatures when introducing new fish, it will be impossible to establish the correct temperature for the shocked fish because the bag water will have been introduced with the fish. Hence prevention is paramount.

Comment: Temperature shock is a problem for which there is absolutely no excuse. Equalising temperatures is one of the fundamental principles of fishkeeping.

1.5 SHOCK AND STRESS

Shock and stress are physiological responses of the fish to adverse stimuli, such as inappropriate environmental factors; they are generally regarded in aquarium circles as short- and long-term reactions respectively, although shock may equally be regarded as an extremely acute form of stress.

It is normal for all higher organisms to experience some degree of stress throughout their lives, but under some circumstances long-term (chronic) stress can pose a serious threat to health. In the aquarium, stress should be avoided whereever possible, particularly in fish whose health has already been compromised (e.g. by disease or injury) and following transportation.

1.5.1 SHOCK

A physiological response to sudden trauma of various kinds, commonly too abrupt an alteration in one or more environmental factors. Specific types of shock have been covered under the relevant environmental problem sections of this chapter, and include Nitrate shock (1.2.9), Osmotic shock (1.1.2), pH shock (1.1.3), Temperature shock (1.4.2). Chemical shock may be osmotic shock, pH shock, or a combination of the two. Toxic shock is a term sometimes used to describe acute Poisoning (1.2.1), including a severe adverse reaction to chemical medications.

Signs: Variable, depending on the nature and severity of the trauma, but they may include: loss of colour; increased or decreased respiratory rate; resting on the bottom (commonplace) with occasional jerky movement to another location, and often hiding among plants or other decor items. Sometimes, by contrast, shock manifests as an escape response, with the fish swimming frantically up, down, and along the tank sides as if trying to find a way out. In severe cases, the fish may lie on its side or even belly-up. Death from shock is not uncommon, particularly in highly susceptible species.

Cause: Sudden changes in one or more environmental parameters. Shock is most commonly seen in newly-introduced fish, but also following partial water changes where insufficient attention has been given to matching water parameters of the new water to that of the aquarium. Susceptibility varies between species and individuals.

Even where there is no major change in water parameters involved, badly-stressed fish may exhibit shock symptoms when introduced into an aquarium, particularly after transportation, as a reaction to the unfamiliar environment. This syndrome is sometimes termed 'post-introduction shock' or 'post-introduction (or post-transportation) stress'.

Prevention: Fish should never be exposed to sudden changes in water parameters, and, obviously, poisoning of any kind. When using chemical medications, particularly as short-term high-dosage baths, the fish should be constantly observed for signs of trauma and removed if necessary (See also Chapter 24).

Treatment: Where the onset of shock is rapid and obvious (such as when caused by a change in temperature, or acute poisoning), then the underlying cause should be identified by testing the water and rectified immediately. Where all aquarium occupants are affected, such as when an ill-considered water change is the cause, then conditions in the aquarium should be rectified. By contrast, where newly-introduced fish have been traumatised by exposure to different water parameters, they should be transferred to more suitable water conditions. Never alter the water chemistry in the main aquarium to suit new fish, as this risks shocking the residents!

Newly-introduced fish which are shocked simply by the effects of transportation and the strangeness of their environment, should be left strictly alone to adjust to their situation and recover from their stress. They should *never* be poked or prodded in an attempt to stimulate them into leaving cover, or to encourage swimming if they are resting on the bottom, as this additional stress may have fatal consequences. It is often beneficial to turn the aquarium lights off – a period of darkness will have a calming effect on many fish – until the next day, by which time most fish will have recovered and integrated into their new surroundings.

1.5.2 STRESS

Stress can be a serious problem in aquarium fish, with chronic stress commonly resulting in eventual death, e.g. caused by slow starvation, or by lowered immunity and hence increased susceptibility to infection. Unfortunately, its effects are often underestimated or attributed to other causes (e.g. an imagined pathogenic disease).

The life of a fish in nature undoubtedly involves stress – fear of predation being a prime example of a natural stressor. Within the confines of an aquarium, however, many stress situations can develop, which, if they occurred in nature at all, could be evaded simply by swimming away to a more congenial spot. It is well known that the noisy clumsy angler hardly ever catches a fish!

Signs: Signs of stress are numerous and non-specific (so diagnosis must often be on the basis of circumstances, i.e. a known possible cause such as obvious bullying, or a high nitrate reading), and may include: loss of appetite and, in the longer term, resultant emaciation; hiding, including hanging in corners head down or up; nervousness and a tendency to panic ('pancaking', along the surface, jumping, looking for a way of escape through the aquarium glass); abnormal coloration (usually much darker, sometimes paler than normal); increased respiratory rate.

Cause: Adverse environmental factors – incorrect water chemistry; poor water quality; incorrect temperature; inappropriate or inadequate shelter; aggression by other fish or fear of aggression from larger and/or more boisterous tankmates (even though the latter may actually be peaceful and harmless); extraneous stimuli such as tapping on the aquarium glass; constant or unusual activity near the tank, loud noise (and attendant vibration).

In addition, diseases can themselves be stressors, as can some medications and the treatment process. Aquarium maintenance, unless performed discreetly and quietly, can cause stress, as can constant alterations to the decor and other 'fiddling', even with the best intentions. Any form of handling, especially netting, packing, and transportation is a source of stress. Even reproduction can be stressful for many species – the chasing sometimes involved during courtship can be stressful, and there is no escape from a persistent but unwelcome suitor within the confines of the aquarium. Species which practise parental care may, at breeding time, regard normally acceptable tankmates as a dire threat to their brood and suffer (and inflict!) stress.

Prevention: It is probably impossible to avoid all stress in aquarium fish, but every effort should be made to provide as stress-free an environment as possible, by providing suitable environmental conditions for each and every species, i.e. appropriate water chemistry and quality, decor, tankmates, diet, etc. Extraneous causes of stress (resulting from human activity), should also be kept to a minimum. The aquarist should be constantly on the alert – by observing his fish regularly and carefully – for any signs of stress, or potential causes of stress, developing.

Treatment: Identify and rectify the cause(s). This may sometimes mean re-homing fish that have proved incompatible. Bear in mind that the best solution to bullying is often to remove a single bully rather than the multiple victims.

Comment: A stress-free aquarium is the hallmark of a skilled aquarist.

1.6 ACCIDENTS, INJURIES, AND ASSOCIATED PROBLEMS

These relate to physical traumas which are not the direct result of disease or adverse water conditions. Many are the result of unsuitable aquarium furnishings, aggressive tankmates, or rough handling by the aquarist.

1.6.1 ACCIDENTS AND INJURIES

Accidents and injuries are here classified as environmental problems – even though a fish may damage its skin against a rock or jump out of the tank owing to parasite irritation, the rock is part of the environment and the inadequate tank cover an environmental deficiency.

Injuries may be external and/or internal. Some are trivial, others more serious, even life-threatening.

External injuries may include puncture wounds, abrasions, lost scales, torn or split fins, eye loss, gill damage, and so on. Burns (from heating equipment) are also included under this general heading. Because the skin helps maintain the fish's internal physiological salt balance (see Chapter 17), any extensive (or localised but serious) skin damage may lead to Osmotic stress (1.6.2). Moreover, even minor external injuries may become infected and, unless the problem is dealt with, possibly lead to the death, or permanent disfigurement, of the fish.

Internal injuries may cause serious damage to vital organs. It is sometimes possible to diagnose internal injury from the recent history and behaviour of the fish, but specific diagnosis and treatment are generally not possible.

Signs: External injuries are normally obvious. Burns can be difficult to distinguish from other injuries or skin infections, but suspect a burn in the event of unexplained injury to a fish with a predilection for resting on/under the heater.

Internal injuries are sometimes indicated by unusual behaviour following a known cause of injury – for example, a damaged swimbladder, following an attack (ramming) by another fish, may manifest as loss of buoyancy.

Causes: The majority of injuries are caused by aggressive behaviour by other fish, either directly (e.g. bites) or when a fleeing fish collides with decor or equipment. Panic – for example if the fish is frightened by activity outside the aquarium – can also result in collision injuries, as can dashing around the aquarium and scratching against decor when affected by parasites or adverse water conditions. Large parasites may also directly injure fish at their point of attachment, creating a wound that may become infected, especially after the parasite has detached.

Unsuitable decor may lead to minor damage (but with possibly serious implications): coarse substrates may abrade the mouths/gills of fish that dig/sift the substrate, and similarly damage the undersides and/or barbels of bottom-dwellers. Even a minor collision with very coarse-textured or sharp-edged rocks (and other decor items) can cause a serious wound. Unstable decor may collapse and crush aquarium residents, who may also occasionally get stuck in any suitable aperture – filter inlets, holes in bogwood/flowerpots, rock crevices, etc. Some species are more prone to this type of behaviour than others. Likewise species that like to rest on or under the heater are particularly prone to burns; these include some catfish (notably loricariids) and loaches, plus cichlids and other hole-dwellers.

Jumping out of the tank can cause serious injury, (external and internal). Inept handling – netting, incorrect packing (Chapter 6) – can cause minor or major damage.

Prevention: Injuries can often be prevented by common sense in choosing fish, decor, equipment etc, although there is always a danger of aggression between individuals where two or more fish are kept together. Researching each species will often reveal any specific suicidal tendency (jumping, getting stuck, sitting on heaters), so that suitable precautions can be taken.

If burn-prone fish are kept, then consider using an undertank heating mat, or a heater guard which fits over the heater tube. Positioning the heater at a steep angle (rather than horizontally) will discourage its use as a perch, and it can be sited at a distance from the bottom so that any fish resting underneath will not actually come into contact. Providing adequate hiding-places may also help.

Treatment: Most minor injuries will heal without treatment. If the injured fish is feeding and otherwise behaving normally, it is better to let well alone, as any treatment may cause a degree of stress. If, however, the fish is patently in difficulty, or the injuries are extensive and/or showing signs of infection, then treatment will be necessary. To avoid medicating healthy fish, this should take place in a hospital tank unless topical application of the medication is feasible (see Chapter 24). Hospitalisation will also provide a stress-free environment (especially important if aggression was the cause of the injuries).

A prophylactic treatment with salt (Chapter 27) can be used to prevent secondary bacterial or fungal infection in salt-tolerant species, and reduce Osmotic stress (1.6.2) where there is extensive skin damage. Raising the temperature within the fish's tolerance range will increase the metabolic rate and encourage healing.

Deep wounds and severe burns should be treated with an antiseptic such as mercurochrome (Chapter 27), while large ones can be sealed with Vaseline (pharmacy grade petroleum jelly), or (check with the vet) a non-toxic skin-dressing cream to create an artificial barrier to infection, and possibly reduce Osmotic stress (1.6.2), while the wound heals.

Comment: Some injuries may be so severe as to require euthanasia (Chapter 25), for example, if there is clearly no chance of survival, or if the degree of suffering is deemed unacceptable given the minimal likelihood of recovery (for example in cases of total loss of buoyancy control due to swimbladder damage).

1.6.2 OSMOTIC STRESS

Disruption of a fish's osmoregulatory system due to extensive skin permeability (e.g. arising from injury or disease) or as a result of incorrect water chemistry (dealt with under 1.1.2 above).

Osmoregulation is the process by which fish maintain the appropriate salt/water balance in their bodies in order to provide optimal internal conditions for various physiological and biochemical processes. Where the skin's natural impermeability is compromised by injury or disease, then osmotic forces may cause water to enter and body salts to be lost via the wound(s), creating additional work for the osmoregulatory system, which in severe cases may be unable to deal with the overload, leading to death from osmoregulatory failure.

Signs: If a fish with one or more deep wounds, ulcers, or extensive skin damage exhibits typical signs of stress (1.5.2), such as abnormally light or dark coloration, unusual behaviour (lethargy or hyperactivity), clamped fins, increased respiratory rate and, in severe cases, loss of balance, then osmotic stress should be suspected.

Cause: Serious skin injury or disease.

Prevention: Deep wounds and extensive areas of skin damage should be treated topically with an antiseptic such as mercurochrome (Chapter 27), then sealed with Vaseline (pharmacy grade petroleum jelly) or a non-toxic (check with the vet) skin-dressing cream to create an artificial barrier to infection, and help reduce osmotic stress while the wound heals.

Treatment: Add a proprietary balanced physiological salt (from the aquarium store) to the water, at the rate of 1 g/litre for soft-water species, or 3 g/litre for hard-water species. This will reduce the osmotic pressure (the difference between the internal and external salt content), helping to alleviate osmotic stress. The salt will also help prevent secondary fungal attack of skin wounds.

Comment: Unfortunately there is a risk of salt treatment doing more harm than good in the case of fish accustomed to mineral-depleted, acidic water, because of the effects of the attendant change in water chemistry on the fish's biochemical processes.

Table 14 Additional Diseases and Conditions in which Environmental Parameters may be a Contributory Factor.

Cloudy eye (6.2)
Dropsy (6.3)
Fin and tail rot (3.2.2)
Fish tuberculosis (3.2.3)
Fungus infections (3.3)
Hole-in-head disease (4.1.10)
Malawi bloat (6.4)
Pop-eye (exophthalmus) (6.5)
Skin slime disease (4.1.18)

2.0 DIETARY PROBLEMS

These usually result from incorrect feeding, but may be the consequence of
other health or environmental problems. Most are largely avoidable, and
their occurrence often reflects negligence on the part of the aquarist.
   Nutritional disorders often take a long time to manifest, usually weeks
or months rather than days, and the symptoms may be vague. Sometimes irreversible
physiological damage will have occurred before the aquarist suspects any problem.
Prevention, by correct feeding, should be the keynote.
   Like environmentally-induced diseases (1.0), nutritional diseases are not infectious.
Certain live foods, however, can introduce pathogens and parasites.
 (See also Chapter 7).

2.1 CONSTIPATION
Blockage of the gut with food, preventing normal defecation. Potentially fatal.
Signs: Absence of faeces is the key sign (the others are non-specific), often coupled
with loss of appetite. The fish may be lethargic, sometimes resting on the substrate.
In serious cases the body may become distended and the respiratory rate increased.
Usually limited to a single fish at any given time.
Cause: Usually unsuitable diet, normally over a period of time. For example, some
fish are prone to constipation if fed nothing but dry foods, this being a notorious
problem with the Oscar (*Astronotus ocellatus*). Sometimes, however, a single meal of
a totally inappropriate food may cause constipation. Fry of some species are prone to
gut blockages if inadvertently fed *Artemia* cysts ('eggs') or the empty cysts ('shells').
   Occasionally blockages may be caused by totally inedible items that have been
ingested, e.g. pieces of gravel (some large fish may even swallow pieces of
equipment!), although most fish are efficient at rejecting or ejecting anything inedible
before it enters the lower digestive tract.
Prevention: The type and size of food items and the frequency of feeding should be
appropriate to the species. Feeding nothing but dry foods, even of the very best
quality, may carry some risk of constipation.
Treatment:
• If the affected fish is still feeding, then live foods with a high roughage element may
be sufficient remedy; aquatic invertebrates such as *Daphnia*, and the various types of
mosquito larvae, as well as earthworms, are often recommended.
• Epsom salts (magnesium sulphate, Chapter 27) applied via bath immersion are
sometimes effective, and a slight increase in temperature (within the tolerance range
of the species) may be beneficial by increasing metabolic rate and gut activity.
• Large fish may be offered whole earthworms which have been injected with a very
small amount of dissolved Epsom salts, or even liquid paraffin.
When the fish begins to produce faeces again, it should be offered foods with a high
roughage content, as above. Rectify the diet to avoid recurrence. Supplementing the
normal diet with high fibre foods may be sufficient.

2.2 FATTY LIVER (FATTY DEGENERATION OF THE LIVER)
A pathological condition of the liver which may eventually prove fatal.
Signs: Usually no outward signs, the condition often being detected only upon
autopsy, although fish suffering from Obesity (2.3) are prime candidates.

Cause: Long-term consumption of unsuitable dietary fats (highly saturated fats), such as are found in mammal and poultry meat. Such fats are not easily digested and are instead accumulated in the liver.

Prevention: Avoid feeding mammal or poultry meats to fish. Very cheap aquarium fish foods, and those designed for food fish (where growth rather than longevity is the prime objective), may also contain unsuitable fats, and should be avoided.

Treatment: None. Rectify diet to prevent further fat deposition.

2.3 OBESITY

Aquarium fish, in common with many other pets, are commonly obese. Obesity in fish may cause difficulty in swimming, be accompanied by unseen internal problems such as Fatty liver (2.2), digestive tract disorders, and functional Sterility (6.6) caused by fat deposition around the gonads. It is also unsightly to anyone who appreciates the natural elegance and functional design of a healthy, properly-fed fish.

Signs: Abnormal girth, particularly as regards the abdomen; in some fish the condition may affect the area between the pelvic (ventral) insertion and the head. Fish are rarely obese when purchased (unless from other aquarists!), and many aquarists do not realise their fish are becoming obese because of the slow advance of the condition. Remember, however, that female fish increase, often considerably, in girth as they fill with ripening eggs!

Prevention: Correct diet and feeding (Chapter Seven). Comparison of fish with photos of wild-caught individuals of the same species, or specimens on sale in shops (provided not obviously emaciated), should permit monitoring of 'waistlines'.

Treatment: Remedy diet and feeding regime. It will not harm fish to reduce their food intake to a bare minimum pending their return to the shape nature intended.

Comment: Obesity is a common feature of fish belonging to showing enthusiasts (Chapter 9), where it is the result of gross overfeeding on unsuitable foods in the interests of achieving maximum size (and hence maximum points for size). It is not, of course, in the interests of the fish, whose health may be seriously compromised by its owner's unthinking cruelty. The authors believe show rules should be amended to penalise, or even ban the entry of, obese fish, as a deterrent.

2.4 UNDERNOURISHMENT AND MALNUTRITION

Unlike Obesity (2.3) this condition is rare in the domestic aquarium, although it is sometimes seen in newly-imported fish.

Signs: Gradually decreasing girth, ultimately emaciation, and a hollow belly (however, some diseases, e.g. Fish tuberculosis (3.2.3) may also cause these signs); lethargy.

Cause: Food is unsuitable or inadequate for the fish in question, and/or is offered at times when the fish is inactive, e.g. if tanks containing nocturnal species are fed only by day. Loss of appetite resulting from environmental problems (including Stress (1.5.2) or other disease) may be responsible, as may inability to compete for food properly, or at all, with tankmates.

Prevention: Correct feeding, plus regular monitoring of food intake and behaviour at feeding time. Avoidance of stress and other environmental problems (1.0).

Treatment: Rectify cause(s). If the problem is not general to all the aquarium occupants, consider isolating (in a hospital tank) those badly affected, so they can recover on an improved diet without disturbance or competition from other fish. In the case of aggression-inhibited feeding, it may be necessary permanently to re-house some fish (the bullied – or the bullies!), or else the problem is likely to recur.

Comment: While Obesity (2.3) can perhaps be forgiven (except where deliberately induced), visible undernourishment is unacceptable. The caring aquarist will be aware that his fish are not feeding and should take the necessary remedial action, before any signs of starvation manifest. It is simply a matter of careful observation.

2.5 VITAMIN DEFICIENCY

Fish require certain vitamins in their diet, without which various physiological problems may occur. Vitamin deficiencies are, however, rare in aquarium fish.

Signs: Vitamin deficiency problems may take weeks or more to manifest and the symptoms are non-specific. A common symptom of vitamin deficiency is reduced growth in young fish. Reproductive Sterility (6.6), and increased susceptibility to infections (immunosuppression) are sometimes caused by vitamin deficiencies.

Deficiencies in specific vitamins may give rise to different signs, as follows:
• Vitamin A: eye disorders such as Exophthalmia (6.5) and/or Cloudy eye (6.2); haemorrhages in the skin/fins.
• Vitamin C: fin erosion ; fin/skin haemorrhages; skeletal deformity.
• Vitamin E: Exophthalmia (6.5).

Note: most of the above symptoms are more likely to be the result of environmental problems or infectious diseases, and a vitamin deficiency should be suspected only if the fish have received a poor or inadequate diet over a prolonged period.

Cause: Normally, long-term feeding on poorly balanced or vitamin-deficient foods (some very cheap brands of fish food may be deficient in certain vitamins), especially if the diet is monotonous. Some vitamins (the vitamin B complex; vitamin C) are water-soluble and may leach from dry foods in the aquarium water, the extent of the problem varying from brand to brand. Vitamin C may also degrade in dry foods during storage, and because of this, and its water-solubility, is the vitamin most likely to be deficient in fish fed on such foods. Fish which have starved for a long period may suffer vitamin deficiency, especially as regards water-soluble vitamins, which are not stored in the tissues.

Prevention: Good-quality dry foods contain all the vitamins necessary, nevertheless varying the diet is a sensible precaution against vitamin deficiency and many other nutritional problems. Dried foods should be properly stored (in airtight containers in a cool, dry place) to guard against vitamin degradation (and other forms of deterioration). Once opened, packs of dry foods should be regarded as having a maximum useful life of two or three months.

Treatment: Improve the diet. Suspected cases of vitamin deficiency can also be treated with a course of proprietary vitamin supplements, but the root cause of the deficiency must be remedied to prevent recurrence.

Table 15 Additional Diseases and Conditions in which Nutritional Factors may be a Contributory Element.

Aflatoxin poisoning (1.2.2)
Bacterial infections (3.2) of the skin
Cloudy Eye (6.2)
Exophthalmus (6.5)
Hole-in-head disease (4.1.10)
Malawi bloat (6.4)
Skeletal deformities (5.3)

3.0 PATHOGENIC DISEASES

These are infectious diseases, which can be transmitted from one fish to another.

A **pathogen** is an organism that, in the course of its life cycle, lives in or on another organism and thereby causes harmful effects, i.e. disease. ('Pathogenic' derives from Greek words meaning 'causing disease'). Fish pathogens include species of Viruses (3.1), Bacteria (3.2), and Fungus (3.3). Various species of protozoa (4.1), together with helminths and crustaceans (4.2), may also cause disease in fish, and hence are also pathogens, however these are often grouped separately as **parasites**, and we have followed the latter convention in this book.

Fish pathogens are normally transmitted directly from one fish to another, sometimes with a free-living phase occurring off the fish (c.f. some parasites (4.0) where transmission may be indirect, involving one or more intermediate hosts). Direct transmission may be subdivided into **horizontal transmission**, where the pathogen spreads from one fish to another via the aquarium water or physical contact (including eating or being eaten!), while **vertical transmission** involves the disease being passed from parent to offspring via the eggs, sperm, or embryos. In most cases, pathogens are spread by horizontal transmission, although some viruses and bacteria are known also to be transmitted vertically.

It is likely that all established aquaria will contain an array of fish pathogens, just as our own environment harbours human viruses, bacteria, and the like. It is also quite normal for fish to sustain a few pathogens either on or in their bodies, but the numbers are usually kept in check by the fish's immune system such that no clinical disease occurs. Thus not all pathogens, even if present in the aquarium, pose an immediate threat to the healthy fish. They may, however, proliferate and cause disease where the fish's health or immunity is compromised by traumas such as Injury (1.6.1), chronic Stress (1.5.2) and adverse water conditions (1.1-1.3).

Infections can be categorised as being primary or secondary. A **primary infection** occurs when the pathogen invades healthy tissues of a fish, causing disease and damage. Many viral and bacterial pathogens are capable of causing primary infections. On the other hand, some bacteria and most fungi more commonly cause **secondary infections**, i.e. they invade tissues which have already been damaged by another infectious agent (or by injury). These secondary invaders are also known as **opportunistic pathogens**, since they take the opportunity to infect tissues which are already weakened. Prophylactic medication with antifungal and antibacterial remedies is sometimes advisable where secondary infections are likely.

Aquarists sometimes use common names for describing various disease conditions of fish, often because the causative organism is invisible to the naked eye and thus impossible to identify precisely by clinical signs alone. Thus a number of disease conditions have hobby names descriptive of their effects, such as cotton wool disease or cauliflower disease. In some cases, such a disease condition may be caused by any of a number of pathogens producing similar clinical signs. Nevertheless, the aquarist is likely to come across the scientific names of many fish pathogens, particularly the more common ones (e.g. *Saprolegnia* 3.3.7, *Flexibacter* 3.2.4) in the aquarium literature. In recognition of this situation, the common names of diseases have been used to catalogue them in this section (with the causative pathogens mentioned). In addition, the more commonly encountered pathogens are also briefly entered under their scientific names, with cross-references to the common names of the diseases they cause.

3.1 VIRUSES AND VIRAL DISEASES

Viruses are extremely small pathogens that can be seen only using a high-powered electron microscope. They are intracellular pathogens, i.e. they must invade living cells of their host to multiply. Viruses proliferate by controlling the genetic material of the host cells and instructing it to manufacture duplicate viruses, which then invade adjacent cells. Release of the newly-formed viruses is often by host-cell disruption (cell lysis) with resultant damage. The viruses spread to adjacent cells, or are carried to more remote host tissues via the bloodstream. Some types of virus cause the host cells greatly to enlarge to the extent that they form visible lumps or clusters which can be confused with Tumours (6.7). Extensive cell lysis and tissue damage may ultimately kill the host.

The outcome of a virus infection depends partly on the host's immunity and partly on other factors. In some situations, the immune system will destroy the virus, sometimes before any clinical symptoms develop. Or the virus may win the battle and ultimately kill the host. Another scenario is that the host does not develop clinical disease but nevertheless continues to harbour viruses, and is termed a '**carrier**'. These seemingly healthy carriers are an undetectable source of infection and may remain infective for prolonged periods, perhaps for the rest of their lives, posing an unsuspected health risk to others. As far as aquarium fish are concerned, this means that quarantine is far from totally effective in preventing the introduction of viral diseases. (This is not to say fish should not be quarantined!)

It is not yet possible to cure virally infected fish, though some of the antiviral drugs developed for human use may in the future find applications as regards fish diseases. Antibiotics do not destroy fish viruses. The free virus particles (i.e. those existing off the fish) can, in some cases, be eliminated by certain disinfectants, but these are generally ichthyotoxic and can be used only on equipment, *never* in the occupied aquarium, and must be throughly rinsed off before the equipment is used again. Because of the danger of disinfectant residues, virus-contaminated decor (such as gravel) or porous equipment (such as filter media) should be replaced.

Fortunately, most common viral infections of aquarium fish are rarely fatal, and it is not uncommon for the host gradually to develop acquired immunity to the pathogen and ultimately eradicate the disease. Thus the most sensible action is to quarantine any aquarium in which viral infection is suspected, and to ensure that the quarantined fish are maintained under optimal conditions (which should, of course, already be the case!) so that their immune systems are not compromised.

It must be stressed that it is totally unethical to sell or give away any fish known to have been in contact with a highly pathogenic virus infection, as there is a risk of spreading the disease to other aquarists' aquaria.

The most commonly reported viral infections of aquarium fish are those which cause visible and characteristic external signs, but others may cause undiagnosable systemic problems, and be responsible for non-specific symptoms such as haemorrhages or conditions with a number of possible causes, e.g. Dropsy (6.3). Accurate diagnosis of such non-specific viral diseases requires complex and expensive laboratory investigations and for this reason is rarely undertaken.

3.1.1 CAULIFLOWER DISEASE (LYMPHOCYSTIS DISEASE)

A chronic viral disease of fish, restricted to highly-evolved groups, such as the cichlids, and which does not affect cyprinids or catfish. It is the most commonly reported virus disease of tropical aquarium fish.

The common name is derived from the appearance of the whitish cysts that characterise the disease, which in some cases coalesce to form structures resembling miniature cauliflowers (whose shape has also been compared to that of a raspberry or bunch of grapes). The *Lymphocystis* virus causes infected cells greatly to enlarge and, as the infection proceeds, adjacent cells are invaded as well, such that eventually clusters of giant cells (up to 5mm or more across) (the cysts) are formed. The disease is unsightly but rarely dangerous, although large growths on the lips may cause the fish to starve to death by preventing feeding.

Signs: Small white, grey-white, or pinkish growths, most commonly on the fins but also on the head and body. The developing cysts can initially be confused with those of Whitespot (4.1.23), but eventually grow much larger and are typically far less numerous. In addition, whitespot spreads rapidly to other fish, while cauliflower disease is only mildly infectious; and fish with the virus infection rarely exhibit an increase in respiratory rate or any signs of irritation (such as flashing), in contrast to those infected with whitespot. Cauliflower disease may, however, cause loss of appetite and eventually emaciation, by which time diagnosis should be obvious on the basis of the growths.

Cause: The *Lymphocystis* (3.1.3) virus. It has been suggested that there may be several closely-related *Lymphocystis* viruses, each with a limited host range; this might, if true, explain the apparent low infectivity of the disease.

Transmission: Infection is probably via damaged skin. It has also been suggested that the virus could be contracted orally, by picking at the cysts on an infected fish, or by ingesting detached cysts or free viruses in the water (the virus can survive for several days in the water).

Predisposing factors: It seems likely that adverse environmental conditions and Stress (1.5.2) may trigger (where the virus is dormant), or aggravate, an outbreak.

The disease appears common in fish that have been artificially coloured by dye injection, particularly glassfish (family Chandidae), but it is unclear whether this results from the stress of the injection procedure or if the virus is transmitted via the hypodermic needle.

Prevention: The risk of introducing the virus can be reduced by long-term (about 8 weeks) quarantine, which is generally sufficient for most cases to manifest, although it is thought that the virus can remain dormant in a fish for longer periods, so it is impossible to be absolutely sure that any fish is *Lymphocystis*-free.

Visibly affected fish should not normally be purchased; nevertheless, in view of the usually harmless nature of the disease, some aquarists consider it acceptable to buy an unusual or otherwise unobtainable fish affected by the virus. Such fish should, however, be quarantined until they have been free of *Lymphocystis* growths for a period of 8 weeks.

Treatment: No known chemical treatment. The cysts normally eventually disrupt and disappear. Affected fish may develop acquired immunity.

The growths can be removed surgically, but this is undesirable because of the stress involved, and is not generally necessary unless the fish is discommoded (e.g. by cysts preventing feeding). In any case, surgery may be impracticable on small fish and, in severe cases, euthanasia may be (Chapter 25) the only humane option.

Comment: Scarring may occur, especially at the sites of large cysts.

3.1.2 FISH POX (CARP POX)

A common disease of coldwater fish, but rare and not normally infectious under tropical aquarium conditions. Although unsightly, the disease generally does little harm to the fish, and is only rarely fatal.

Signs: Irregular (in shape, size, distribution), usually clearly defined and separate, gelatinous grey-white or pinkish growths, up to 1-2 mm thick, anywhere on the fins, head, and/or body. They are initially soft but may eventually harden to a waxy consistency. In severe cases much of the surface of the fish may be affected, but this rarely occurs in tropical aquaria. Fish pox growths can be distinguished from excess mucus by the fact that they are more raised and have well-defined edges.

Cause: A herpes virus, sometimes referred to as *Herpesvirus cyprini*.

Transmission: Little is known about the virus; it appears to have an incubation period of about 6 months. The disease appears only slightly infectious.

Predisposing factors: Susceptibility to the disease may be influenced by factors such as genetic predisposition, poor nutrition, poor water quality and, in the case of coldwater fish, (seasonal) changes in water temperature.

Prevention: Good husbandry. Obviously affected fish should not be purchased.

Treatment: No known treatment. The immune response of affected fish may eventually eliminate visible signs of the disease, although not necessarily permanently.

3.1.3 *LYMPHOCYSTIS*

An iridovirus (a group of DNA viruses) which causes Cauliflower disease (3.1.1).

> **Table 16 Additional Diseases and Conditions in which Viruses may be the Causative Agent.**
>
> Dropsy (ascites) (6.3)
> Pop-eye (exophthalmia) (6.5)
> Tumours (6.7)

3.2 BACTERIA AND BACTERIAL DISEASES

Bacteria are microscopic unicellular organisms which occur singly or in groups/colonies, and are invisible to the naked eye except when they form large colonies. There are innumerable species, which are classified in broad categories based on shape, e.g. cocci (spheres), and bacilli (rods).

Not all bacteria are pathogenic. Numerous harmless species are normally present in the aquarium: in the water, on the equipment and decor, and living on the skin of the fish or in their guts. Some are actually beneficial to the health of the aquarium, for example, those responsible for breaking down nitrogenous wastes and thus providing biological filtration, and those which synthesise vitamins in the fish's gut.

A number of bacteria species are, however, potentially pathogenic to fish and responsible for a number of diseases, both internal and external. Some of these species may be present in the healthy aquarium or even form part of the normal intestinal flora of its occupants, and become pathogenic only under certain circumstances, for example immunosuppression due to environmental or dietary problems (1.0, 2.0 respectively) or where a fish is already weakened by other pathogenic disease. Bacterial pathogens may also cause secondary infection of tissues previously damaged by other pathogens or parasites.

The small size of bacteria and their lack of external features makes it impossible to identify them using microscopy alone. For the same reasons, it is not possible visibly to distinguish between those which are pathogenic and those which are harmless. Instead, special staining methods, culture techniques, and biochemical tests are used.

It should be obvious from the above that the aquarist will be unable positively to identify the species of bacteria involved in any suspected bacterial disease of his fish. Although it is possible to arrange laboratory tests via the veterinarian, this is not only expensive, but time-consuming – the fish may all be dead by the time the results become available. Hence, diagnosis is usually based simply on clinical signs. Treatment is normally initially with bactericides (Chapter 27) available over-the-counter from the aquarium retailer or pharmacist, or with antibiotics (Chapter 27) if the condition fails to respond.

3.2.1 *AEROMONAS*
A genus of bacteria common in aquatic environments. Some species are pathogenic, causing skin infections such as Ulcers (3.2.9).

3.2.2 FIN ROT (INCLUDING TAIL ROT)
The progressive erosion and disintegration of the fins.

Signs: An attack of fin rot may be preceded by abnormal red streaks in the fins caused by congestion of blood vessels (fin congestion). This is followed by abnormal lightening of the outer edge of the affected fins, then fraying of the fin membrane and ultimately the fin rays as well. The rotting edge of the fin may become inflamed and the infection, if left untreated, advances towards the base of the fin, which may ultimately rot away completely. The infection may even progress on to the body, and death then commonly occurs.

Secondary fungal infection (3.3) of the affected fin(s) is common.

Cause: Several bacteria species have been associated with fin rot: *Aeromonas* (3.2.1) (*A. liquefaciens*, *A. formicans*), *Pseudomonas* (3.2.8), and *Flexibacter* (3.2.4) (*F. columnaris*).

Transmission: Infection is usually by opportunistic bacteria in the water or already harmlessly residing on the fish.

Predisposing factors: These bacteria may become pathogenic as a result of environmental factors such as Injury (1.6.1), adverse water conditions (1.1, 1.2), or where the fish is immunosuppressed, perhaps due to Stress (1.5.2). Often a combination of these is involved, e.g. fin damage accompanied by poor water quality – fin damage does not invariably lead to fin rot in an otherwise healthy fish.

Prevention: It is impossible to avoid all the circumstances that may predispose fish to fin rot, but good husbandry and careful choice of compatible fish will minimise the likelihood of the disease. In cases of serious fin injuries, prophylactic treatment with salt or gentian violet (see Chapter 27) will usually prevent the condition developing. Because the disease is obvious, and normally (but not always) progresses slowly, serious infection and possible permanent fin loss can be prevented by prompt treatment.

Treatment:

• Bath immersion of the affected fish in a solution of salt (provided the species is salt-tolerant) or a phenoxyethanol-based proprietary medication (Chapter 27) .

• If only one or two fish are affected, gentian violet, applied topically. This treatment has also proved effective in cases that have failed to respond to other medications. These medications will also act as a treatment for, or prophylactic against, secondary fungal infection.

In addition, any contributory environmental causes should be eliminated, to speed recovery and the regeneration of the fins, and to prevent any recurrence.

Comment: Fin rot is also a common secondary condition in cases of serious systemic bacterial infection, where it is often accompanied by other signs of such infection, for example ulcers and body distension (c.f. Dropsy, 6.3).

3.2.3 FISH TUBERCULOSIS (FISH TB, MYCOBACTERIOSIS)

A systemic disease caused by various species of *Mycobacterium*. Mycobacterial infections are fairly common in aquarium fish, particularly in gouramis, barbs, tetras, and livebearers.

Signs: General ill health, with signs including loss of appetite, lethargy, emaciation (a hollow belly), exophthalmia (6.5), skin ulcers, and abnormally pale coloration. Generally speaking, the disease progresses over a period of time, sometimes eventually causing deformities of the skeleton. Usually fatal if not treated. Post-mortem examination may reveal white nodules around 2-3 mm in diameter in the internal organs. Note: nodules may sometimes be the result of other pathogens such as *Ichthyophonus* (3.3.6), and confirmation of the diagnosis requires laboratory testing (acid-fast staining).

Cause: *Mycobacterium marinum* and *M. fortuitum* are known to cause fish TB in aquarium fish.

Transmission: Mycobacteria may enter the water from open ulcers or faeces or rotting carcasses of infected fish. Infection is considered to be via the ingestion of infected faeces or by foraging on the infected bodies of dead/dying tankmates. There is evidence that the disease can sometimes be transmitted vertically via the eggs (or embryos in the case of livebearing species).

Predisposing factors: Poor husbandry (especially regarding aquarium hygiene) may predispose fish to this disease, which is not highly contagious. Persistent poor tank hygiene may result in a succession of fish developing the disease.

Prevention: Fish showing signs of fish TB should never be purchased; any specimen suspected of having the disease should be isolated to minimise the risk of infecting others, and never used for breeding purposes. Good aquarium hygiene will make for healthy fish with optimal disease resistance, and also avoid transmission via corpses.

Treatment: Mycobacterial infections are difficult to cure, although antibiotics (Chapter 27) such as kanamycin and erythromycin are sometimes effective. In some cases, combination antibiotics may be prescribed. Euthanasia (Chapter 25) should be considered in the case of badly affected fish.

Comment: There is a slight risk of humans contracting mycobacterial infection from diseased fish or infected aquarium water, especially via open cuts or grazes. (See Chapter 25).

3.2.4 *FLEXIBACTER* (*CHONDROCOCCUS*, MYXOBACTERIA)

A genus of bacteria that can cause necrosis of the skin, fins, gills, and mouth of fish. *Flexibacter* is the infective agent in diseases such as Mouth fungus (3.2.5) (not a fungus at all), also known as columnaris disease, and Fin rot (3.2.2).

The species most commonly reported in freshwater fish is *F. columnaris*, a gram-negative bacterium which affects many different types of fish and is thought to be more pathogenic at tropical temperatures. This bacterium has also been implicated in causing bacterial gill disease although other types of bacteria may, in fact, be the cause.

3.2.5 MOUTH FUNGUS (MOUTH ROT, COLUMNARIS DISEASE)

The name 'mouth fungus' derives from the clinical resemblance to some fungus infections (3.3) – but the condition is in fact caused by a bacterium. The disease commonly affects the mouth but may also attack other parts of the surface of the fish, when it is generally termed columnaris disease.

Signs:

• Chronic form: initially small, off-white to grey, marks, usually on the head, but sometimes on the fins and gills. The lips are particularly likely to be affected, and the infection may extend into the mouth cavity. The initial lesions develop into off-white fluffy growths, resembling cotton wool, hence the confusion with external fungal infections, which are often similar in appearance. Mouth fungus, however, has a coarser, more granular appearance, and is often greyer in colour than true fungus. Investigation under a high-power microscope will reveal rod-shaped bacteria rather than fungal hyphae. The disease progresses slowly over a period of time and can be fatal if not treated.

• Acute form: a systemic infection, usually occurring at tropical temperatures, with an incubation period of a few days. The fish do not always show external symptoms but may die within as little as 2-3 days. Diagnosis is normally possible only on post-mortem examination of infected tissue, and this disease may be responsible for some unexplained deaths.

Cause: *Flexibacter columnaris.*

Transmission: The bacterium is commonly present in aquarium water, on dead organic material, and even on healthy fish skin, and may invade damaged or unhealthy skin and spread to the surrounding tissues. *Flexibacter columnaris* appears to be more pathogenic under hard water conditions with a pH above 6.

Predisposing factors: These include existing damage to the mouth (e.g. from injury), or adverse environmental conditions, such as high levels of nitrogenous wastes, incorrect pH, or low oxygen content (see Chapter 10 and 1.0 above). A possible predisposing factor is Vitamin deficiency (2.5).

Mouth fungus usually occurs at temperatures above 20 °C (68 °F).

Prevention: Good husbandry. It is inappropriate to keep fish at low temperatures or those from hard or alkaline conditions in soft acid water. Ill health due to incorrect environmental factors is far more likely than *Flexibacter* infection.

Treatment: Bath immersion using a proprietary treatment containing phenoxyethanol (Chapter 27) is normally effective. Because this medication is also fungicidal, it will cater for misdiagnosis, resulting from the similarity of the disease to some genuine fungal infections. In serious cases, especially if internal tissues are affected, an antibiotic, such as oxytetracycline (Chapter 27), may be required.

Comment: Survivors of this infection may develop a degree of acquired immunity.

3.2.6 *MYCOBACTERIUM*

The genus *Mycobacterium* contains several species, two of which (*Mycobacterium marinum* and *M. fortuitum*) affect aquarium fish, causing the systemic disease known as Fish tuberculosis (3.2.3) or mycobacteriosis.

3.2.7 *NOCARDIA*

A genus of bacteria, some species of which affect freshwater fish. *Nocardia* infections are very similar to those caused by *Mycobacterium* (3.2.6), with laboratory testing necessary to differentiate the two types of bacteria. Signs, prevention and treatment are, essentially, as for *Mycobacterium* infection.

3.2.8 *PSEUDOMONAS*

A genus of gram-negative rod-shaped bacteria, some of which affect fish, causing problems such as Fin rot (3.2.2) and Ulcers (3.2.9).

3.2.9 ULCERS

Skin ulcers may occur through bacterial infection of an injury or be an outward manifestation of a systemic bacterial infection.

Signs: Open sores on the head and/or body, with reddened edges. If they are the result of a systemic infection, then one or more other signs of the underlying problem are likely, e.g. body distension (Dropsy, 6.3), exophthalmia (6.5), Fin rot (3.2.2), and emaciation. Secondary infection with Fungus (3.3) is common.

Cause: Various bacteria, including *Aeromonas* (3.2.1), *Mycobacterium* (3.2.6), *Pseudomonas* (3.2.8), and *Vibrio* (3.2.10). (But note, some poisons (1.2) can cause ulcerative necrosis of the skin.)

Transmission: The causative bacteria species are commonly found in aquarium water where they are generally harmless to healthy fish, but may opportunistically invade any open wound.

Predisposing factors: Skin damage, Stress (1.5.2) and adverse water conditions (1.1, 1.2) may predispose fish to ulcerative infections.

Prevention: Good husbandry, minimisation of stress, and avoidance of situations likely to lead to skin injury.

Treatment: Small superficial ulcers can be treated by bath immersion using a proprietary anti-ulcer or anti-systemic-bacteria medication, preferably one with fungicidal properties (e.g. one containing phenoxyethanol, to deal with any secondary fungal attack. Minor lesions that fail to respond to proprietary treatment, and larger, deeper or more numerous ulcers, should be treated with antibiotics, administered in food, by bath immersion, or by injection (in larger fish).

Where environmental problems are implicated, these must be remedied as part of the treatment, and to help minimise the likelihood of the disease recurring.

Ulcers may develop secondary infections, and, where there is extensive skin damage, Osmotic stress (1.6.2) may occur. If the fish is to stand any chance of recovery, these additional traumas must be treated, or, if possible, avoided. A long-term salt bath (1-3 g/litre for several days) will help reduce osmotic stress and act as a prophylactic against fungus. However, this treatment can be used only where compatible with the antibacterial medication chosen, and on salt-tolerant species. See Chapter 27 for further details of treatments.

3.2.10 *VIBRIO*
A genus of bacteria found predominantly in brackish or marine waters. However, a strain of *Vibrio anguillarum* ('Type C') has been recorded as causing Vibriosis (3.2.11) in freshwater fish.

3.2.11 VIBRIOSIS
A systemic disease predominantly of marine and brackish-water fish, but occasionally found in freshwater aquaria. It occurs in two forms, chronic and acute, both of which can be fatal.
Signs:
• Chronic vibriosis: external signs include exophthalmus (6.5) and skin lesions or Ulcers (3.2.9), while post-mortem investigation may reveal lesions of the musculature and inflammation of the intestine.
• Acute vibriosis: skin haemorrhage may occur, as well as body distension (Dropsy, 6.3), but equally there may be no external signs except those generally associated with most types of disease (e.g. increased respiratory rate, lethargy, and loss of appetite). Death is rapid. Post-mortem may reveal necrosis or enlargement of internal organs. Because of the similarities between systemic bacterial infections, diagnosis can be confirmed only by laboratory tests.
Cause: *Vibrio anguillarum* (3.2.10).
Transmission: Infection may occur through bacteria entering the tissues via skin injuries (1.6.1) or by feeding on infected corpses or faeces.
Predisposing factors: Adverse water conditions, particularly organic pollution with Ammonia (1.2.3), Nitrite (1.2.10), and/or Nitrate (1.2.8). Other causes of Stress (1.5.2) may be contributory factors in an outbreak of this disease.
Prevention: Good husbandry and minimisation of stress. Fish which show any signs of systemic bacterial infection should not be purchased.
Treatment: Normally antibiotics, such as chloramphenicol or furazolidone, administered orally, are required effectively to treat vibriosis. Certain other bactericides (e.g. oxolinic acid) may also be effective. See Chapter 27 for further details. Chloramphenicol should be administered in food for 6 days, at the rate of 50 mg (1.764 oz) per kg (220.462 lb) of fish on the first day, and 30mg (1.058 oz) per kg of fish per day for the following 5 days. Dosage for furazolidone, again via food, is 100 mg (3.527 oz) per kg of fish daily for 6 days.

Table 17 Additional Diseases and Conditions in which Bacteria may be a Causative Factor.

Dropsy (ascites) (6.3)
Hole-in-head disease (4.1.10)
Malawi bloat (6.4)
Pop-Eye (6.5)

3.3 FUNGUS AND FUNGAL INFECTIONS
Fungal infections are among the most commonly encountered pathogenic diseases in aquarium fish. These diseases are generally characterised by the presence of fluffy hyphae – the source of the generic term Cotton wool disease (3.3.3).

Most fish-pathogenic fungi are opportunistic, and normally attack only where tissues have previously been damaged (commonly by Injury (1.6.1) but also by other disease) allowing access to their spores (and possibly other stages). These are frequently present in the aquarium water, as evidenced by the growth of fungus that rapidly appears on corpses or uneaten food left in the tank by the slovenly fishkeeper. Fungus may also attack fish eggs – usually those which are infertile or damaged but it can quickly spread to healthy eggs (see Egg fungus, 3.3.4).

Most species of fungi attack only the external tissues or gills of fish, and only rarely are 'atypical' fungi encountered which invade the internal tissues. External fungal infections are easily treated with a number of readily available fungicidal chemicals and aquarium remedies (Chapter 27), but Systemic fungal infections (3.3.8) are commonly regarded as untreatable, although bath immersion in a solution of malachite green (Chapter 27) has been suggested as a possibility.

Poor aquarium hygiene, Stress (1.5.2), Chilling (1.4.1), old age, chronic malnutrition (2.4), and other health problems are all factors which may weaken fish and make them more vulnerable to fungal attack – fungus is not an inevitable consequence of injury if the fish and the aquarium are in the best of health.

3.3.1 *ACHYLA*
A genus of fungus belonging to the class Oomycetes, one of the possible causative agents in Cotton wool disease (3.3.3) and Egg fungus (3.3.4).

3.3.2 *BRANCHIOMYCES*
A genus of fungus (class Phycomycetes), responsible for the disease known as Gill rot (3.3.5) or Branchiomycosis. Not commonly encountered in tropical aquaria.

3.3.3 COTTON WOOL DISEASE
A general term used by aquarists for external fungal infections characterised by fluffy, usually whitish, cotton-wool-like growths.

Signs: Fluffy, usually white or whitish, growths, sometimes extensive, sometimes just small tufts, commonly at the site of an Injury (1.6.1) or where skin integrity has been damaged by diseases, including wounds left by large parasites (4.2). Untreated fungal growths may turn grey to reddish-brown with time, as they accumulate dirt or algae. If the condition is neglected, the fungus may eventually spread to adjacent healthy tissue. Neglected cases can ultimately prove fatal.

Fungus is often seen as a secondary infection, including of the fins in cases of Fin rot (3.2.2).

Cause: A number of genera of fungi, including *Saprolegnia* (commonly but erroneously used by aquarists as a generic for all fish-pathogenic fungi) (3.3.7) and *Achyla* (3.3.1). Other genera of fungi may be involved, and a single site may be attacked by multiple species of fungi.

Transmission: Fungi may be found in most aquaria, where they exist as saprophytes, feeding on organic matter including rotting fish carcasses. They can, however, attack damaged tissues of live fish, or fish which are severely immunosuppressed. Infection is via the fungal spores, and possibly other stages, which are present in the water or attached to organic matter.

Predisposing factors: Poor aquarium hygiene, Stress (1.5.2), Chilling (1.4.1), old age, Injury (1.6.1), and other diseases.

Prevention: Good husbandry, minimisation of stress.

Some lazy and slovenly aquarists, whose aquaria are so badly maintained that they are prone to constant fungal problems, sometimes attempt to 'solve' the problem by the prophylactic use of fungicides. This approach does not address the underlying problems, with the result that other diseases are also likely to manifest owing to continuing poor aquarium conditions, and the repeated dosing with fungicides may eventually cause chemical toxicity to the fish.

However, prophylaxis against fungus is sometimes a sensible precaution in cases of injury, using bath immersion or topical application, as under Treatment, below.

Treatment: If numerous fish are affected (and they should not be, in a properly-maintained aquarium with compatible tankmates!) then treatment can take place in the main aquarium. Under normal circumstances, however, long-term bath immersion in the hospital aquarium is preferable to medicating healthy fish together with sick ones.

• Most fungal infections should respond to a prolonged salt (Chapter 27) bath (which can also be used for prophylaxis), provided all species (and plants) are salt-tolerant.

• Alternatively an aquarium fungicide, e.g. one containing phenoxyethanol (Chapter 27) can be used.

• A third option, provided the fish is not in need of rest and recuperation (i.e. in the hospital tank) as well as fungal treatment, is topical application of gentian violet (Chapter 27), which is also bactericidal and hence a doubly useful prophylactic treatment for skin damage. This method has the advantage that the fish can immediately be returned to its normal environment, avoiding the stress of experiencing a strange environment and subsequent reintroduction.

The underlying causes of repeated injuries, or fungal attacks triggered by poor conditions and/or general ill health, should be remedied.

Comment: The bacterial disease known as Mouth fungus (3.2.5) or columnaris also produces fluffy whitish growths similar to those caused by fungi, and is sometimes also known as cotton wool disease.

3.3.4 EGG FUNGUS
Fungal infection of fish eggs.

Signs: Eggs affected by fungus are typically covered in fluffy white fungal hyphae.
Cause: Various species of fungus, including members of the genera *Achyla* (3.3.1) and *Saprolegnia* (3.3.7).
Transmission: Fungal spores are normally present in the aquarium water and will readily attack any decomposing organic matter, including non-viable decaying eggs. The fungus may subsequently spread to adjacent fertile eggs.
Predisposing factors: The degree of susceptibility varies, with some species producing tough-skinned eggs which are comparatively resistant to fungal (and bacterial) attack. Viable eggs which are scattered, or attached singly to substrates such as plant leaves, are normally safe from fungal spread. However, this can be a problem where clutches are laid close-packed, as in the case of bubble-nest-building anabantids and substrate-spawning cichlids and gobies. Fortunately, part of the parental care practised by most such fish involves carefully picking out any unhealthy eggs.
Prevention: In general, the problem arises only where parental species have

neglected or abandoned their clutch, or where the aquarist is endeavouring to hatch eggs artificially (Chapter 8). In the former case, any eggs affected by fungus can be carefully picked out using a pipette, needle, or fine-pointed forceps, while in the latter, normal procedure is prophylactic use of a suitable fungicide (Chapter 27), methylene blue being particularly popular.

Treatment: Once any egg has been attacked by fungus no remedial treatment is possible.

Comment: Many aquarists incorrectly assume that white or opaque eggs are fungused even if no fluffy hyphae are apparent. Some normal healthy eggs are in fact opaque and whitish (or yellowish/pinkish) when laid. Eggs which are clear at spawning but infertile usually turn white within 24 hours due to internal decomposition, but fungus does not normally appear until later.

3.3.5 GILL ROT (BRANCHIOMYCOSIS)

An uncommon fungal infection of the gills.

Signs: Increased respiratory rate, gasping at the surface, hanging in well-oxygenated areas (e.g. near the surface or in filter outflows). The gills may exhibit clearly visible mucus hyperproduction and be mottled (dark red and lighter patches); in extreme cases, the gill may rot away. Secondary infections of fungi such as *Achyla* (3.3.1) and *Saprolegnia* (3.3.7) may be apparent. Death from Hypoxia (1.3.3) may occur within 2-4 days at tropical temperatures.

Cause: *Branchiomyces* (3.3.2) species.

Transmission: *Branchiomyces* spores may already be present in the aquarium water, or introduced by infected fish.

Predisposing factors: High levels of organic toxins such as Ammonia (1.2.3), Nitrite (1.2.10), and Nitrate (1.2.8); overcrowding; and algal blooms (Chapter 22). Gill rot usually occurs at temperatures above 20 °C (68 °F).

Prevention: Good husbandry.

Treatment: No proven remedies, however some aquarists have advocated a long-term bath, in the affected aquarium, using a proprietary fungicidal medication containing phenoxyethanol (Chapter 27). Increase aeration to improve oxygen levels in order to alleviate hypoxia, both during treatment, and, if successful, while the gill tissue regenerates. Contributory factors should be remedied by improving husbandry.

3.3.6 ICHTHYOPHONUS

A genus of fungus (in fact the taxonomic status of this pathogen is unclear, and it may not be a true fungus) that causes systemic infection, usually in marine, and only very rarely in freshwater, fish (and then apparently as a result of feeding on marine trash fish, e.g. in aquaculture). In the past, it was thought to be a far more frequent cause of systemic infection in freshwater species, hence the name is sometimes used in older aquarium literature with reference to any type of systemic fungus.

3.3.7 SAPROLEGNIA

A genus of fungus belonging to the class Oomycetes. The name *Saprolegnia* is commonly, but erroneously, used by aquarists to describe any fluffy fungal infection – in fact, other genera from the same class also produce this type of growth.

3.3.8 SYSTEMIC FUNGAL INFECTIONS

These infections are difficult to diagnose without post-mortem examination, and are thought to be rare, and generally regarded as untreatable, hence their impact on aquarium fish has been little studied. The following brief summary encapsulates what is generally known.

Signs: Usually only non-specific signs of ill health, possibly no signs at all until the disease is advanced or if it affects a vital organ. In some systemic infections, tiny tufts of fungus may appear protruding from under the edges of several or numerous scales.

Cause: One systemic fungus which has very occasionally been recorded in freshwater fish is *Ichthyophonus* (3.3.6), which is more usually found in marine fish.

Transmission: Little is known. Adverse environmental conditions and Stress (1.5.2) may be contributory factors. *Ichthyophonus* is known to have been transmitted via contaminated dead marine fish fed as food, e.g. in aquaculture.

Prevention: As with most diseases, good husbandry and stress minimisation may help fish to resist this type of infection.

Treatment: A long-term bath immersion in malachite green solution (Chapter 27) has been suggested as a possible treatment.

4.0 PARASITES

This group of fish enemies includes a number of protozoa (protozoan parasites, 4.1), as well as larger parasites (4.2), such as various helminth worms, *Argulus* (Fish louse, 4.2.7), and leeches (4.2.6).

Parasites, like pathogens (3.0), are organisms which may cause ill health in the animal on or in which they live (the 'host'). Sometimes parasites exist on the host in small numbers ('light parasite burden') such that they may not cause any significant problem and produce no noticeable signs. However, a heavy parasite burden, or a single large parasite on/in a relatively small host, can cause serious damage and even death.

Parasites are commonly subdivided into two groups: **ectoparasites**, which live on the outside of the host (in the case of a fish, this is usually taken to include the mouth and gill cavities as well as the skin and fin surfaces); and **endoparasites**, which live in the tissues, blood, and/or organs (including the stomach/intestine).

Some fish parasites encountered under aquarium conditions, in particular ectoparasitic protozoa and skin/gill flukes, are transmitted directly from fish to fish, typically involving a free-living phase in the water or substrate. Many larger parasites, however, have a complex life cycle involving two or more hosts (including a fish) and, in such cases, transmission is indirect. Intermediate hosts include aquatic snails or aquatic crustaceans such as copepods. In the case of some fish parasites, notably tapeworms, a terrestrial, rather than an aquatic, intermediate host may be involved, for example a piscivorous bird or mammal – obviously such life cycles cannot be completed under aquarium conditions!

In the aquarium hobby, infections caused by protozoa are generally known by the external signs they cause (e.g. whitespot, velvet disease), whereas infestations caused by many of the macroscopic parasites are referred to by the parasite's common name (e.g. gill flukes, anchor worm). Accordingly, they are grouped separately here, as Protozoan Parasites (4.1) and other Parasites (4.2).

4.1 PROTOZOAN PARASITES

Protozoa are single-celled organisms, usually detectable only under a microscope, although some are just visible to the naked eye. Some are grouped according to their locomotory method. For example, ciliate protozoa are fringed with hairs (cilia) which are beaten to propel the organism, while flagellate protozoa use one or more flagella (singular flagellum, a whip-like appendage) for the same purpose. They include both free-living and parasitic species, and a number are parasites of fish; some of the most common diseases of aquarium fish are caused by protozoa, including probably the best-known of all ornamental fish ailments, whitespot (ichthyophthiriasis, 4.1.23), which is caused by the protozoan parasite *Ichthyophthirius* (4.1.12).

Protozoa parasites can be ectoparasitic (explained above), while others are endoparasitic and invade the tissues, including the blood. Some attack both external surfaces and internal tissues. In the case of protozoan parasites of fish, those which are ectoparasitic or invade the skin are normally easy to treat, with a variety of proprietary medications being available for the purpose, while those that invade deeper tissue and the blood are generally far more difficult to eliminate.

Many protozoan parasites are commonly present in small numbers on or in seemingly perfectly healthy fish. Their numbers can, however, multiply to disease proportions under certain circumstances, e.g. if the host's immune system is compromised, commonly by environmental factors (1.0), in particular poor water quality (1.2) and Stress (1.5.2). Treatment commonly includes remedying any underlying causes of the parasite escalation, but chemical medication is generally required as well. If not treated, many of these protozoan diseases can prove fatal.

Most protozoan fish infections have been given common names (e.g. whitespot, skin slime disease) by aquarists, based on the visible manifestations of the disease. For this reason, where the disease and the parasite have different names in aquarium terminology, they have been catalogued separately below, for ease of reference. In such cases, the cause of the disease is simply stated to be the relevant parasite, with no additional data on the parasite itself; such information (e.g. on the life cycle) can then be found under the parasite entry. This information may be of interest in understanding the disease, but is not essential to recognising or treating it.

Table 18 Protozoan Parasites and the Diseases they Cause.	
Parasite	**Disease**
Apiosoma	No common name
Chilodonella	Skin slime disease (costiasis)
Epistylis	No common name
Heterosporis	No common name
Hexamita	Hole-in-head disease (hexamitiasis; head & lateral line erosion)
Ichthyobodo	Skin slime disease (costiasis)
Ichthyophthirius	Whitespot (Ich)
Piscinoodinium	Velvet ('Oodinium'; rust disease; gold-dust disease)
Pleistophora	Neon tetra disease
Trichodina	Skin slime disease (costiasis)
Tetrahymena	Guppy disease
Trypanosomes	No common name

4.1.1 *APIOSOMA*

A genus of stalked ciliate protozoa which are usually free-living but sometimes colonise the skin, fins, and gills of freshwater fish. They are considered to be commensals rather than true parasites since they do not usually harm the fish and do not feed on its body tissues, although large aggregations may produce visible 'growths', which may cause the aquarist concern. Very occasionally, large numbers on the gill tissues may lead to gill dysfunction and a degree of physiological Hypoxia (1.3.3). *Apiosoma* sometimes colonise areas of damaged skin in large numbers.

Signs: Small numbers of *Apiosoma* are unlikely to produce any signs, but aggregations may appear as whitish growths on the skin or fins, easily confused with Whitespot (4.1.23) or Cauliflower disease (Lymphocystis disease) (3.1.1), both of which are more common. Diagnosis can be confirmed by microscopical examination, but this is unlikely to be necessary: whitespot can be differentiated by the fast proliferation of spots over the fish and by its rapid spread to other fish; cauliflower disease typically forms globular growths which aggregate as grape- or cauliflower-like clusters.

Cause: One common species is *A. piscicolum*, which may be found on a wide range of tropical freshwater species, notably those from southern Africa.

Predisposing factors: Adverse environmental factors, particularly poor water quality (1.2) and Stress (1.5.2).

Transmission: Possibly by contact of fish with substrate or other surfaces containing *Apiosoma* colonies. Some of the stalked ciliates produce swimming forms.

Prevention: *Apiosoma* is unlikely to be a problem if the predisposing factors are avoided.

Treatment: In the event of a serious outbreak, a long-term salt (Chapter 27) bath (2 g per litre, for 3-7 days) should prove effective; if salt-intolerant species are present, then a proprietary anti-protozoan treatment can be used instead.

4.1.2 *CHILODONELLA*

A genus of ciliate protozoans, one of a number of pathogens which may cause Skin slime disease (4.1.18). The fish-pathogenic *Chilodonella* are obligate parasites (i.e. can survive only on the host) and feed mainly on dead skin cells. Small numbers cause little, if any, harm but if the fish becomes immunosuppressed by environmental factors, or if there is heavy organic pollution in the aquarium, then the parasites can rapidly proliferate and attack healthy tissue.

4.1.3 *COSTIA*

A synonym of *Ichthyobodo* (4.1.11). This now obsolete generic name may still be encountered in aquarium literature, as may the derivative Costiasis, also known as Skin slime disease (4.1.18).

4.1.4 *CYCLOCHAETA*

A synonym of *Trichodina* (4.1.20), one of the causative agents in Skin slime disease (4.1.18).

4.1.5 *EPISTYLIS*

A genus of stalked ciliate protozoa which sometimes attach themselves to fish and may colonise tissue infected by bacteria, on which they feed. They are regarded as commensal rather than parasitic, but there is evidence that the stalk of *Epistylis* may penetrate the skin and add to the damage caused by the bacterial infection (which is believed to be the main cause of any clinical problems).

Signs: Colonies of *Epistylis* may resemble small tufts of fungus (4.3), typically on harder external surfaces such as the opercula and the tips of fin rays, often with concomitant signs of bacterial infection (3.2) and in association with an infected Injury (1.6.1).

Cause: Several species are known, including *E. colisarum* which has been recorded in gouramis. Prevention and treatment are the same for all species.

Predisposing factors: Organic pollution (1.2.3, 1.2.8, 1.2.10) and an existing bacterial infection are major contributory factors to colonisation of fish by these protozoa. However, *Epistylis* rarely cause problems in aquarium fish.

Transmission: Via a free-swimming migratory stage (called a telotroch) which detaches from the parent colony.

Prevention: Good husbandry and prompt treatment of injuries and external bacterial infections.

Treatment: Long-term bath immersion in salt solution (Chapter 27).
Comment: The associated bacterial infection must, of course, be treated as well.

4.1.6 GUPPY DISEASE

A protozoan disease sometimes encountered in tropical aquaria and principally associated with guppies (*Poecilia reticulata*), but which may also affect other poeciliid livebearing species and occasionally other groups of fish.

Signs: Small white patches (colonies of protozoa) on the skin (in guppies the parasites sometimes congregate around the eyes). Bristly protruding scales. Occasionally, the musculature and internal organs may be affected, and the disease can be rapidly fatal. Definitive diagnosis requires microscopical examination of skin scrapings from the infection site.
Cause: *Tetrahymena corlissi* (4.1.19).
Transmission: Direct, via the free-swimming stage.
Prevention: Livebearing fish showing signs of this disease should not be purchased.
Treatment: Mild infections of the skin may respond to treatment with a proprietary anti-protozoan treatment, but more serious attacks involving internal tissues are generally incurable, and euthanasia (Chapter 25) may be necessary.

4.1.7 HEAD AND LATERAL LINE EROSION

See Hole-in-head disease (4.1.10).

4.1.8 *HETEROSPORIS*

A genus of microsporidian protozoa, closely related to *Pleistophora* (4.1.16). In the tropical freshwater aquarium, most noted for attacking the musculature of angelfish (*Pterophyllum* spp.), with a high mortality rate, particularly in young fish.
Signs: Emaciation; greyish patches/spots on the skin.
Cause: In angelfish, *H. finki*.
Transmission: Thought to be by cannibalism of infected corpses.
Prevention: Isolation of suspected cases to prevent spread. Prompt removal of corpses.
Treatment: None. Badly-affected fish may require euthanasia (Chapter 25).
Comment: Adult angelfish appear to be more resistant than juveniles.

4.1.9 *HEXAMITA*

A genus of flagellate protozoa, regarded by some authorities as synonymous with *Octomitus* (4.1.14) or *Spironucleus* (4.1.17). These protozoa are commonly found in small numbers in the intestines of cichlids, and occasionally in other families of fish, and are thought to be a causative factor in Hole-in-head disease (4.1.10) (also known as head and lateral line erosion).

4.1.10 HOLE-IN-HEAD DISEASE (HEXAMITIASIS)

A disease primarily of cichlid fish (family Cichlidae), thought to be at least partially protozoan in origin, but apparently sometimes accompanied by systemic bacterial infection (3.2). It remains unclear to what extent the manifestations of the disease are attributable to protozoa or bacteria, or whether both agents in fact play an essential role in the progress of the condition. Death occurs in many, but not all, untreated cases.

Signs: White stringy faeces (generally regarded as the diagnostic sign, if not attributable to diet), sometimes accompanied by enlargement and erosion of the sensory pores of the head (and/or occasionally the lateral line = head and lateral line erosion). Affected pores usually become filled with whitish pus, which may ooze from them in severe cases. Abnormally dark coloration, loss of appetite, and eventually emaciation, are other characteristic signs, although body distension (Dropsy, 6.3) occasionally occurs, perhaps as a result of concomitant bacterial infection or disruption of osmoregulation.

Cause: Protozoa of the genus *Hexamita* (4.1.9), perhaps coupled with systemic bacterial infection by, for example, *Aeromonas* (3.2.1).

Predisposing factors: Any factor that may compromise the fish's immune system: other diseases, environmental problems (1.0), Stress (1.5.2), or even old age.

Transmission: Readily transmitted from cichlid to cichlid; the exact route is unknown, although this is probably via the aquarium water as cross-infection occurs even where no cannibalism of corpses has taken place. Coprophagy has also been suggested as a possible method of transmission, but cichlids do not normally forage on faeces.

Prevention: Although prophylaxis is possible, this is not normally advisable because of the danger of the parasite developing resistance to the only effective drugs known. It is preferable to eliminate predisposing factors, especially stress. Cichlids that have been effectively treated for hexamitiasis are thought to remain free of the parasite unless untreated cichlids are subsequently introduced, in which case re-infestation is likely.

Treatment: It is normal to treat only fish exhibiting signs of the disease. Metronidazole and di-metronidazole (Chapter 27) are sometimes effective provided the strain of *Hexamita* has not developed resistance. Di-metronidazole is usually kept in reserve for situations where metronidazole fails to effect a cure. There is no evidence that other treatments (including proprietary aquarium remedies for use against *Hexamita*) have any significant effect.

Some aquarists have reported a better cure rate (provided the disease is not too advanced) using metronidazole in conjunction with an antimicrobial (to treat any concurrent systemic bacterial infection), e.g. furanace (nifurpirinol) at the rate of 2g/100 litres of aquarium water.

Comment: Many mystery deaths of cichlids may be due to *Hexamita* infestations where the sensory pores have remained unaffected. It has long been thought that the characteristic pus-filled holes develop if (and only if) the protozoa affect the sensory pores, although recent veterinary investigations have failed to locate *Hexamita* in the pus itself.

4.1.11 *ICHTHYOBODO*

A flagellate protozoan ectoparasite of fish (synonym *Costia*), one of the causative agents of Skin slime disease (4.1.18). As well as the parasitic stage, this protozoan has a free-living stage in the water and is commonly present in small numbers in the aquarium, apparently proliferating to problem levels only if fish are immunosuppressed by environmental factors (including Stress, 1.5.2) or other disease. It can infect a wide range of fish species, feeding on its host's skin. Young fish may be particularly susceptible, even under good environmental conditions.

This parasite prefers a temperature of less than 25 °C (77 °F) and dies at about

30 °C (86 °F). There have been reports of a resistant cyst stage which could represent a potential source of reinfection.

4.1.12 *ICHTHYOPHTHIRIUS*

The parasitic protozoan responsible for what is probably the best-known disease of aquarium fish, Whitespot (4.1.12) (ichthyophthiriasis, also known as Ich).

There appears to be only one species of *Ichthyophthirius*, *I. multifiliis*, although several different strains have been identified. This parasite has a multi-stage life cycle, which includes both infective and free-living forms. Although commonly thought of as an ectoparasite, the infective stage of *Ichthyophthirius* in fact lives in, rather than on, the skin of its host, and is thus an endoparasite, even though it does not invade the underlying tissues. It also attacks the gills, eye cornea, and the inside of the mouth cavity. This protozoan tolerates a wide temperature range and can thus easily be transmitted from coldwater to tropical species and *vice versa*.

(See page 258 for life cycle).

4.1.13 NEON TETRA DISEASE

This disease is caused by an endoparasitic protozoan, which infects primarily the musculature (but sometimes the internal organs) of certain species of tetra and a few other fish, including a small number of cyprinids.

Signs: Slight infections may exhibit no symptoms, but in moderate to serious cases there is fading of coloration and grey or white patches may appear under the skin. The parasites destroy muscle tissue and this may cause contortion of the body and abnormal swimming. In advanced cases there may be emaciation. Death is commonplace.

Cause: *Pleistophora hyphessobryconis*.

Transmission: Via accidental ingestion of spores, for example as a result of foraging on an infected fish corpse. Once inside the host's intestine, the parasite invades the surrounding tissues where it multiplies and spreads, eventually forming masses of spores which may in their turn eventually be ingested by other fish.

Prevention: Visibly affected fish should not be purchased, and should be isolated if the disease develops subsequent to purchase. Corpses should always be promptly removed from the aquarium to avoid spreading this and other diseases. Unfortunately, the spores may remain viable for a long time, making it difficult totally to eradicate the parasite; if repeated outbreaks are a problem then the aquarium should be re-stocked with species from outside the host range.

Treatment: Experimental studies using toltrazuril (Chapter 27) have shown some promise, but as no effective treatment is commercially available at present, prevention is essential. In some cases the host's immune system appears to combat the infection and bring about self-cure.

4.1.14 *OCTOMITUS*

A genus of flagellate protozoa of dubious taxonomic standing, regarded by some authorities as synonymous with *Hexamita* (4.1.9).

4.1.15 *PISCINOODINIUM*

(Synonym *Oodinium*, which is still commonly cited in the aquarium literature although no longer scientifically valid for this taxon.)

Life Cycle of Ichthyophthirius

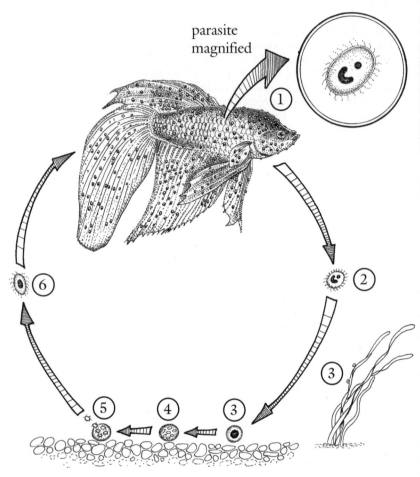

parasite
magnified

Stages not to scale.

1. Parasitic feeding-growing stage (trophont) beneath skin of fish.

2. Mature parasite leaves fish and falls to the substrate.

3. Reproductive stage (tomont or "cyst") on substrate. This stage may also be found attached to plants.

4. Cyst begins to divide.

5. Cyst releases between 250 and 2000 infective stages.

6. Infective stage (theront or "swarmer") swims in the water in search of a fish to infect.

A genus of ectoparasitic dinoflagellate protozoa (phylum Mastigophora), which causes the freshwater fish disease known as Velvet (4.1.22) (also known as freshwater velvet, gold-dust disease, or rust disease). Two species – *P. pillulare* and *P. limneticum* – have been recorded from freshwater aquarium fish (although *P. limneticum* is now considered by some authorities to be a synonym of *P. pillulare*). The parasite attacks a broad range of species but is more commonly seen in barbs and other cyprinids, gouramis, and killifish.

The parasite's life cycle involves both parasitic and free-swimming stages; the duration of the life cycle is temperature-dependent, becoming more rapid the higher the temperature. *Piscinoodinium* is capable of photosynthesis, and light is important for its development.

These parasites can proliferate extremely rapidly in the tropical aquarium, leading to resident fish being exposed to successive waves of infective dinospores and acquiring a parasite burden numbering hundreds or thousands of individual protozoa. (See page 260)

4.1.16 *PLEISTOPHORA*

A genus of endoparasitic (intracellular) protozoa (phylum Microspora) which attack the muscle tissues of fish. As far as aquarists are concerned, the only species of importance is *P. hyphessobryconis*, which causes Neon tetra disease (4.1.13). This parasite was originally described from two Amazonian tetras, the neon tetra (*Paracheirodon innesi*) and the glowlight tetra (*Hemigrammus erythrozonus*). It has subsequently been recorded in a few other tetra species, plus a number of cyprinids including zebra danios (*Brachydanio rerio*), and certain barbs.

A related microsporidian genus, *Heterosporis* (4.1.8), affects freshwater angelfish (*Pterophyllum* spp.) and at least one species of loricariid catfish (*Ancistrus cirrhosis*).

4.1.17 SPIRONUCLEUS

A genus of flagellate protozoa of dubious taxonomic standing, regarded by some authorities as synonymous with *Hexamita* (4.1.9).

4.1.18 SKIN SLIME DISEASE (COSTIASIS)

A general term for an infection whose primary sign is 'slimy skin' (i.e. mucus hyperproduction) caused by certain genera of ectoparasitic protozoans.

The alternative name, costiasis, derives from a now obsolete scientific name of one of these genera, *Costia*, now regarded as a synonym of *Ichthyobodo* (4.1.11).

Signs: Mucus hyperproduction causes the skin to take on a cloudy appearance, often between the head and the dorsal insertion, or covering much of the head and body. The skin may appear rough, and scales and skin may peel away in strips in severe cases. Fin erosion may occur. Irritation may lead to flashing (scratching against the substrate and other decor/equipment). If the gills are affected, there will be signs of Hypoxia (1.3.3), e.g. gasping at the surface and coughing. Other generalised signs of ill health include lethargy and loss of appetite. Areas where the skin is badly damaged may develop secondary infections of bacteria (3.2) or fungus (3.3). In the absence of treatment, death from hypoxia and/or Osmotic stress (1.6.2), *inter alia*, is commonplace.

Cause: *Chilodonella* (4.1.2), *Ichthyobodo* (4.1.11), *Trichodina* (4.1.20), or a combination of any of these.

Predisposing factors: It is not uncommon for small numbers of the causative protozoans to be present on seemingly healthy fish; however, if the latter are immunosuppressed due to adverse environmental factors, including Stress (1.5.2), then the parasites may proliferate to problem levels.

Transmission: Via the aquarium water or direct contact between fish. *Chilodonella piscicola* is thought to spread entirely by direct contact and hence is more commonly found in heavily-populated aquaria.

Prevention: Good husbandry, sensible population levels and stress avoidance. Although the causative protozoa may be present even in healthy aquaria, prophylaxis is neither necessary nor desirable; avoidance of the predisposing factors is preferable, as these are equally likely to contribute to other health problems.

Treatment: Treat the whole aquarium and its occupants, since it is best to assume that all fish within the affected tank will be infected to varying extents.

Treatment is normally by bath immersion using a proprietary anti-protozoal intended to combat this disease, administered in accordance with the manufacturer's instructions. Some authorities advocate raising the temperature to 28 °C (83 °F) during the treatment period, normally for 10-12 hours. If this treatment proves ineffective, formalin (Chapter 27) or metriphonate (Chapter 27) can be tried. Care must be taken to avoid mixing medications: several successive partial water changes should be made to remove the proprietary remedy, or the fish transferred to a medication-free tank.

It is vital to identify and eliminate the underlying cause(s) of the protozoan proliferation, to avoid recurrence.

4.1.19 *TETRAHYMENA*

A genus of ciliate protozoa. Most species are free-living, although a few are known occasionally to cause disease in fish; in particular *T.corlissi* is sometimes encountered in tropical aquaria where it can cause Guppy disease (4.1.6). Although chiefly a parasite of the guppy (*Poecilia reticulata*), *T. corlissi* may also attack other poeciliid livebearing species and occasionally other groups of tropical fish.

4.1.20 *TRICHODINA*

A genus of ciliate protozoa which may occur as harmless commensals on the body surfaces of fish, but can become parasitic under certain conditions, causing Skin slime disease (4.1.18). Several species of trichodinids (*Trichodina* and related genera) are associated with fish, but precise identification is unnecessary as far as treatment is concerned. Most (but not all) species have a broad host range. In their parasitic mode they feed on the skin/gills of their host and, if present in large numbers, can cause serious damage. Some species spend most of their lives on their host but are able to survive off the fish for up to two days, so transmission may occur via the water as well as by direct contact with an infected fish.

4.1.21 TRYPANOSOME INFECTION

An endoparasitic protozoan infection of the blood, uncommon in aquarium fish but sometimes present in wild-caught or pond-reared individuals.

The trypanosomes are a group of flagellate protozoa, named after the included genus *Trypanosoma*.

Signs: Mild infections may be asymptomatic. Fish which are heavily parasitised may exhibit lethargy and emaciation, which are, however, generalised symptoms of ill health and more likely to be symptomatic of more common problems. If no other cause can be found, then microscopical examination of a blood sample will confirm or rule out trypanosome infection.

Cause: Protozoa of the trypanosomes group.

Transmission: By bloodsucking leeches, which occasionally are found in aquaria. Leeches introduced from the wild could infect aquarium fish. Wild-caught and pond-reared fish, which are commonly exposed to leech attack, may occasionally harbour trypanosomes, but will be unable to transmit them to other fish in the absence of leeches.

Prevention: Avoid introducing bloodsucking leeches, whose feeding habits in any case render them undesirable aquarium inhabitants!

Treatment: None available.

4.1.22 VELVET DISEASE

(Also known as freshwater velvet, *Oodinium*, rust disease, or gold-dust disease)

An ectoparasitic protozoan disease sometimes encountered in the tropical freshwater aquarium.

Signs: Depending on the severity of the disease in individual fish, signs may include flashing, clamped fins, fin-twitching, shimmying, mucus hyperproduction, increased respiratory rate, lethargy, and loss of appetite. Fish with heavy infestations may appear peppered with gold (hence 'gold-dust disease') or their skin may appear to have a yellowish velvety coating. If untreated, the disease can result in death, with fry and young fish particularly vulnerable.

Cause: Two species of *Piscinoodinium* have been recorded from freshwater aquarium fish: *P. pillulare* and *P. limneticum* (though some authorities consider *P. pillulare* the only valid species).

Predisposing factors: Different species or even individuals of a species may be affected to varying degrees, but it is unclear whether this reflects innate or acquired immunity, or susceptibility to contributory environmental factors such as poor water quality (1.2) or Stress (1.5.2).

Transmission: See life-cycle information under 4.1.15.

Prevention: Quarantine for 3-4 weeks will usually prevent the introduction of velvet into the main aquarium.

Treatment: It is thought that only the free-living stages are vulnerable to chemical treatments, which include proprietary anti-velvet medications, quinine, copper treatments and salt, (Chapter 27).

Increased temperature will accelerate the life cycle of the parasite, so that all encysted stages hatch more rapidly and become vulnerable to the medication, thus reducing the overall treatment period necessary. However, this technique should be avoided in severe infestations because of the danger of exacerbating existing respiratory problems (see Hypoxia, 1.3.3).

The proliferation of the parasites can be reduced by keeping the aquarium in darkness, thus preventing photosynthesis in the parasitic free-living stages. This technique is useful for minimising further proliferation of the protozoa in cases where the fish already have a serious parasite burden, but should be used only in conjunction with chemical treatment.

Life Cycle of Piscinoodinium.

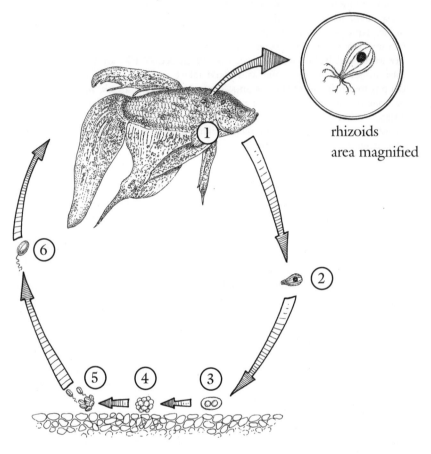

rhizoids
area magnified

Stages not to scale.

1. Parasitic stage (trophont) attached to the skin of fish. The penetrating root-like rhizoids are used to anchor the parasite to its host.

2. Trophont leaves fish.

3. Reproductive stage (tomont or "cyst").

4. Cyst begins to divide.

5. Cyst releases up to 256 infective stages.

6. Infective stage (dinospore) swims in the water in search of a fish to infect.

4.1.23 WHITESPOT (ICHTHYOPHTHIRIASIS, ALSO KNOWN AS ICH)

An extremely common and highly infectious protozoan disease, which seems to affect all species of freshwater fish, coldwater as well as tropical.

Signs: Typically, characteristic raised white spots on the fins, head, and body (and on the gills and in the mouth), more obvious on dark-coloured fish, and also clearly visible on transparent fins, especially against a dark background. The spots are usually discrete, but several may cluster together if the infection is very severe. There is a possibility of confusion with small *Lymphocystis* (3.1.3) cysts and small colonies of *Apiosoma* (4.1.1), however whitespot can be differentiated easily by its speed of proliferation and its rapid spread to other fish.

Fish with only slight infections may show little in the way of behavioural signs apart from occasional scratching and flashing in an attempt to alleviate the irritation caused by the parasites. More heavily infected individuals will scratch more frequently, and behave restlessly, darting, shimmying, and twitching their fins. Parasite damage to the gills may result in increased respiratory rate; the fish may gasp at or near the surface and eventually while resting, exhausted, on the bottom. The fins may become ragged, and the skin pale, with patches of it sloughing off. If this degree of gill and/or skin damage occurs, the fish is unlikely to survive, dying of physiological Hypoxia (1.3.3) or osmoregulatory failure (1.6.2) or a combination of both. All fish are susceptible, but small individuals, and especially fry, are likely to die within a couple of days from heavy exposures, unless treated promptly.

Cause: *Ichthyophthirius multifiliis* (4.1.12).

Predisposing factors: The degree of susceptibility seems to vary from species to species – for example the clown loach (*Botia macracanthus*) is reported to be highly susceptible. Whitespot commonly manifests in fish which have been chilled. See also Comment, below.

Transmission: See life cycle diagram under 4.1.12. The parasite tolerates a wide temperature range and can thus be passed from coldwater fish to tropical species, and *vice versa*.

Whitespot may be introduced into an aquarium by:

• Infected fish.

• Water harbouring infective free-living stages (e.g. in fish bags or accompanying aquatic live-food organisms (e.g. *Daphnia*, *Tubifex* worms) if these have recently been collected from whitespot-infected waters).

• Possibly on aquatic plants to which the reproductive cysts may attach.

Contrary to popular belief, however, it is highly unlikely (at least, in developed countries) that whitespot could be introduced via tap water; the infective stage can survive only a few hours without a fish host (not long enough to pass through the water supply system), and may also be harmed by chlorination.

Prevention: Quarantine of newly-acquired fish, by far the most common source of whitespot in the domestic aquarium. If all aquarists took this simple precaution, whitespot would not be the problem it is.

Treatment: Fortunately, whitespot is normally easy to treat, and deaths avoidable, provided treatment is administered at the early stage of infection. Chemical remedies destroy only the free-swimming stage, so treatment must continue for a few days after all spots have disappeared. This will allow any encysted stages to 'hatch', so that the final waves of infective free-swimming stages can be eliminated. Raising the temperature will accelerate the life cycle of the parasites, but should be used with care, if at all, where the gills are badly affected, because of the risk of exacerbating existing Hypoxia (1.3.3).

Chemical remedies include a number of proprietary treatments. Methylene blue (Chapter 27) is highly effective, but should be used only where its deleterious side-effects on nitrifying bacteria and plants are unimportant, e.g. in the quarantine/hospital tank. Salt (Chapter 27) can also be used, and has the virtue of remaining effective, without re-dosing, until the outbreak is over (when the salt content should, of course, be progressively eliminated by partial water changes).

Because the free-living infective stages die quickly in the absence of a host, an infected tropical aquarium, and its decor/equipment, can be rid of whitespot by leaving it free of fish for 5-7 days (longer at cooler temperatures).

Extensive skin disruption in the course of this disease may render the fish susceptible to secondary bacterial infections (3.2), which may ultimately cause death, even in the absence of further parasite damage.

WARNING: some types of fish, including scaleless species, are extremely intolerant of some commercial whitespot remedies; the instructions should list fish species which need to be moved prior to administering the treatment. Some species are also intolerant of salt. If necessary, sensitive species can be removed to the hospital tank and treated with a different medication suitable for the species in question.

Comment: Those fish which survive an outbreak of whitespot may develop partial immunity to any subsequent exposure to this parasite. This may explain the fact that some fish experience a heavy infection during an outbreak of whitespot while others appear uninfected.

Acquired immunity may also provide an explanation for the supposedly resistant or dormant forms of whitespot that have been reported, with outbreaks occurring long after any fish or other possible vector of the disease was last introduced into the aquarium. (This phenomenon may also be the source of the belief that whitespot can be introduced via tap water.) What is more likely is that the disease has been present all along but at an imperceptibly low level because of acquired immunity from earlier infection. If the fish become immunosuppressed, as the result of adverse water quality or other stress, then parasite numbers may increase to levels causing visible signs, resulting in an apparently spontaneous outbreak with no obvious source.

Fish which have lived, with no signs of whitespot, in a dealer's aquarium for weeks, and are therefore thought to be free of the disease, may nevertheless develop it after purchase. There are two possible reasons for this:

• The new fish have a low level infection of whitespot which is triggered by the stress inherent in transportation and introduction to a strange aquarium. The resident fish may become infected if they have little or no acquired immunity.

• The new fish are whitespot-free and have no acquired immunity, but the fish already resident in their new home have a low-level infection. The new fish, lacking immunity, typically suffer a severe infection, while the residents remain unaffected. The new fish – and the dealer – invariably get the blame!

Chilling is known to be a stressor which reduces immunity to whitespot. This is why so many fish develop the disease after transportation home from the shop or, commonly, a large water change where the aquarium has (incorrectly) been refilled with cold water.

Table 19 Categories of Commonly-encountered Non-protozoan Fish Parasites.	
Crustacean parasites	The class Crustacea includes a number of species that are parasites of fish. Crustacean ectoparasites sometimes seen in freshwater aquaria include the anchor worm (*Lernaea*) (4.2.1), the fish louse (*Argulus*) (4.2.7) and the gill maggot (*Ergasilus*) (4.2.9).
Flukes	The generic term used for a number of helminth parasites of fish. Flukes are commonly subdivided into monogenetic flukes (Monogenea) and digenetic flukes (Digenea) depending on whether the parasite requires just one (monogenetic) or multiple (digenetic) hosts during its life cycle. Flukes may be ecto- or endo-parasitic, and the site colonised (e.g. gills, skin, eye, various internal organs) depends on the genus or species of parasite involved. Flukes sometimes encountered in the freshwater aquarium include eye flukes (*Diplostomum*) (4.2.5), gill flukes (*Dactylogyrus*) (4.2.8), skin flukes (*Gyrodactylus*) (4.2.11), and those causing black spot disease (4.2.2).
Leeches	Elongate annelid worms, up to several centimetres long, characterised by their anterior (oral) and posterior suckers and by their typical looping movements. A number of species occur in fresh waters, including the fish leech (*Piscicola*) (4.2.6).
Trematodes	See Flukes, above
Worms	A collective common name used for several groups of helminth parasites, including flukes (above), roundworms (nematodes) (4.2.10), tapeworms (cestodes) (4.2.13), and spiny-headed worms (Acanthocephala) (4.2.12). It is also, rather misleadingly, used in some other common names of fish parasites, e.g. anchor worm (a copepod crustacean). Some non-parasitic worms, e.g. earthworms, *Tubifex*, and Whiteworms are used as fish foods.

4.2 OTHER PARASITES

This section includes those non-protozoan parasites sometimes found on or in tropical freshwater fish kept in aquaria, and encompasses a size range extending from microscopic to a centimetre or more in length. Unlike the protozoan parasites, they do not form a discrete taxonomic group, and may be found under different subheadings elsewhere in the aquarium literature. Table 19 shows the subheadings most likely to be encountered.

Many of these parasites have been given common names in the aquarium hobby,

> ### Table 20 Scientific Names of Some Non-protozoan Fish Parasites and their Corresponding Common Names.
>
> | | |
> |---|---|
> | Acanthocephala | Thorny- or spiny-headed worms (4.2.12) |
> | *Argulus* | Fish louse (4.2.7) |
> | *Camallanus* (4.2.3) | No common name (genus of nematodes) |
> | *Capillaria* (4.2.4) | No common name (genus of nematodes) |
> | Cestodes | Tapeworms (4.2.13) |
> | *Dactylogyrus* | Gill fluke (4.2.8), gill worm |
> | *Diplostomum* | Eye fluke (4.2.5) or eye worm |
> | *Ergasilus* | Gill maggot (4.2.9) |
> | *Gyrodactylus* | Skin fluke (4.2.11) |
> | *Lernaea* | Anchor worm (4.2.1) |
> | Nematodes | Roundworms or threadworms (4.2.10) |
> | *Piscicola* | Fish leech (4.2.6) |
> | Platyhelminthes | Flatworms (includes tapeworms (4.2.13) and flukes) |

and, as in the sections on pathogens (3.0) and protozoa (4.1), we have used these, where available, in the catalogue below. However, in this case, the common names mostly refer to the parasite itself (e.g. fish louse) rather than the disease it causes. The format of this section, therefore, differs from that used for the protozoa, in that the biology of the parasite is included, under a single heading, with the signs and treatment of infestation. Scientific names of parasite genera and other groups are shown in Table 20, together with the equivalent common names.

Generally speaking, the larger, clearly visible, parasites are not often seen in the aquarium, although they are relatively commonplace in the wild and outdoor breeding/rearing facilities. Because of their visibility, they are usually eliminated before the fish reach retail outlets and the domestic aquarium.

4.2.1 ANCHOR WORM

A general term for ectoparasitic copepod crustaceans with anchor-like structures for attachment to their host. Where tropical aquarium fish are concerned, the most important genus is *Lernaea*, with *L.cyprinacea* being the most commonly reported species.

Transmission and biology: *Lernaea* has a direct life cycle, i.e. there are no intermediate hosts.

Like other crustaceans, anchor worms exist as separate sexes, and mating occurs on the surface of the fish. After mating, the male dies and the female becomes parasitic, partially embedding herself into the skin of the host by means of a special organ known as the holdfast. She now develops a pair of egg sacs which give her a distinctive and characteristic Y-shaped appearance. The ripe eggs are released into the water; after hatching, there are a number of free-swimming, and subsequently parasitic, larval stages. The parasitic larvae usually colonise the gills. The female may subsequently produce further pairs of egg sacs.

Signs: The adult parasite is elongate (1cm/0.4 in or more long) and Y-shaped, with the foot of the Y attached to the fish.

The Life Cycle of the Anchor Worm.

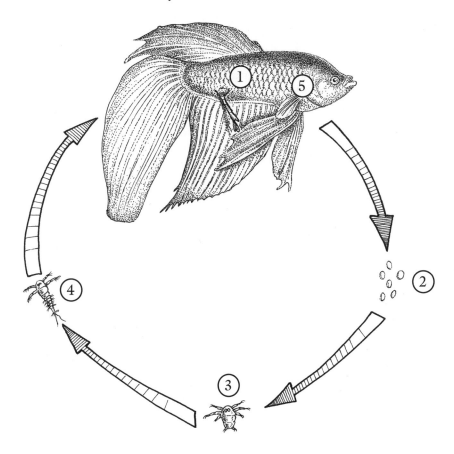

Stages not to scale.

1. Parasitic female anchor worm attached to skin of fish. The male is not parasitic.

2. Female anchor worm releases eggs into the water.

3. Free-swimming larval stage. The larva undergoes several moults.

4. Infective stage larva.

5. Larva attaches to the fish's gills.

The gill-dwelling larval stages are invisible to the naked eye.

Parasitised fish may scratch and flash as a result of irritation, and heavy infestation of the gills with larvae may result in signs of Hypoxia (1.3.3), for example as increased respiratory rate. The entry wounds made by the parasites may be the site of secondary bacterial (3.2) and/or fungal (3.3) infection.

The extent of the damage caused by *Lernaea* varies greatly. Medium to large fish may be apparently unaffected by quite large numbers of adult *Lernaea*, while small fish can be severely weakened by just one or two parasites, and die. Gill damage caused by heavy larval parasitisation may also lead to death, through hypoxia.

Prevention: Do not buy fish with visible parasites, or from a tank containing visibly infested fish (because of the possibility of juvenile stages in the water or on the gills). Tadpoles may harbour *Lernaea*, but should in any case not be housed with fish, and certainly not fed to fish because of the increasingly endangered status of many amphibian species. Water from natural sources (e.g. that accompanying wild-caught live foods such as bloodworm and *Daphnia*) may harbour free-swimming stages of *Lernaea* if fish are present in the pond or stream in question.

Treatment: Isolate fish with adult parasites to prevent the eggs from being released into the aquarium.

Provided the host fish is large enough to withstand the attendant trauma, small numbers of adult *Lernaea* can be removed using forceps. The resulting deep puncture wounds should be treated topically with an antiseptic such as mercurochrome (Chapter 27) to prevent infection or treat any secondary infection already present.

Large numbers of parasites should not be removed all at the same time, because of the attendant trauma and the danger of Osmotic stress (1.6.2). Instead, the adult *Lernaea* should be removed in small batches and the resulting wounds allowed to heal between batches. Use a long-term trichlorfon (Chapter 27) bath (see below) to prevent re-infestation during this possibly lengthy process.

The larval stages can be eradicated using a trichlorfon bath. Because this chemical gradually degrades in water, re-dosing will be necessary at weekly intervals for 4-6 weeks in order to ensure eradication of all stages.

4.2.2 BLACK SPOT

A condition caused by the presence in the skin or fins of larval digenetic flukes belonging to a number of species. The condition is usually harmless, albeit unsightly, unless the infestation is very severe.

Transmission and biology: Because digenetic flukes have a multi-host life cycle, in which the fish is only one in a succession of animals parasitised, they cannot be transmitted from fish to fish in the aquarium. It is just possible that snails recently collected from the wild may harbour an intermediate stage in the life cycle and thus transmit the parasites to fish. Under normal circumstances, however, black spot is seen only in fish which are wild-caught or pond-reared.

Typically the life cycle of digenetic flukes entails sequential transmission involving a snail, a fish, and a bird (the final host). The fluke metacercaria (= larva) encysts on the skin/fins or in the tissues of the fish, and if it becomes impregnated with host melanophores (pigment cells) the characteristic black spots appear, otherwise it may remain invisible. The parasite cannot multiply within the fish host, nor can the fish-parasitic stage infect snails present in the aquarium.

Signs: One or more small dark spots, roughly circular and 1-2mm in diameter, on the skin and/or fins. No apparent ill-effects even when present in large numbers.

Prevention: It is always unwise to introduce wild-collected snails into the aquarium because of the risk of their carrying disease. There is no need to isolate affected fish, or to refrain from buying them.

Treatment: None.

4.2.3 *CAMALLANUS*

A genus of nematode worms (see also 4.2.10) (family Camallanidae). The species most commonly recorded from aquarium fish is *C. cotti*, reaching 12 mm (0.5 in) in length.

Transmission and biology: Normally the life cycle of *Camallanus* involves a copepod as intermediate host, but in the aquarium this parasite may multiply for several generations without any intermediate host, via the ingestion of larvae in faeces or through cannibalism of corpses. The adult worms live in the fish's gut and feed on their host's blood. Severe infestations can cause ulceration of the gut.

Predisposing factors: Poeciliid livebearers seem susceptible to this parasite.

Signs: Typically, the first sign of *Camallanus* infection is red-brown worms protruding from the fish's anus. Severe infestations may lead to spinal deformity and emaciation.

Prevention: Avoid using copepod live foods collected from fish-populated waters. Good husbandry (siphoning off faeces, removal of corpses) will help reduce spread if parasitised fish are inadvertently introduced.

Treatment: An anthelminthic (Chapter 27) such as fenbendazole, administered via medicated food (0.25% inclusion) or long-term bath immersion.

4.2.4 *CAPILLARIA*

A genus of nematode worms (see 4.2.10) parasitic in the gut or liver of some fish species, in particular cichlids.

Transmission and biology: The life cycle is direct (no intermediate hosts); the adult worms produce eggs that hatch into infective larvae. Outbreaks of *Capillaria* usually result from recent introduction of infested fish.

Signs: Light infestations may be asymptomatic. Heavy infestations may cause loss of appetite and emaciation. Faeces may appear thin and white, or as light and dark segments, independent of recent diet.

Predisposing factors: Discus (*Symphysodon* spp.), and angelfish (*Pterophyllum* spp.) are reputed to be particularly susceptible.

Prevention: Isolation of fish suspected of being infested with *Capillaria* is advisable, to avoid transmission via cannibalism or coprophagy.

It has often been stated that discus should not be kept with angelfish because of the danger of cross-infection with *Capillaria*. However, infection can just as easily be from other discus (and discus can infect angelfish!) so the precaution has little practical value. What is important is to be aware that both fish genera are susceptible and remain alert for signs of infestation.

Treatment: An anthelminthic such as levamisole or piperazine (Chapter 27).

4.2.5 EYE FLUKE

The name given to digenetic flukes of the genus *Diplostomum* (phylum Platyhelminthes) whose intermediate metacercarial stage infects the eyes of fish. Also sometimes known as eye worm.

Transmission and biology: Because digenetic flukes have a multi-host life cycle, in which the fish is only one in a succession of animals parasitised, they cannot be transmitted from fish to fish in the aquarium. The life cycle of *Diplostomum* entails sequential transmission involving a snail, a fish, and a bird (the final host). The fish host is normally invaded via the gills, after which the larval flukes are carried via the blood to the small capillaries within the fish's eye; some authorities consider that they may also be able to penetrate the eye lens directly from the water. Inside the eye, the flukes grow to full size within 4-5 weeks and may remain in the lens for up to 4 years, causing impaired vision and occasionally severe eye damage and blindness.

It is just possible that snails recently collected from the wild may harbour an earlier stage in the life cycle and thus transmit the parasites to fish. Under normal circumstances, however, eye fluke is seen only in fish which are wild-caught or pond-reared. *Diplostomum* cannot multiply within the fish host, nor can the fish-parasitic stage infect snails present in the aquarium.

Signs: One or both eyes may appear cloudy (but bear in mind that eye cloudiness (see Cloudy eye, 6.2) may have other, more common causes. Small white 'cataracts' may occur. Exophthalmia (6.5) is sometimes seen in association with eye fluke infestation, but, again, has commoner causes.

If eye flukes are introduced by wild-caught snails, larval invasion of the fish may occur in such vast numbers, within the confines of the aquarium, as to cause massive gill damage and death.

Prevention: Avoid introducing wild snails, either deliberately or accidentally, e.g. on plants or with live foods collected from the wild. There is no need to isolate affected fish unless impaired vision causes them problems (e.g. inability to compete effectively for food) in the community aquarium.

Treatment: None. There is evidence that some anthelminthics (Chapter 27) may kill the larval flukes, but, as they cannot infect other fish and the eye(s) will already be damaged, there is little point.

Occasionally a fish which is badly discommoded by impaired vision may require euthanasia (Chapter 25).

4.2.6 FISH LEECH

The leeches (phylum Annelida – annelid worms) include a number of terrestrial and aquatic species, but only a few are parasites of fish, the best-known being members of the genus *Piscicola*. Thus the presence of aquatic leeches in the aquarium, although not particularly desirable, does not necessarily represent a danger to the resident fish.

Leeches feed on their host's blood, and while rarely causing serious harm directly by this activity, may transmit fish-parasitic protozoa (blood parasites) such as Trypanosomes (4.1.21) (and possibly bacteria and viruses).

Leech infestations are rarely encountered in aquaria but are common in fish ponds and in the wild.

Transmission and biology: Leeches are temporary parasites which may leave their host (to lay eggs) and can survive off the fish for up to three months. The eggs are laid in cocoons on, for example, plants or stones. Depending on the temperature, the eggs take 13-80 days to hatch from the cocoon, and the young leeches, which need to find a fish host after hatching, are mature after 19-24 days.

Life Cycle of the Fish Leech.

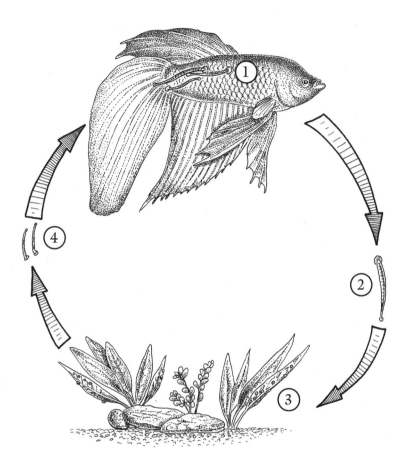

Stages not to scale.

1. Adult leeches feed on fish blood for 2-3 days at a time (not to scale).

2. Leeches leave the fish to digest or to lay eggs.

3. Leech eggs laid in cocoons attached to rocks and plants.

4. Newly hatched leeches need fish on which to feed.

When seeking a host on which to feed, the leech lurks in ambush – on the bottom, a rock, or a plant – until a fish passes close enough for it to attach. It then moves around on the host until it finds a suitable place to feed, where it pierces the skin with its mouth parts and extracts blood.

Adult leeches are generally too large (1-5 cm/0.5-2 in) to be introduced unnoticed into the aquarium, whether on fish or decor items, but eggs are sometimes accidentally introduced on plants or stones collected from outdoor, fish-inhabited, waters. There is also a small risk of introducing leeches via wild-collected live foods.

Signs: Adult leeches are often obvious by virtue of their size and recognisable by their worm-like appearance. They have an extensible segmented body with a disc-shaped sucker at each end, the anterior (oral) sucker usually being noticeably smaller than the other. Leeches may be seen both on, but more often off, the fish – in the latter case swimming with undulating movements or crawling over surfaces with a stretching-looping motion. Although they may hide among decor after leaving the fish, the possible existence of a leech problem should nevertheless be obvious from the residual red or whitish circular bite wounds, which are susceptible to secondary infection with Bacteria (3.2) and/or Fungus (3.3). Other types of tissue damage, such as Ulcers (3.2.9), are similar in appearance (and more likely), so if a leech problem is suspected, seek confirmation by examining the undersides of rocks and stones, and the bases of plants, for any signs of their egg cocoons, which are brown to black, oval, and sometimes in clusters.

Behavioural signs may include lethargy (due to anaemia resulting from blood loss); conversely, the fish may be abnormally restless.

As not all aquatic leeches are parasitic on fish, the presence of adult leeches (unless on the fish) or cocoons is not necessarily indicative of a problem unless accompanied by bite wounds. Unfortunately, the fish-parasitic and harmless leech species are not always easy to differentiate.

Prevention: Wild-collected aquatic live foods should be carefully inspected for the presence of adult leeches. Never use pond plants in the aquarium as they may harbour leeches or their eggs. Stones, wood, and/or gravel collected from fish-inhabited waters should be plunged into boiling water as a safeguard. Inspect potential fish purchases closely for leeches and other large parasites.

Treatment: Salt (Chapter 27) can be used to encourage a feeding leech to detach from its host. Non-attached leeches may be individually removed from the substrate/water using an aquarium net or siphon tube. Leeches may be eradicated chemically from aquaria using organophosphorus compounds such as trichlorfon (Chapter 27). Because the cocoon stage is resistant to chemicals, re-dosing is usually necessary after 2-3 weeks. In view of the toxicity of organophosphorus compounds, it is better to move the fish (after ensuring they are leech-free) to alternative accommodation (if available) and then treat the infested tank. (See page 271 for life cycle.)

4.2.7 FISH LOUSE

A general term for members of the crusacean genus *Argulus* (family Branchiura), which are ectoparasitic on fish. Although fish lice are more common on coldwater fish than tropicals, these parasites are occasionally introduced into the aquarium with live foods collected from waters populated by fish. Of some 30 known species, two have been reported from aquarium fish, namely *A. foliaceus* and *A. japonicus*.

DISEASES

Cloudy eye.

Mary Bailey.

Dropsy.

Mary Bailey.

Fin rot (edges of fin)
and fungus.

Mary Bailey.

Injury, probably from collision with a sharp decor item. If such wounds are left untreated, fungal or bacterial infection may follow.

Mary Bailey.

Stress in an undecorated, crowded, shop tank. Note the clamped fins and poor coloration, typical signs of ill-health.

Mary Bailey.

Whitespot. Note the clamped fins as well as the small white spots on the fins and body.

Mary Bailey.

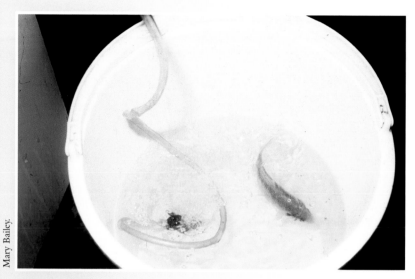

Short-term bath in a bucket.
Note the aeration – often essential during such treatment.

Skin slime disease.
Note the grey mucus on the upper half of the fish. The fact that this
upper-water gourami is resting on the bottom is a sign that it is very unwell.

FISH IDENTIFICATION

Dwarf gourami
Colisa lalia
Family Belontiidae
(Labyrinth).

Siamese fighting fish or Siamese fighter (mal
Betta splendens
Family Belontiidae
(Labyrinth fish).

Opaline gourami
Trichogaster trichopterus
Family Belontiidae
(Labyrinth).

Pearl lace gourami
Trichogaster leeri
Family Belontiidae
(Labyrinth).

Bronze corydoras
Corydoras aeneus
Family Callichthyidae
(Catfish).

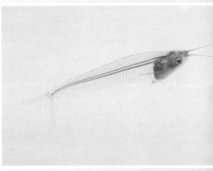

Glass catfish
Kryptopterus bicirrhis
Family Siluridae
(Catfish).

Spotted corydoras
Corydoras punctatus
Family Callichthyidae
(Catfish).

Celebes rainbow
Telmatherina ladigesi
Family Atherinidae
(Rainbowfish).

Chequer barb
Barbus oligolepis
Family Cyprinidae
(Cypriniform).

Silver shark
Balantiocheilus melanopterus
Family Cyprinidae
(Cypriniform).

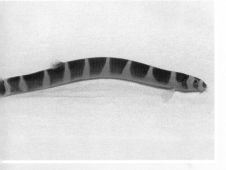

Khuli loach
Pangio sp.
Family Cobitidae
(Cypriniform).

Golden rosy barb
Puntius conchonius
Family Cyprinidae
(Cypriniform).

Red-tailed black shark
Epalzeorhynchus bicolor
Family Cyprinidae
(Cypriniform).

Rosy barb
Barbus conchonius
Family Cyprinidae
(Cypriniform).

Zebra danio
Brachydanio rerio
Family Cyprinidae
(Cypriniform)

Tiger barb
Barbus tetrazona
Family Cyprinidae
(Cypriniform).

Green sailfin molly (male)
Poecilia sp.
Family Poeciliidae
(Cyprinodont).

Green swordtail (male)
Xiphophorus helleri
Family Poeciliidae
(Cyprinodont).

Guppy (male)
Poecilia reticulata
Family Poeciliidae
(Cyprinodont).

Black lyretail molly (female)
Poecilia sphenops
Family Poeciliidae
(Cyprinodont).

Red swordtail (male)
Xiphophorus sp.
Family Poeciliidae
(Cyprinodont).

Chocolate molly (male)
Poecilia sphenops
Family Poeciliidae
(Cyprinodont).

Yellow wagtail platy (female)
Xiphophorus maculatus
Family Poeciliidae
(Cyprinodont).

Half-black angel
Pterophyllum scalare
Family Cichlidae
(Cichlid).

Silver hatchet
Gasteropelecus sternicla
Family Gasteropelecidae
(Characiform).

Penguin tetra or penguin fish
Thayeria boehlkei
Family Characidae
(Characiform).

X-ray tetra
Pristella riddlei
Family Characidae
(Characiform).

Neon tetra
Paracheirodon innesi
Family Characidae
(Characiform).

Black phantom tetra
Megalamphodus megalopterus
Family Characidae
(Characiform).

Head and tail light tetra
Hemigrammus ocellifer
Family Characidae
(Characiform).

Life Cycle of the Fish Louse.

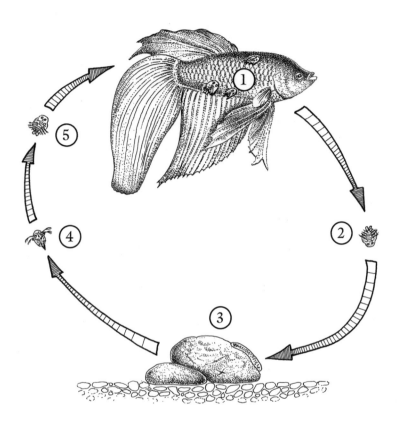

Stages not to scale.

1. Fish lice attached to skin of fish.

2. Female louse detached from fish in order to lay eggs.

3. String of eggs laid on rocks or other hard surfaces.

4. First stage larva free-swimming in the water. The larva moults several times before becoming an adult.

5. Adult louse. Only the female is parasitic.

Transmission and biology: Fish lice are temporary parasites, which probably find a host by chance encounter. *Argulus* mate in open water, after which the female lays her eggs on solid surfaces. The eggs of *A. japonicus* hatch after about two weeks at 25 °C (77 °F); the juveniles are initially free-swimming, attaining the parasitic adult stage at a size of 3-3.5 mm ($^1/_8$ in) (after around 5 weeks). On encountering a host fish they attach to its skin with suckers, using their needle-like mouth parts to inject an anti-coagulant before feeding on the fish's blood. The fish louse is able to move around on the host and may thus cause multiple wounds. When replete with blood, it may leave the host and swim free for a time before attaching to another host; in aquarium terms, this means that a single parasite may cause damage to more than one fish, if not eradicated.

The severity of the effects of a fish louse infestation will depend on the number of parasites in the aquarium and the sizes of the fish parasitised. Severe infestations can lead to significant loss of blood and the concomitant damage to the skin may result in Osmotic stress (1.6.2). Moreover, *Argulus* wounds may become infected with Bacteria (3.2) and Fungus (3.3).

It has been suggested that fish lice may be carriers of pathogenic bacteria.

Signs: The adult parasite is visible to the naked eye as a semi-transparent flattened disc 5-12 mm ($^1/_4$-$^1/_2$ in) in diameter. A pair of dark compound eyes are clearly visible near the anterior end. Small red wounds may be apparent on the fish where lice have detached. The parasites may cause skin irritation, leading to restlessness (darting, jumping, scratching) in affected fish. Heavy infestations may cause lethargy, loss of appetite, and a degree of mucus hyperproduction.

Prevention: Carefully inspect potential purchases. Seriously infested individuals should not be purchased; mild infestations can be dealt with during quarantine (see Treatment, below). Bear in mind that water from a tank showing signs of *Argulus* infestation (parasites or wounds) may contain free-swimming adults or juveniles, even if the fish purchased is parasite-free. Free-swimming *Argulus* may be accidentally netted along with *Daphnia* and other 'pond foods' collected from fish-populated waters, and plants/rocks taken from such waters may harbour eggs.

Treatment:

• Fish lice can be eradicated using bath immersion in a solution of metriphonate, formalin, or potassium permanganate (Chapter 27). Proprietary anti-crustacean parasite treatments are also available. The fish should be observed for some time subsequently for signs of secondary bacterial/fungal infection of the wounds, which should be treated if necessary.

• Small numbers of fish lice may be removed from large fish using forceps. Each wound should be treated with a topical antiseptic (Chapter 27) to guard against secondary infection. After treatment the fish must be introduced into an *Argulus*-free aquarium; the infested aquarium can then be treated chemically (as above) or allowed to remain fish-free for 5-6 weeks until any eggs have hatched, the juveniles stages have been completed, and the eventual adults have died through lack of any host. (See page 273.)

4.2.8 GILL FLUKES

Strictly, any fluke that parasitizes the gills, but in aquarium usage applied to the monogenetic flukes of the genus *Dactylogyrus*.

Some 50 species are known, with a size range of 0.15 to 2 mm in length. All are gill parasites, found only in fish, and occasionally also occurring on other parts of the body.

Transmission and biology: No intermediate host is required. The female fluke releases her eggs, which drop to the bottom where they hatch into free-swimming larvae. These have a limited time (hours) in which to find a host, otherwise they will die. On locating a host, they attach to the gill region, where they mature and eventually lay eggs to renew the cycle. The time taken for eggs to hatch, and larvae to mature, varies from species to species and with water temperature.

Signs: variable, according to the extent of the parasite burden.

• Fish with only a few flukes may show no signs, or just occasional irritation (flashing or scratching).

• Heavier infestations may manifest as gasping and an increased respiratory rate, sometimes with 'coughing'. Flashing and scratching are more frequent, sometimes practically continuous, and the fins may be clamped. Loss of appetite may occur.

• Acute infestation may occur if an infected fish is introduced into an aquarium containing fish which have not previously been 'challenged' by gill flukes and have no acquired immunity. Vast numbers of larval flukes colonise their gills and cause severe damage resulting in acute physiological Hypoxia (1.3.3), manifesting as heightened coloration, loss of swimming control, and immobile, staring eyes (as also seen in acute Poisoning, 1.2). The carrier fish, which may have only a light parasite burden due to partial acquired immunity, often shows only mild signs of illness, if any.

In all cases the gills may appear pale with grey edges, and mucus hyperproduction around the gills is likely.

Heavy infestations are likely to prove fatal if untreated, and acute infestations may cause such massive trauma as to be lethal despite prompt treatment.

Prevention: Unfortunately, because slight infestations are often asymptomatic, there may be no obvious signs during the quarantine period. It is thought that many fish may harbour very small numbers of these parasites and be able to resist further infestation by virtue of acquired immunity; provision of minimum-stress conditions will help ensure that the fish's immune system is not compromised. Serious and acute infestations seem in any case to be rather uncommon.

Treatment: Bath immersion with a proprietary anti-fluke remedy is the normal treatment of choice. It is essential to complete the course of treatment according to the manufacturer's instructions to ensure total eradication, as the egg stage is resistant to chemical treatment. A common error is to stop treatment because the fish have apparently recovered, only to have them re-infected by newly-hatched flukes, when the whole course needs to be started again from scratch.

Alternatives are bath immersion using formalin (Chapter 27), or an anthelminthic such as praziquantel (Chapter 27).

Comment: Scratching is not necessarily a sign of gill fluke parasitisation; in very many cases, it is the result of environmental problems (see 1.0), which should be ruled out before fluke infestation is suspected. (See page 276).

4.2.9 GILL MAGGOTS

A term used for *Ergasilus*, a genus of crustacean (copepod) parasites of the gills. Approximately 65 species of ergasilid parasites are known from freshwater fish, but, from the aquarist's viewpoint, exact identification is unnecessary.

Transmission and biology: Direct, with no intermediate host required.

Life Cycle of the Gill Fluke.

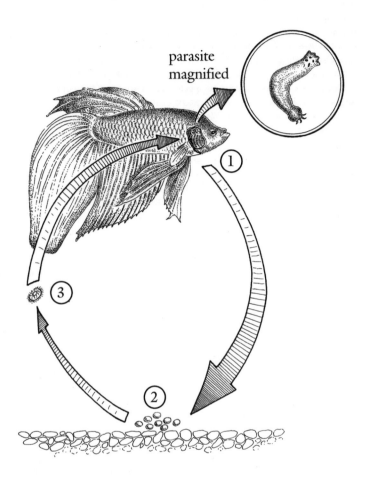

parasite
magnified

Stages not to scale

1. Parasitic flukes attached to gill filaments. Adult flukes release eggs into the water.

2. Eggs on the substrate.

3. Infective stage (oncomiracidium) swims in the water in search of a fish to infect.

Only the female *Ergasilus* is parasitic – the male and larval stages are free-swimming. After fertilisation, the female uses her antennae to attach to a gill filament. She then develops egg pouches from which nauplii hatch after about 3-5 days (at normal tropical aquarium temperatures), after which the next batch of eggs is produced. The nauplii mature after 8-10 weeks and mate. A female can produce more than 40,000 offspring in a single year.

Luckily gill maggots are rarely a problem in aquaria, though they are relatively common on wild and pond-reared fish. They are usually introduced on infected fish or as free-swimming larvae in fish-bag water. There is also a possibility of introducing larval stages with wild-collected live foods from fish-inhabited waters, if the food organisms were transported in water taken from their source.

Signs: Behavioural signs are those normally associated with gill problems: gasping, 'coughing', and increased respiratory rate. If the gills are examined, then the parasite (0.5-3 mm long) and her maggot-like egg pouches (1-3 mm long), should be visible to the naked eye, as well as mucus hyperproduction on and around the gills.

Prevention: Quarantine and care in collecting live foods from the wild.

Treatment: Proprietary anti-crustacean medication, metriphonate, or potassium permanganate (Chapter 27).

4.2.10 ROUNDWORMS AND THREADWORMS

This large group, properly known as nematode worms, includes both free-living and parasitic species. These worms have cylindrical, non-segmented, bodies and are variable in size and coloration. More than 5,000 species of parasitic nematodes are known, and some 650 have been identified as adults in fish. Possibly the best known species encountered in tropical aquarium fish are *Camallanus* (4.2.3) and *Capillaria* (4.2.4), but infestation with other types of roundworms, too numerous to catalogue specifically, is possible. The following is, therefore, a generalised summary.

Transmission and biology: The nematode life cycle may involve one or more hosts depending on species, i.e. transmission may be direct (by worm eggs in faeces) or indirect (e.g. via some aquatic invertebrates, including some used as live foods, which may be intermediate hosts).

In the case of some fish-parasitic nematode species, it is the larvae which infect the tissues of the fish, while in others, the adult worm resides in the host's gut, where it lives off the gut contents, mates, and releases eggs which are voided with the faeces. Some nematode species require two different fish hosts, one infected by the larvae, and the other harbouring the adult worms.

Severe larval infestation can damage internal organs, and large numbers of adults commonly weaken the host.

Signs: Low-level infestations may be asymptomatic. Severe infestations may cause swelling of the abdomen and lethargy due to insufficient nutrient uptake even though the fish is feeding well. Spinal deformity may occur in extreme cases.

Prevention: It is likely that many fish carry a light nematode burden which causes no noticeable harm to an otherwise healthy fish. Filter/siphon off faeces to avoid transmission and re-infection via coprophagy. Although there is a risk of introducing nematodes via some live foods, in practice, this seems rarely to cause problems and the beneficial effects of live foods probably outweigh the risk.

Treatment: Anthelminthics (Chapter 27) such as piperazine.

4.2.11 SKIN FLUKES

Monogenetic ectoparasitic flukes of the genus *Gyrodactylus*, numerous species of which have been recorded from fish. Skin flukes, as the name suggests, are generally found on the skin, but may also parasitise gills and fins.

Transmission and biology: Transmission is from fish to fish, by direct contact.

Gyrodactylus are obligate parasites, that is, they cannot survive away from the host fish, although they are able to move around freely on its surface. All are hermaphroditic, producing live young. They typically attain a length of 0.4 mm (a few exceed 1 mm). They are generally cylindrical in shape and characterised by suckers and hooks which they use to attach to the skin of the host, where they feed on epithelial mucus and cells.

Under optimal conditions (for the flukes), *Gyrodactylus* are able to proliferate very rapidly, causing serious infestations within a short period (days rather than weeks) and possibly leading to host death.

Signs: Mild infestations may be asymptomatic apart from occasional scratching and flashing. In the case of heavier infestations, there is likely to be mucus hyperproduction as a response to tissue damage, and severe cases may involve reddened areas, secondary infections, Ulcers (3.2.9), and fin erosion. The scratching is likely to be more frequent, even frenzied, although the fish may otherwise be lethargic. The fins may be clamped. If the gills are severely affected, there may be respiratory distress, as with Gill flukes (4.2.8).

Diagnosis can be confirmed using a low-powered microscope to examine a skin scrape for the presence of flukes.

Predisposing factors: Poor aquarium hygiene (e.g. heavy organic pollution, 1.2) and stress may reduce the immune response of the fish. Because transmission is by direct contact, overcrowding may increase the likelihood of spread from fish to fish.

Prevention: Quarantine. Avoid the predisposing factors. It seems probable that fish develop an immune response to *Gyrodactylus*, as otherwise it is difficult to see how any individual, once infected, could avoid heavy infestation.

Treatment: Bath immersion using a proprietary skin and gill fluke medication. Salt and anthelminthics (Chapter 27) (such as mebendazole) can also be used. Stubborn cases may require a short-term bath using formalin (Chapter 27).

4.2.12 SPINY-HEADED WORMS

A phylum of worms (Acanthocephala), also known as thorny-headed worms, several species of which are intestinal parasites of fish. They are associated largely with cyprinids, and generally restricted to wild-caught and pond-reared fish.

Transmission and biology: Acanthocephalans have a multi-host life cycle and cannot be transmitted directly from fish to fish.

The adult worms vary in length (typically 1.5-3 cm/0.75-1.25 in) according to species, and attach to the gut wall using their elongate proboscis equipped with spines and hooks. The females release eggs into the gut, subsequently to be voided with the faeces, where they may be consumed by the intermediate host, an aquatic crustacean. The eggs next develop in the crustacean's gut, and the cycle is completed if a fish eats the crustacean. It is thus possible for infection to occur via aquatic crustaceans harvested from fish-inhabited waters for use as live food.

Signs: Often asymptomatic if the parasite burden is light. In heavy infections there may be emaciation, as with other intestinal parasites, e.g. Roundworms (4.2.10) and

Tapeworms (4.2.13). Confirmation of possible diagnosis requires specialist identification of worm eggs present in faecal samples, or post-mortem examination of a specimen.

Prevention: Infection can be avoided by not using crustacean live foods, notably amphipods, collected from fish-populated waters. However, as acanthocephalan infestations are rarely serious, the benefits of using such live foods may be deemed worth the very slight risk.

Uneaten water hog-lice (*Asellus*) sometimes colonise aquarium filters, where they can provide the necessary intermediate host for acanthocephalans. This risk can largely be avoided by feeding these crustaceans in small quantities, using a worm-feeder (rather than tipping them into the tank), thus minimising the likelihood of any escaping the notice of the fish long enough to take refuge!

Treatment: None. However, the adult worms have a limited lifespan (a few months) and cannot re-infect the host, so the infection disappears in time.

4.2.13 TAPEWORMS

Tapeworms (scientifically known as cestodes) are ribbon-like segmented worms. About 1,500 species have been recorded from fish, all of them endoparasitic.

Transmission and biology: Tapeworms are multi-host parasites: in some species, the fish is an intermediate host, harbouring the larval stages in the tissues or body cavity; in others, it is the final host, harbouring adult parasites in the gut. Other hosts include aquatic invertebrates and birds. Because of the complexity of the life cycle, these parasites cannot be transmitted from fish to fish directly, although fish can be infected by some live foods, notably copepods. Copepods taken from fish-free waters can be infected, acquiring the parasite from infected bird droppings.

Fish-parasitic tapeworms may range in length from a few centimetres up to 40 cm, depending on the species.

Signs: Both adult and larval tapeworms generally cause no visible harm to their fish hosts such that the aquarist is often unaware that his fish are affected. However, heavy worm burdens with adults or larvae can cause problems (emaciation, swelling of the abdomen), and a heavy burden of larvae in the abdominal cavity can damage internal organs, cause impaired buoyancy and swimming difficulties, and may even rupture the body wall.

Diagnosis can be confirmed by post-mortem dissection or microscopic examination of faecal samples (the latter method will confirm only the presence of adults in the gut, not of larvae in the body cavity).

Prevention: Avoidance of some live foods (copepods, *Tubifex*) from natural waters (even fish-free waters, because of the transmission by birds). However, tapeworms are rarely a serious problem in aquarium fish, even where wild-collected live foods have been extensively used.

Treatment: Anthelminthics (Chapter 27), but before using chemical treatments it is essential to ensure that the problem is due to adult tapeworms in the gut (confirmed by presence of tapeworm eggs in the fish's faeces) and not to larvae. Dead, decomposing, larval stages in the body cavity cannot be vented from the fish, but anthelminthics can safely and effectively be used to eliminate adult stages in the gut. Suitable drugs include niclosamide or praziquantel, administered in food.

5.0 GENETIC DISEASES AND DISORDERS

A number of genetically-induced conditions and diseases are sometimes seen in tropical aquarium fish. These are probably more common in captive-bred fish as a result of using poor-quality or inbred breeding stock.

Some genetic disorders are normally apparent in fry from their first few days of life. If only one or two fry in a large brood are affected, the cause is likely to be random mutation. If, however, most of a brood are affected, then this is commonly an inherited problem, possibly associated with inbreeding, although not all such malformations are genetic in origin.

In general, the likelihood of all the conditions described in this section can be reduced, if not totally prevented, by careful selection of breeding stock and avoidance of inbreeding (see Chapter 8).

There is no way of remedying genetic defects; if they are likely to cause suffering (as in the case of severe deformities of the body), then the affected fish should be euthanased (Chapter 25). This is not necessary in the case of colour mutations and minor deformities such as a missing gill cover or mis-formed fin. Such fish should not, however, be used as breeding stock.

Because the cause, prevention, and treatment of genetic disorders are the same in each case (as outlined above), these have not been repeated in the sub-sections below.

5.1 BELLYSLIDING

Dysfunction of the swimbladder, in newly-hatched or newly-released (in the case of mouthbrooding species) fry.

Signs: Fry are lacking in buoyancy, and 'slide' or 'hop' along on their bellies. (Note: this may be normal behaviour in some bottom-dwelling species in which reduced buoyancy is the norm.)

Comment: Bellysliding fry commonly die within their first few days of life, rendering euthanasia unnecessary.

5.2 COLOUR MUTATIONS

A number of these occur in tropical aquarium fish, the best known being albinism and melanism.

Albino fish lack pigmentation and are white/cream with red eyes; the white 'colour' is actually an absence of any pigment, and the likewise unpigmented eyes are 'coloured' red by the blood in their capillaries. Albino fish are thought to be less hardy than normal individuals, possibly because of associated physiological weaknesses. Their eyes are particularly light-sensitive, hence they should be kept under subdued lighting and provided with areas of shade. A number of tropical aquarium fish species are available in albino form, e.g. *Corydoras aeneus* and the Oscar (*Astronotus ocellatus*). Albino forms sometimes also occur naturally, particularly in subterranean-living populations or species ('cave fish'), such as the blind cave tetra, the hypogean form of *Astyanax mexicanus*, which has no need of pigmentation as it is blind and lives in perpetual darkness.

Melanism is caused by overproduction of the dark pigment melanin, leading to permanent black or abnormally dark coloration. Again, melanistic forms of some aquarium fish are available, e.g. the black angel (a form of *Pterophyllum scalare*).

Melanistic forms are sometimes less vigorous than their normal ancestors, and may be more prone to blindness and tumours (6.7).

Other pigmentation mutations include:

• Leucism – white, but pigmented, usually with normal or black eyes. Leucism is less common than albinism, but can be seen in the white molly (*Poecilia* var.), an aquarium strain, and occasionally in nature, e.g. white males of the Malawi cichlid *Metriaclima callainos*, in which normal male coloration is blue.

• Xanthism – yellow-pigmented. Probably the best-known xanthic aquarium variety is the gold form of the severum cichlid (*Heros severus*). Another cichlid, the Midas cichlid or yellow devil (*Amphilophus citrinellus*), has a naturally-occurring xanthic morph.

• Erythrism – red/orange pigmented. Artificial forms exhibiting this trait include orange swordtails (*Xiphophorus* var.), while naturally-occurring red/orange morphs are known to occur in a number of species, e.g. the Midas cichlid's close cousin *Amphilophus labiatus*, the red devil.

Sometimes partial melanism is seen in combination with leucism, xanthism, or erythrism, producing individuals with an irregular blotched or marbled pattern. This phenomenon is also known from a few species in nature, most notably the two *Amphilophus* species mentioned above and a number of Lake Malawi cichlids.

5.3 DEFORMITIES

These may be broadly categorised as follows:

• Deformities of the head, particularly the jaws, producing a twisted or foreshortened appearance. Not very common. Occasionally one or both eyes may be missing or atrophied.

• Deformities of the spine: scoliosis (lateral, visible from above) and lordosis (vertical, visible from the side). Scoliosis and lordosis may occur in combination in a single individual. Twisting of the caudal peduncle is commonly genetic in origin. Spinal deformities are common and may cause displacement and/or distortion of the internal organs, leading to swimming difficulties and other less obvious forms of suffering.

• Deformities of the operculum, which may be wholly or partly missing, on one or both sides. Common, especially in inbred strains of some species, e.g. angelfish (*Pterophyllum scalare*). Such deformities seem to cause no distress, but are unsightly, and undesirable because they leave the delicate gills unprotected.

• Deformities of the fins. Fins may be wholly (usually the pectorals) or partially missing; sometimes both rays and membranes are absent, sometimes just a single membrane such that the fin is divided into two parts. Other fin deformities include multiple fins and variations from the norm as regards shape and size.

• Siamese twins are sometimes seen in livebearer fry, and very occasionally in those of egg-laying species. Euthanasia (Chapter 25) should be regarded as obligatory.

Comment: Deformities may also occur during the fish's early development or later in its life, from other causes including Environmental problems (1.0), Injury (1.6.1), Fish tuberculosis (3.2.3), Vitamin deficiency (2.5), and Parasite infestation (e.g. with nematodes, 4.2.10). Such deformities do not automatically preclude use of the fish as breeding stock; however, never purchase a deformed fish as there is usually no way of telling how it acquired its deformity.

6.0 DISEASES WITH MORE THAN ONE POSSIBLE CAUSE

A small number of general physiological conditions which may be caused by one or more of a number of factors.

6.1 ANAEMIA
A deficiency of haemoglobin in the blood, often due to insufficient numbers of red blood cells.

Signs: The gills appear very pale (they are normally bright red). Post-mortem dissection may reveal abnormally pale internal organs.

Possible causes:
- Heavy infestations of blood-feeding ecto- or endo-parasites.
- Large numbers of blood-dwelling Trypanosomes (4.1.21).
- Certain systemic bacterial or viral infections.
- High levels of Nitrite (1.2.10) may also reduce haemoglobin levels, but, in this case, the gills normally turn brownish.
- Dietary deficiency, including Vitamin C deficiency (2.5).

Prevention: Avoidance or early diagnosis and treatment of the cause (i.e. before it leads to anaemia).

Treatment: Identify and remedy the cause.

6.2 CLOUDY EYE
A term used by aquarists to describe any cloudiness or opacity of the eye.

Signs: One or both eyes may be clouded and/or have an opaque pupil.

Possible causes:
- Bacterial infection (3.2).
- Fungal infection (3.3).
- Vitamin deficiency (2.5), notably vitamin A deficiency.
- Chlorine (1.2.5) damage (usually mild and very short-term cloudiness).
- Eye fluke (4.2.5) usually affects the pupil internally, turning it whitish.
- Old age.

Predisposing factors: In the case of pathogenic infection, the problem may be triggered or exacerbated by poor aquarium hygiene and water quality. Stress (1.5.2) may lead to a reduced immune response and increased susceptibility to infections.

Prevention: Very few aquarists can truthfully claim never to have had a case of cloudy eye, usually resulting from environmental factors. However, good husbandry should avoid regular problems.

Treatment: Identify, and if possible remedy, the cause. In the majority of environment-associated cases, simply improving water quality is sufficient to effect a cure, without resorting to chemical treatments.

Comment: Clouding over of the outer surface of the eye in one or more fish is often the first sign of a developing problem with water quality.

6.3 DROPSY (ASCITES)
The name given by aquarists to a uniform swelling of the abdominal region.

Signs: Significant swelling of the abdomen, often causing the scales to protrude, resulting in a pine-cone-like effect, particularly noticeable when viewed from above. This protrusion of the scales distinguishes dropsy from other conditions that may cause abdominal swelling, such as Tapeworms (4.2.13) and pregnancy/ripening eggs.

Other symptoms may include lethargy, gasping, increased respiratory rate, and loss of colour. In chronic cases, there may be skin ulceration (3.2.9). Exophthalmia (6.5) is sometimes seen in conjunction with dropsy.

Possible causes:
• Bacterial infection (*Aeromonas* – 3.2.1, *Mycobacterium* – 3.2.6, *Nocardia* –3.2.7). Outbreaks of dropsy affecting several fish simultaneously or in rapid succession are commonly bacterial in origin.
• Virus infection (3.1).
• *Hexamita* infection (4.1.9).
• Osmoregulatory problems (1.1.2; 1.6.2).

Predisposing factors: Adverse water conditions (such as poor water quality and incorrect water chemistry); immune suppression (often caused by long-term stress); poor nutrition; genetic weakness; old age.

Outbreaks of bacterial dropsy often coincide with the presence of a virulent strain of bacteria combined with adverse environmental conditions.

Prevention: Minimise stress, ensure correct nutrition, and maintain optimum environmental conditions, to avoid predisposing fish to the disease. Pay particular attention to aquarium hygiene, as transmission of bacterial dropsy is primarily via ingestion of infected faeces and/or corpses.

Treatment: If bacterial dropsy is suspected, treat with a proprietary internal bacteria medication, or an antibiotic (e.g. oxytetracycline or chloramphenicol; Chapter 27) administered with food. In all cases, ensure water conditions are optimal.

6.4 MALAWI BLOAT

A condition affecting mouthbrooding cichlids from the lakes of the East African Rift Valley, first reported from Malawian species. It is similar to Dropsy (6.3) in some respects, but differs in others (notably the invariably rapid progress of the illness), and is regarded by aquarists as a quite different disease. Very little formal scientific or veterinary research has been conducted into this disease.

Signs: Typically the fish initially exhibits lethargy, loss of appetite, and an increased respiratory rate, sometimes gasping in mid-water or at the surface. Severe swelling of the abdomen follows, generally within 24 hours of the first signs of ill health. The fish loses buoyancy and rests on the bottom in obvious distress, usually dying within 72 hours (generally much less).

Possible causes: Bloat has been formally associated with bacterial infection and/or an inappropriate or unvaried diet. On the very rare occasions that several fish are affected simultaneously, then bacterial infection should be suspected. Typically, however, cases occur singly at intervals of a few weeks to 2-3 months, and investigations by aquarists suggest that the vast majority of these are primarily the result of dietary and environmental factors – although these could be simply predisposing factors to some pathogenic infection. However, as it is possible to prevent bloat almost completely by eliminating these factors, the question may be regarded as academic!
• Unsuitable diet. A diet entirely of dried foods, containing large amounts of dried food or mammal meat (beef heart), has been implicated.
• Poor water quality, in particular where there are high levels of nitrate.

• The (long-term) addition of salt (sodium chloride, NaCl) to the aquarium water (in the mistaken belief that this replicates natural water chemistry/increases hardness).

Prevention: Avoid the possible causes/predisposing factors!

Treatment: Broad-spectrum antibiotics (Chapter 27) may help bacterial bloat, but no data are available to confirm this. There is no known treatment for environmental or dietary bloat, so prevention is essential. The vast majority of cases are fatal, and because of the degree of suffering evidently experienced by the victim, euthanasia (Chapter 25) should be considered even though death is usually rapid.

6.5 POP-EYE

An eye condition, also known as bubble-eye among aquarists, but correctly termed exophthalmia or exophthalmus. It is often a symptom of an internal pathogenic disease or an environmental health problem rather than a disease in its own right, but is almost invariably regarded by aquarists as the latter.

Signs: One or both eyes swell and protrude from the orbit. In extreme cases, the eye may literally 'pop' out of the orbit and be lost. Clouding of the entire outer surface of the eye (6.2) often accompanies (and commonly precedes) exophthalmus. If associated with a systemic infection (see below), there may also be other signs of the underlying disease, such as abdominal swelling (see Dropsy, 6.3).

Possible causes: The protrusion of the eye is caused by a build-up of fluid in or behind the eye. This build-up has a number of potential causes:

• Eye fluke (4.2.5).
• Systemic bacterial infection (3.2).
• Virus infection (3.1).
• Systemic fungal infection (3.3.8).
• Vitamin deficiency (2.5).
• Any dysfunction of the physiological processes of the fish, e.g. Osmoregulation (1.1.2).

Predisposing factors: Poor water quality is a major predisposing factor – many cases respond to an improvement in water quality without any need for chemical treatment. Incorrect water chemistry may affect osmoregulation and other biochemical processes.

Prevention: Optimum husbandry.

Treatment: Identify and treat/remedy the underlying cause. Prompt action, at the first sign of swelling, is essential to prevent permanent damage to or loss of the eye(s). If there are no indications of pathogenic or parasitic disease, suspect an environmental problem, i.e. water chemistry or quality. Even if these are within acceptable parameters for the species, it is worth performing a partial water change each day for 2-3 days, as this will often effect a cure. It may take a week for the swelling to subside completely, but, if water quality is at the root of the problem, the eye cloudiness that almost invariably accompanies this type of exophthalmus will normally disappear much more quickly, indicating that the treatment is proving effective.

6.6 STERILITY

Signs: Apparently healthy adult fish, with both sexes present, fail to breed. Either eggs are laid but fail to hatch, or no eggs are laid.

Possible causes:
• Inappropriate lighting; usually insufficient light causing underdevelopment of gonads due to lack of stimulation of the pituitary gland (see Chapters 12 and 17).
• Inappropriate water chemistry for the species and/or poor water quality affecting production/viability of eggs and/or sperm.
• Incorrect diet affecting development/production of eggs/sperm.
• Fish too young (not yet capable of producing eggs/sperm).
• Fish too old (no longer producing eggs/sperm).
• Genetic sterility (functional sterility resulting from genetic mutation (5.0) or hybridisation).
• Disease (e.g. Tumours (6.7), Fat deposition (2.2; 2.3) resulting from incorrect diet); Fish tuberculosis (3.2.3) can affect the gonads, causing sterility.
• Certain chemical remedies, notably malachite green and acriflavine (Chapter 27), are thought sometimes to cause sterility in fish.
• Genetic manipulation (by commercial breeders).
Prevention: Avoidance of factors under the control of the aquarist (including fighting, poor water quality, incorrect water chemistry, inappropriate diet, use of potentially harmful chemicals, inbreeding, hybridisation of species).
Treatment: Remedy the cause, where possible (i.e. the first three listed; the fourth should remedy itself given time!). However, some forms of sterility are permanent.

6.7 TUMOURS
(Also known as neoplasms and neoplasias)
All teleost fish are potentially at risk of developing tumours. Some fish groups seem to be particularly prone to certain types of tumour – for example, some poeciliid hybrids, and characins, appear more prone to melanomas (pigment cell tumours).

Some types of tumour are benign (harmless), but others can be malignant (cancerous) and spread throughout the body. Large tumours, even if benign, may cause swimming difficulties or affect vital organs simply by virtue of their size. Tumours on the lips may cause feeding difficulties.
Signs: These will vary considerably depending on the type of tumour and its position on or in the fish. A number of other conditions may cause external 'growths', e.g. the cauliflower-like cysts of Lymphocystis disease (3.1.1) or those seen in Black spot (4.2.2), and these should be ruled out before suspecting a tumour. Internal tumours are unlikely to manifest unless large enough to cause external distortion (usually asymmetric) of the fish's outline.
Possible causes: Although it is virtually impossible to identify the exact cause of any tumour, certain causes have been associated with certain types of tumour, for example Aflatoxin contamination (1.2.2) with liver tumours, melanoma with inbreeding and hybridisation. There is also some evidence that tumours can be caused by extreme pollution levels and virus infections.

The susceptibility of any individual fish may be influenced by its species, sex, age (the likelihood of a tumour developing increases in old age), hereditary factors, and probably by its immune status.
Prevention: Prevention cannot be guaranteed, but good husbandry and avoidance of inbreeding may help reduce the likelihood of tumours occurring.
Treatment: Surgical removal of skin or other external tumours is occasionally performed (by a vet) where the tumour is likely to cause problems or distress, by

encroaching on the mouth, vent, or gills, or by causing swimming difficulties by virtue of its weight. Normally, however, treatment is impossible. Tumours do not always cause the fish any apparent distress or inconvenience, and some may stop growing after a time. If there is any sign of suffering then euthanasia (Chapter 25) is the kindest course.

CHAPTER 22

AQUARIUM PESTS

Aquaria are sometimes invaded and colonised by organisms which, while generally inherently harmless, often cause the aquarist concern. Sometimes the concern is justified, as the presence of such organisms in 'epidemic' proportions may be a sign of environmental degradation or other lack of attention to detail by the aquarist (including failure to check live foods for 'nasties', collecting decorative material from fish-inhabited natural waters). So although these pests may be simply unsightly or a nuisance, and not directly harmful to the fish, their presence is often a warning sign, and should never be ignored.

1. ALGAE

Algae are primitive aquatic plants which, depending on the species, attach to underwater surfaces or live free in the water. They vary in colour (green, brown, red, grey, yellowish) and in form – from a slimy coating to fluffy tufts, and from a moss-like carpet to long filamentous strands (e.g. the so-called 'blanketweed' seen in ponds in summer). True algae differ, however, from the so-called 'blue-green algae', which are now scientifically classified as Cyanobacteria (see below).

The presence of algae is inevitable where water, nutrients, and light are found in combination; and as all three elements are found in every aquarium, the aquarist should learn to accept that algae are a natural (and inevitable) part of the aquarium ecosystem. Indeed, algae offer a number of positive benefits in the aquarium, as in nature: they provide natural food for some herbivorous fish; they, and the micro-organisms they harbour, are an excellent source of first foods for fry; they reduce the amount of nitrate (which they use as a nutrient) in the water; and they give otherwise stark decor such as rocks a more natural appearance (rocks in natural waters are generally algae-coated). And if algae grow too rampantly, they provide a warning of possible water quality problems.

Different aquaria may be colonised by quite different types of algae. In part, this may be a function of the aquarium lighting, with low light levels favouring the brown, slime-like types, and bright lighting encouraging vivid green forms.

Algae are regarded as a particular nuisance when they coat the aquarium glasses and the leaves of plants. However, it is easy to keep the front glass clean using an algae scraper or algae magnet; algae can be left on glass panels not used for viewing, where they will help remove nitrate and provide food for fish. An additional benefit, for aquarists with a photographic bent, is that a coating of algae on the back glass will prevent flash reflection.

In nature, it is quite normal for the older leaves of aquatic plants to be colonised by algae. Such leaves are generally moribund and are successively replaced by new growth. If algae on aquarium plants are a problem, this generally signifies that there is too much algal growth, or insufficient higher plant growth. Aquarists often make the mistake of reducing the aquarium lighting (intensity and/or period) to try to curb algae, and instead curb the growth of the higher plants, making the problem worse! Healthy plants also help limit algae by competing for available nutrients.

Rampant algal growth (e.g. when it is necessary to remove algae from the viewing glass(es) every few days) can take place only where there are sufficient nutrients available, hence a genuine algae problem is commonly a sign of high levels of nitrate and/or phosphate. This may in turn be due to overdosing with aquarium fertiliser to promote plant growth, but is more commonly indicative of poor husbandry – overcrowding, overfeeding, inadequate water changes, excessive amounts of mulm, or a combination of these factors. Levels of nitrate and other nutrients may also be high in the tap water used for water changes. Whatever the reason, it is not the algae, but the underlying problem that requires attention, as otherwise adverse effects on fish health are likely – from the pollution, *not* the algae!

Free-swimming algae, invisible to the naked eye, may sometimes proliferate to the extent that the water becomes clouded and pea-soup-like – this is termed 'green water', and is common in ponds in summer, but may also occur where an aquarium is exposed to bright sunlight for a significant part of the day. Again, the problem is likely to be indicative of high nutrient levels.

Although proprietary aquarium algicides are available, this easy 'solution' to the problem is, in fact, no solution at all. The death and decay of large amounts of algae may overload the filtration system, bringing to a head the background pollution problem at the root of the algal plague. Even if this does not happen, the dead algae will simply add to the nutrient content of the aquarium, so that when algae recolonise (as they inevitably will), the recurring problem may turn out to be even worse than before. A repeated cycle of chemical dosing and biological overloading is almost certain to have adverse effects on the fish. It is thus far better to identify and remedy the cause of any excess of algae, and to regard any normal growth as a friend rather than an enemy.

A number of fish species – such as the sucking loach (*Gyrinocheilus aymonieri*) and some suckermouth catfish – are well-known 'algae-eaters' and can be used to keep algae within bounds, but should not be regarded as a substitute for maintaining low levels of organic wastes in the aquarium.

2. *ASELLUS*

These aquatic isopods (Crustacea), also known as water hog-lice, have a passing resemblance to woodlice (to which they are related). They may be introduced with, or as, live food and colonise inaccessible crannies in the decor, as well as the filter. They are not directly harmful to fish, but may act as intermediate hosts for acanthocephalan parasites (spiny-headed worms, Chapter 21, section 4.2.12). However, the latter are rarely a problem in aquarium fish, so concern on this account is unnecessary. A large population of *Asellus* may, however, imply heavy organic pollution, to which these creatures may additionally contribute.

3. BRISTLE WORMS

Annelid worms of the family Naididae, measuring up to 2 cm (0.75 in) in length, characterised by the presence of bristles (which probably render them unpalatable to fish). They are typically white to pink, and reproduce by budding or by laying eggs. They can be introduced on plants, inside the shells of aquatic snails, or in the water accompanying collected wild live foods. In the aquarium, they may also live on or in the substrate, where they feed on detritus, hence their presence in significant numbers may be indicative of poor aquarium hygiene and possible danger to the fish from pollution. The worms themselves are harmless. Improving hygiene will control their numbers, and benefit the fish by improving their living conditions.

4. COPEPODS

Copepods are small aquatic crustaceans, most species of which are harmless to fish. Some free-living types (e.g. *Cyclops*) are used as live foods, while a few are fish-parasitic (Chapter 21, section 4.2).

Free-living (harmless) copepods are generally semi-transparent and up to 3mm (0.125 in) long, and typically swim in short, hopping movements, but may also rest on underwater surfaces, including the aquarium glasses. They may be introduced into the aquarium deliberately (as live food), or accidentally (on plants). Few survive long, as most fish find them irresistible, although large fish may ignore them as too small to be worth eating. An infestation of free-living copepods is thus likely only if they are not being eaten, either because they are unsuitable food for the fish kept, or because the fish are so unwell that they have lost interest in even this tempting food source. This may be due to environmental pollution (heavy organic loading) which should also be suspected if copepods start to proliferate in the aquarium.

If the underlying problem is resolved, the fish will generally solve the copepod problem with great relish!

5. CYANOBACTERIA

A group of micro-organisms responsible for the algae-like growth known to aquarists as 'blue-green algae'. Its appearance seems to be related to high levels of nitrate and phosphate, although not all aquaria with a high level of organic wastes are affected. It can blanket the entire aquarium decor, including the substrate, with a rather slimy, bluish-green coating, almost overnight. It is not known to be directly harmful to adult fish (though underlying poor water quality may be), but may blanket and suffocate fry which rest on the substrate or decor at night, and may also smother plants.

Blue-green algae are extremely difficult to eradicate from the aquarium completely, such that subsequent blue-green blooms may occur at the least subsequent deterioration in water quality. The only remedy is to reduce levels of organic wastes, and to keep siphoning off as much of the green mess as possible at every water change. Unfortunately, 'blue-green algae' appear to be totally unpalatable to fish. Malayan burrowing snails are said to feed on it, but this has not been the experience of one of the authors, and the snails may prove to be just as much of a nuisance as the Cyanobacteria (see Snails, below).

6. *HYDRA*

These small coelenterates are freshwater relatives of the sea anemones, and measure from a couple of millimetres to about 2 cm (0.8 in) in length (including tentacles). Their form – a stem crowned with tentacles at one end, the other anchored to a solid substrate – makes them unmistakable, although they can also contract into tiny jelly-like blobs. Their colour varies from cream to grey or light brown.

Hydra are occasionally introduced into aquaria with live foods or wild-collected decor, and subsequently establish themselves on the decor and aquarium glasses, where they can provide an extra element of interest almost as fascinating as the intentional occupants of the aquarium!

They are harmless to adult fish, but may capture fry and other very small fish, as well as small items of food intended for fish! Occasionally their numbers reach pest proportions, and, as with many pests, this may indicate an underlying husbandry problem.

Complete eradication normally involves stripping down the aquarium, scrubbing its surfaces, and washing gravel, decor, and underwater equipment, in hot (above 40 °C, 105 °F) 2-5% salt solution. If the aquarium is planted (plants will not take kindly to being scrubbed in hot salty water!), an alternative method is to remove the fish (and snails, if welcome residents) to temporary accommodation and raise the tank temperature to 42 °C (110 °F) for 30 minutes. Biological filter media should be removed from internal filters during the heating, but filters themselves left in place, as *Hydra* may be attached to their surfaces. External filters should be switched off (for no longer than an hour, or the bacterial population may start to die through lack of oxygen). The tank should be allowed to cool to normal temperature (or be cooled by performing a partial water change, refilling with cold water) before the fish (and snails) are replaced and the filtration restored.

The *Hydra* population can be controlled in a stocked aquarium by adding salt (Chapter 27) to produce a 0.5% solution, which should be maintained for about a week, then progressively eliminated by partial water changes. This method can be used only if all the fish are salt-tolerant; otherwise, the aquarium glasses must be regularly wiped/scraped, the detached *Hydra* siphoned off, and rocks and other 'hard decor' items routinely removed and scrubbed in hot salty water.

Some types of fish (notably gouramis but also some young rock-browsing cichlids) feed on *Hydra* and can be used to control the population, if – and only if – these fish are suitable occupants for the aquarium in question.

7. LEECHES

Leeches are sometimes accidentally introduced into the aquarium and may be seen on decor or swimming free in the water. Some species are fish parasites, and full details can be found in Chapter 21, section 4.2.6.

8. NEMATODE WORMS

A large group of thread-like worms, also known as threadworms or roundworms, which includes both free-living and parasitic species. Non-parasitic nematodes –

1-3 cm (0.4-1.2 in) long, non-segmented, red-brown worms – may occasionally colonise the substrate and biological filter. They may be introduced with live foods, and are quite harmless. If they become numerous, this may indicate that an improvement in aquarium hygiene/feeding regime is required. This remedial action should be all that is necessary to achieve a reduction in their numbers.

For details of fish-parasitic nematodes see Chapter 21, section 4.2.10.

9. OSTRACODS

Kidney-bean-shaped crustaceans up to 4 mm (0.15 in) long, which can sometimes be seen scuttling around the substrate like tiny mobile spots. They are usually yellowish or brown-black in colour. They attach their eggs to plants and hence may be introduced with them, as well as with live foods. Aquaria may very occasionally harbour small numbers, which can proliferate to plague proportions if aquarium hygiene is poor. Thus, although these creatures are harmless, their presence indicates an underlying environmental and/or feeding problem that could itself affect the fish. Improving husbandry is the solution to both controlling the ostracods and eliminating the underlying problems.

10. PLANARIANS

Planarians are harmless, non-parasitic, flatworms which nevertheless frequently strike panic into the hearts of aquarists, who mistake them for parasites such as leeches. They are typically 2-10 mm (0.08-0.4 in) in length, and are usually creamy-white, grey or brown. The light ones often appear semi-transparent when they are seen on the aquarium glass, while the dark ones can resemble tiny slugs. Characteristic features are a V-shaped head and a slow gliding motion over aquarium surfaces.

Planarians may be accidentally introduced into the aquarium via aquatic plants or live foods. It is possible for an aquarium to have a small and totally unnoticed planarian population living in or on the substrate. Occasionally, they reach epidemic numbers and are then usually spotted crawling across the front glass or even floating free in the water. This proliferation is usually indicative of overfeeding, the uneaten food being consumed by the planarians which undergo a progressive population explosion. The feeding regime must be reviewed and water quality improved if this has suffered as a result of the overfeeding.

Planarians are often a problem where large fish are fed on foods which disintegrate in their mouths such that a shower of particles issues from the gills and falls to the bottom. The particles are too small to be of further interest to the large fish. In such cases, it may be not the quantity, but the type, of food that is the real problem. Possible solutions are a change of diet or the use of bottom-scavenging fish to clear up the 'fall-out'.

Some types of fish, e.g. gouramis, may feed on planarians and control their numbers, but this method of control does not eliminate the other dangers (pollution) posed by uneaten food, and should not be regarded as the optimal solution to the problem.

11. SNAILS

Some aquarists introduce aquatic snails deliberately, as scavengers; others accidentally, on plants (including plants from aquatic retailers). Whatever the method of their arrival, eliminating snails, if they subsequently prove undesirable, is far less easy. This is particularly true of the livebearing Malayan burrowing snail (*Melania tuberculata*), which lives in the substrate, where it may proliferate to an alarming extent without the aquarist realising it is there at all.

The presence of large numbers of snails is a sure indication of an unhealthy aquarium. Not only must the snails be finding organic material on which to feed, but they will also be using up oxygen and producing organic wastes. Some may predate on fish eggs; and wild-caught snails, or those taken from ornamental ponds, may introduce a number of parasites (Chapter 21, section 4.2) for which they are intermediate hosts.

A snail population can be kept within bounds by regularly removing all those visible, e.g. by scooping them up in a net or siphoning them out. Large specimens can be individually picked out by hand. Snail removal is best performed after the aquarium light has been off for some time, as most are more active nocturnally. Burrowing snails often leave the substrate at night, to forage on the decor and aquarium glasses.

Proprietary snail destroyers are available, but their use is inadvisable in tanks populated by fish. Most molluscicides contain copper (Chapter 27), which is toxic to fish so an overdose can prove lethal. Snail corpses may severely pollute the aquarium, in particular where the Malayan burrowing snail is the problem, as, even if the chemical is used at night, innumerable dead snails are likely to remain hidden in the substrate. If a molluscicide is deemed necessary to deal with burrowing snails, the fish should be removed to alternative accommodation, the tank treated, and then cleaned out completely and set up afresh with new substrate.

To avoid accidentally introducing snails, however, it is quite acceptable to treat plants with molluscicide prior to introduction – bear in mind that tiny snails may not be noticeable during a visual check. Avoid buying fish from tanks containing

Malayan burrowing snails and quarantine any tank infested with them until complete eradication has been achieved, as it is very easy for tiny new-born individuals to stowaway in nets, fish bags, siphon tubes, and other equipment.

12. *TUBIFEX* WORMS

Tubifex worms are commonly used as live food despite the likelihood of their introducing disease. If they are simply dropped into a tank containing substrate, some may escape being eaten by burrowing into it. This may also occur if too many worms are fed at a time using a worm feeder, as those left uneaten will eventually wriggle out of the feeder and drop to the bottom. The result will be a colony of *Tubifex* in the substrate, visible as small red-brown worms partially protruding from it. The best solution is to stop feeding the fish, who, hungry from lack of easier pickings, will soon take the trouble to capture the worms and eradicate the problem.

Note: small red-brown worms protruding from the anus of a fish are not *Tubifex* that have survived the digestive process, but *Camallanus*, a parasitic nematode (Chapter 21, section 4.2.3).

CHAPTER 23

PROFESSIONAL SERVICES

1. The veterinarian
2. Fish health consultant
3. 'Helplines'
4. The pharmacist
5. The aquarium retailer

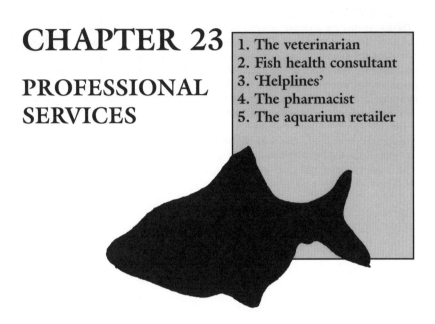

There are a number of professionals from whom the aquarist can seek advice and assistance in diagnosing and treating diseases in aquarium fish. It is strongly recommended that such assistance be sought sooner rather than later if the aquarist is unable quickly to diagnose, and effectively remedy, a health problem. Failure to do so may lead to unnecessary suffering and deaths.

Obviously, the aquarist should also research the availability of such assistance *before* it is actually needed, for example by locating a veterinarian who has specialist training in fish health (if there is one in the locality), and a pharmacist, and by finding out how to contact a fish health consultant if required.

Hints on these topics are included below.

1. THE VETERINARIAN

As we have seen in the introduction to this section of the book, it is not normal practice to take fish to the vet or have the vet make a home visit. However, it is useful – essential for the serious aquarist – to have certain veterinary services available should the occasion require. Such services may include:
• Provision of prescription-only drugs.
• Advice on dosages and methods of treatment.

- Actual treatment (such as injection of drugs, or operations).
- Euthanasia (Chapter 25) of incurably diseased fish.
- Post-mortem examination.
- Laboratory examination of tissue/blood/faecal samples.
- Laboratory analysis of water samples.

(The last three of these may be required for diagnostic purposes, and may involve the material being sent away for examination.)

It is neither reasonable nor fair to expect the vet to provide these services without prior warning that they may one day be required, as he may need to make sure the necessary information or external services are available. It is pointless to turn up at morning surgery one day clutching a fish – dead or alive – or water sample, and to expect immediate service from a totally unprepared vet.

Instead, telephone the local veterinary practice when you start keeping fish, and enquire if there is a fish specialist available there, or if they know of one within a reasonable distance. If not, then discuss with them your possible requirements for advice and assistance, in advance of any actual requirement.

2. FISH HEALTH CONSULTANTS

Whereas vets have to be registered before they can practise, anyone can set himself up in business as a fish health consultant, so the level of knowledge and service can be extremely variable. Personal recommendation (by another aquarist, retail store, or even the vet) can be a safer method of seeking this type of professional help than consulting the telephone directory or advertisements in specialist magazines.

Ideally, the fish health consultant will have completed formal training in the field of fish biology, including diseases, and have documented qualifications. Do not be afraid to enquire about these qualifications or to ask to see the relevant certification – the properly qualified consultant will have nothing to hide.

The range of services offered by fish consultants is variable. Some will make home visits. Unlike vets, however, fish health consultants are not allowed to provide prescription-only medications, and this can often be a serious limitation to their value. However, a well-informed and experienced consultant may prove invaluable in identifying the cause of a problem or diagnosing a disease, and in suggesting a course of action/treatment, if necessary using medication obtained from the vet. In some cases, it may be advantageous for the fish health consultant to liaise directly with the vet, and this is often mutually beneficial, especially if the vet has limited experience with fish.

3. 'HELPLINES'

A number of aquarium magazines, major fish food manufacturing companies, and specialist aquarium societies, offer telephone or postal helplines, often free of charge. Again, the quality of service may range from excellent to diabolical, although the organisations providing the service normally endeavour to use reliable consultants, in order to protect their own reputations. Bear in mind that, if the consultant is unable to view the fish and its surroundings, then often only a best-guess diagnosis can be made, or advice provided as to possible causes. In the case of postal services, consider the time delay between enquiry and reply – many fish diseases are acute and the fish may be dead and buried by the time a response is received, even if the service is prompt. But for non-urgent health enquiries, these services are often very good, and many extend to providing advice on general fishkeeping, husbandry requirements of particular species, etc.

The World Wide Web (Internet) also has sites where one can seek advice. Again, there may be a delay before a response is received, though response from some sites may be rapid. It is not always easy to ascertain whether the source of advice is reliable, especially when dealing with personal rather than company websites.

4. THE PHARMACIST

As with the veterinarian, it may prove worthwhile to approach a pharmacist to discuss the possibility of his assistance as and when required. In general, a sympathetic ear is more likely from the pharmacist running his own business than the one on the prescription counter of a busy chain store, who may also be limited as to what he can supply by company rules and policy.

As with the vet, it may help to take along some back-up literature. One of the authors once experienced some difficulty in buying preserving alcohol from a pharmacist obviously suspicious that it was intended for human consumption!

Bear in mind that most pharmacists will have no knowledge of fish health, so do not expect them to assist with treatment advice or dose rates, etc.

5. THE AQUARIUM RETAILER

Many aquarium retailers are experienced aquarists (this does not always include the weekend staff) who will have seen many fish diseases in the course of their personal fishkeeping and while running the store; they may be able to help you identify your problem and advise on the best method of dealing with it. Unfortunately, it is not always easy to distinguish between the genuinely informed and sincerely helpful retailer and the one whose main interest is in selling you the remedy he has on his shelf. If he has no idea what your problem is, but suggests a remedy, remember our warnings about the pointlessness and dangers of administering chemicals without first making an accurate diagnosis. If he is able to diagnose the disease, then check, using this book, whether the remedy suggested is likely to be effective. The honest dealer will not be offended by your common sense!

If you have just purchased a fish from a retailer, and it has become unwell, he may already be treating the same problem if it has also appeared in his stock. Approach the subject with tact and do not imply he has sold you a sick fish intentionally or through negligence, at least not if you want his help. Tip: if the fish in the tank(s) from which you bought your fish are all in good health, then your problem is almost certainly a reaction to the stress of transportation (Chapter 6) or too large a change in environmental conditions (Shock – see Chapter 21, section 1.5.1).

Some aquarium stores will test a water sample for a customer, free of charge or for a small fee. However, the aquarist should always have available test kits for pH, ammonia, nitrite and nitrate, as stores are not open 24 hours per day, seven days per week, and rapid identification of a water chemistry or quality problem is commonly the key to saving fish lives.

SECTION III

CHAPTER 24

TREATMENT
OF DISEASES

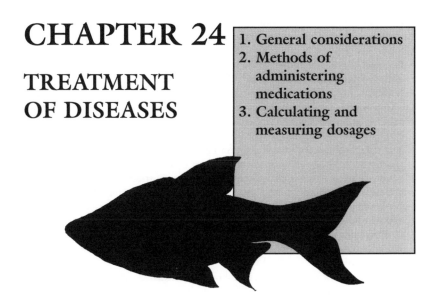

1. General considerations
2. Methods of administering medications
3. Calculating and measuring dosages

This chapter addresses the procedures involved in the administration of drugs to fish by the aquarist. It is assumed that any surgical procedures required will be performed by the veterinarian or other professionally qualified individual (Chapter 23). Treatment of environmental problems (other than first aid for injuries) and many dietary disorders will normally be a matter of improving the environment (refer to Chapters 10, 11, 12) and diet (Chapter 8) respectively, and is not covered here.

1. GENERAL CONSIDERATIONS

Medications can be administered to fish in a number of ways, which are discussed later in this chapter. The following introductory section discusses a number of topics which are relevant to the treatment of fish in general.

THE HOSPITAL TANK
Every aquarist should have a spare aquarium, which can be used either to hospitalise, quarantine, or breed fish, or for the isolation of aggressive individuals (see also Chapters 4, 5, 6, 8, 19). When used as a hospital tank, it may serve several functions:

• Isolation of a fish for observation.
• Isolation of a fish for rest and recuperation from aggression, stress, post-spawning/parturition fatigue (if necessary, e.g. in livebearers).
• Isolation of a single fish requiring chemical treatment (avoids unnecessary medication of healthy fish).
• Isolation of one or a succession of fish for short-term chemical treatment (where treatment of the main aquarium is inappropriate – see short-term bath, below).
• Isolation of fish where the medication to be used may affect biological filtration or is harmful to plants (hence unsuitable for the main aquarium).
• Isolation of one or a number of fish likely to react badly to a medication used in the main aquarium. The isolated fish may be treated with an alternative medication, depending on circumstances.

The ancillary equipment of the isolation tank will vary depending on the specific usage. For example, it will normally be used simply as a container – without heating, filtration or decor (but often with aeration) – for short-term treatments. Longer treatments will require heating and perhaps chemical filtration with zeolite (to remove ammonia), and maybe some sort of shelter if required by the species in question, to avoid stress. For rest and recuperation, it will probably be set up as a proper temporary home, with equipment (including biological filtration), substrate, a slate as background, and other appropriate decor, but arranged so that the fish can easily be viewed.

The volume of the hospital aquarium should be calculated, and note of it kept (e.g. in the medicine chest, or the tank itself can be labelled) to avoid the need to calculate the figure every time the tank is used.

OTHER USEFUL EQUIPMENT
• A pipette or eye-dropper for dispensing drops of liquid remedies. Do not use 'second-hand' droppers as they can easily be contaminated with the previous solution. New ones can be obtained from the pharmacist.
• A small measuring cylinder, 25 or 50 ml capacity for example, for measuring liquid remedies. The cylinder should be calibrated in 1 ml gradations and ideally made of glass rather than plastic. Available from the pharmacist.
• A fine artist's paintbrush or cotton buds (swabsticks) for topical application of antiseptic/fungicide.
• Long-nosed forceps for removing large skin parasites and items stuck in the mouth/gullet.
• A clean cloth or towel for immobilising the fish, or as an 'operating surface' during out-of-water procedures. This must have been thoroughly and repeatedly rinsed in fresh water to ensure it contains no traces of detergent or soap.
• Letter-scales for weighing fish or drugs. Electronic food scales, accurate to 2g or better, are adequate for weighing large fish.
• A sharp knife, scissors, or angler's 'priest' for use in euthanasia (Chapter 25).
• A large glass jug or jar for pre-diluting/pre-dissolving medications before addition to the aquarium. This container must be soap- and detergent-free, and should not be plastic, as it may react with some chemicals or retain residues in surface scratches.
• Rubber gloves for protection (see also Chapter 26). Again, they should be soap-

and detergent-free, and reserved for fish use.
• A lidded plastic bucket (less stressful than a plastic bag for a visit to the vet).

THE BASIC MEDICINE CHEST
(Numbered references are to subsections in Chapter 21, and details of the medications listed, and their availability, will be found in Chapter 27.)

To avoid any temptation to try a remedy to see if it works on an undiagnosed 'mystery disease', it is inadvisable to keep a large selection of remedies 'in stock'. Many have a limited shelf life, and may not be needed – if ever – before their expiry date. Some antibiotics and anaesthetics – have special storage requirements (e.g. refrigeration, but they should never be stored in a domestic refrigerator to which children have access. See also Chapter 26).

It is, however, sensible to have available a small number of medications for the commoner problems likely to be encountered:
• Salt (sodium chloride, NaCl), which has numerous uses (Chapter 27). A packet of aquarium salt is a wise investment.
• Methylene blue (Chapter 27). Can be used to treat external bacterial (3.2) and fungal (3.3) infections and whitespot (4.1.23), as well as prophylactically against bacterial and fungal infection of eggs (3.3.4). Although this chemical has the disadvantage of adversely affecting biological filtration, such that it will normally be used only in the hospital aquarium, its versatility makes it an invaluable standby medication.
• A topical antiseptic/fungicide such as mercurochrome (Chapter 27) or gentian violet (Chapter 27), which can be used to treat localised bacterial/fungal infection of injuries (1.6.1), fin rot (3.2.2), or as a prophylactic against such infections.

Aquarists who do not have quick and easy access to suppliers of drugs and chemicals may wish to stock additional items, e.g. treatments for flukes (4.2.8, 4.2.11), skin slime disease (4.1.18), and systemic bacterial infection (3.2). Special filter media for use in emergencies are also useful, e.g. zeolite for removing ammonia, and carbon for removing some contaminants and chemical medications.
  The medicine chest (which should be kept locked for safety reasons, Chapter 26) should also contain test kits for pH, ammonia, nitrite, and nitrate (and others, if required), as well as any water conditioning treatments required – to remove chlorine, and adjust pH, for example.

HANDLING FISH
It is essential to remember that a sick fish is already a stressed fish, and that stress will adversely affect the fish's ability to counter its illness; hence any handling required to treat the illness must be made as stress-free as possible. Fish may become extremely stressed when removed from water, so their exposure to the air must be kept to a minimum. Moreover, fish should be handled carefully to avoid actual physical damage, including to the protective body mucus.
• Make all preparations for hospital or out-of-water (e.g. topical) treatment before catching the fish. This is particularly important for out-of-water procedures, where it is unwise to keep the patient waiting on the table while you look for the antiseptic

or something with which to apply it!

• Do not chase the fish round the tank to catch it (stressful even to healthy fish). Use two nets (or a net and a hand), in a pincer movement, to guide the fish slowly and gently to the front. Sick fish are usually easier to catch than healthy ones.

• For out-of-water procedures, wrap the fish in a damp, soap- and detergent-free, cloth, leaving only the area to be treated exposed. Small fish can be held immobile in the net. Avoid dislodging mucus and scales, and try not to touch the gills unless absolutely necessary (for example, when you need to locate gill parasites). Protect the gills by loosely covering the opercula with a damp cloth.

• Remember that even a sick fish will flap when out of water, and the transfer from net to cloth is fraught with danger. One method of avoiding trouble is to place the cloth over the mouth of the net, and hold it in place with one hand; next, invert cloth, fish, and net on to the working surface, so the fish is on the cloth and under the net; keeping the net in place, raise the edges of the cloth to stop lateral motion; and remove the net before actually wrapping the fish.

• Complete the transfer to 'hospital', or the out-of-water procedure, as quickly as possible, but carefully. It will not benefit the fish to be dropped on the floor!

2. METHODS OF ADMINISTERING MEDICATIONS

Four methods are normally used to administer medications to fish:

• Via the water (bath treatment) – the most usual method. Used to treat both external and internal/systemic diseases (including endoparasites).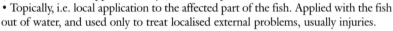
   Bath treatment may be long- or short-term, the former usually (but not always) taking place in the main aquarium, the latter requiring a short period (minutes/hours as opposed to days) in the hospital tank.

• Topically, i.e. local application to the affected part of the fish. Applied with the fish out of water, and used only to treat localised external problems, usually injuries.

• Orally, usually via the food. The oral route is used mainly to treat systemic diseases and endoparasites (particularly those affecting the gut). Drugs can also be delivered directly into the fish's gut via a stomach tube, but this technique is rarely used for aquarium fish, as it can be applied only to large specimens and requires specialised professional knowledge and expertise – hence it will not be discussed further here.

• Injection. Some treatments for systemic disorders, notably antibiotics, are sometimes administered by injection. This method can be used only for larger fish, and is a task for the veterinarian or other fish health professional. It should not be attempted by the aquarist, and hence is not covered further in this chapter.

There are advantages and disadvantages to each method (see below, under the appropriate subsections), and not all are suitable for all sizes of fish.

   In some cases, the choice of administration route may be dictated by the nature of the disease (for example, whether it is systemic/internal or external). Moreover, some medications can be administered by only a single route, or are more effective when given by one route as compared to another. Where options exist, it is wise to evaluate the advantages and disadvantages of each, in particular as regards stress minimisation.

BATH TREATMENT
Bath treatment can be applied in a number of different ways, depending on the medication to be used and/or the circumstances:

• **Long-term bath in the main aquarium.** Usually used where all or most of the fish require treatment, because they are actually unwell, or because the condition is highly infectious such that they probably soon will be. Also necessary where infective agents may be present on the decor and equipment and in the water.

The requisite dose of medication is added to the fish's normal quarters. Re-dosing at intervals may be necessary if the treatment period exceeds the effective 'life' of the medication once added to water. A partial water change is sometimes required before re-dosing.

If the drug does not degrade naturally, it must be removed either by partial water changes or by chemical filtration, as appropriate to the medication, at the end of the treatment period. The latter is usually several days, sometimes weeks.

The advantages of this method are that it avoids the need to catch and handle the fish (which increases stress), and it eliminates any infective agents in the aquarium itself. However, the method has a number of disadvantages:
– Not all fish present may actually require treatment.
– Not all fish present may tolerate the medication.
– The medication may be harmful to biological filtration.
– The treatment may be harmful to plants/snails/crustaceans.
– The treatment may stain decor items.
– If the fish react badly to the treatment, alternative accommodation may not be available.

• **Long-term bath in the hospital aquarium.** This method is used where one or a few fish require treatment for a non-infectious or only slightly infectious condition. It avoids most of the disadvantages associated with treating fish in the main aquarium, but should not be used to treat highly infectious pathogens or parasites which can exist off the host (as the main aquarium might then remain infected). An added benefit is that the amount of medication required, and hence the cost, is less. The method does, however, have its drawbacks, namely that the fish have to be moved twice (stressful), and that where reintroducing territorial species, such as cichlids, is concerned, there may be problems with reintroduction.

• **Short-term bath in the hospital aquarium** or other appropriate container (see below). This method is used where only a short treatment period is necessary (e.g. minutes or hours) or where the medication may be highly ichthyotoxic if the fish are exposed to it for longer periods, and hence it cannot be added to the main aquarium. In the case of potentially ichthyotoxic medications, the fish must be observed continuously during treatment, and removed if they show signs of distress (loss of balance, rapid gill rate, jumping). Sometimes, the actual length of the quoted treatment period is limited to the amount of time that elapses before signs of distress occur, or a stated maximum time, whichever proves the shorter.

The disadvantage of this method of treatment is the high degree of stress involved, which may, however, be necessary to eradicate some types of ectoparasites. Advantages as for long-term bath in the hospital aquarium.

If the medication to be used for a short-term bath is expensive, it is acceptable to use a smaller container (and hence less medication) and, if necessary, immerse the

301

fish in succession. To avoid re-infection (from untreated fish) it may be necessary to accommodate treated fish temporarily in the hospital aquarium. When all have been treated, they can be returned to the main aquarium. This procedure can be operated in reverse, i.e. the fish are all placed in the hospital tank, treated individually in the small container, and returned immediately to their normal home.

Whatever the type of bath treatment, certain rules should be followed (in addition to those applying to all treatments – always follow the dosage instructions, and always complete the course of treatment unless the fish is exhibiting an adverse reaction).

• *Always* monitor the fish for any signs of adverse reaction to the chemical.
• *Always* fill the hospital aquarium (or other treatment container) with water from the main aquarium, or aged water with parameters close to those of the main aquarium.
• *Never* allow concentrated chemicals directly to contact fish. When using the hospital aquarium, add the required dose of medication and mix well, *before* adding the fish. When treating in the main aquarium, dilute or pre-dissolve the medication in a container of aquarium water, then distribute the resulting solution evenly around the aquarium, either by adding it to the outlet stream from the filter, or by pouring it along the length of the tank and then mixing by hand.
• Increase aeration. Sick fish often have respiratory difficulties which may be helped by increasing the oxygen level in the water. The stress of being treated may increase their oxygen requirement further. In addition, some medications, and any increase in temperature required during treatment (see thermal treatment, Chapter 27), may reduce oxygen levels and require compensating.
• Do not use chemical filter media (e.g. carbon) during treatment, as some chemical media may remove certain medications.

TOPICAL APPLICATION

Topical treatment involves 'painting' certain medications, usually antiseptics, on to small areas of the body/fins. It is often used to treat localised bacterial and fungal infections, or prophylactically to prevent such infections where the skin has been damaged. It is an 'out-of-water' procedure (see Handling fish, above). The medication is applied using an artist's paintbrush or a cotton bud (swabstick). The fish should be returned to water as soon as possible.

The advantages of topical treatment are that only the affected parts of the fish are exposed to the medication, and it also enables certain chemicals to be used at concentrations which would be otherwise harmful if allowed to contact the fish's gills (such as when if administered by bath). The procedure is more stressful than treatment in the main aquarium, but, if it is performed rapidly and carefully, the fish can quickly be returned to familiar surroundings. It is almost certainly less stressful than the double move from tank to tank, and change of surroundings, required for hospital tank treatment. It also avoids any problems in reintroducing the fish into the social hierarchy of the main aquarium after an absence, and hence is particularly useful for territorial fish (e.g. cichlids).

ORAL APPLICATION VIA MEDICATED FOOD.

This method is usually used to treat systemic infections or intestinal parasites, commonly using prescription drugs, including antibiotics.

The major benefit of oral application is that it delivers the medication directly to the gut, and hence is very efficient for treating gut parasites and pathogens. Furthermore, many medications pass more readily into the internal tissues via the gut than they would via the skin, and for this reason, the oral route is generally far superior to bath delivery for the treatment of systemic infections.

Another advantage is that only affected fish need be treated, though this may involve moving them to the hospital aquarium (with the attendant advantages of separate treatment, see Bath treatment, above).

However, there are also serious disadvantages. A sick fish may be reluctant to feed, the more so if moved to unfamiliar surroundings. If several fish are to be medicated together, there is no guarantee that each will consume the right amount of the medicated food. It may be necessary to weigh the fish to calculate the correct dose per feed (see Calculating dosages, below), and then estimate how much food to mix it with. Fortunately for the aquarist, many dosages are expressed in terms of weight of medication per weight of food rather than weight of fish, with a stipulated number of medicated feeds offered for a specified number of days.

Medicated foods usually have to be prepared specially, sometimes by the veterinarian or fish health consultant, sometimes by the aquarist. In some countries, commercial medicated foods are available from the aquarium store, and specialist fish food manufacturers may be willing to provide a customized batch of medicated flake or pellet foods for veterinary use. Drugs can be incorporated into pelleted foods by dissolving the drug in a small amount of water in which the food is then soaked. The pellets should, obviously, be of an appropriate size for the fish to be treated. Gelatine solution can be used to help bind the drug to the food and minimise leaching into the aquarium water. The dissolved medication may, alternatively, be injected into earthworms to tempt the appetites of larger fish.

The moisture content of 'home-made' medicated foods renders them particularly liable to rapid invasion by moulds, so they should be stored at a low temperature, ideally in the freezer. Store them in a plastic bag or container and include a label detailing the composition and date of preparation. For safety reasons, they should not be kept in the domestic refrigerator if there are children in the house (see also Chapter 26). 'Leftovers' should not be fed to healthy or recovered fish (because of the danger of encouraging drug resistance in pathogens). If they cannot be stored for future reference, they should be disposed of safely (Chapter 26).

3. CALCULATING AND MEASURING DOSAGES

Dosages quoted in Chapter 27 are expressed in various ways, according to the nature of the medication (dry/liquid) and method of administration. Those for dry chemicals (powders/crystals) are expressed in terms of weight, e.g. milligrams (mg) or grams (g), whereas liquids are generally expressed in terms of volume, e.g. millilitres (ml). Drug dosages for bath treatments relate to the volume of water to be treated, e.g. 10 mg per litre; 10 ml of a 10% solution per litre, etc. Where drugs are to be administered in food the dosage may be based on the weight (or estimated weight) of the fish – e.g. 10 mg drug per kilogram weight of fish; 0.1 ml per 100 g of fish, etc. Alternatively, medicated foods may be based on the relative proportions of drug to food, e.g. 1 mg drug per 100 g pellet food.

CALCULATING AQUARIUM VOLUME

The volume of an aquarium is usually expressed in litres or gallons. To calculate volume:

• Multiply length x width x depth (all in cm) and divide by 1,000 for volume in litres.

• Multiply length x width x depth (all in feet) and multiply by 6.23 for volume in imperial gallons.

(For conversion of litres to gallons and vice versa, and for US gallons, see Table 21, Weights and Measures).

When calculating the volume of a decorated aquarium, remember to allow for the volume displaced by the substrate and decor. This can be difficult to estimate, so when first filling the aquarium with water (with the decor in place), use a container of known volume for the job, and keep a tally of how many times you fill it. From this you can calculate the actual volume of water used, a note of which should be kept in a safe place, e.g. the medicine chest, or written on the side of the tank in indelible pen (which can be removed with surgical spirit – or similar – at a later date, if necessary).

If the treatment is to be applied as a short-term bath (see Methods of Administering medications, above) in a small volume of water, then it may be simpler to measure out an appropriate volume of water rather than calculating the volume of the container.

Some drugs are expensive, and there is little point in medicating 10 litres of water to treat a 3 cm fish for 5 minutes, after which water and medication are thrown away.

WEIGHING FISH

It is impracticable, stressful and dangerous (to the fish) to weigh a fish 'dry'. Instead, it should be weighed in a container of water (using letter or kitchen scales for small fish/containers; a spring suspension balance and a bucket of water may be needed for larger ones). The container and water are first weighed; the fish is then netted and placed in the container, which is weighed again. The fish should immediately be returned to its own (or the hospital) aquarium. The weight of the fish is the total weight (fish + container + water) minus the combined weight of container and water.

Table 21 Weights and Measures.	
Imperial	**Metric**
1 imperial gallon* of water weighs 10 lbs	1 litre of water weighs 1 kilo
1 lb = 16 oz	1 kilo = 1,000 g
1 lb = 0.454 kilos	1 kilo = 2.205 lb
1 cubic foot of water = 6.23 gallons	1000 cc (ml) = 1 litre
1 imperial gallon = 4.55 litres*	1 litre = 0.2198 gallons
1 pint = 0.568 litres	1 litre = 1.756 pints
1 inch = 2.54 cm	1 cm = 0.3937 inches

*1 US gallon = approximately 0.8 of an imperial gallon or 3.79 litres.

STOCK AND WORKING SOLUTIONS

Dosages quoted for many (non-proprietary) medications in Chapter 27 commonly refer to a 'stock solution' (e.g. a 3% stock solution of hydrogen peroxide). In such cases, if the chemical has been purchased in dry form, then a stock solution must first be prepared. It is easiest to perform this task in metric units, where the percentage figure quoted is the number of grams of chemical to be added to one litre of water (e.g. a 1% solution will be 10 g of chemical to one litre of water, or 1 g to 100 ml).

The aquarist may encounter problems in preparing stock solutions, however, as he may not have the necessary equipment (a laboratory balance) for weighing the very small amounts of chemicals often required to create manageable volumes of stock solution. While he has the option of using larger amounts of dry chemical and water, he will then be faced with the problem of disposing of or storing the surplus! Hence it is preferable to obtain ready-prepared stock solutions wherever possible.

Sometimes the available stock solution may be a different strength to the one quoted for treatment. For example, the aquarist may find his stock solution of drug X is 30% but the quoted dosage is based on a 6% stock solution.

In such cases there are two options:

1) The stock solution can be diluted to that cited (i.e. in cases where a weaker stock solution is required). Thus, using the drug X example above, one volume of the 30% stock is added to 4 volumes of diluent (e.g. distilled water) to give the required 6% stock. The dosage can then be followed exactly as quoted.

2) The dosage can be recalculated to compensate for the differences in stock strengths. For example: a dosage is based on a 40% stock solution of drug Y which is to be administered at the rate of 2 ml per litre of aquarium water. However, the aquarist's stock bottle of drug Y is a much weaker 5% solution. To adjust for stock differences, divide 40 by 5, and multiply by the dosage rate. Thus, $40/5 = 8$, multiplied by 2 ml per litre = 16 ml per litre. Hence the aquarist must administer his stock solution at the rate of 16 ml per litre.

Most proprietary aquarium remedies, by contrast, come in the form of stock solutions with specific dosage instructions, which should be followed to the letter. It should never be necessary to adjust the stock solution strength of these remedies.

The eventual solution of the medication, created by adding the required dose of stock solution or dry chemical to the water to be treated (the aquarium, hospital tank, or other short-term bath container – see under Bath Treatment, above, for precautions to be taken when so doing), is termed the 'working solution' (or 'working strength'). For example, a 20% stock solution of drug needs to be administered at the rate of 3 ml per litre of water. Thus, the working strength is 20% x 3/1000 = 0.06% solution.

Occasionally (but not always), e.g. where the stock solution is applied topically or to the food, the stock solution and the working solution may be the same concentration (i.e. the stock solution is sometimes used 'neat').

It is vital that fish are exposed to the correct working solution, and never, under any circumstances, to higher concentrations, otherwise serious damage or death may ensue.

SECTION III

CHAPTER 25

EUTHANASIA

1. Acceptable methods of euthanasia.
2. Unacceptable methods of euthanasia.

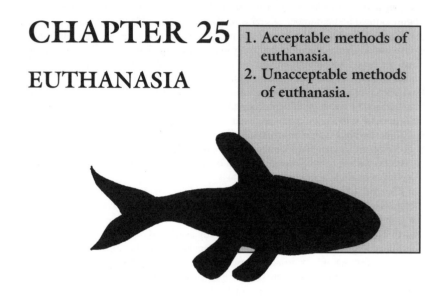

Sometimes it is necessary to kill a fish that is suffering from, or severely incapacitated by, incurable disease or serious injury. Sooner or later, almost every aquarist will have to face up to this need to end suffering; and because the situation may arise suddenly and unexpectedly, it is as well for him to think over the possible options dispassionately at the beginning of his fishkeeping career, so as to be prepared when the time comes.

On occasion, the need for euthanasia is obvious; unfortunately, there are many less clear-cut cases and, if uncertain, the aquarist should seek a second opinion from the vet or a more experienced aquarist. One thing is certain – it is never right to allow suffering to continue because of ignorance of how to euthanase a fish, or through squeamishness. If the latter is an insurmountable problem, then assistance (again, vet or experienced aquarist) must be sought rather than leaving the fish to suffer.

In addition, the fish must be despatched as quickly and as painlessly as possible. Many 'traditional' methods of fish euthanasia are convenient and 'comfortable' for the aquarist but result in prolonged stress and physical suffering for the fish, rather than a quick 'clean' ending. If the aquarist cannot stomach killing a fish humanely himself, then he must take it to the vet for euthanasia.

1. ACCEPTABLE METHODS OF EUTHANASIA

• Anaesthetic overdose. This may require a visit to the vet in countries
where the necessary chemicals are available only on prescription. Phone the
vet first – he may be willing to supply the chemical for home use (minimises stress
for the fish by avoiding a journey to the vet), but may insist on performing the task
himself. In this case, the aquarist must decide whether to take the fish to the vet or
arrange a home visit. This method of euthanasia is suitable for any size of fish, and
is particularly suitable where numbers are involved, e.g. where a brood is to be culled
(see also below). For suitable anaesthetics and dosages, see Chapter 27.
• Concussion, with destruction of the brain. The fish should be netted and wrapped
in a cloth (for grip) with its head exposed. The head is then hit forcefully against a
hard object (doorstep, edge of a table, large rock). Alternatively, a hard object (rock,
hammer) can be brought down on the head of the fish. Fishing (angling) shops
stock a type of club, known as a 'priest', used for despatching salmon, trout, etc,
which is ideal for killing larger fish. Unless the head has been completely crushed
during the operation, then the brain should subsequently be pierced, via the top of
the head, with a sharp instrument (e.g. a knife or scissors), to ensure the fish is dead
and not just stunned.
• Decapitation, with destruction of the brain. If the fish is small and elongate, its
head can be severed using a sharp knife or scissors. This method of euthanasia is
unsuitable for larger or deep-bodied fish as the operation may take some time and
cause acute suffering. The fish should be held in a cloth, as for concussion, and,
because the brain may remain conscious for a while after decapitation, the brain
should be pierced and destroyed, as for concussion, above.
• Predation. It is sometimes necessary to dispose of genetically deformed or stunted
fry, or surplus numbers, by culling. (It is normally impracticable for the amateur to
rear and find homes for the hundreds or thousands of fry produced by some fish.)
It is generally regarded as humane to feed such fry to a piscivore (this is the normal
and natural fate of most fry in the wild) with the following provisos:
– The fry must be healthy (apart from any genetic problems).
– The size of the predator(s) must be such that each fish is eaten quickly.
– The numbers of fry fed at any one time should be such that they are all eaten
quickly, and none left to share the predator's tank, in terror, until it is hungry again.
   Note: in some countries it may be illegal to feed any live fish to another fish or
other animals.

2. UNACCEPTABLE METHODS OF EUTHANASIA

The following methods of euthanasia cause suffering, and are totally
unacceptable:
• Flushing a live fish down the lavatory or sink waste disposal unit (see also
Disposal of dead fish, Chapter 26).
• Breaking the neck without subsequent destruction of the brain; the fish
may remain alive for some time, and still be conscious when its 'corpse' is disposed
of.
• Suffocation, by removal from water.
• Dropping a live fish into boiling or iced water.

• Slow chilling (with or without water). (This method is often suggested in aquarium literature, on the basis that the metabolism slows and the fish slips away. However, it is now thought that the physiological processes involved are painful and the suffering considerable.)

Diseased fish, alive or dead, should never be fed to other fish, as this may transmit infection. Corpses should be disposed of safely and responsibly, as discussed in Chapter 26.

CHAPTER 26

HEALTH AND SAFETY

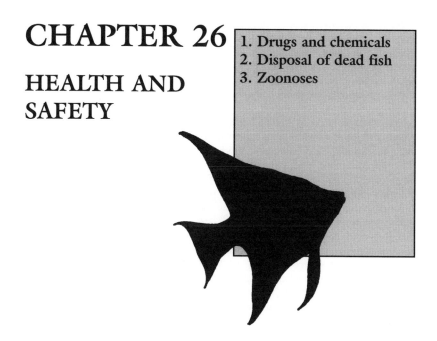

1. Drugs and chemicals
2. Disposal of dead fish
3. Zoonoses

It is vital to be aware of potential dangers (to the aquarist, his family, his fish, and the environment) inherent in the 'do-it-yourself' approach to treatment.

1. DRUGS AND CHEMICALS

HANDLING AND STORAGE OF DRUGS AND CHEMICALS
Many fish disease remedies and water-testing reagents are potentially toxic to humans. In most countries, legislation requires that a suitable caution be printed on the packaging of dangerous chemicals, but it is wise to assume that all chemicals are potentially toxic unless specifically stated otherwise. Specific warnings are given for some especially hazardous chemicals under the appropriate entries in Chapter 27. The following safety precautions are suggested in the case of all chemicals:

• All chemicals should be kept in clearly labelled containers, and stored in a locked box or cabinet with a key which is kept out of the reach of children.
• Always follow the manufacturer's specific instructions regarding special storage conditions (e.g. specific temperature constraints) and safety precautions.
• Wear rubber gloves when handling chemicals or immersing the hands in medicated water.

• Do not suck on the siphon tube when performing a water change on a medicated tank (in fact, any tank!); use an automatic siphon-starter.
• If chemicals accidentally come into contact with the skin or eyes, wash away immediately with plenty of clean water. It is strongly advised that medical attention is sought if chemicals come into contact with the eyes.
• Never hesitate to seek medical assistance urgently if a chemical has been swallowed, or if you suspect this may have happened. This applies even if only medicated aquarium water is involved, rather than the neat chemical.
• Always open bottles and other containers over a sink, so any spillage is contained and can be washed away (but see also Disposal of chemicals, below). Some chemicals can irrevocably damage or stain clothing and soft furnishings.

SAFE USE OF DRUGS AND CHEMICALS

Many chemical treatments are actually ichthyotoxic (poisonous to fish), but can be used at sublethal concentrations to eradicate pathogens or parasites. Overdosing, however, may prove fatal. Some fish are especially sensitive to particular chemicals. Some drugs, in particular antibiotics, can, if misused, lead to the evolution of drug-resistant strains of pathogen (some fish pathogens are already resistant to some formerly effective drugs owing to excessive use).

The following rules should be adhered to strictly:
• Use a medication only where a specific disease has been diagnosed and the medication is appropriate to that disease. *Never* use drugs at random in the hope of curing an undiagnosed condition.
• Use antibiotics only where no alternative is available or where alternatives are proved ineffective.
• *Never* overdose – this is unlikely to hasten or increase the likelihood of a cure, but may kill the fish.
• *Always* complete the course of treatment recommended. Failure to do so may leave the disease unremedied but the fish weakened by the exposure to chemicals, and hence less able to withstand the disease. That is to say, the problem may actually be exacerbated by the incomplete treatment.
• *Always* follow any other instructions to the letter.
• *Never* mix chemicals unless the treatment instructions specifically advise this. *Never* unintentionally mix drugs by using them in succession without ensuring the previous treatment is no longer present (naturally degraded, or removed by chemical filtration or partial water changes).
• *Always* check whether any fish species present is sensitive to the treatment. Chapter 27 warns of known species sensitivity to specific medications, and proprietary remedies usually carry warnings, if relevant, which should be heeded.
• Even if a fish is supposedly tolerant of the treatment, *always* watch carefully for any adverse reaction. This is particularly necessary with short-term baths, but also monitor for adverse effects with long-term baths, particularly when the treatment is first administered.
• *Always* check to see if the intended treatment is harmful to biological filtration; a sudden ammonia or nitrite surge may be more harmful than the disease, or have a 'final straw' effect.

DISPOSAL OF DRUGS AND CHEMICALS

Any surplus, date-expired, or otherwise unwanted chemicals or drugs must be disposed of safely. Consult the vet or pharmacist as to suitable disposal methods which comply with any local legislation. Never dispose of chemicals in the domestic rubbish or pour them down the drain; such irresponsible behaviour may lead to contamination of the environment and/or harm to other people.

In some cases, disposal of medicated aquarium water may require special care, e.g. where antibiotics (danger of drug resistance) or particularly toxic chemicals have been used. Again, seek professional advice. One solution may be to dig a deep soakaway in the garden, provided this is not located adjacent to a natural water source such as a stream or lake. A soakaway will at least limit contamination to a small known area. Bear in mind that in some countries it is illegal, with stringent penalties, to contaminate a natural water source.

2. DISPOSAL OF DEAD FISH

Ideally, dead fish should be incinerated (the domestic fire or garden bonfire will suffice for small to medium specimens without offending the household or neighbours with the smell). If this is not possible, or undesirable for reasons of sentiment, they should be buried. A third option is to wrap the corpse in polythene and dispose of it in the domestic rubbish. Corpses should not be put down the lavatory or sink waste-disposal unit, as this could conceivably result in the infection of native fish with exotic pathogens. Likewise, dead or sick fish should not be fed to other fish because of the risk of spreading disease or, if the dead fish has been medicated, unintentionally dosing the predator.

For this latter reason, dead fish should not be fed to other domestic pets, and, if the corpse is buried, precautions should be taken to ensure that it cannot be exhumed and consumed by pets or wildlife. A slate, piece of paving slab, or layer of stones immediately above the corpse is usually effective.

3. ZOONOSES

These are diseases which can be transmitted from animals to man. Fortunately, only one fish zoonosis is of importance to aquarists, namely fishkeeper's or fishtank granuloma. This disease is an infection with the bacteria which cause fish tuberculosis (Chapter 21, section 3.2.3), namely various species of *Mycobacterium (ibid.,* 3.2.6), and is cut rare. It is not normally serious unless the patient is severely immunosuppressed, and should not be confused with the far more serious human tuberculosis caused by *Mycobacterium tuberculosis*.

The condition manifests as a skin infection, normally on the hands or forearms and usually at the site of an earlier cut or graze, that refuses to clear up under normal treatment (i.e. with proprietary antiseptic creams). The area may be inflamed, with suppuration, encrustation, and irritation.

The causative bacteria enter via broken skin during the handling of infected fish or when the hands/arms are immersed in infected aquarium water. The risk of infection can be minimised by avoiding contact with aquarium water and fish if there is broken skin on the hands/arms, especially if the presence of fish TB is suspected. In such circumstances, rubber gloves should be worn, or, for deep tanks, veterinary arm-length gloves.

Treatment is by antibiotics, under medical supervision. However, this disease is so rare that many doctors may not necessarily consider it, hence misdiagnosis can occur. It may thus be necessary for the aquarist to inform his doctor of the possible cause, and, if necessary, request referral to a dermatologist for a specialist opinion.

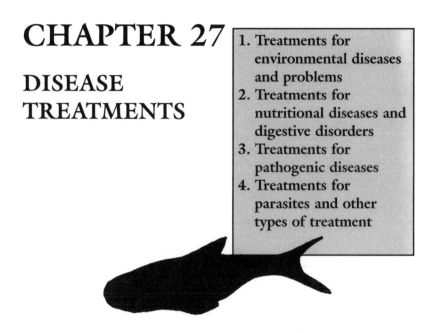

CHAPTER 27

DISEASE
TREATMENTS

1. Treatments for environmental diseases and problems
2. Treatments for nutritional diseases and digestive disorders
3. Treatments for pathogenic diseases
4. Treatments for parasites and other types of treatment

This chapter catalogues chemical and other methods of treatment generally used to treat or prevent disease in tropical aquarium fish. For ease of reference we have, where possible, grouped these treatments in parallel with the disease groupings used in Chapter 21, Fish Diseases, and references are made to subsections within that chapter (e.g. Hypoxia, 1.3.3). There is, however, generally no direct one-to-one correlation between specific diseases and specific treatments, so the latter are simply listed alphabetically within each group. These main groups are followed by a number of other types of treatments with less specific usages. An alphabetical index of all the treatments covered is provided in Table 22; Chapter 24 should be consulted for practical details of preparing and administering medications.

Sourcing of chemical treatments will vary from country to country, depending on local legislation. Antibiotics, for example, are prescription-only drugs in some countries, but available freely over-the-counter in others. Thus some aquarists may have to approach their veterinarian to obtain the drugs or chemicals they require. In any case, veterinary assistance may be required as regards dosage, and sometimes administration, for example where injection is necessary. Other chemicals may be available from the pharmacist or the aquarium store. Wherever possible, potential sources have been indicated under the entry for each medication.

In addition to the medications listed in this chapter, a number of proprietary aquarium remedies are available from aquarium stores. Their availability has been mentioned where relevant, but specific brand names have not been included. These remedies should always be used strictly in accordance with the manufacturer's instructions and warnings.

Note: Gallons quoted in dosages are imperial gallons 1 US gallon = 0.8 imperial gallon.

1. TREATMENTS FOR ENVIRONMENTAL DISEASES AND PROBLEMS

This category includes chemical treatments used to remedy environmental diseases and problems, including pests (Chapter 22). It must be stressed that avoidance and prevention of adverse environmental factors should be the norm. The regular need to use chemicals to resolve environmental problems is a sure sign of ignorance, sloppiness, or laziness on the part of the aquarist. Environmental problems for which chemical treatments are available include oxygen depletion (Hypoxia, 1.3.3), nitrite poisoning (1.2.10), and various pests such as snails, algae, planarians and copepods.

It is important to bear in mind that destroying pests, whether animal or plant, does not remove their residues from the aquarium, and that the resulting increase in organic wastes may cause a temporary filter overload with concomitant ammonia/nitrite toxicity. The greater the bio-mass of the pests being treated chemically, the greater the likelihood of serious after-effects.

Some treatments for environmental problems include:

Copper
Copper is an effective molluscicide (snail destroyer). Several copper-based snail treatments are commercially available; however, all copper treatments are potentially toxic to fish. Moreover, the general warning about filter overload applies. In the case of substrate-dwelling snails, the use of a molluscicide will result in innumerable dead snails remaining hidden in the substrate, their rotting corpses posing a serious pollution threat. For these reasons, mechanical removal of live snails is safer.

Hydrogen peroxide
For general discussion see under Treatments for Bacterial Diseases P.315.

Hydrogen peroxide can be used as an 'oxygen donor', for rapid emergency rectification of hypoxic conditions (1.3.3), in the aquarium. Dosage is at the rate of 1-2 ml of 3% solution per 10 litres (5-10 ml per 10 gallons) of aquarium water. The hydrogen peroxide stock solution should be partially diluted before it is added to the aquarium – that is to say, mix the required amount of stock solution with approximately 10 times as much aquarium water. The resulting solution should ideally be poured in front of the filter outlet to ensure rapid dispersal throughout the tank, failing which manual stirring of the aquarium is suggested. The tank should be aerated during treatment. Overdosing will cause further stress and possibly serious physical harm to the fish, and *must* be avoided.

It is also important to identify the underlying cause of the hypoxia, and under normal conditions this, together with increased aeration, will be sufficient treatment without resorting to the use of hydrogen peroxide.

Table 22 Alphabetical List of Drugs and
Other Treatments Discussed in Chapter 27.

(Note: in the following list 'anti-parasite' refers to the larger parasites covered in Chapter 21, section 4.2; treatments for protozoan parasites are categorised as 'anti-protozoan'.)

Drug/Treatment	Group	Page
Acriflavine	Bactericide	P318
Benzocaine	Anaesthetic	P330
Bleach	Disinfectant	P331
Chloramphenicol	Bactericide (antibiotic)	P318
Copper	Environmental/anti-protozoan	P314/323
Di-metronidazole	Anti-protozoan	P324
Epsom salts	Dietary	P316
Fenbendazole	Anti-parasite	P327
Flubendazole	Anti-parasite	P327
Formalin	Anti-protozoan/anti-parasite	P324/327
Furanace	Bactericide	P319
Gentian violet	Bactericide/fungicide	P319/323
Hydrogen peroxide	Environmental/bactericide	P314/319
Iodine	Bactericide	P319
Iodophors	Disinfectant	P331
Kanamycin	Bactericide (antibiotic)	P318
Levamisole	Anti-parasite	P327
Magnesium carbonate	Dietary	P316
Malachite green	Anti-protozoan	P325
Mebendazole	Anti-parasite	P328
Mercurochrome	Bactericide	P319
Methylene blue	Bactericide/fungicide/anti-protozoan	P320/325
Metriphonate (trichlorphon)	Anti-parasite	P319
Metronidazole	Anti-protozoan	P325
MS222	Anaesthetic	P330
Neomycin	Bactericide (antibiotic)	P318
Niclosamide	Anti-parasite	P328
Nifurpirinol	Bactericide	P320
Oxolinic acid	Bactericide	P320
Oxytetracycline	Bactericide (antibiotic)	P318
Ozone	Bactericide	P320
Phenoxyethanol	Bactericide/anaesthetic	P321/330
Piperazine	Anti-parasite	P328
Potassium permanganate	Bactericide/anti-parasite/disinfectant	P321/331
Praziquantel	Anti-parasite	P328
Quinines	Anti-protozoan	P326
Salt (sodium chloride, NaCl)	Environmental/bactericide/fungicide/protozoan/anti-parasite	P316/321/323/326/328
Sodium thiosulphate	Environmental	P316
Thermal treatment	Other	P332
Toltrazuril	Anti-protozoan	P326
Tricaine methanesulphonate	Anaesthetic	P330
Trichlorfon	Anti-parasite	P329
Ultra-violet irradiation	Environmental/bactericide/anti-protozoan	P316/322/326
Vitamin supplements	Dietary	P317

Salt (Sodium Chloride, NaCl)
For general discussion see under Treatments for bacterial diseases, below.
1) Salt can be used to combat infestations of *Hydra*. Complete eradication may prove difficult without stripping down and scrubbing the aquarium surfaces and washing the gravel, decor, and underwater equipment in hot salt solution (above 105 °F; 2.5% salt). However, *Hydra* can be kept within bounds in stocked aquaria by adding salt to produce a 0.5% solution, which is maintained for about a week then reduced by several partial water changes at 24-hour intervals. It should be borne in mind that not all fish species are salt-tolerant.
2) Salt can also be used to reduce nitrite toxicity (1.2.10), using a dosage of 50-100 mg per litre. This treatment is useful if the nitrite level is too high to be reduced to safe levels by partial water changes within a reasonable period of time (i.e. before the nitrite kills or seriously harms the fish). This low salt level is tolerated by most fish species, however some may react as badly to the treatment as to the original problem.

Sodium thiosulphate ($Na_2S_2O_3$)
Perhaps better known for its use as a photographic developer (known as 'Hypo'), this chemical is effective in neutralising toxic chlorine (1.2.5) in the domestic water supply. Pure sodium thiosulphate is a white powder, although it is usually purchased from the aquarium retailer in liquid form, as a proprietary aquarium water conditioner or dechlorinator. Commercial formulations vary in strength so the manufacturer's instructions regarding dosage must be followed. Sodium thiosulphate will also neutralise chloramine, but not the toxic ammonia released during the chemical reaction; hence where chloramine is present, it is essential to use a proprietary dechlorinator also intended for chloramine, as this will contain an ammonia remover.

Under normal circumstances these chemicals should be used only to treat tap water before aquarium use, but, in an emergency, they can be used to combat chlorine/chloramine toxicity in the aquarium. There is, however, normally no excuse for this situation arising.

Ultraviolet (uv) irradiation
UV is sometimes used to eliminate blooms of free-floating unicellular algae ('green water'), particularly in ponds. For full discussion of the usage of UV, see under Treatments for Bacterial Diseases.

2. TREATMENTS FOR NUTRITIONAL DISEASES AND DIGESTIVE DISORDERS

Included in this category are treatments used to remedy problems arising from incorrect feeding. It must be stressed that prevention is far better than cure in the case of such ailments. See also Chapter 8, Nutrition; Dietary Problems (2.0).

Some treatments used for digestive and dietary problems:

Epsom salts (hydrated magnesium carbonate, $MgSO_4: 7H_2O$)
Epsom salts are sometimes effective against Constipation (2.1) in fish. Treatment is

via a long-term bath (1-3 days), normally in a hospital tank, using a dosage of 1 level teaspoon per 4 gallons (2.5 g per 18 litres), dissolved in a small volume of aquarium water and added to the aquarium. Raising the temperature slightly (within the tolerance limits of the fish) may assist by increasing metabolic rate. If the treatment is effective, the fish should start to produce faeces within 1-3 days.

Vitamin supplements
Most reputable brands of dried aquarium fish foods contain all the vitamins necessary for good health. Where vitamin deficiency (2.5) problems do occur, vitamin supplements are available from aquatic retailers; they should be administered in accordance with the manufacturer's instructions. The effective routes of administration are orally (i.e. by feeding a vitamin-enriched food) or by injection (by a veterinarian).

It must be stressed that it is neither necessary nor desirable to use vitamin supplements on a regular basis if the fish are fed an appropriate, balanced and varied diet of good quality foods. Feeding excessive amounts of certain vitamins can lead to vitamin toxicity problems in fish.

3. TREATMENTS FOR PATHOGENIC DISEASES

TREATMENTS FOR BACTERIAL DISEASES

Bacterial diseases (3.2) and infections are generally treated with bactericides, a generic term for chemicals which kill bacteria. Bactericides may be used to kill pathogenic bacteria living on the external surface of the fish or in their tissues (internal bacteria), or elsewhere in the aquarium.

Bactericides include antibiotics, antiseptics, and disinfectants. Some of these anti-bacterials are, strictly speaking, bacteriostatic rather than bactericidal, i.e. they prevent bacteria from multiplying rather than killing them. Bactericides used to treat or prevent external infections (i.e. of the skin or wounds) are termed antiseptics, while those used solely to sterilise equipment are called disinfectants. Disinfectants are often toxic to fish and should not be used where they are present. Some bactericides are also fungicidal, and some disinfectants may also eliminate some parasites.

Bactericidal treatments which can be used in the presence of fish are catalogued here (subdivided into antibiotics and other bactericides), while disinfectants are dealt with later. As well as the treatments included here, a number of proprietary aquarium bactericidal treatments, commonly referred to as anti-bacteria or anti-internal-bacteria remedies, are available from aquarium retailers.

ANTIBIOTICS
Antibiotics are a type of bactericide, but usually treated as a discrete group. Some of the antibiotics produced for human use are also used in veterinary medicine, including in the treatment of bacterial diseases of fish. The majority of antibiotics used for treating fish are those effective against gram-negative bacteria, the group to which most fish-pathogenic bacteria belong.

In some countries, antibiotics for aquarium use are available only via a vet-erinarian; in others, a whole range of these drugs can be bought over-the-counter in aquatic shops. Even where antibiotics are freely available, it is wise to seek veterinary advice regarding their selection and use. Ill-considered and excessive usage of these drugs has led to an ever-increasing number of antibiotic-resistant strains of bacteria, including fish-pathogenic types. In addition, fish which are regularly exposed to antibiotics may suffer diminished immunity to bacterial pathogens. The prophylactic use of antibiotics in some commercial breeding establishments may explain the apparently high susceptibility to bacterial infections of some commercially-reared fish. Many bacterial infections of aquarium fish can, in fact, be treated successfully with other types of medication, allowing antibiotics to be kept in reserve for situations where they are genuinely necessary.

Fish species vary in their tolerance of some antibiotics, so avoid overdosing and monitor fish during treatment for signs of any adverse reaction.

Some antibiotics used for treating fish:

Chloramphenicol
This antibiotic, available as chloramphenicol succinate, is effective against *Aeromonas* (3.2.1) causing Ulcers (3.2.9). It is normally administered by injection as it is not very effective when applied by bath immersion. Injection dosage: 25-40 mg per kg of fish, repeated weekly, or as often as daily in certain circumstances.

Kanamycin
Kanamycin, in the form of kanamycin sulphate, is used particularly for treating Mycobacteria (3.2.6) in fish. It can be administered via a long-term bath: dosage and duration of the treatment may depend on the species and/or the severity of the infection, but is usually between 10 and 100 mg/l for 5-10 days, re-dosing every 1-3 days, with a total of 50% of the aquarium water changed between doses. Kanamycin may also be administered orally in food or by injection (intraperitoneal), but this latter method has been reported as causing toxicity in some fish species.

Neomycin
Neomycin sulphate is used against some gram-positive bacteria and many gram-negative bacteria species. Treatment is by bath immersion at the rate of 250 mg per 4.55 litres (1 gallon), repeated after 2-3 days. The drug is known to destroy nitrifying bacteria, and hence should not be used in aquaria with biological filtration, but in a hospital tank.

Oxytetracycline
Oxytetracycline hydrochloride is used to treat systemic bacterial infections (3.2). It can be administered by bath immersion (long-term bath of 5 days, at 20-100 mg/litre, repeated if necessary), injection (10-20 mg per kg of fish, again, repeated if necessary), or orally, in food (60-75 mg per kg of fish per day, for 7-14 days).

OTHER BACTERICIDES:

Acriflavine
Acriflavine was formerly often used to treat (by bath immersion) various bacterial (3.2) and protozoan (4.1) infections, and even today is a component of some proprietary remedies as well as being used as a topical treatment for superficial skin

damage. Several problems with the use of acriflavine have come to light. Notably, it has been proven to cause reproductive failure in *Poecilia reticulata* (the guppy) and possibly other species. It is also harmful to aquatic plants. The emergence of acriflavine-resistant strains of fish bacteria has further diminished its usefulness.

Furanace (also known as Nifurpirinol)
Furanace is an antimicrobial chemical used to treat internal (systemic) bacterial infections. In some countries it is available only on prescription. It can be administered by short- or long-term bath (dosage: 1-10 mg/litre for 5-10 minutes, or 0.01-0.1 mg/litre for several days, respectively), or orally in medicated food (2-4 mg per kg of fish, daily for 5 days, with medicated food being fed exclusively during the treatment period).

Hydrogen peroxide (H_2O_2)
This chemical has powerful oxidising properties but decomposes into harmless water and oxygen; hence it is commonly used as a disinfectant in human medicine since it leaves no undesirable residues. It is also sometimes used as an aquarium antiseptic, as well as for treating external protozoan infections and as an emergency remedy for hypoxic aquarium conditions.

Hydrogen peroxide is available from pharmacists as an aqueous solution, whose strength is given either as the percentage H_2O_2 in water, or as the number of volumes of oxygen produced by 100 ml of the solution on decomposition. Typical pharmacy strength solutions are 6% (= 20 volumes) in the UK, or 3% (= 10 volumes) in the USA.

Antiseptic/anti-protozoal treatment is normally by short-term bath at the rate of 10 ml of 3% solution to 1 litre of water (40 ml per gallon), for a maximum of 5-10 minutes, less in the event of visible distress (jumping, respiratory distress). Tolerance is species-dependent.

Gentian violet
Gentian violet, available from pharmacists, is a combination of three dyes: methyl rosaniline, methyl violet, and crystal violet. It has bactericidal and fungicidal properties. A 1% solution is sometimes used for the topical treatment of external conditions such as bacterial Fin rot (3.2.2) as well as bacterial (3.2) and/or fungal (3.3) infections of wounds. It is important not to allow the chemical to come into contact with the fish's eyes or gills. Warning: gentian violet stains human skin, clothing, aquarium nets etc, a vivid purple colour.

Iodine
This has long been used in human medicine. Pharmaceutical iodine is not normally used for aquarium fish, but some proprietary aquarium antiseptics contain this chemical. Dosage and treatment should be according to the manufacturer's instructions.

Mercurochrome
Mercurochrome, available from pharmacists, is often used as a topical aquarium antiseptic and fungicide for the treatment of wounds. A 2% stock solution should be applied to the affected area, with the treatment repeated every other day, if

necessary, until the condition is healed. The chemical should not be allowed to contact the gills, and for this reason it should not be applied as a bath immersion.

Methylene blue

Methylene blue is a thiazine dye with bactericidal and fungicidal properties, formerly much used as an aquarium treatment but nowadays somewhat superseded by other medications without its disadvantages: it is harmful to biological filtration, and stains everything (hands, clothes, rocks, gravel, and even silicon sealant) blue. It is also considered to be toxic to plants. Even so, it is a relatively safe and effective treatment for external bacterial and fungal infections as well as certain skin parasites such as *Ichthyophthirius* (4.1.12), the cause of whitespot (4.1.23). It is also a popular treatment for preventing fungal or bacterial attack of eggs (3.3.4). It is available from aquatic retailers in a number of proprietary brands, as a 1 or 2% stock solution. Dosage:

• Treatment of infections in fish: normally by long-term bath, preferably in a hospital tank because of the harmful effects on biological filtration and decor, at a rate of 2 ml of 1% stock solution per 10 litres of water. The dye degrades slowly over a period of days, particularly in the presence of organic materials, so repeat dosing may be necessary.

• Prophylactic treatment against bacterial and fungal infection of eggs: nominal dosage is 2mg/litre, but the usual approach is to add the dye solution to the hatching container a drop at a time, allowing each drop to disperse, until the water is light to medium blue with the eggs still visible to permit observation of their development. The dye is allowed to degrade naturally such that when the larvae become free-swimming and need to feed, first food micro-organisms are not harmed by the dye (but note, in species which have an incubation period of more than 4 days, re-dosing may be needed every second or third day, until the eggs hatch). To help remove the dye and to compensate for the lack of biological processing of wastes in the hatching container, it is advisable to make small (5%) partial water changes daily post-hatching, using carefully matched water (chemistry, temperature).

Nifurpirinol

See Furanace

Oxolinic acid

Oxolinic acid is a synthetic antibacterial compound used to treat systemic bacterial infections caused by *Vibrio* spp. (3.2.11) and other gram-negative bacteria. In some countries it is available only on prescription. It can be administered orally, via medicated food (10 mg of medication per kg of fish, daily for 10 days), or by long-term bath (0.5-2.0 mg/litre for 1-2 days). The effectiveness of bath treatment may decline relative to the degree of alkalinity of the aquarium water, i.e. the higher the pH the less effective the medication.

Ozone (O_3)

Ozone is an unstable form of oxygen produced by the action of ultraviolet radiation or electrical discharge on the free oxygen molecule O_2. The chemical instability of ozone makes it a powerful oxidising agent, whose extra oxygen atom associates readily with both organic and inorganic substances.

Aquarium 'ozonisers' are available which deliver ozone to a special separate chamber through which the aquarium water is pumped. The outflowing water must be vigorously aerated or passed through activated carbon (to remove all ozone residues) before being returned to the aquarium. Even relatively low concentrations of ozone can be ichthyotoxic, such that the residual ozone concentration should be kept below 0.002 mg per litre to avoid stressing, or perhaps even killing, the fish.

Ozone is frequently used in marine aquaria as a potent disinfectant and for its ability to prevent organic discoloration of the water. However, it is rarely used in freshwater systems, largely due to its high running costs. It is effective only in destroying certain free-living stages of pathogens which happen to be sucked into the ozonization chamber.

The effective dosage for killing bacteria and viruses is in the range 1-8 mg ozone per litre per minute, with a contact time of between 2-6 minutes. In the freshwater aquarium, regard with suspicion any signs of distress (especially respiratory distress or other gill problems) or irritation.

Ozone is also potentially dangerous to humans, causing ailments such as nausea, headaches, and depression. Any smell of ozone indicates a level considerably in excess of the safe residual level for fish (and humans too).

Phenoxyethanol (also known as Phenoxethol)

Phenoxyethanol is used as a fish sedative or anaesthetic but also has bactericidal properties, and hence is widely used during surgical procedures on fish. Its main aquarium use is for combating bacterial infections (3.2) and, for this reason, it is a constituent of some proprietary aquarium remedies, which are administered by bath immersion using the dosage recommended by the manufacturer.

Potassium permanganate ($KMnO_4$)

Potassium permanganate is a powerful oxidizing agent which is sometimes used to treat bacterial skin infections and ectoparasites in pond fish, but is not generally recommended for aquarium fish because of the sensitivity of many species to this chemical. Its toxicity increases in line with the degree of alkalinity. It is available from pharmacists in crystal form or as a stock solution. See also Disinfectants, Treatments for Large Parasites.

Salt (common salt = sodium chloride, NaCl)

Salt has been used as an aquarium antiseptic and fungicide for many years, and is still commonly used prophylactically against fungal (3.3) and bacterial (3.2) infections of wounds, although nowadays proprietary aquarium fungicides are preferred for combating existing fungus outbreaks. Salt was also formerly commonly used as a 'tonic', with little or no regard for its appropriateness to the water chemistry requirements of the fish involved, and, erroneously, to 'increase hardness and pH levels' (which it doesn't!).

Because most freshwater aquarium remedies are intended for use on brackish-water fish as well, they can generally be used in conjunction with salt, unless otherwise stated in the manufacturer's instructions. However, it should be remembered that some freshwater fish, likewise many aquarium plants, are highly intolerant of salt, hence treatment should ideally take place in a hospital tank.

It is important to use the correct type of salt for treatment of fish: the product of choice is 'aquarium salt'. Block cooking salt and crystallised sea salt are normally safe, but domestic table salt should be avoided as it usually contains potentially toxic additives. The salt should be pre-dissolved in a small amount of aquarium water, which is then added to the aquarium. Prophylactic dosage is 1-2 level teaspoons of salt per gallon (1-2g/litre), producing a 0.1-0.2% solution. For treatment of established fungal/bacterial infections, use a solution of strength up to 1% (10g/litre) provided the fish shows no signs of distress. This concentration should be achieved gradually over a 24-48 hour period to avoid the risk of osmotic stress and osmotic shock (both 1.1.2), starting with the prophylactic level (0.1-0.2% solution, as above) and increasing the concentration in 0.1% increments every 4-6 hours. In the event of the fish exhibiting distress after any increment in the salt concentration, reduce it again by an immediate partial water change.

Salt is also used to counter nitrite toxicity (see Treatments for Environmental Diseases), for the treatment of Piscinoodinium (see Treatments for protozoan infections), and to dislodge leeches (see Treatments for large parasites).

Ultraviolet (UV) irradiation

UV irradiation is used to eliminate bacteria (as well as some free-swimming parasites and unicellular algae) in the aquarium, and hence is included here. However, it does not eradicate all types of bacteria, etc, so may only reduce, and not necessarily prevent, disease transmission in the aquarium. The efficacy of UV depends on its ability to penetrate the tissues of the target organism. For this reason it is virtually useless in destroying large parasites and cyst- or spore-forming pathogens.

As with ozone, it is employed chiefly in marine aquaria, reflecting the higher monetary value of the occupants. In the freshwater aquarium UV is sometimes used in wholesale or retail premises, for controlling disease in tanks where new stock is constantly being introduced, and for reducing disease transmission in aquaria linked by a centralised filtration unit. However, the use of UV in the domestic aquarium is generally unnecessary, and perhaps actually undesirable, as there is a possibility that the fish's natural defences may be compromised by lack of immunological stimulation (by exposure to bacteria) in UV-treated aquarium water. Such a reduction in immunity could cause problems if the fish were subsequently transferred to an aquarium not treated with UV, and thus exposed to bacteria against which they may not have acquired immunity. UV should never be used as an alternative to quarantine or to compensate for lack of aquarium hygiene.

UV is administered by means of a UV steriliser. It is essential to use only a type designed specifically for aquarium use, always to follow the manufacturer's instructions, and never to look directly at the UV light, as this may cause serious eye damage.

TREATMENTS FOR FUNGAL INFECTIONS

A number of chemicals generally available from pharmacists, and proprietary aquarium fungicides (from aquarium retailers), can be used to treat external fungal infections (3.3) on aquarium fish, usually by long-term bath or topical application. Systemic (internal) fungal infections (3.3.8) are more difficult to combat. Some fungicides can be used to prevent egg fungus (3.3.4).

Unfortunately, some aquarists endeavour to compensate for poor aquarium maintenance and hygiene – which often result in repeated fungal attacks – by using fungicides routinely or prophylactically instead of remedying the underlying problems. Poor conditions are, however, likely to cause other, less obvious, health problems, and constant exposure to fungicidal and other chemicals may itself prove harmful. Some aquarium fungicides include:

Gentian violet
For general details see under Treatments for Bacterial Diseases.

A 1% solution can be applied topically to areas of fungus, but should not be allowed to contact the fish's eyes or gills. Topical application has the advantage of being quick, easy, effective, and of avoiding overall exposure to chemicals in cases where one fish has a small and localised area of fungus.

Methylene blue
For general details, dosage, and administration, (including as a prophylactic against egg fungus), see under Treatments for Bacterial Diseases.

Salt (sodium chloride, NaCl)
For general discussion see under Treatments for Bacterial Diseases, above.

Strong salt solutions were formerly used to treat outbreaks of *Saprolegnia* (3.3.7) and other fish-pathogenic fungi, but this treatment has largely been superseded by proprietary aquarium fungicides. A mild (0.1-0.2%) salt solution, preferably administered in a hospital tank, remains a useful prophylactic following injury.

4. TREATMENTS FOR PARASITES

TREATMENTS FOR PROTOZOAN INFECTIONS
Protozoa are single-celled organisms, mostly microscopic, although a few are just visible to the naked eye. Some species are parasitic, either on the surface of the fish (ectoparasitic) or within its body (endoparasitic). Generally speaking, treatments for ectoparasitic and endoparasitic protozoa are quite different, the latter being far harder to eradicate because the fish's tissues afford a degree of protection against contact with chemical treatments. Partly for this reason, it must not be assumed that all anti-protozoals are equally effective against all protozoa. For instance, the vast majority of anti-protozoal treatments available from the aquarium store are ineffective against blood- or tissue-dwelling protozoa, although they may be quite effective in combating many (but not all) of the ectoparasitic types.

When administering anti-protozoal treatments, the normal precautions should be observed: establish whether the fish to be treated may be sensitive to the chemical in question, and be alert for any signs of distress during treatment.

Some anti-protozoal treatments used for fish:

Copper
Copper is effective against some ectoparasitic protozoa. The form usually employed is hydrated copper sulphate ($CuSO_4.5H_2O$), available from pharmacists as crystals or a commercially-prepared stock solution. Proprietary aquarium remedies containing copper, available from aquatic retailers, use chelated copper, which is less ichthyotoxic and more stable. All copper treatments are, however, potentially toxic to fish, and overdosing may cause major tissue damage or even death. The risk of toxicity is greater

in soft water. Tolerance of copper varies from species to species. In addition, copper must never be used where freshwater crabs, shrimps, or certain other invertebrates are present, as it severely affects their respiratory function.

Treatment is administered by a long-term bath (several days) using a concentration of between 0.15mg and 0.20 mg of free copper per litre of water (higher doses are potentially lethal to some fish). Test kits for monitoring copper levels are available from aquatic retailers. The effectiveness of copper treatments is dependent on aquarium conditions: efficacy decreases the higher the pH or the organic load, and in tanks containing calcareous materials.

Di-metronidazole
See Metronidazole, below.

Formalin
(Sometimes incorrectly referred to as formaldehyde, the gas of which it is an aqueous solution).
Formalin has antiseptic, anti-protozoal, anthelminthic (against ectoparasitic flukes), and preservative properties. It was formerly commonly used to treat the ectoparasitic protozoa responsible for Skin slime disease (4.1.18). Although still used widely in aquaculture it has been largely superseded by safer (for both fish and aquarist) treatments in the aquarium hobby. It is normally sold as a 37-40% solution ('commercial strength formalin').

Formalin is administered as either a long-term (several days) or a short-term (10-30 minutes) bath. Quoted dosages in the aquarium literature tend to be somewhat variable, perhaps because of the varying tolerance of different species; and the effects of treatment – beneficial or otherwise – are unpredictable, especially in the case of high-dosage short-term baths, during which the fish should be monitored closely and removed if distressed (e.g. exhibiting respiratory distress, jumping). For this reason, and because the chemical may adversely affect biological filtration, short-term treatment should always take place in a hospital tank, so that the fish can be returned to their normal, unmedicated environment if necessary. The bath should be prepared in advance so that the formalin is properly dispersed – formalin added to a tank containing fish may cause chemical 'burns' to the skin, or gill damage.

Treatment for ectoparasitic protozoa is by long-term (2-3 days) bath in a hospital tank, using 0.15-0.25 ml of commercial strength (37-40%) formalin per 10 litres (approximately 1-2 drops per gallon), mixed with some aquarium water and added to the treatment tank.

Warning: formalin is extremely dangerous to humans if it contacts skin or eyes, and must be washed off immediately with copious amounts of water. Medical attention should be sought. It produces toxic fumes, and hence should never be opened in a confined area. It should be kept in a dark bottle, as when it is exposed to light, paraformaldehyde (which is highly toxic to fish even in very small concentrations) may be formed as a whitish deposit. Paraformaldehyde is potentially explosive and should be disposed of carefully, preferably with expert help.

Malachite green
Formerly a popular aquarium medication used in the treatment of a wide range of pathogens and parasites, especially ectoparasitic protozoa such as *Ichthyophthirius*

(4.1.12) and those causing Skin slime disease (4.1.18). Nowadays it is less commonly used because of possible harmful effects to humans (particularly when used in powder/crystal form, which might be inhaled). It may also harm biological filtration and plants, is poorly tolerated by some fish, and stains hands, clothing, and equipment. It is still, nevertheless, an ingredient of a number of (liquid) proprietary aquarium and pond remedies. Aquarists wishing to use the unadulterated chemical should obtain a ready-mixed 1% stock solution of the zinc-free grade from a pharmacist, and leave handling the dry form to professionals.

Treatment is by bath immersion, and can be either long-term (0.1-0.2 ml of 1% stock solution per 10 litres, repeated once or twice at 4-5 day intervals, each repeat treatment to be preceded by a 25% partial water change) or short-term (1-2 ml of 1% stock solution per 10 litres for 30-60 minutes, repeated on alternate days for a maximum of 4-5 treatments). Treatment should, ideally, be in a hospital tank as the chemical is easily deactivated by the presence of organic residues.

Methylene blue
Methylene blue has been used for many years as an effective treatment against the whitespot (4.1.23) protozoan (*Ichthyophthirius*) and remains a popular choice against this parasite. It is also an effective bactericide and fungicide. For general discussion and dosage/administration, see under Treatments for Bacterial Diseases.

Metronidazole and di-metronidazole
Metronidazole and di-metronidazole were originally developed for the human treatment of anaerobic bacterial and protozoan infections, and have also shown to be valuable in combating Hole-in-head disease (4.1.10) of cichlids, which is believed to be caused, at least in part, by protozoa of the genus *Hexamita*.

In some countries, these drugs are available only on veterinary prescription. Di-metronidazole is normally used only where metronidazole has failed to produce a cure – some strains of *Hexamita* appear to have developed resistance.

Prophylactic use of these drugs is sometimes advocated, especially for discus (*Symphysodon* spp.), but, given good husbandry and attention to stress minimisation, *Hexamita* should not be a problem in otherwise healthy fish.

Treatment is normally by bath immersion, at the following dosages:

• Metronidazole: normally supplied as tablets, which must be crushed and pre-mixed with a little aquarium water, which is then stirred into the tank. Use 50 mg/4.5 litres (1 gallon) of aquarium water, repeated on alternate days for a total of 3 treatments, with an optional 25-30% water change between treatments.
• Di-metronidazole: 5 mg/litre (25 mg/gallon), administered as above, but with 3 treatments at 3-day intervals. Serious or persistent cases can be given a 48-hour bath, in a hospital tank, at a concentration of 40 mg/litre.

Whichever drug is used, all cichlids in the affected aquarium will need to be medicated, but, if this involves only one or two fish, a hospital tank should be used to reduce cost and avoid unnecessary exposure of healthy fish to the drug. Otherwise, the normal aquarium must be medicated. Neither drug appears to have any harmful effect on biological filtration.

If the fish are feeding, then metronidazole-medicated food can be given. The recommended dosage is 1% (by weight), but most aquarists use 'rule of thumb', soaking pellets/flake in metronidazole solution, or mixing a little powder with foods to which it will adhere, for example, chopped prawn or earthworm.

Quinines

Quinines (available from pharmacists and veterinarians) are perhaps best known for their role in the prevention and treatment of malaria in humans, but have also been widely used to combat some protozoan parasites, notably *Ichthyophthirius* (4.1.12). Nowadays, alternative aquarium remedies are more commonly used, although quinine still appears to have value in the treatment of the dinoflagellate protozoa which cause marine velvet disease.

The following quinine treatment has shown success in killing the free-living stage of *Amyloodinium* (marine velvet disease) and may therefore be worth considering for cases of freshwater velvet (4.1.22) (caused by *Piscinoodinium*). Chloroquine diphosphate is applied as a long-term bath (3 days) at a concentration of 10 mg/litre. A repeat dose can be given if necessary. Treatment may be given in the main aquarium or a hospital tank; in the former case, although the drug will decompose with time, it is preferable to make a number of partial water changes, spread over several days, after treatment. Alternatively, filtering over activated carbon removes quinines.

It should be noted that some fish species, and many aquatic invertebrates, have very low quinine tolerance, and it is important to monitor for signs of toxicity (respiratory and other distress) during treatment.

Salt (sodium chloride, NaCl)

For general information see under Treatments for Bacterial Diseases.

Salt can be used to treat *Piscinoodinium* (freshwater velvet disease, 4.1.22) by means of a long-term bath in a solution of 10 g salt/45 litres of aquarium water.

Toltrazuril

This triazinone drug has been used for combating certain protozoan diseases of birds, and, more recently, has been applied experimentally as a bath immersion for the treatment of various fish parasitic protozoa. For example, it appears effective in destroying the parasitic stage of *Ichthyophthirius* (4.1.12) but not the free-swimming infective stage. At present, it is available only on veterinary prescription in some countries, and further research is required before its use by aquarists can be advocated.

Ultraviolet (UV) irradiation

UV has the ability to eliminate some free-swimming organisms, including some protozoa. For general details and administration, see under Treatments for Bacterial Diseases.

TREATMENTS FOR LARGE PARASITES

The majority of the treatments listed here are anthelminthics, chemicals which are effective in eliminating various helminth parasites ('worms'). In the case of fish parasites, this group includes flukes (4.2.8, 4.2.11), nematodes (roundworms, 4.2.10), and cestodes (tapeworms, 4.2.13). These drugs are generally administered via medicated food, though some are effective as a bath treatment. Some anthelminthics are also effective, applied as a bath treatment, against non-helminth ectoparasites such as *Argulus* (fish louse, 4.2.7). Veterinary advice should be obtained where no dosage is given.

Many of the anthelminthics used for fish are also important in human medicine, and hence available only via a veterinarian in many countries. Others, e.g. trichlorfon, are organophosphorus compounds, highly toxic chemicals whose availability is often strictly regulated.

It is important to be aware that the life cycles of some ectoparasites are complex and involve stages which are resistant to chemical treatments and others which are more vulnerable. As the resistant stages can remain viable for extended periods of time, repeat dosing may be necessary to eradicate the parasite completely. For this and other reasons, it is important always to consult the section on the relevant parasite in Chapter 21 before attempting treatment.

As well as the chemicals listed below, a number of proprietary aquarium remedies are available for combating some large ectoparasites. These should be used in accordance with the manufacturer's instructions. Again, it is essential to complete the recommended course of treatment so as to allow time for chemical-resistant eggs to hatch or encysted stages to emerge.

Fenbendazole (proprietary names include 'Panacur')

Used mainly for worm infestations in horses, fenbendazole is also useful in the treatment of fish nematodes, such as *Camallanus* (4.2.3). It can be purchased as a proprietary equine wormer; the powder/granular form, rather than paste, should be used for aquarium purposes. A 3-week course of treatment is required, via a long-term bath at a dose of 2-3 mg/litre, with repeat doses on days 7 and 14.

Flubendazole

A chemical analogue of Mebendazole (qv, below)

Formalin

A 37-40% aqueous solution of formaldehyde gas (this solution is sometimes incorrectly referred to as formaldehyde). For general details see Treatments for Protozan Infections.

For a short-term bath to eliminate flukes (and other large ectoparasites, e.g. *Argulus*, 4.2.7), a dosage of 2 ml of commercial strength (37-40%) formalin per 10 litres (approximately 17 drops/gallon) may be tried, with aeration provided during the treatment, which should last for a maximum of 30 minutes and then only if the fish is not distressed. The bath should be prepared in advance so that the formalin is properly dispersed – formalin added to a tank containing fish may cause chemical burns to the skin, or gill damage.

Levamisole

This drug, available as levamisole hydrochloride, is soluble in water, and used for treating nematode infections (4.2.10). It seems to have only a limited, if any, effect on the eggs of these worms. It is normally administered orally via medicated food, or, for large fish, by tube. Suggested dosage is 5-10 mg levamisole hydrochloride/kg of fish, in medicated food, daily for 7 days.

Mebendazole (proprietary names include 'Vermox')
Used to treat intestinal tapeworms (Cestodes, 4.2.13) and monogenetic flukes
(4.2.8; 4.2.11). It is only poorly soluble in water. For intestinal tapeworms
treatment is orally, once per week for 3 weeks, via food medicated at the rate of
25-50 mg/kg of fish. For monogenetic flukes treatment may be via short-term bath
(100 mg/litre for 10 minutes) or long-term bath (1 mg/litre for 24 hours).

Niclosamide
(Proprietary names include 'Yomesan' and 'Nicloside')
Niclosamide can be used to treat intestinal tapeworms (Cestodes, 4.2.13) and
Spiny-headed worms (acanthocephalans, 4.2.12), but appears to have little or no
effect on the egg stage of the former. It is administered in food at the rate of 50-100
mg per kg of fish per day, with medicated food fed exclusively for 7 days.
Alternatively – and avoiding the need to calculate the weight of the fish – mix 1%
niclosamide with food (e.g. 10 mg of drug/g of food), the medicated food again
being fed exclusively for 1 week. A repeat course of treatment may be needed in both
cases.

Piperazine
Piperazine is supplied as piperazine citrate or piperazine sulphate, and is sometimes
used for the treatment of intestinal nematodes (4.2.10), e.g. *Camallanus* (4.2.3). It
is administered orally, via a medicated food comprising 2.5 mg drug mixed with 1g
of moistened flake or pellet food. This is fed exclusively for 7-10 days. A repeat
course may be necessary after a further 10-14 days.

Potassium permanganate
For general discussion see under Treatments for Bacterial Diseases.
Potassium permanganate has been used to kill some of the larger fish ectoparasites,
but is not the treatment of choice owing to its potential ichthyotoxicity. It can be
used in exceptional cases to combat heavy infestations of *Argulus* (4.2.7), using a
short-term bath (5-10 mg/litre, for 30 minutes).

Praziquantel
Praziquantel is sometimes used to combat intestinal tapeworms (Cestodes, 4.2.13)
and monogenetic flukes (4.2.8; 4.2.11). To eliminate tapeworms it is administered
via medicated food, at the rate of 50 mg/kg of fish per day, the medicated food being
used exclusively for 1-2 days. For monogenetic flukes treatment is by short-term
bath, 2 mg/litre, for 2-3 hours. A repeat bath may be required a week later.

Salt (sodium chloride, NaCl)
For general information see under Treatments for Bacterial Diseases.
Salt can be used to detach leeches (e.g. *Piscicola*, 4.2.6) feeding on fish. This
method is preferred to manual removal with forceps which can result in the leech's
mouthparts being left in the wound where they may cause an infection. The strength
used will not kill the leeches, but encourages them to withdraw their mouthparts
and leave the host in an attempt to evade the saline conditions. The treated fish can
subsequently be placed in a leech-free aquarium while the problem of any remaining
non-feeding leeches or their cocoons is combated with stronger, possibly

ichthyotoxic, chemicals or by breaking down and sterilising the aquarium.

Leech detachment is by short-term bath in 2.5% salt solution. It is usually, but not always, effective. Bear in mind that not all fish are salt-tolerant.

Trichlorfon (also known as Metriphonate)

Trichlorfon is an organophosphorus compound, sometimes used to eradicate a number of fish ectoparasites such as gill (4.2.8) and skin (4.2.11) flukes, *Argulus* (Fish louse, 4.2.7), *Lernaea* (Anchor worm, 4.2.1), but also as an insecticide in horticulture and agriculture. The use of organophosphorus compounds in aquaculture (including the aquarium) is now restricted in many countries, because of the potential neuro-toxicity of these chemicals to man, animals, and the environment. Although the chemical may be available from horticultural and agricultural outlets, it should be used only under veterinary supervision. The percentage content of trichlorfon in proprietary solutions varies and this must be taken into account when calculating the dosage for treating fish.

Trichlorfon is normally applied as a long-term (about a week) bath at the rate of 0.25 mg/litre. It may be added directly to the aquarium and is not known to affect biological filtration. Some fish, notably characins, may be particularly sensitive to trichlorfon, and should be closely monitored during treatment and removed in the event of respiratory distress or other abnormal behaviour (e.g. jumping). The water should be well aerated during treatment, and temperature should not exceed 27 °C (80 °F) or chemical effectiveness may be reduced.

Trichlorfon becomes less effective not only with increasing temperature but also with increasing alkalinity (pH above 7.0), with the result that further dosing may be needed to maintain a therapeutic concentration. The manufacturer's instructions for re-dosing should be followed wherever possible. In the absence of such information, however, as a rough guide (re)dose the average freshwater aquarium (25 °C/ 77 °F, pH 6.5-7.5) as follows: a full dose (0.25 mg/litre; 1 mg/gallon) on day 1, followed by a half dose on day 3 or 4 to compensate for degradation. The fish should remain in the bath for 7 days.

Because of the danger of residual chemical activity after the treatment period in very acid water, it is prudent, where such conditions obtain, to make several partial water changes following treatment.

5. OTHER TYPES OF TREATMENT

ANAESTHETICS

Anaesthetics are sometimes used prior to surgical procedures, for euthanasia (Chapter 25), and for long-distance (especially international) transportation. Mild sedation is sometimes required for calming a fish in preparation for extensive wound treatment and similar out-of-water procedures where the fish may otherwise struggle and injure itself. Deep sedation is needed for procedures such as X-rays and the taking of blood samples, where any movement of the fish would be undesirable or dangerous. Anaesthetics also possess analgesic function, which is necessary to reduce pain during invasive procedures, such as surgery to remove a tumour.

A number of different types of anaesthetic have been used for fish but chemical anaesthetics are nowadays those most commonly used for ornamental fish. In some countries, they are available only from a veterinarian. If incorrectly administered, they may cause unnecessary stress and pain, perhaps even unintended death, so they should normally be used by aquarists only under veterinary supervision.

Chemical anaesthetics are usually administered by immersion (being taken up, and subsequently excreted, via the gills) rather than by injection. Accordingly, dosage is calculated on the basis of water volume rather than on fish body weight, although optimal dosage may vary depending on the species of fish and the health of the specimen to be anaesthetised, as well as environmental factors (e.g. water temperature). Fish that are able to utilise atmospheric oxygen may take longer to become anaesthetized. Because of these influencing factors, it may be advisable slowly to increase the dosage over a period of time until anaesthesia is achieved, particularly when anaesthetising a species for the first time.

Exposure to the dose of anaesthetic required to induce heavy sedation may cause the fish to fall into increasingly deeper stages of anaesthesia until respiratory arrest and death occur. For this reason, the fish should be constantly monitored during treatment and returned to anaesthetic-free water as soon as possible.

Rubber gloves should always be worn when working with anaesthetics as some are considered to be potentially toxic to humans.

Some chemical anaesthetics used for fish:

Benzocaine (chemical name: ethyl-p-aminobenzoate)
Benzocaine is applied by bath immersion. It usually comes in the form of a white powder which is poorly soluble in water and must first be dissolved in absolute alcohol or acetone. A stock solution (e.g. 10 g benzocaine per litre of solvent) will retain its potency over several months of storage under light-free conditions.

The dosage required for anaesthesia or euthanasia is variable, as discussed above. As a starting point, for anaesthesia with recovery 40-100 mg per litre of water (i.e. 4-10 ml of the stock solution (10 g/litre of solvent, suggested above) will induce anaesthesia within a few minutes. The fish should subsequently be transferred to aerated, anaesthetic-free water for recovery. For euthanasia, use an overdose level of 200-300 mg/litre (i.e. 20-30 ml of stock solution/litre). Higher concentrations may be required for some species.

Phenoxyethanol (also known as phenoxethol)
Phenoxyethanol, obtained as a liquid, is applied as a bath immersion, the anaesthetic dose being variable. as mentioned above. It also has bactericidal properties and is thus sometimes used by veterinarians for surgical procedures on fish, and is also a component of a number of proprietary aquarium remedies.

Tricaine methanesulphonate (Alternative chemical name: 3-aminobenzoic acid ethyl ester. Also known under the brand name 'MS222' and as TMS)
Tricaine methanesulphonate is possibly the most widely used fish anaesthetic. Like benzocaine, it comes as a white powder, but has the advantage of being readily soluble in water, although it is more expensive. It is applied as a bath immersion.

The specific dose required for anaesthesia or euthanasia will vary as discussed above. As a rough guide, a dosage of 40-100 mg/litre will induce anaesthesia in many species, allowing recovery if the fish is subsequently transferred to aerated, anaesthetic-free water. Tricaine tends to reduce the pH of water, particularly soft, unbuffered water, and this may stress the fish, so twice the amount of sodium bicarbonate (i.e. to give a final bicarbonate concentration of 80-200 mg/litre) should be added to buffer the pH, before immersing the fish. For euthanasia, use an overdose level of 300 mg/litre mixed with twice the quantity of sodium bicarbonate (i.e. to give a final bicarbonate concentration of 600 mg/litre) before adding the fish.

DISINFECTANTS
Disinfectants are sometimes used on aquarium equipment, but normally only after an outbreak of serious pathogenic disease, especially if involving highly pathogenic microbes (such as some bacteria and viruses) which may persist on equipment that has been in contact with infected fish or water. Disinfectants may also be used on second-hand equipment, as a precaution prior to use.

Aquarium disinfectants include chlorine- and iodine-based chemicals. Both groups of chemicals are inactivated by organic matter so any dirty equipment should be washed before disinfection. Moreover, these disinfectants should never come into direct contact with fish or other aquatic animals, so it is essential thoroughly to rinse the equipment prior to re-use. Likewise, great care is needed if disinfecting porous items – for example some types of substrate materials and filter media - as it may prove impossible to eradicate all disinfectant residues; the safest course may be replacement. (See also Chapter 21, Poisoning, 1.2).

Some disinfectants sometimes used for aquarium equipment:

Bleach
Bleach is a solution of sodium hypochlorite, i.e. a chlorine-based chemical, and readily available as a domestic disinfectant. However, it is highly toxic to fish and is not recommended for aquarium use even though sometimes advocated in the older literature. Even trace amounts may lead to serious skin and gill tissue damage. Bleach is also highly corrosive, and may ruin nylon nets and some other items of aquarium equipment, e.g. those made of metal. It is also lethal to plants.

Iodophors
Iodophors are iodine-based disinfectants, and safer than bleach, although they should nevertheless be used with extreme caution as mentioned above. Commercial iodophor solutions may be purchased from some aquatic retailers or the veterinarian, as a stock solution which requires dilution. Equipment is normally disinfected via immersion or surface wipe, and it is important to adhere to the manufacturer's instructions regarding dilution and exposure time.

Potassium permanganate
For general data see under Treatments for Bacterial Diseases.

Potassium permanganate can be used to sterilise aquarium plants in situations where there is a risk that the plants may be carrying fish pathogens or pests. The plants are immersed in a very dilute solution (rosé-wine-coloured) for 5-10 minutes.

THERMAL TREATMENT
Raising the aquarium temperature may help combat an infectious disease in some situations. Thermal treatment can be beneficial in one or more ways:
• Thermally-induced death of parasites. The protozoan parasites *Ichthyophthirius*

(4.1.12) and *Ichthyobodo* (4.1.11) (= *Costia*) are normally unable to complete their life cycles above 30 °C (86 °F), so raising the temperature to just beyond this critical value for 1 week will effectively eradicate these parasites, assuming the affected fish species are able to tolerate this degree of heat (many cannot).

• Acceleration of parasite metabolism. Increasing the water temperature will generally speed up the life cycles of parasites, and thus shorten the periods spent as chemical-resistant stages (e.g. cysts). When used in combination with a suitable chemical remedy, thermal treatments often effect a faster cure.

• Increasing the water temperature can sometimes influence a fish's ability to combat diseases – within physiological limits, the speed and efficacy of the immune response increases with water temperature. Likewise, an increase in temperature may speed up the metabolic rate, helping the healing process. After treatment the temperature should be returned to the normal, natural level for the fish concerned. Although some aquarists, in particular those keeping discus (*Symphysodon* spp.), routinely keep their fish at unnaturally high temperatures in the belief that this wards off disease, long-term overheating can cause respiratory distress and general stress.

When considering thermal treatments, ensure that the increased temperature will be within the fish's tolerance range. Any increase in water temperature should be effected gradually, e.g. 2 °C (3.5 °F) per hour maximum, to avoid thermal shock.

Raising the temperature carries the disadvantage of increasing the oxygen requirement of the fish and reducing the oxygen-carrying capacity of the water, such that extra aeration may be needed to compensate. Because of the possibility of increased temperature making respiratory activity more arduous, thermal treatment is best avoided where there is, or is likely to be, existing gill damage/inflammation, (e.g. caused by gill infections or parasites).

APPENDIX A

THE ORNAMENTAL FISH INDUSTRY

1. Sources of ornamental fish
2. Conservation of wild fisheries
3. The live fish chain
4. The retail trade
5. Current trends in the industry
6. The influence of the hobbyist

A knowledge of the tropical fish industry is not essential to the successful maintenance of an aquarium. However, the keen aquarist with a thirst for further knowledge may find a little background information of interest.

The tropical aquarium hobby spans well over a century, from 1868 when Chinese paradise fish (*Macropodus opercularis*) were brought to Europe (Paris), where they were successfully kept and spawned in aquaria. By the turn of the century, tropical freshwater aquaria had become very popular, such that opportunities existed for the commercial production of fish to satisfy growing demand. Much of the pioneering work in tropical aquarium maintenance is credited to the Germans, and was later developed on a large commercial scale by the Americans, who built several outdoor ornamental fish farms in southern Florida. Nowadays, literally hundreds of ornamental fish farms exist throughout the world. The ornamental fish hobby currently supports a worldwide industry involved in the supply of livestock as well as the manufacture of associated goods such as aquaria and their equipment, medications, fish foods, books and magazines.

1. SOURCES OF ORNAMENTAL FISH

Advances in fish husbandry techniques, particularly in relation to captive spawnings and fry-rearing successes, have resulted in an increasing number of species being bred under farm or aquarium conditions, rather than wild-caught. Several hundred tropical freshwater fish species are now routinely bred either in outdoor fish farms or indoors in 'fish houses'.

In terms of numbers of fish, the majority of tropical freshwater fish are captive-bred (however some exporting countries, such as those in South America, trade mostly in wild-caught stock). This contrasts markedly with the tropical marine fish trade where virtually all specimens are taken from the wild, mostly from coral reefs.

FISH FARMS
Numerous large-scale ornamental fish farms exist in the United States (especially Florida), Africa, Sri Lanka, Malaysia, Singapore, Thailand, Indonesia, and China (Hong Kong), as well as other regions of the world, preferred localities being those where year-round temperatures are high enough for artificial heating to be unnecessary. Many of the smaller fish farms, such as many of those in Asia, are family-run businesses, and often the whole family live, sleep and work on the farm premises.

The majority of tropical ornamental fish are bred in countries other than those where they originated, often for reasons of infrastructure and facilities (many species come from difficult-of-access regions of Third World countries), but occasionally fish farming takes place close to the natural habitat. Examples are fish-breeding facilities around the shores of Lakes Malawi and Tanganyika in east Africa, which take advantage of the unlimited supply of water with the right chemistry and temperature practically on the premises.

Europe, despite its long history of involvement in the aquarium hobby, is not a significant tropical fish producer, although many high-quality cichlids are produced in Germany. The UK and Germany remain the market leaders in Europe, but the Czech Republic is currently establishing itself as an important European producer of high-quality tropical freshwater fish.

Ornamental fish farms are generally run according to the same principles as food-fish aquaculture, with the emphasis on mass production under intensive conditions. Profit margins per fish can be very small, and the risks of complete wipe-outs due to water pollution or infectious diseases mean that fish farming is a high-risk business.

A brief insight into the mechanics of ornamental fish farming is given below.

FISH FARMING – THE GUPPY
The guppy (*Poecilia reticulata*) continues to be one of the most popular of all tropical aquarium fish. Some fish farmers breed guppies in addition to other ornamental fish species; however several farms are devoted exclusively to guppy production. On many guppy farms, the fish are kept in outdoor concrete tanks or in net cages suspended in ponds. The water depth is typically about 0.3-0.6 metres, and the ambient temperature around 23-28 °C. Guppy farms are often sited where there is a steady supply of brackish water because guppy farmers typically culture their fish in slightly salt water. It should be noted, however, that the guppy is found mostly in freshwater habitats in the wild.

Each farm may hold literally millions of guppies at any one time. About four generations can be produced per year. The cycle of events is basically as follows: selected guppies are used for breeding by the time they reach four to six months of age (the broodstock is usually replaced before it reaches one year old). Pregnant females carry their young for approximately one month, and typical brood size is between 20 and 80. The fry are removed to separate quarters for the early rearing stage. By the time they are about three weeks old, they can be sexed, enabling the males and females to be raised separately to prevent undesirable matings. At two to three months of age, the youngsters are large enough to be sold, but the best specimens are held back as the next batch of broodstock.

Guppy farming is a labour-intensive business, with considerable effort and skill being required to match the appropriate males with females to achieve the desired colours, size, and finnage. Sexing the youngsters is extremely laborious – each tiny fish is transferred to a Chinese soup spoon and sexed by eye!

CAPTIVE BREEDING BY AQUARISTS

At the other end of the scale from fish farming, significant numbers of ornamental tropical freshwater fish are home-bred by aquarists, sometimes simply as an incidental to keeping an aquarium, sometimes as a deliberate source of additional enjoyment and interest, with the added benefit of financial help towards defraying the purchase and running costs of the additional tanks normally involved. In fact, some aquarists progress to becoming semi-professional breeders. The young fish are normally sold to the retail trade or to other hobbyists, although some serious and committed breeders establish professional relationships with wholesalers, sometimes being commissioned by the latter to try to breed new imports otherwise available only as wild-caught specimens, or species where demand outstrips supply from other sources. In general, the market for home-bred fish is restricted to commonplace species for which demand is high, or to unusual or rarely-bred species for which there is a smaller, but otherwise unmet, demand.

WILD-CAUGHT STOCKS (ornamental fisheries)

Large numbers of freshwater tropical fish are still taken from the wild, particularly from the Amazon region of South America, which is home to more than 3,000 freshwater fish species, including aquarium favourites such as tetras and *Corydoras* catfish. Many of the wild-caught species are either technically difficult to spawn in captivity, or simply not economically viable for farming on a commercial basis, perhaps due to limited demand. Wild-caught specimens often command a premium price over captive-bred stock.

The collection of live fish for the aquarium trade provides a source of monetary income for many rural communities, often in remote locations where alternative forms of employment may be scarce or non-existent.

In contrast to the situation in food-fisheries, the type of fishing gear used to collect aquarium species is generally unsophisticated, and includes hand nets, seine nets, cast nets, and fish traps, the choice of gear depending on the species to be caught and the physical nature of the body of water.

COLLECTION OF WILD FISH BY AQUARISTS

Aquarists living in, or visiting, tropical countries, may wish to collect their own stocks of wild fish. It must, however, be remembered that this may require a government licence or other permit, particularly where the fish are subsequently to be exported. Careful research and planning is required. An import permit and other paperwork (e.g. fish health certification) may also be required to bring the fish into the aquarist's own country. National or state agricultural/fisheries departments usually deal with fish export and import documentation.

Even where the necessary official permission has been obtained, the would-be collector should bear in mind that the fish he plans to collect may represent the livelihood of local people, to whom government permission to catch fish is a meaningless formality, and who may resent what they regard as poaching. Local permission must, therefore, always be obtained as well – not only as a matter of courtesy, but also to ensure the safety of the collector.

Consideration must also be given to the conservation status of the fish (see below).

2. CONSERVATION OF WILD FISHERIES

Many freshwater species occur over very limited ranges, perhaps just a few small ponds, and could easily be overfished simply by keen hobbyists (and scientists!). Certain African killifish populations have apparently been fished to extinction by private collectors.

Obviously, there is also a risk that the commercial collection of large numbers of fish from the wild may eventually compromise the viability of natural populations, even where the species is common and widespread. For example, one of the most popular aquarium fish, the cardinal tetra (*Paracheirodon axelrodi*), is still fished from its wild habitats in Brazil rather than mass-produced on fish farms. Moreover, evidence from zoologists in Singapore suggests that overfishing for the aquarium trade has led to the demise of the local populations of six-banded barbs (*Puntius johorensis*), khuli loaches (*Acanthophthalmus semicincta*), harlequin rasboras (*Rasbora heteromorpha*), and pygmy rasboras (*Rasbora maculata*).

Concerns that the cardinal tetra, and other high-demand species, may be overfished for the aquarium industry have prompted research programmes to investigate and develop sustainable ornamental fisheries. One such programme is currently in progress in the Brazilian Amazon, and it is hoped that similar schemes will be established in other heavily-fished regions. At present, however, studies on the impact of commercial aquarium fish collectors on wild stocks remain scant, due largely to insufficient money and resources being channelled into this field of conservation research. A recent, and constructive, innovation is a levy on exports of ornamental fish, in order to fund such research.

RELEASE OF ORNAMENTAL FISH INTO THE WILD

The release of aquarium fish by aquarists and fish farmers (be it accidental or intentional) has sometimes had a serious impact on native fish faunas. Often the exotic escapees out-compete the native fish, as has happened in North America, Mexico, and parts of south-east Asia.

Aquarists must therefore never release their aquarium (or pond) fish into the wild. In many countries, this is illegal and punishable by a fine or imprisonment.

3. THE LIVE FISH CHAIN

Most of the tropical fish encountered in the aquarium trade have been transported for hundreds or thousands of miles from their place of origin. The long-distance transportation of aquarium fish is therefore an important part of the ornamental fish trade.

Moreover, an ornamental fish may pass through several hands between the time it leaves the fish farm or place of capture to the point where it is released into the aquarist's aquarium. The chain of handlers typically involves the fish farmer or fisherman, exporter, carrier, importer, wholesaler (who is sometimes, but not always, the importer), retailer, and finally the aquarist. In some cases, there may be extra links in the chain, for example various holding facilities necessary in order to consolidate a consignment for export.

HOLDING FACILITIES

Much of the collection of wild-caught fish is undertaken piecemeal by native fishermen and at scattered and remote localities, generally far from easy contact with the countries for which the stocks are ultimately destined. In consequence, the next step is for the fish to be assembled at some convenient point prior to the next stage in their journey to the domestic aquarium. They may initially be kept in containers – often cages suspended in their native waters – for days, or even weeks, until sufficient numbers have been accumulated to justify the effort and/or expense of transporting them to a holding station, which will usually receive stocks from many different (groups of) fishermen throughout the surrounding area.

Like the native fishermen, the holding station will normally retain the fish until a worthwhile consignment has been accumulated. Sometimes, local holding stations will themselves supply larger, 'central' ones in the same way, with the fish passing along this established chain of communication until ultimately they arrive at an export station, which will normally be within easy reach of an international airport.

PACKING FOR AIR FREIGHT

Most fish are transported by air, which means that air-freight charges have a significant influence on the final retail price. Bear in mind that fish, unlike other livestock, have to be transported in water, which adds considerable weight (and hence freight costs) to the cargo. Thus, through economic necessity, live fish must be packed at high density in order to minimise the freight cost per fish. The actual density of fish relative to volume of water varies according to size and species.

Typically, fish are packed in plastic (polythene) bags which are filled with approximately one-third water and two-thirds oxygen. Ornamental fish exporters have developed several techniques which maximise packing density without incurring high mortalities. For example, it helps to starve the fish for a couple of days prior to packing – this minimises the amount of waste matter excreted during shipping, and hence reduces the risk of a water quality problem during transit. Various chemicals may be added to the water, for example, granules of zeolite (clinoptilite) which is an ammonia-remover. Some exporters add anaesthetics such as phenoxyethanol to the transportation water, to sedate the fish, thereby reducing their metabolic rate and hence the amount of toxic wastes they produce. Sedation also reduces aggressive behaviour (which might otherwise be heightened under confined, crowded conditions) and hence reduces the likelihood of battle injuries. The metabolic activity of the fish during transport can also be lowered by reducing the water temperature by a few degrees.

Once packed, the bags of fish are placed in styrofoam boxes, which provide protection and thermal stability, and taken to the airport. The timing of the whole procedure is critical. The packing must be completed and the boxes transported to the airport in adequate time for paperwork formalities and loading, but at the same time as late as possible to minimise the time the fish spend packed. In the event of a greatly delayed take-off, the entire consignment sometimes has to be returned to the export station and unpacked, and eventually despatched some days or weeks later, when the fish have recovered from the attendant trauma.

The whole transportation process, from bagging at the exporters to unbagging at the importers, may span 36 hours, sometimes more. Usually the fish are not inspected during this period. Live fish consignments must, however, comply with the International Air Traffic Association's (IATA) Live Animals Regulations.

FROM IMPORTER TO RETAILER

Once they have arrived in their destination country, the fish are collected from the airport by the importer who has ordered them, and taken back to his facility, where they will normally be kept in holding tanks to recover from their journey, pending sale to a wholesaler. Sometimes the importer is also a wholesaler; in either case, it is the wholesaler who eventually supplies retailer customers, normally spread throughout the country.

Importer/wholesaler facilities are generally very large indoor fish-houses, with space heating rather than separate heating for each tank or vat. Many employ separate filtration systems, commonly air-driven, for each tank, as the likelihood of disease is high in newly-imported stock, and the risk of this being spread by a centralised filtration system proportionately high. Because of the likelihood of disease, new stock is commonly treated prophylactically, in particular for ectoparasites. The stock is observed for signs of other diseases and any that manifest are, of course, treated. Some losses from the stress and other problems associated with transportation (see below) are, unfortunately, inevitable.

For each subsequent stage in their journey to the retailer the fish must be re-packed, again in polythene bags, with oxygen but not usually anaesthetics (as the journey is shorter), and then in styrofoam boxes. They are generally transported to their destination by a professional carrier service or by the importer/wholesaler's private transport.

At the retail outlet, they are again unpacked and, ideally, allowed a quarantine/recovery period before sale to the hobbyist.

Fish which have been subjected to the various stages of the transportation chain are inevitably stressed and this stress can have a deleterious effect on the immune system, rendering the fish susceptible to disease.

The increased likelihood of health problems during or after transportation means fish should be quarantined at one or more stages in the chain, the quarantine period serving not only to allow any latent disease to manifest and be treated, but also to enable the fish to recuperate after their ordeal. Ideally, they should receive a final quarantine period in the retailer's tanks before being made available to the customer. Unfortunately, this does not always happen.

4. THE RETAIL TRADE

Under normal circumstances, the retail trade will be the only part of the fish chain with which the average aquarist has any contact.

Retail outlets can be highly variable in type and quality (Chapter 1). They may range from a few tanks in a general pet store to massive emporia of warehouse dimensions, by way of small, old-fashioned shops, specialist dealers concentrating on one or more types of fish, and departments in garden centres and home-improvement outlets. It is impossible to make any general value judgement regarding quality of stock and service from the size, type, or location of the retail store, although specialists are usually among the better outlets because they depend on drawing custom from far afield by virtue of their reputation, as they are unlikely to find a sufficiently large local market for their speciality. Moreover, the proprietors of such outlets tend themselves to be enthusiasts regarding their speciality, i.e. their interest extends beyond their immediate profits.

THE PRICE OF FISH

Those aquarists who complain about the high retail price of fish should bear in mind the various costs involved in bringing tropical fish to the hobby: the expense of culture or capture; cost of air freight; and wages for the suppliers, exporters, importers, wholesalers, and retailers. As mentioned earlier, the live fish industry is a high-risk business – a disease outbreak or water quality problem can result in heavy mortalities and hence great economic losses.

It is also worth reflecting that many aquarium species were far more expensive in the past than they are now, even without taking inflation into account. In fact, several species of tropical freshwater fish can nowadays be purchased for little more than a bar of chocolate, partly as a result of overproduction by fish farmers, and this low price has led to some despicable hobbyists treating their fish as little more than disposable items. Overheard comments in aquarium shops, such as, "If it dies, we'll get another next week", reveal an uncaring mentality which is sadly not uncommon. In the authors' opinion, the ornamental fish industry would benefit if the retail prices of many species were significantly increased; the care afforded to the fish by the aquarist and by traders/shippers would probably improve as a result.

5. CURRENT TRENDS IN THE INDUSTRY

QUANTITY RATHER THAN QUALITY

Although many fish farmers make every endeavour to produce quality fish, mass-production of some species has led to a serious loss of quality, not only in visible characteristics such as colour, but also in vigour. The results are commonly colourless, stunted, and unhealthy, compared to their wild forebears. Of course, at least part of the blame must fall upon the aquarist for demanding cheap fish, or for buying such poor-quality stock and thus supporting the market, even though this is often the result of ignorance of what good stock looks like, because it is so rarely available.

Another problem derives from techniques used in mass-production. Eggs are usually hatched artificially, even in species where the parents would naturally tend eggs and fry (see Chapter 8). This method not only ensures that there is no danger of egg cannibalism, but may also increase yields in species where a replacement clutch is produced if the first is lost. Unfortunately, there is increasing evidence that parental care may be a learned, rather than an inherited, characteristic in one group of fish, the cichlids, much of whose popularity with aquarists lies in their guarding of their eggs and fry. Artificially hatched and reared stock, lacking in parental care behaviour, is increasingly a source of frustration for many would-be cichlid breeders.

'MAN-MADE' FISH

There is a long-established and continuing trend among fish farmers towards diversifying their stock by developing new strains of aquarium fish, especially the popular species such as guppies, mollies (*Poecilia* spp.), platies (*Xiphophorus* spp.), and angelfish (*Pterophyllum scalare*). By skilful selective breeding techniques they have produced new colour patterns, longer fins, and even different body shapes. For instance, several popular species are nowadays available in an albino form.

Some concern has been expressed regarding the production of strains with abnormal – deformed – body shapes. The so-called 'balloon molly', as its name suggests, has an 'inflated' stumpy body rather than the streamlined shape of the normal wild form. In common with the extremely long-finned strains, these stumpy-bodied fish often exhibit swimming difficulties and, partly for this reason, the ethics of producing such abnormal varieties has come into question.

Selective breeding techniques are a traditional, though often labour-intensive, method of creating new colour strains. In recent years, however, new colour forms have been created by simply injecting fish with brightly-coloured dyes. Pale-bodied fish, such as albinos, or those with semi-transparent bodies, are most commonly used for this form of artificial coloration. As with the stumpy-bodied varieties, there is much condemnation of the injection process, which is known to cause high mortalities and may induce stress-related disease outbreaks in the injected fish.

Hybridisation provides another method of achieving new forms. An aquarium example of hybridisation is the red parrot cichlid which is thought to be the product of three distinct genera of cichlids, though its exact origins are a well-kept trade secret. The red parrot hybrid also has a deformed body shape, and is prone to buoyancy problems.

NEW TECHNOLOGIES
New technological advances are increasingly being applied to ornamental fish production. Some of these advances are outlined below.

Hormone-induced breeding
Artificially induced spawning techniques, in which the broodstock is injected with hormones, have enabled difficult-to-breed species to be produced on a commercial basis, examples being the freshwater 'sharks' (e.g. *Labeo* spp.) and synodontid catfish. Hormone injection is unsuitable for use on many tropical freshwater fish, due to their small size, but recent advances, such as using hormones delivered via the food or as a bath immersion, may soon avoid this size limitation, enabling more of the smaller species to be commercially produced in captivity.

Single-sex offspring
The production of single-sex offspring, using hormone-induced sex reversal, is well established in food-fish culture and is now being applied to the commercial production of certain ornamental species.

The ability to produce batches of all male fish is economically advantageous for those species in which the males are more attractively coloured or have larger fins than the females, and hence command a higher price. Examples are the guppy, mollies, the dwarf gourami (*Colisa lalia*), and the Siamese fighting fish (*Betta splendens*). Males of these species sell (export price) for between two and four times the price of females. To achieve all-male fish, the youngsters are given a course of food impregnated with an androgen (male hormone). Sex manipulation has one additional benefit, namely that the fish farmer, who has invested time and effort in developing a new strain, can maintain his monopoly on production by selling mono-sex fish and hence prevent others from propagating the bloodline.

Not all batches of exclusively male fish are the result of hormone treatment, however.

In the case of some species, where males are polygynous (mate with multiple females) rather than breeding in pairs, there is some evidence that the reason for the imbalance of the sexes is that the majority of females are being retained by the breeders in order to maximise output. Only relatively few males are needed for fertilisation purposes.

Given that, for many aquarists, a major part of the enjoyment of fishkeeping lies in producing the next generation, the ethics of both techniques are again questionable.

Hormone-induced sterility

Male hormones are also sometimes used, in overdose, to effect sterility in male fish, the object being to prevent the amateur aquarist from successfully breeding the stock he has purchased and thus competing with the professional. Hormone-sterilised males appear normal, exhibit normal courtship behaviour, and even go through the motions of fertilising the eggs, but viable sperm is not produced. This technique has reportedly been used on dwarf cichlids, particularly species which have only recently been introduced from the wild. This use of hormones must, therefore, be regarded as unethical, as there is, obviously, no question here of the fish farmer protecting years of effort in producing a man-made strain, and the customer is unknowingly purchasing stock which is useless for breeding purposes. The authors' view is that sterile stocks should be labelled accordingly, so that the customer can make an informed decision as to whether or not to buy.

6. THE INFLUENCE OF THE HOBBYIST

Like any type of business, the ornamental fish industry has both positive and negative aspects. In the final analysis, the customer – the aquarist – has the power to encourage the good and weed out the abuses, provided he is able to recognise what is beneficial to the hobby and what is detrimental.

The key, as in so many aspects of life, is education and knowledge. Unless the aquarist knows that a fish is deformed, poorly coloured, or unsuitable for his aquarium, he may unknowingly support abuses through ignorance. Few people buy balloon mollies or red parrots when it has been explained to them that these fish are deformed and probably suffering as a result. People who have seen photographs of beautiful, vibrantly-coloured wild fish usually want to see similar specimens in their own aquaria, not those that have been mass-produced without any thought for maintaining natural characteristics and vigour. Some commercial breeders breed selectively and produce good-quality fish – poor quality is not an inevitable adjunct of mass-production.

Every aquarist can play a part by buying on an informed and selective basis, rather than simply accepting what is conveniently available or cheapest. By insisting on quality fish and equipment, and by refusing to buy what is unnecessary, undesirable, poor-quality, or unfriendly to the environment, every aquarist can help encourage his retailer to apply the same principles in his own dealings with his suppliers and so on, back down the chain of supply. The best aquarium stores, wholesalers, importers, breeders, and manufacturers require no such 'coercion', already valuing their reputation for quality, service and fair dealing as an essential part of their success and prosperity. They deserve the aquarist's support.

APPENDIX B

SOURCES OF FURTHER INFORMATION

The list of books and journals below is far from exhaustive, and new books are constantly being published. A sensible approach is to borrow books from the public library (or other aquarists) for evaluation, and to then buy those thought likely to be of continuing use or interest. Most good books contain a bibliography, which may prove a fruitful source of further suggestions for additional reading.

Aquarium and pet stores sometimes stock a (usually) limited range of books, but it may be necessary to order books specially from a general bookstore or a specialist supplier (mail order). A number of specialist suppliers are listed at the end of this Appendix.

1. BOOKS

GENERAL BOOKS ON AQUARIUM
FISH AND/OR AQUARIUM KEEPING
(Some titles embrace groups of fish other
than freshwater tropicals, e.g. coldwater,
tropical marine.)

Axelrod, H.R., Burgess, W.E., Pronek, N.,
and J.G. Walls (frequently updated editions;
co-authors may change with editions), *Dr
Axelrod's Atlas of Freshwater Aquarium Fishes*.
TFH Publications, Inc., Neptune City, NJ,
USA. (A mammoth illustrated catalogue
covering thousands of freshwater fish species.)

Bailey, M. and G. Sandford (1995), *The
Ultimate Aquarium*. Anness Publishing Ltd.,
London. 256pp. (Sound practical advice on
setting up and maintaining an aquarium (part
1), plus details of the care and breeding of
major groups of ornamental fish (part 2). The
two parts are also available separately, as
Caring for your Aquarium and *The New Guide
to Aquarium Fish*.)

Bailey, M., and N. Dakin (1998), *The
Aquarium Fish Handbook*. New Holland,
London. 159pp. (The biotope approach to
keeping freshwater, brackish, and marine
tropicals.)

Coffey, D.J. (1986), *The Encyclopaedia of
Aquarium Fish*. Treasure Press, London. 224
pp. (An A-Z of fish and aquarium terms,
covering freshwater and marine systems.)

Riehl, R. and H. Baensch (1987), *Aquarium
Atlas*, Vols. I, II, III. Mergus, Germany.
(Comprehensive three-volume encyclopaedia
of species.)

Sterba, G. (1967), *Freshwater Fishes of the
World*. Studio Vista, London. 879 pp.
(Restricted in scope because of its age, but
still a useful guide to species that have been
in the aquarium hobby for many years. Out
of print, but should be available from
libraries.)

Van Ramshorst, J.D. (managing editor) (1991), *The Complete Aquarium Encyclopaedia of Tropical Freshwater Fish*. The Promotional Reprint Company Ltd., Leicester, for Bookmark Ltd. 391 pp.

BOOKS DEALING WITH SPECIFIC GROUPS OF FISH

Au, D. (1998), *Back to Nature Guide to Discus*. Fohrman, Sweden. 126pp. (Up-to-date sensible basic guide to maintenance and breeding.)

Axelrod, H.R. and W.E. Burgess (1979), *Freshwater Angelfishes*. TFH Publications, Neptune City, NJ, USA. 93pp.

Burgess, W.E. (1989), *An Atlas of Freshwater and Marine Catfishes*. TFH Publications, Neptune City, NJ, USA. 784pp.

Dawes, J. (1991), *Livebearing Fishes – A Guide to their Aquarium Care, Biology and Classification*. Blandford, London. 240 pp.

Géry, J (1977), *Characoids of the World*. TFH Publications, Neptune City, NJ, USA. 672 pp.

Hellner, S. (1990), *Killifish*. Barrons Educational Series, New York. 72 pp.
Keenleyside, M. (ed.) (1991), *Cichlid Fishes: Behaviour, Ecology, and Evolution*.

Chapman & Hall, London. 378pp. (A compendium of scientific papers, of interest to the serious cichlid aquarist.)

Konings, A. (ed.) (1991), *Enjoying Cichlids*. Cichlid Press, Germany. 240pp. (Good general guide to the family and its maintenance.)

Konings, A. (1995), *Malawi Cichlids in their Natural Habitat* (2nd edition). Cichlid Press, Germany. 352pp.

Konings, A. (1998), *Tanganyika Cichlids in their Natural Habitat*. Cichlid Press, Texas, USA. 272pp.
Lambert, D. and P. Lambert (1995), *Platies and Swordtails*. Blandford, London. 124 pp.

Lambourne, D. (1995), *Corydoras Catfish*. Blandford, London. 127 pp.

Linke, H. & W. Staeck (1994), *African Cichlids I: Cichlids from West Africa*. Tetra Press, Germany. 200pp.

Linke, H. & W. Staeck (1994), *American Cichlids I: Dwarf Cichlids*. Tetra Press, Germany. 232pp.

Loiselle, P.V. (1994), *The Cichlid Aquarium*. Tetra Press, Germany. 447pp.
S cheel, J.J. (1990), *Rivulins of the Old World*. TFH Publications, Neptune City, NJ, USA. (Old world killifish by a recognised authority.)

Schulte, W. (1988), *Piranhas in the Aquarium*. TFH Publications, Neptune City, NJ, USA. 128 pp.

Scott, P.W. (1987), *A Fishkeeper's Guide to Livebearing Fishes*. Salamander, London. 117 pp.

Seuss, W. (1993), *Corydoras*. Dähne Verlag, Germany. 218pp.

Stawikowski, R. & U. Werner (1998), *Die Buntbarsche Amerikas*, Vol. I. Eugen Ulmer, Germany. 540pp. (By far the most comprehensive work available on large and medium-sized neotropical cichlids, available at present only in German. A second volume, covering the remaining species, is in preparation. Possibility of English versions later.)

Walker, B. (1974), *Sharks and Loaches*. TFH Publications, Neptune City, NJ, USA. 160pp.

Wischnath, L. (1993), *Atlas of Livebearers of the World*. TFH Publications, Neptune City, NJ, USA. 336 pp.
In addition the following series of books on ornamental fish are available, with further titles likely in the future:

Aqualex (Dähne Verlag, Germany; website at http://www.aquanet.de). (Pictorial softback catalogues of groups of fish, with maintenance and behaviour hints. Volumes on Malawi and Tanganyika cichlids published to date. Accompanying CD-ROM available for both books, plus CD-ROM *Digital Lexicon of Tropical Freshwater Fish* covering 800 species.)

Aqualog (Verlag A.C.S, Germany; website at http://www.aqualog.de). (Very similar to *Aqualex* in concept, but no CD-ROM versions). Most recent volumes hardback. Also maintenance guides, with background information on the groups covered. Published to date: Catalogues of Neotropical Cichlids (3 vols), Discus and Angelfish, Malawi Cichlids (two volumes), Livebearers, Old World Killifish (two volumes), Labyrinth Fish, Loricariid Catfish, *Corydoras* Catfish, Rainbowfish, Freshwater Stingrays; maintenance guides on Malawi Cichlids; Freshwater Shrimps, Crayfish, and Crabs; Loricariid Catfish; Discus; Rainbowfish; Freshwater Stingrays.)

Back to Nature (Fohrman Aquaristik, Sweden). (Basic guides to groups of fish, with general maintenance details and catalogue of species with specific details. Published to date: Malawi Cichlids; Tanganyika Cichlids; Catfish; Discus; Plants.)

REGIONAL FISH FAUNAS:
Note: Some of these books are hard to track down, and some are occasional publications which are either scarce or only locally available. See below for a list of specialist book suppliers. There are very few books in the English language which cover the freshwater fish faunas of Central and South America. J = Published in a Journal.

Allen, G.R. (1982), *A Field Guide to the Inland Fishes of Western Australia*. Western Australian Museum, Australia. xvi + 86 pp. (+ plates).

Allen, G.R. (1989), *Freshwater Fishes of Australia*. TFH Publications, Neptune City, NJ, USA. 240 pp.

Allen, G.R (1991), *Freshwater Fishes of New Guinea*. Publication No. 9 of the Christensen Research Institute, New Guinea. 268pp.

Ataur Rahman, A.K. (1989), *Freshwater Fishes of Bangladesh*. Bangladesh Zoological Survey, Bangladesh. 364 pp.

Bell-Cross, G. and J.L. Minshull (1988), *The Fishes of Zimbabwe*. Zimbabwe National Museums and Monuments, Harare, Zimbabwe. 294 pp.

Brichard, P. (1978) *Cichlids and all the Other Fishes of Lake Tanganyika*. TFH Publications, Neptune City, NJ, USA. 544 pp.

Datta Munshi, J.S. and M.P. Srivastava (1988), *Natural History of Fishes and Systematics of Freshwater Fishes of India*. Delhi: Narendra Publishing House. xviii + 403 pp.

Eccles, D.H. (1992), *Field Guide to the Freshwater Fishes of Tanzania*. (FAO species identification sheets for fishery purposes). Food and Agricultural Organisation, Rome. v +145 pp.

Inger, R.F and P.K. Chin (1990), *The Freshwater Fishes of North Borneo*. (Reprint of the 1962 edition by the Sabah Zoological Society, Sabah, Malaysia) 268 pp. (plus supplementary chapter by P.K. Chin, 47 pp.).

Jayaram, K.C. (1981), *The Freshwater Fishes of India, Pakistan, Bangladesh, Burma and Sri Lanka – a handbook*. Zoological Survey of India, Calcutta. xxii + 475 pp.

Konings, A. (1990), *Cichlids and all the Other Fishes of Lake Malawi*. TFH Publications, Neptune City, NJ, USA. 495pp.

Kottelat, M. (1985), Fresh-water Fishes of Kampuchea. *Hydrobiologica* 121: 249-279. (J)

Kottelat, M. and A.J. Whitten (1993), *Freshwater Fishes of Western Indonesia and Sulawesi*. Gadja Mada University Press, Yogyakarta.

Leggett, R. and J.R. Merrick (1987), *Australian Native Fishes for Aquariums*. J.R.Merrick publications, Australia. 241 pp.

Lim, K.K.P and P.K.L. Ng (1990), *A Guide to the Freshwater Fishes of Singapore*. Singapore Science Centre, Singapore. 160 pp.

Mohsin, A.K.M. and M.A. Ambak, (1983), *Freshwater Fishes of Peninsular Malaya*. Penebrit Universiti Pertanian Malaysia, Kuala Lumpur. xvii + 284 pp.

Munro, I.S.R. (1967), *The Fishes of New Guinea*. Department of Agriculture, Stock and Fish, Port Moresby. 650 pp.

Pandey, A.K. and G.S. Sandhu (1992), *Encyclopaedia of Fishes and Fisheries of India*. Anmol, New Dehli. 7 volumes.

Page, L.M. and B.M. Burr (1991), *A Field Guide to the Freshwater Fishes, North America north of Mexico*. Peterson Field Guide Series. Houghton Mifflin Company, Boston. xii + 432 pp. (+ plates).

Pethiyagoda, R. (1991), *Freshwater Fishes of Sri Lanka*. The Wildlife Heritage Trust, Colombo. xiii + 362 pp.

Roberts, T.R. (1989), *The Freshwater Fishes of Western Borneo (Kalimantan Barat, Indonesia)*. (Memoirs of the California Academy of Sciences, number 14). California Academy of Sciences, San Francisco. xii + 210 pp.

Skelton, P. (1993), *Freshwater Fishes of Southern Africa*. Southern Book Publishers, Harare. xiii + 388.

Smith, N.J.H. (1981), *Man, Fishes, and the Amazon*. Columbia University Press, New York. x + 180 pp. (Not an ichthyofauna book as such, it deals with the fisheries of the Amazon, but contains a useful checklist of foodfish of the Itacoatiara region, Brazil, plus notes on habitats.)

Suvatti, C. (1981), *Fishes of Thailand*. Royal Institute, Thailand. 379pp.

Talwar, P.K. and A.G. Jhingram (1991), *Inland Fishes of India and Adjacent Countries*. Oxford and IBH Publishing Company, New Delhi. 2 volumes.

FISH ANATOMY AND PHYSIOLOGY

Norman, J.R (1975), *A History of Fishes*. 3rd edition, by P.H. Greenwood. Ernest Benn Limited, London. xxv + 467 pp.

FISH NUTRITION

Hepher, B. (1988), *Nutrition of Pond Fishes*. Cambridge University Press. xii + 388 pp. (Scientific text containing a vast amount of information on fish metabolism, digestive enzymes, growth, energy pathways, and the various nutritional requirements of fish.)

FISH HEALTH

Andrews, C., Exell, A., and N. Carrington (1988), *Manual of Fish Health*. Salamander Books Ltd., London. 208 pp.

Burgess, P., Bailey, M., and A. Exell (1998), *A-Z of Tropical Fish Diseases and Health Problems*. Ringpress Books Ltd., Lydney, UK. 392pp. (Comprehensive study of avoidance, diagnosis, and treatment of ill health in fish.)

Butcher, R. (1992), *Manual of Ornamental Fish*. British Small Animal Veterinary Association publication, Gloucestershire, UK. 200 pp. (Aimed primarily at veterinary surgeons.)

Carrington, N. (1990), *The Healthy Aquarium*. Salamander Books, London. 116 pp.
Untergasser, D. (1989), *Handbook of Fish Diseases*. TFH Publications, Inc., Neptune City, NJ, USA. 160 pp.

Noga, E.J. (1996), *Fish Disease, Diagnosis and Treatment*. Mosby-Year Book, Inc., St Louis, USA. ix + 367 pp. (Excellent book, aimed chiefly at vets and advanced fishkeepers.)

FISH BEHAVIOUR

Zupanc, G.K.H. (1985), *Fish and their Behaviour*. Tetra, Germany. 188pp.

FISH BREEDING

Breder, C.M. and D.E. Rosen (1966), *Modes of Reproduction in Fishes*. TFH Publications, Neptune City, NJ, USA. xv + 941 pp. (Still regarded as the definitive work on reproductive strategies.)

Wickler, W. (1966), *Breeding Aquarium Fishes*. Studio Vista, London.

FISH COLORATION
Voss, J. (1980), *Color Patterns of African Cichlids*. TFH Publications, Neptune City, NJ, USA. 125pp. (An interesting insight into the variability and function of colour patterns of one group.)
TAXONOMY
Nelson, J.S. (1994). *Fishes of the World*. John Wiley and Sons, New York. xvii + 600 pp.

Various authors and editors (1985), *International Code of Zoological Nomenclature*. International Trust for Zoological Nomenclature, in association with the British Museum (Natural History), London. 338 pp. (The rules of nomenclature, probably of interest to the advanced aquarist only.)

FOSSIL FISH
Fricklinger, K.A. (1995). *Fossil Atlas – Fishes*. Mergus, Germany. 1,088 pp.
Maisey, J.G. (1996) *Discovering Fossil Fishes*. Henry Holt and Company, New York. 223 pp.

ORNAMENTAL FISH INDUSTRY
Fernando, A.A and V.P.E. Phang (1994). *Freshwater Ornamental Fish Aquaculture in Singapore*. Singapore Polytechnic, Singapore. 123pp.

COLLECTING AND WATCHING FISH
Coad, B.W. (1995), *Fishes – Expedition Field Techniques*. 2nd edn. Expedition Advisory Centre, Royal Geographical Society, London. 97 pp. (Provides practical information on equipment, techniques and the planning of a fish collecting trip. Available from: Expedition Advisory Centre, Royal Geographical Society, 1 Kensington Gore, London SW1 2AR.)
Lavett Smith, C. (1994), *Fish Watching – An Outdoor Guide to Freshwater Fishes*. Cornell University Press, New York. x + 216 pp. (Describes techniques for watching freshwater fish in the wild, from the shore or boat. Information on North American freshwater fish and their habitats.)

AQUARIUM PLANT BOOKS
Christensen, C. (1999) *Back to Nature Guide to Plants*. Fohrman, Sweden. 128pp.

James, B. (1986) *A Fishkeeper's Guide to Aquarium Plants*. Salamander, London. 117 pp.

Muhlberg, H. (1982) *The Complete Guide to Water Plants*. EPP Publishing Ltd. 392 pp. (Extremely detailed reference work covering the biology of aquatic plants plus an extensive systematic catalogue of aquatic plant families, genera and species. Out of print – try library.)

BIOTOPE AND ECOLOGY
Coulter, G.W. (1991), *Lake Tanganyika and its Life*. Oxford University Press. vi + 354pp.

Fryer, G. and T.D. Iles (1972), *The Cichlid Fishes of the Great Lakes of Africa*. Oliver & Boyd, London. 641pp. (Still the definitive general study of the East African lakes. Out of print, but available from libraries.)
Golding, M. (1989), *Amazon, the Flooded Forest*. BBC Books, London. 208pp.

Goldschmidt, T. (1996), *Darwin's Dream Pond*. M.I.T. Press, USA. 274pp. (Lake Victoria – the evolutionary rise and fall of the Lake Victoria cichlid species flock.)

Lowe-McConnell, R.H. (1987), *Ecological Studies in Tropical Fish Communities*. Cambridge University Press. 382pp.

Reid, G.M. (1989), *The Living Waters of Korup Rainforest*, World Wildlife Fund report 3206/A8:1. (West Africa).

2. AQUATIC MAGAZINES AND JOURNALS IN THE ENGLISH LANGUAGE

(Countries are those where published, and do not necessarily reflect availability. Titles are monthly unless otherwise stated.)
aqua geographia (Italy) (quarterly).
Aqualog News (Germany) (bi-monthly).
Aquarist and Pondkeeper (UK).
Aquarium Fish Monthly (USA).
Aquarium Sciences and Conservation (International) (quarterly).
Cichlid News (USA) (quarterly).
Freshwater and Marine Aquarium (FAMA) (USA).
Practical Fishkeeping (UK).
Tropical Fish Hobbyist (USA).

3. SPECIALIST AQUARIUM BOOK SUPPLIERS:

Several companies and individuals deal with specialist, second-hand, and antiquarian titles. Some advertise their services in the aquarium magazines. Here are just a few:

USA:
Aquatic Promotions Inc. PO Box 522842, Miami, Florida, FL 33152.
Tel/Fax +01-305-593-0088.

Gary Bagnall, Bookseller. 310 McMilan Road, San Luis Obispo, CA 93041.
Cichlid Press, 417 Val Plano Drive, El Paso, Texas, TX 79912. email info@cichlidpress.com; website: http://www.cichlidpress.com (Own specialist cichlid publications only).

Finley Aquatic Books, 150 North Road, Pascoag, RI 02859. Email: lfinley@loa.com
Raymond M. Sutton, Jr. Fish Books. PO Box 330, Williamsburg, Kentucky 40769.

The Fish Factory, 676 Mississinewa Road, Chesterton, IN 46304. Tel/fax: 219 929 9575. Email: fishbooks@niia.net

UK:
Animal House (UK), QBM Business Park, Gelderd Rd., Birstall, Batley, West Yorkshire. Tel. +44 1924 479946; Fax. +44 1924 444854. Email: fishadvice@aol.com (Mail order and shop, good selection of up-to-date, good-quality, hobby books.)

Cichlid Press (UK), 1, Copper Oak, East Village, Crediton, Devon, EX17 4DW. Tel/Fax +44 1363 866509. Email: 106326.3671@compuserve.com; website: http://www.cichlidpress.com (Mail order cichlid books/videos and *Back to Nature* series; subscriptions to *aqua geographia* and *Cichlid News*; free advice on obtaining other book/magazine titles.)

Steven Simpson Natural History Books, Rising Sun, Kelsale, Saxmundham IP17 2QY. Tel. +44 1728 604777; Fax. +44 1728 604555. (Specialises in new/second-hand/antiquarian fish books.)

APPENDIX C

GLOSSARY
(What did the authors mean by...?)

This book contains a number of technical and scientific terms, as well as words which form part of fishkeeping 'jargon', which may not be immediately familiar to the reader. It is hoped that this glossary will provide the necessary clarification.

Acclimatisation: adjustment to conditions different to those to which a fish is accustomed or to those a species experiences in nature.

Acoustico-lateralis system: a sensory system in fish, sensitive to vibration, consisting of the ears and head/lateral line (qv) sensory canals.

Acute: (of illness) short-term and severe. cf chronic.

Adsorption:(re filtration) the process whereby contaminants are removed from the water and collected on the surface of a chemical filter medium.

Adipose: fatty.

Aeration: passing air through water in order to circulate it and enhance gas exchange at the surface.

Aerobic: requiring free oxygen for life processes.

Agastric: lacking a stomach.

Albinism: absence of pigment.

Algae: primitive aquatic plants, some of which grow on surfaces in the aquarium. cf green water.

Allopatric: not found in the same area in nature. cf sympatric.

Amelioration: improvement, remedying.

Amphipod: a type of crustacean.

Anaerobic: not requiring free oxygen for life processes.

Anoxic: lacking in oxygen.

Anterior: front.

Anthelminthic: a medication used against helminth ('worm') parasites.

Aquarist: strictly, a person who keeps fish or other aquatic organisms in an aquarium; sometimes also used of pondkeepers, and often interchangeably with 'fishkeeper'.

Asymptomatic: exhibiting no symptoms.

Atrophy: shrink in size with a reduction in, or total loss of, function.

Auricle: external part of the ear (not present in fish).

Bactericide: a chemical that kills bacteria.

Bacteriostat: a chemical that restricts the proliferation of bacteria.

Barbel: a paired sensory structure adjacent to the mouth of certain types of fish.

Batrachian: any member of the group of amphibians that includes the frogs and toads.

Binocular vision: using both eyes in unison to produce a single visual image.

Biotope: a habitat (qv) and the living things it contains.

Buccal: of the mouth cavity.

Buccopharyngeal: of the mouth cavity and pharynx.

Calciferous: (of rocks, gravel, soil) containing calcium salts.

Capillary: a very fine blood vessel (or other tube).

Carnivore: an animal that eats meat. In the case of fish, applied to species that eat other creatures of any type. Piscivores, insectivores, molluscivores (all of which qv) are specialised carnivores.

Caudal: of the tail.

Caudal peduncle: base of the tail.

Chelating: chemical method of 'locking up' metal ions, used in some water treatments.

Chromatophore: a pigment cell.

Chronic: (of illness) long-term, continuing over a long period. cf acute.

Ciliate: (of protozoa) fringed with hairs. cf flagellate.

Circadian: pertaining to the daily (24-hour) cycle.

Coelenterate: member of the taxonomic grouping that includes jellyfish, sea anemones, freshwater *Hydra*, coral polyps, *inter alia*.

Colostrum: a mammal's first milk after giving birth.

Commensalism: the biological relationship where two organisms live together, to the advantage of one or both, without any element of detriment to either (cf parasitism) and without the reciprocally active partnership seen in symbiosis (qv).

Community aquarium: an aquarium containing a number of different fish species that are able to live together in relative harmony.

Community fish: fish suitable for a community aquarium, (qv).

Conspecific: belonging to the same species. cf heterospecific.

Copepod: type (group) of small aquatic crustacean.

Coprophagy: feeding on faeces.

Crepuscular: active during twilight periods (dawn and dusk).

Ctenoid: (of scales) comb-like. cf cycloid.

Culling: the elimination of defective or superfluous livestock, e.g. fish fry.

Cycloid: (of scales) round. cf ctenoid.

Dentition: the teeth; (in taxonomy) the form, number, and position of the teeth.

Dermis: the inner layer of the skin. cf epidermis.

Detritus: debris, rubbish.

Dichromatism: the condition of having two different colour forms. cf polychromatism.

Digenetic: (of parasites) having two (or more) hosts at different stages of the life cycle. Usually in reference to helminths (qv). cf monogenetic.

Diluent: any liquid used to dilute a solution

(normally the same liquid as used to create the original solution).

Dimorphism: the condition of having two forms of a feature. Sexual dimorphism of size, for example, means that male and female are different sizes. cf polymorphism.

Diffusion: free movement of a substance (e.g. gas, solution) to achieve a concentration equilibrium.

Diffusion gradient: free movement of substances to a variable higher or lower concentration.

Diurnal: active by day.

Dorsal: of the back.

Dysfunction: partial or complete loss of function.

Ectoparasite: a parasite that lives on the outside of its host. cf endoparasite.

Elasmobranch: a member of the Elasmobranchii, the cartilaginous fish.

Emaciation: the process of wasting away or becoming abnormally thin; the condition resulting from such wasting.

Emergent vegetation: above-water growth by plants growing in water.

Emerse: out of water. Used to describe the seasonally out-of-water stage of an otherwise underwater plant.

Endoparasite: a parasite that lives inside its host. cf ectoparasite.

Epidermis: the outer layer of the skin. cf dermis.

Epilithic: growing on rock.

Epiphytic: growing on a plant.

Epithelial: of the skin.

Erythrocyte: a red blood cell.

Euthanasia: humane killing.

Exophthalmia, Exophthalmus: eye protrusion.

Extant: surviving, currently existing.

Facultative: of feeding, able to feed on a particular item when available, but not restricted to that dietary item. Also used in other contexts, e.g. facultative plant-spawner. cf obligate.

Family: a group of closely-related genera (see genus) thought to have a common ancestry. See also Chapter 2.

Flagellate: (of protozoa) having a flagellum, a whip-like appendage. cf ciliate.

Flashing: scratching while simultaneously turning on one side.

Fluke: a type of parasite.

Fluviatile: of, or living in, rivers.

Fry: baby fish.

Genetic survival: the survival of an individual organism's genetic material, by passing its genes to a new generation by breeding.

Genus (plural genera): a group of closely-related species (qv) thought to have a common ancestry.

Gibbosity: hump.

Gonads: the organs that produce reproductive cells (eggs and sperm).

Green water: phenomenon caused by the proliferation of free-swimming unicellular green algae (qv) in the aquarium or pond.

Gustatory: of taste.

Habitat: the natural environment of an organism.

Haemoglobin: the red pigment in red blood cells.

Hardness: a measure of certain dissolved minerals in water.

Hardy fish: fish which do not require specialised aquarium conditions, especially vis-a-vis water.

Helminth: a type of worm belonging to the phylum Platyhelminthes.

Herbivore: an animal (incuding fish) that eats vegetable matter.

Herptile: reptile.

Heterospecific: belonging to a different species. cf conspecific.

Horizontal transmission (of disease): spread from individual to individual by contact or via the environment. cf vertical transmission.

Host: the organism on which a parasite lives.

Hybridisation: the cross-breeding of two species.

Hyperproduction: abnormally high production.

Hypha (plural hyphae): strand (of fungus).

Hypogean: underground.

Hypoxic: oxygen-depleted.

Ichthyotoxic: poisonous to fish.

IEX: abbreviation for ion exchange, qv.

Immunoglobulins: special protein molecules which have immune function.

Inbreeding: the mating of closely-related individuals. cf line-breeding.

Insectivore: an animal (including fish) that eats insects (including their larvae).

Insertion (of a fin): the point where the fin is attached to the body.

Interspecific: between different species.

Intracellular: inside a cell.

Intraperitoneal: (of injection) into the abdominal cavity.

Intraspecific: within a species.

Invertebrate: an animal without a backbone, e.g. insects, spiders, worms, crustaceans. cf vertebrate.

Ion: an atom or groups of atoms which possesses an electrical charge.

Ion exchange: process used to treat water, usually to soften it or neutralise pollutants.

Iridocytes: cells in the skin of a fish that reflect light.

Isopod: a member of the Isopoda, a family of crustaceans.

Labial: of the lips.

Labyrinth fish: member of the sub-order Anabantoidea, fish that have a labyrinth, an accessory respiratory organ that enables them to breathe atmospheric air.

Lacustrine: of, or living in, lakes.

Lamella (plural lamellae): (strictly) a thin plate or layer; (of the gills) a filament.

Lateral line: a row of sensory pores along the side of a fish.

Laterally compressed: flattened sideways, i.e. the fish is 'thin' from side to side.

Lepidophage: a scale-eater.

Lineage: ancestry, family tree.

Line-breeding: the careful selective breeding (qv) of a 'pedigree' strain of fish. Line-breeding involves a degree of planned inbreeding (qv), but care is taken to avoid deleterious effects.

Lipid: a type of fat (strictly, a form of fatty acid).

Livebearer: a fish that gives birth to live young instead of laying eggs.

Lymphocyte: a type of white blood cell.

Lysis: breaking down, disruption.

Malaise: ill health.

Marginal: (of plants), growing along the margins of water, commonly with roots in water and (most of the) foliage above the surface.

Maxillary: of the jaw(s).

Melanism: an excess of the dark pigment melanin.

Melanoma: a black or dark tumour.

Melanophore: a dark (black) pigment cell.

Metacercaria: the larval stage of some parasites.

Microbial: pertaining to microscopic organisms.

Milt: fish sperm.

Molluscicide: a chemical that kills molluscs, e.g. snails.

Molluscivore: an animal (including fish) that

eats molluscs (e.g. snails, shellfish).

Monogenetic: (of parasites) having just one host during the life cycle. Usually in reference to helminths (qv) cf digenetic.

Moribund: dying.

Morph: form.

Mouthbrooder: a fish that carries its eggs and/or fry in its mouth to protect them.

Mulm: organic debris that may accumulate in the aquarium.

Myotome: a block of muscle.

Naked: without scales or scutes.

Nares: nostrils.

Nauplius (plural nauplii): a newly-hatched aquatic crustacean.

Necrotic: (of animal tissue) dead (and often decaying).

Nematode: a type of worm.

Neoplasia, Neoplasm: tumour.

Neural: of nerves.

Nocturnal: active at night.

Nomenclature: naming; biologically speaking, the scientific naming of animals and plants.

Nuchal: of the top of the head.

Obligate, Obligatory: of feeding, obliged to feed on one type of food. An obligate piscivore, for example, feeds only on fish. Also used in other contexts, thus an obligate plant-spawner spawns only on plants. cf facultative, opportunistic.

Olfactory: relating to the sense of smell.

Omnivore: an animal (including fish) that eats all types of foods.

Oocyte: egg cell.

Operculum (plural opercula): gill-cover.

Orbit: eye socket.

Osmoregulation: the regulation of the mineral salt concentration of a fish's body fluids vis-a-vis the mineral salt concentration of the water in which it lives.

Osmosis: the flow of water (or other solution) across a semi-permeable membrane.

Outage: (regarding the electricity supply) a break in supply.

Pancaking: a panic reaction involving skimming along the water's surface on one side, usually in flat-sided fish.

Parasitism: the biological relationship where one organism (the parasite) lives on or inside another (the host), with the parasite gaining benefit to the detriment of the host (usually the parasite feeds on the host's tissues). cf commensalism, symbiosis.

Pathogen: an organism that causes disease.

Parturition: the process of giving birth.

Pectoral: of the breast.

pH: the measure of the acidity or alkalinity of water.

Pharyngeal: of the pharynx (the part of the throat opening off the mouth).

Photoperiod: period (within a 24-hour day) during which light is present.

Phytochemicals: literally, chemicals from plants. Phytochemicals are the secondary products of plant metabolism, i.e. the trace compounds (rather than main ones such as carbohydrates and vegetable proteins) used by herbivores and then carnivores as important nutritional elements in the food pyramid.

Phytoplankton: plant plankton (qv).

Piscivore: an animal (including fish) that eats fish.

Plankton: small organisms, animal (zooplankton) and/or plant (phytoplankton), drifting or floating in water.

Plasma: the liquid component of blood.

Poeciliid: a member of (noun), or belonging to (adjective), the family Poeciliidae.

Poikilothermic: cold-blooded.

Polychromatism: the condition of having multiple colour forms. cf dichromatism.

Polymorphism: the condition of having multiple forms. cf dimorphism.

Posterior: rear.

Primary infection: an infection of previously healthy tissue. cf secondary infection.

Prophylactic: preventive of disease.

Protozoa: a group of microscopic unicellular animals.

Reagent: a substance with characteristic reactions, used in chemical tests.

Respiratory distress: difficulty in obtaining sufficient oxygen, usually evidenced by increased respiratory (gill) rate and gasping.

Reverse osmosis (RO): a method of purifying water.

Rheophile, Rheophilic: living in fast-flowing water (e.g. rapids).

Ripe: of female fish, filled with eggs that are ready to be laid.

Riverine: of rivers.

Runt: an individual whose size is stunted.

Saprophytic: living on decaying organic matter.

Scalation: the coating of scales on a fish; (in taxonomy) the type, arrangement, and numbers of scales on a fish.

Scutes: bony plates which protect the skin of some catfish.

Secondary infection: infection of tissue damaged by some other agency. cf primary infection.

Selective breeding: the breeding together of selected individuals, usually to fix or establish a particular characteristic or set of characteristics. Selective breeding sometimes, but not always, involves line-breeding (qv) – it is possible selectively to breed unrelated individuals whereas line-breeding involves an element of inbreeding (qv).

Shimmying: moving the body from side to side, often while 'swimming on the spot'.

SL: abbreviation for standard length, (qv).

Spawn: lay eggs (in aquatic/amphibious animals (e.g. fish, batrachians)).

Spawning medium: anything on or in which a fish spawns; usually refers to materials specially supplied for the purpose by the aquarist.

Spawning substrate: any surface on which a fish spawns.

Species: a group of individuals with common characteristics and able to interbreed, and distinguishable from other such groups. See also Chapter 2.

Species aquarium: an aquarium devoted to a single species of fish.

sp.: abbreviation for species (singular).

spp.: abbreviation for species (plural).

ssp.: abbreviation for subspecies.

Standard length (SL): the length of a fish's head and body, not including the tail. cf total length.

Styrofoam: expanded polystyrene, a type of plastic with excellent insulating and cushioning properties, used, *inter alia,* to make fish transportation boxes and to cushion tank bottoms.

Subcutaneous: beneath the skin.

Subspecies: a group of individuals of a species (qv) which have their own special characteristics but are still interfertile with all members of the species. See also Chapter 2.

Substrate: literally, 'under layer'. Used of the material covering the bottom of a natural body of water or of the aquarium (strictly speaking, the 'bottom substrate'); of any surface on which a fish spawns (spawning substrate, qv) or feeds (feeding substrate).

Substrate-spawner: a fish that attaches its eggs to a substrate (qv).

Symbiosis: the relationship where two organisms live together to their mutual benefit, by virtue of a reciprocally active partnership. cf commensalism, parasitism.

Sympatric: found in the same area in nature. cf allopatric.

Syntopic: living together in the same biotope in nature.

Systematics: the classification of living (and extinct) organisms. See also Chapter 2.

Systemic: pervading the system, e.g. systemic disease.

Tactile: of touch.

Taxon (plural taxa): any division of the animal or plant kingdoms.

Taxonomy: the classification of living (and extinct) organisms. See also Chapter 2.

Teleost: a member of the Teleostei, bony fish.

Terrestrial: of land.

TL: abbreviation for total length, (qv).

Topical: (of treatment) localised, restricted to the affected area.

Total length (TL): the length of a fish from tip of snout to end of tail. cf standard length.

Trematode: a type of parasite.

Trinomial system: the system of nomenclature used for members of the animal kingdom.

Unicellular: single-celled.

var.: abbreviation for variety.

Vector: carrier.

Ventral: of the belly.

Vertebrate: an animal with a backbone, e.g. fish, mammals, birds. cf invertebrate.

Vertical transmission (of disease): spread of disease from parent to offspring via sex cells or embryos. cf horizontal transmission.

Viviparous: giving birth to live young (as opposed to laying eggs).

Vomerine: of the vomer (a bone in the roof of a fish's mouth).

Water butt: a barrel or similar, used to collect rain water from the roof.

Water chemistry: the chemical make-up of a sample of water plus any substances dissolved in it

Water column: the vertical dimension of a body of water, e.g. reference is often made to aquatic creatures migrating up and down the water column on a daily basis.

Zoonosis (plural zoonoses): a disease that can be transmitted from an animal to humans.

Zooplankton: animal plankton (qv).